MORE PRAISE FOR
SUICIDE: WHAT REALLY HAPPENS IN THE AFTERLIFE?

"Heath and Klimo have put together a masterful tome that addresses a very complex and difficult subject. They shy away from neither the scientific nor the moral complexity of after-death research and its implications for our understanding of suicide. And, in spite of the many ambiguities in interpreting mediumistic data, they provide us with the best guide book to this material now available."
  –Jeffrey Mishlove, Ph.D., author of *The PK Man* and dean of
   Consciousness Studies at the University of Philosophical Research

"Klimo and Heath's book brings together two very controversial topics: channeling/mediumship and suicide. This is the first book to bring together so many disparate sources from over a century of apparent spirit communication-source material one would have to truly dig for otherwise. I applaud the authors for having done such an amazing job with this difficult research proposition.

"But more than laud the authors for the work done, it is the context and setting of the research material and commentary they provide that gives us much to think about. This is especially true of the section on murder-suicide/suicide bombers, a subject that holds much relevance for the targets of terrorism.

"All in all, this is a thought-provoking and well-researched book, and an amazingly interesting read."
  –Loyd Auerbach, M.S., director of The Office of Paranormal
   Investigations and author of *A Paranormal Casebook*

"This book is a sensitive exploration of what it means to take one's own life. Messages from purported spirits deal with all kinds of suicide, from assisted suicide to the suicide bomber who murders himself and others in the name of God. The central theme, that we are all 'part of an interconnected whole' and that 'ripples ... spread from each of our decisions,' needs to be heard by anyone who thinks of suicide and by the rest of us as well."
  –William Roll, Ph.D., Department of Psychology at the University of
   West Georgia, author of *Unleashed of Poltergeists and Murder* and *The
   Poltergeist*

"Get ready for an extensive, utterly fascinating, in-depth look at suicide, the first book ever to consider the topic from all possible and previously impossible angles—ethical, physical, mental, and spiritual. ... This book allows us to listen to what those who have taken their lives have to say—and it's not what you think!"
  –Chris Fleming, Sensitive, paranormal investigator, and co-host on the
   syndicated TV show *Dead Famous*

"This book addresses one of the most important questions in science, religion, and society. Anyone interested in the implications of suicide afterlife communications for the evolution of humanity should read this book."
    –Gary E. Schwartz, Ph.D., author of *The Afterlife Experiments,*
    The Truth About MEDIUM, and *The G.O.D. Experiments*

"Pamela Heath and Jon Klimo have written a timely book that may save thousands of lives. It should be read by anyone who has contemplated suicide, or knows someone who has committed suicide. The section on murder-suicide contains groundbreaking information which sheds new light on what is happening in the world today. This book is compelling reading that clearly shows that death is not the end."
    –Richard Webster, author of more than eighty books, including
    Soul Mates and *The Practical Guide to Past Life Memories*

"This book is a bold study of today's tragic rise of suicide. American teenagers and suicide bombers are doing the unthinkable. The authors probe the psychological and spiritual roots of this disaster. There is much practical wisdom here, and much intriguing data about the mystery of life turning against itself. I recommend this book, especially for its novel perspectives on suicide."
    –Michael Grosso, Ph.D., author of *Experiencing the Next World Now*

SUICIDE

What really happens in the afterlife?

channeled conversations with the dead

PAMELA RAE HEATH and **JON KLIMO**

North Atlantic Books
Berkeley, California

Copyright © 2006 by Pamela Heath and Jon Klimo. All rights reserved. No portion of this book, except for brief review, may be reproduced, stored in a retrieval system, or transmitted in any form or by any means—electronic, mechanical, photocopying, recording, or otherwise—without the written permission of the publisher. For information contact North Atlantic Books.

Copyright acknowledgments begin on page 436.

Published by
North Atlantic Books
P.O. Box 12327
Berkeley, California 94712

Cover and book design © Ayelet Maida, A/M Studios
Printed in the United States of America
Distributed to the book trade by Publishers Group West

ISBN 13: 978-1556-43621-5

Suicide: What Really Happens in the Afterlife? is sponsored by the Society for the Study of Native Arts and Sciences, a nonprofit educational corporation whose goals are to develop an educational and crosscultural perspective linking various scientific, social, and artistic fields; to nurture a holistic view of arts, sciences, humanities, and healing; and to publish and distribute literature on the relationship of mind, body, and nature.

North Atlantic Books' publications are available through most bookstores. For further information, call 800-337-2665 or visit our website at www.northatlanticbooks.com.

Substantial discounts on bulk quantities are available to corporations, professional associations, and other organizations. For details and discount information, contact our special sales department.

Library of Congress Cataloging-in-Publication Data

Heath, Pamela Rae.
  Suicide : what really happens in the afterlife? / by Pamela Rae Heath and Jon Klimo.
    p. cm.
  Includes bibliographical references.
  ISBN 1-55643-621-1 (pbk.)
  1. Future life. 2. Channeling (Spiritualism) 3. Suicide victims. 4. Spirit writings.
  I. Klimo, Jon. II. Title.
  BF1311.F8H43 2006
  133.9'3--dc22
                              2006005945

1 2 3 4 5 6 7 8 9 DATA 12 11 10 09 08 07 06

This book is dedicated to all the souls who have
suffered due to suicide—whether the suicides themselves,
their family and friends, or the victims of suicide bombers.
May they find peace, healing, and enlightenment.

Acknowledgments

We would like to acknowledge all of the psychics, mediums, and channels who try to bring comfort and understanding to both those stranded in the lower astral and those left behind, trying to cope with their sorrow. Thank you for your work.

Contents

Introduction... 1
    The Purpose of This Book 2
    How Knowledge about Survival Could Affect Our Lives 8
    How This Book Came to Be 11
    A Few Words about Channeling 14
    Survival Research: A Brief Overview 17
    The Approach Taken in This Book 25

PART I – *Traditional and Assisted Suicide*

1 – Overview of Traditional Suicide................................ 31
    Historical Overview 32
    Suicide Today 34
    Socio-Cultural Perspectives 36
    Psychological Perspectives 39
    Attempted Suicides and NDEs 44
    Treating the Suicidal Person 49
    Existentialism and Death 51
    Suicide and the Afterlife 56

2 – General Spirit Attitudes toward Suicide 65

3 – Why People Kill Themselves.................................... 82
    A True Accident 85
    Bids for Attention 87
    Getting Even 87
    Irrational Moments 89
    Depression and Lack of Hope 90
    To Provide Relief to Their Family 92
    They Feel There Are No Other Options 92
    Possession 93
    Desire to Return to the Afterlife 96
    Karma 98

4 – Transitioning to the Afterlife................................ 100

5 – Afterlife Experiences 111
    Reactions to Death   112
    Being Greeted by Spirits   116
    Funerals   118
    Life Review and Self-Judgment   121

6 – Adjustment Problems 129
    Psychological Baggage   130
    Refusal to Believe They Are Dead   133
    Failure to Recognize Helpers   137
    Harm Caused to the Living   139

7 – Moving On 144
    Problems Due to Lifespan   148
    Special Assistance   151
        The Value of Prayer   153
        The Use of Sleep   156
        Spiritual Therapy   157
    The Impact of Suicide on Future Lives   163

8 – Messages of Regret 171
    Regret for What Happens to Those Left Behind   172
    Regret Over Being Discarnate   177
    Regret for Wasted Potential   179
    Regret for Karmic Backsliding   180
    Regret for Their Manner of Death   183
    Regret for Their Continued Existence   185

9 – Messages to the Suicidal 187
    Suicide Is a Bad Idea   187
    Life Is Worth Living   189
    Death Is Not a Solution   190
    The Importance of Love   200
    Responsibility for Your Choices   201
    Help Is Available   202

10 – Messages to Those Left Behind 204
    Reassurance   204
    Those Left Behind Are Still Loved   210
    The Need for Loved Ones to Let Go of Grief   212
    Relieving the Family of a Sense of Guilt   216
    Forgiveness   219
    Advice   221
    Warnings   222
    Ongoing Issues   223
    Controversial Statements   225

11 – Assisted Suicide 227
    Spirit Attitudes   233
    What Souls Who Were Involved in Assisted Suicide Say   244

PART II – *Murder-Suicide and Suicide Bombers*

12 – Overview of Murder-Suicide 249
    Suicide Bombers   249
    Psychological and Psychiatric Perspectives   251
    Other Secular Views   257
    Non-Islamic Suicide Bombers   264
    The Islamic Perspective   268
    Case Vignettes   275
    Additional Perspectives from Muslim Scholars and Journalists   280

13 – General Messages 284
    References to Islam   285
    Fighting Over Religion   290
    Self-Sacrifice and Martyrdom   292
    Preconceived Expectations   295
    Death by Explosion   297
    The Role of Emotion   299
    How Murder Is Viewed in the Afterlife   301
    The Karma of Harming Others   308

14 – Experiences in the Afterlife 314
    Initial Experiences   315
    Funerals   321
    Life Review   322
    Adjustment Problems   326
    Interactions with Victims   332
    Moving On   336
        The Value of Prayer   338
        Spiritual Work   339
    Karma and Reincarnation Issues   340

15 – Messages to Those Left Behind 346
    Messages from Victims   346
    Channeled Messages from Suicide-Murderers   347
        Why They Did It   347
        Death Is Not a Solution   349
        Regrets   350
        There Are Other Options   352
        The Importance of Love   352
        Other Messages   353

16 – The Spirit View on Terrorism **358**
    General Spirit Views   **358**
    The View of Spirits Who Specialize in Dealing with Terrorists   **360**
    The Meaning of Catalytic Events   **365**
    The Solution to Terrorism   **369**

17 – Conclusion **376**
    What the Dead Say about Suicide   **376**
    Five Perspectives on What Happens in the Afterlife   **380**
    Key Themes   **383**

Glossary **387**
References **391**
Notes **402**
Permissions **436**
About the Authors **438**

The only real death that ever occurs is when a dream we cherish dies.

– P. M. H. Atwater, *We Live Forever: The Real Truth About Death*

Introduction

The first two-thirds of this book, Part I, is about the after-death experiences of people who have committed suicide. It is based on communications received through mediumship, or channeling, said to be coming from human spirits who have survived their bodily deaths and now exist in what many call the afterlife. Most of these messages claim to be from those who killed themselves, who are now able to share their experience, including the repercussions of their suicides. This major portion of the book begins with an overview of what the academic, medical, and mental health communities have to say about traditional suicide. Part I ends with an overview, again from the scientific and scholarly communities, on assisted suicide and euthanasia.

Part II, the final third of the book, turns to the related topic of murder-suicide—when someone purposefully kills another, or others, in the process of killing oneself. Again, we will first present an overview on this subject from those in *this* world—scientists, clinicians, scholars, and journalists—before turning to hear the perspective from purported spirits in the afterlife, including those who claim to have carried out such murder-suicides.

Let us briefly focus on the second of these two parts of the book, since its topic so dominates our collective consciousness today and perhaps our collective *un*conscious as well. The last few years have been filled with the relentless news stories and searing media images about an ever-more-unsettled world headlined with terrorist suicidal murderers, and the term "suicide bomber" has been added to everyone's vocabulary. There is a decidedly troubled post-9/11 quality to our lives today. Since watching on live television the disintegration of both World Trade Center towers in New York City on September 11th, 2001, we have come to a deep knowing that our lives will never be the same again. Our media now confront us with a central theme of terrorism, featuring a relentless succession of Palestinian, Iraqi, other Arab, Chechen, and Islamic extremist murder-suicide bombings. Many suicide bombers have not been Muslims, such as the Sri Lankan Tamil Tigers. We hear stories of young Middle-Eastern Arab men and women being recruited for these suicide missions. They are being told—and they are telling themselves—that if they choose this route of heroic *jihad,* or righteous holy war, they will be helping their fellow oppressed countrymen. But more: Not only will they be seen as beloved martyrs in the eyes of Allah as a result of their murder-suicide, but the men, and even the boys and women, will also each be gifted with as many as seventy virgins (also sometimes translated as apparitions or spirits) with whom to enjoy the afterlife.

Seeking fulfillment of this promise of pleasing God and receiving great reward, hundreds of these suicide bombers during the last few years have been dutifully taking thousands of their victims with them out of this world in sudden, horrific rupturings of local reality into splattered butcherings of what had once been precious human life. At the same time, the long-standing traditional and present-day teachings of Islam, the Muslim faith, overwhelmingly concur that both suicide and murder are condemned in the strongest terms in the Koran and other core writings based on the teachings of the Prophet Muhammad and his followers.

Even as we try to understand the grounds from which this recent drastic revisioning of long-standing Islamic tradition has been made by its fanatic splinter groups, the fact remains that hardly a day goes by without someone new blowing him- or herself up in order to destroy the lives of others. And it could be argued that this would not be occurring, or not in the numbers that it is, if the promise of divine afterlife rewards for such atrocity was not being embraced in such a deadly, unquestioning manner by each suicide-murderer. Therefore, we are moved to examine the current events topic of suicide bombers, trying to place it within the possibility of an afterlife following death where they experience and report back on their deeds and the repercussions stemming from them.

THE PURPOSE OF THIS BOOK

This book draws from 120 years of published material primarily based on medium-conveyed (channeled) messages and information said to be from human spirits who have survived physical death and are now continuing to exist on a nonphysical level of reality, which is variously termed in the survival literature the afterlife, or the astral plane, or just "the astral," or *bardo,* or *devachan,* or heaven, paradise, purgatory, or hell, depending on the earthly life one had lived up until death. This information is reported to be coming from many different sources, including: (1) from human, and sometimes nonhuman, discarnate (nonphysical) spirits;

(2) from interviews with various survival researchers, psychics, mediums, and channels, and from séances (to use a term carried over from the nineteenth century) that we, the authors, have conducted for purposes of this book; and (3) from sources other than through mediumship and channeling, including out-of-body experiences (OBEs), near-death experiences (NDEs), past-life and reincarnation reports, psi or psychic means (such as clairvoyance and remote viewing), and, to a lesser extent, from dreams and lucid dreams, and from experiences obtained through altered states of consciousness (ASCs).

We believe ours is one of the most thorough attempts ever made to draw from, and picture, the post-death afterlife perspective. Besides providing the broad consensus to be found from a multi-sourced perspective regarding what happens as and after we die, our book's chief contribution is its unique focus on perspectives coming from those who claim to have committed suicide and from other nonsuicide sources on "the other side" who share their experiences and perspectives related to suicide and what kinds of repercussions and learning come from having ended one's life.

This book has been written in order to examine the following interrelated questions: What, if anything, happens when and after we die? Is there some kind of afterlife, and, if so, what is it like? Is there a relationship between the life one has lived prior to death and the life after death, and, if so, what is that relationship? Particularly—and the main focus of this book—what happens after death to people who have taken their own lives? And, especially, what happens after death to those who have purposefully committed murder as part of their suicide? Specifically, did any of those recent, widely publicized yet usually anonymous, Middle-Eastern suicide bombers find themselves, as they had been promised, welcomed and beloved in paradise for the killing they had done? We want to consider these questions from the perspective of those identifying themselves as newly entering, or already inhabiting, the afterlife.

There are two basic paths by which to try to answer such time-honored, still mostly unanswered, questions about life after death. First, we may examine what our fellow still-living humans have to say on these matters from their limited earthly perspective. We can study their research and theories: from psychical investigators, parapsychologists, and other survival researchers, as well as from skeptics and other traditionally trained scientists inclined to doubt the survival hypothesis—that we survive death. We can weigh their opinions, conjectures, and arguments, look at what data they have, listen to their stories, and read their writing. And we can look at the data from polls about what percentage of Americans believe in survival of bodily death. But, in the last analysis, this path must be seen as one of ignorance and personal opinion, of an admitted lack of firsthand experience and evidence about what, if anything, is the case for us human beings following our physical deaths. Each of us is apparently going to have to pass totally alone through that seeming one-way valve at death, that entryway into either a terminal void or a living afterlife. Until we pass into that entryway, each of us will not know *for sure* what happens at and following death.

Or second, we can listen to the experiences of a small group of our still-living fellows who claim to have various kinds of privileged insight, information, and experience regarding the nature of what happens after we physically die, including the claim that we do indeed survive and continue in some meaningful, conscious way that preserves at least some of our previous identity and memory. As mentioned, these insights may come from glimpses through altered states of consciousness, from near-death experiences, out-of-body experiences, and from information gained through assorted psychic means. But especially—and central to this book—there is communication ostensibly received by mediums and channels from afterlife-based human spirits said to have survived their physical deaths.

The purpose of this book is to follow the second of these two paths. In the last 120 years, an entire library of books have been written that purport to provide evidence that when we die we meaningfully survive the deaths of our physical bodies and continue to have experiences and grow in some kind of trans-physical or spiritual realm. Most of the material in these many hundreds of publications is based on various kinds of psychic or spiritual insight and communication, particularly gained by means of the process traditionally called "mediumship" and in recent years also called "channeling." Our book attempts to draw from and add to this rich tradition of collections of communications said to be from surviving spirits in the afterlife realm. In so doing, we hope to provide yet further food for thought about death and the hereafter for those who are still alive. Specifically, we hope to provide the definitive collection of spirit communications that address the topic of suicide and its repercussions following death.

The problem with such privileged information, however, is its authenticity. How believable is it? How do we know we are being told the truth? What are the empirical and epistemological grounds for what these privileged insight-providers and communication-mediators and their supposed disembodied sources claim to know? While many of you at the outset will not be ready to be convinced by such after-death insights drawn from this second path, we still hope you will at least keep an open mind as you read.

We have mentioned that one pressing reason for writing this book at this time is the continued climate of global terrorism punctuated with daily headlines about Middle-Eastern suicide bombers and their victims. Extremist religious, as well as secular and political, arguments about murder-suicide and the promising afterlife repercussions of such acts, when those acts are portrayed as necessary, justified, and heroic, lie at the heart of the stories told to and believed by the current winding parade of anonymous martyrs preparing for their own imminent deaths and the ensuing meteoric flash of their headline-grabbing moment of murderous fame.

We know that it is too much to hope that the stories in our book, focusing on the reported afterlife repercussions of our earthly deeds, suicide in particular, might somehow dissuade future potential suicides, and suicide bombers, from carrying out their acts. Still, we hope to have whatever small positive influence we can.

There is another, even broader, purpose for this book that is addressed to *all* of us, not just to, and about, a small violence-prone subgroup. This has to do with the concept of *karma*—the millennia-old perspective that what we do in and with our earthly lives comes back to us; that "what goes around comes around;" that "as ye sow, so shall ye reap." This is the perspective that our choices and acts have repercussions for others and, particularly, for ourselves, and that if we do not experience and learn from our deeds and their repercussions while still in this lifetime, we will have to experience them in life, or lives, beyond this current one.

More specifically, to use Webster's dictionary, karma is:

> The force generated by a person's action that is held in Hinduism and Buddhism to be the motive power for the round of rebirths and deaths endured by him until he achieved spiritual liberation and freed himself from the effects of such force.... [It is] the sum total of the ethical consequences of a person's good and bad actions comprising thoughts, words, and deeds that is held ... to determine his specific destiny in his next existence.[1]

Whether we believe in the literal truth of karma or simply choose to take it figuratively as a kind of teaching story, it can be helpful to use it to look at our own lives and those of others. Without some kind of larger context within which to understand what is happening here on Earth today, to make sense of, and live with, what is occurring, many of the most troubling things we experience both directly and indirectly can strike us as deeply unfair, meaningless, or without purpose. Therefore, it is the purpose of this book to provide such a larger, or transcendental, context, even if we are ultimately unable to prove it is the true picture of things.

There appears to be an existential climate of increasing numbers of us questioning what is the purpose and meaning of our lives, of life on Earth, given our current deeply troubled and problem-ridden world. Things are getting out of control; traditional ways are no longer working. There is a rising climate of estrangement, fear, violence, and terrorism, with increasing occurrence of depression and despair. In the West, there is the widening use of tranquilizers, in addition to other drugs and alcohol, to numb or disconnect us from the disturbed and disturbing feelings we are having in the face of our lives and the world we are sharing. We are challenged to make sense of this world and of the many disturbing human acts within it. We are about the business of making meaning, though this ongoing activity of meaning-making for most of us is largely taken for granted and not done with much consciousness or time spent. Yet we are being faced with events that strike many of us as deeply unfair, unjust, crying out for restitution and rebalance, if not downright retribution and revenge. At such times, it is natural for the imagination to take what was not right and make it right, to entertain what the proper "just desserts" would be in such a case. But usually it does not seem to be our human job to make this happen in real life. We just play out in imagination whatever the call to justice would look and feel like.

It is an understatement to say that life is not always easy. It can be tremendously difficult, stressful, painful, and depressing. But in spite of these hard portions that make up parts of all of our lives, most of us stick it out through life, striving for as much positive experience, meaning, and fulfillment as we can have, even in the face of how much life can hurt as well. Then, particularly, when we hear how yet another of us has taken his or her own life, we cannot help but wonder: For him or her, was this truly the hoped-for quick release from all existence forever? Was it the longed-for sudden and complete extinguishing for all eternity of any opportunity whatsoever to understand what life was all about, what it was for, what its meaning and purpose was, including its frustration, unfulfilled desires, failure, pain, and suffering? Is suicide truly the quick escape, the easy out it seems to be, that it is made out to be, especially by and for those contemplating it? According to the myriad, admittedly unusual, purported otherworldly sources that fill our book, the answer is a resounding, choral consensus of *Nos*. It would seem that the universe may be wiser, more generous, and even more loving than that.

INTRODUCTION

How many chances do we get to learn the deeper, fuller, truer story? Just one; just this one short life? Can we prematurely sever the warm, pulsing lifeline of a human being—our own or someone else's—and just have that rich existence fall into nothingness forever? There are certainly hundreds of millions of us, perhaps a few billion, in the world today who see things exactly this way—that nothingness alone follows death at the end of this once and only life. But then there are billions more of us in the world—whether following the religious teaching of our culture or simply having worked it out for ourselves—who choose to believe, even claim to *know for sure* beyond just believing or having faith, that when we die, no matter how we die, some kind of existence continues in some kind of personally meaningful way. We embrace a more open-ended story about human existence and its meaning that does not include the view that a life can be so abruptly and irrevocably extinguished, obliterated and annihilated into just nothingness and meaninglessness by natural death, let alone by unnatural suicide or murder.

So, depending upon the religious-spiritual perspective we have been taught and conditioned with, or have personally chosen or developed for ourselves, many of us billions alive today carry within us this open-ended story about how death is not the end. There is a vastly shared continuation story, with its myriad historical and cultural variations, traditions, and texts, with all its respective sources of information and inspiration. And within this overall story, there are further smaller stories about what may happen, or *does* happen, or even *should* happen, to those of us who purposefully kill ourselves or, more narrowly, who purposely kill others in the process of purposefully killing ourselves.

How do we then judge who has the truest story? In today's post-modern world, there may no longer be just one dominant, best story other than the one that works best for each of us alone. Still, to be completely honest, shouldn't we also leave open the possibility that perhaps the truest story of all may turn out to be that none of those stories of hope, continuation, survival, second chances, justice, and additional opportunities for living, learning, and growth—that none of them have any truth to them whatsoever? That they are nothing more than that: stories, fictions to carry comfortingly while alive? If so, we are then faced with what may be the most natural thing there is: the stainless, pristine, undeniable blade of ultimate severance—the event of death that comes to us all and sends us off, each ultimately alone, into nothingness forever. No wonder billions of us choose our survival and continuation stories of a kind of personal immortality in the face of that deadly, ultimately lifeless, reductionist scenario, true though it might turn out to be.

HOW KNOWLEDGE ABOUT SURVIVAL COULD AFFECT OUR LIVES

Entertaining our earlier-imagined scenario—that we *do* survive death—we return to the concept of karma. Now imagine what the world might be like for karma-minded inhabitants who are really living their belief. Would we treat each other better because we really knew—*really knew*—that our acts, even our unacted-upon individually harbored thoughts and intentions, would affect what awaited us, what and how we might be living and experiencing later in this life or in the next one? That by our present thoughts and deeds we are actually preparing a place for ourselves in what occurs on the other side of physical death? Knowing for certain that life does go on following death, would some of us choose to end our life right now because we find it too boring, meaningless, frustrating, frightening, or painful? Could we simply say, "I know I can't just turn it all off completely and forever; but I don't like—or just can't stand—this current television program that is my current life, so I think that by killing myself I'll just change channels, so to speak, to see what else is available, because anything is bound to be better than this"? Or, given survival and karma, would we try to live the very best life we could, full of kindness, compassion, charity, and being of service to others, because, based on what we are doing in this life, we are authoring what comes next for us?

Let's imagine what the world would be like if everyone in it knew from physical birth until death that death was not the end. Imagine what our life would be like, individually and together on this planet, if everyone knew they were going to continue on after physical death; that we continue with awareness and the capacity to experience and make meaning, and with some kind of continuity between who we are and the life we lived prior to death and who we will be and the experiences we will be having following death. Imagine that we all *really* knew that this was the truth of things throughout our lives—that we knew this from birth, through our upbringing, our schooling, and our culture in general. We would have known no other truth, no other scenario, than that physical death was simply a doorway, a transition to the next phase of existence, experience, and growth—a shift from one experiential realm to another. So, then, what would such a world be like and how would we be behaving in it?

Or imagine a situation somewhat more realistic, which starts with the world the way it really is today and our experiences as part of it, which then undergoes some massive event that deeply changes things. Imagine that many of us, most of us, perhaps even all of us, alive right now, were given whatever proof was needed to convince us, either overnight or over a fairly short period of time, that death was not the end and that what occurs after death has some kind of relationship to who we were and to our lives prior to death. Also, if we happened not to have believed in such certain survival of physical death before this imagined conversion, imagine we were at the same time able to remember what it was like for us before we knew this, when we thought that nothing happened after death, or that, if something happened, it was pretty unclear, agnostic, and not much dwelt on.

This second imagined scenario seems more interesting than the first, closer to home, more imaginable. The first is more like trying to imagine a possible world where something had always been the case, knowing that death was just a transition. But this would be a world very different from our current one. In the second scenario, however, we imagine the world the way it really is today and then entertain what it would be like if things changed because something proved to us that death is not the end. Such a scenario could actually happen.

As you try to imagine this second scenario, you may wish for more information. For example, how can you imagine how the world might change, how people and their behaviors might be affected and changed, by irrefutable knowledge of such continuation for each of us beyond death, unless you knew the nature of what occurs after death? How would this post-death afterlife, this next life, be related to the one we know right now? Does who we are and what we did while alive contribute to who we are and what happens after we die? Would it be as many of our world faiths picture it: that we make a place for ourselves in the next life (the afterlife, heaven, purgatory, or hell) by the nature of our earlier life here on Earth, by our deeds, by the lifelong record of our pre-death experience?

In this second scenario, would we wake up knowing without doubt that we continue beyond death, and then go out into the world being as compassionate, generous, loving, and good as we can be? That we would do this because part of what we have now learned is that something like karma is part of how this new, larger reality operates and that the repercussions of our acts are according to the nature and quality of those acts? Would most of us come from a better place and try to live a better life? Or would many of us also try to get away with murder, many literally, because there is now nothing to lose? After all, how can I be punished by you for my misdeeds in this life? Life in prison? Execution? No, my life does not end; it just changes. I have lives to come. And what about all the bored and fickle people who would simply change the no-longer-wanted channel of what they were experiencing by killing themselves just to see what else there was? Could assurance of immortality breed irresponsibility just as much as lead to new-found responsibility to oneself and others? One could only hope that if everyone knew that karma and personal survival were real, that many of our wayward neighbors would make more responsible choices because they would realize they were being responsible to *themselves,* as well as to others, because they would have to live with what they chose to do, what they actually did, and would have to live with themselves, perhaps forever, in light of it.

The information contained in this book may change the minds of some of you about the nature of death, as well as about the nature of choosing death by suicide to end your own life and what the results of that might be. Reading what we are presenting here may open you to the possibility, even the certitude, that life continues after death. But, more likely, many, even most, of you may not be so strongly affected and may still be left in a kind of hazy, agnostic zone of uncertainty about death and the possibilities of survival. Or for those of you already in that zone, you will continue to stick to your own understanding of what will come after death, an understanding that you had prior to reading this book and that you probably had been taught by a particular religion. So, even those of you who brought to the reading of this book an already in-place belief system or faith about an afterlife may not have this belief or faith changed by the contents of this book. Nonetheless, we have chosen to present this book for our earthly family at this time in the hope that it might have some effect, opening us to, or keeping us open to, imaginings of a larger, more meaningful existence where all that we do really *does* matter and really *does* have meaning, repercussions, and continuation. Given the disturbing condition of our world today, and the wanting quality of the inner lives of so many of us inhabiting it, we can no longer afford the state of how narrow, rigid, or closed so many of our minds, imaginations, and hearts have become.

In their recent book *The Afterlife Experiments: Breakthrough Scientific Evidence of Life After Death,* University of Arizona research psychologist Gary E. Schwartz and his co-author William L. Simon use mediums to find apparent evidence that life continues after death, and pose the same basic question we have posed: What if we knew we survive physical death? In Chapter 18, "How Our Lives Might Change," Schwartz uses the term *living soul hypothesis* to refer to the view that we meaningfully and consciously survive the deaths of our bodies. For Schwartz, such a view would encourage people to evaluate how kind and compassionate they have been, how present, or lacking, such qualities have been in their lives in this physical lifetime, which is only part of a larger, longer continuing existence.[2] He asks:

> If you had been cruel to a given person, who then died, how would you feel if you knew scientifically and without doubt that he or she would still be around ... looking over your shoulder—not merely metaphorically but literally? Would you want to face him or her when it was your time to "cross over"?[3]

He further conjectures:

> If the living soul hypothesis is true, and we develop our abilities to "hear" what the dead have to say to us, perhaps human deceit might come to an end. It's possible that we could enter a new era of human caring ... [which] I call integrity love.[4]

If we really do continue living in some form following death, Schwartz proposes:

> ... we would then have to seriously consider and accept where some of "our" thoughts come from. Perhaps it's time for us all to humble ourselves and consider the possibility that to various degrees we may already be receiving communication from those who have walked this earth before us.
>
> If the living soul hypothesis is proven accurate, we'll need to awaken to the realization that the distinction between "our" minds and "their" minds may be far less clear than previously imagined.[5]

HOW THIS BOOK CAME TO BE

About fifteen years ago, one of us (Klimo) met a licensed clinical psychologist in her late forties, who said she was planning to take her own life. However, before she did that, she said she wanted to do a little research about what, according to some, is supposed to happen after you die, including what is said to happen if you take your own life. She was referred to me by a fellow psychologist friend of mine, who told her I had some expertise about death, having specialized in parapsychological and transpersonal viewpoints, including scenarios of what may occur following death.

She told me she was in a great deal of psycho-emotional, not physical, pain and suffering. It stemmed from a cosmetic operation that left parts of her body in what she felt was a sufficiently disfigured condition that she was no longer sexually attractive to men. Still worse, however, in the years following the operation, she had begun to spontaneously, and unpredictably, go through terrifying periods of uncontrollable psychological dissociation. These would fragment the once intact, clear, self-consistent, self-aware subjective space of her conscious awareness and sense of herself into unpredictable and uncontrolled, sharply cut-off passing islands of experience and awareness, like the reflecting shards of a broken mirror.

She had used all her own clinical skills on herself to no avail, and the psychiatrist with whom she was working when I met her, and with whom she continued to work throughout the time I saw her, seemed unable to help either. She told me she preferred death by suicide to this depressing and frightening deterioration of her mind and body. She depicted herself as a Jewish atheist who didn't believe anything was going to happen after she died other than loss of consciousness forever, and so, for her, death would be acceptable, even welcomed.

She told me that before ending her life, however, she wanted to talk to me as a resource person, just out of curiosity, about the so-called afterlife. The first thing I did, between her first and second visit, was to quickly put together a collection, from my own library of perhaps a hundred books about survival of death, of seven or eight passages of communication from the "spirits" of different individuals who said, through mediums or channels, that they had successfully taken their own lives and then found themselves in an afterlife where they experienced the repercussions of their act. The content of this anomalously received material usually related to variations on karma, lesson learning, soul growth, and learning that, by killing oneself, one does not escape what led up to one's death, nor does one escape one's own ongoing experiencing of existence.

The collection I put together was an example of what is called *bibliotherapy*, or "the use of selected reading materials as therapeutic adjutants in medicine and psychiatry."[6] More specific to my work with her, the term means "guidance in the solution of personal problems through directed reading."[7]

She and I began by discussing these readings for a few sessions and then continued on an almost-weekly basis for another four or five months. I thought she was so brilliant and articulate on behalf of her own secular humanist, atheist, and nonbelieving clinician-scientist point of view, obsessively bent on her own eventual suicide, that I asked if I could tape our conversations. I still have the tapes of a number of those sessions toward the end of our time together, when our talks became largely an ongoing debate. In this debate she, on the one hand, was trying to convince me—playing on my compassion for her and my belief in her own passionate free will—to help her end her life, Kevorkian-style[8] (a physician who performed and martyred himself to the cause of assisted suicide) so that she wouldn't have to be alone in the process of leaving this world. And then, on the other hand, there was me in response, after months of seeing her, being forced to dig ever deeper to examine and clarify my own beliefs, values, and ethics, eventually telling her that I could *not* and would *not* help her in this way. I was eventually able to tell her that I thought she should *not* take her own life either, whether by herself or in someone else's company. It so happened that, after those months of my seeing her, she discovered that her mother had developed a serious case of cancer and so she set aside her plans for suicide for the time being in order to take care of her. After that, I never heard from her again, lost any way to reach her, and, being unable to locate her to this day, I don't know if she ever went ahead with her plan to kill herself.

To bring this story full circle, years later (yet long before we had the idea for this book), I shared with Dr. Pamela Heath (now my co-author) my experience of working with this woman. Years then passed, but inspired by my story, it turned out that Pam, by herself and unbeknownst to me, began the laborious task of bringing together a much more extensive collection of mediumistic/channeled material on suicide from an afterlife perspective than I had done for my client, and then she asked me to join her as co-author to help finish working on the book. In this sense, the book you are now reading may be providing food for thought and discussion for a potentially vaster readership than my original little set of bibliotherapy readings did for my suicidal psychologist client. Our much more comprehensive book is now meant to be read by a wide variety of people, including those who might now or someday be contemplating ending their own lives, and hopefully may dissuade at least some of them—some of you—from doing so. This book may also help those of you who, in turn, are trying to help others to not take their own lives.

In addition, we have wondered, perhaps idealistically, whether this book might reach some of that special, troubled and troubling, population of current historically important Islamic-based Muslims considering combining taking their own lives with taking the lives of others—the present generation of suicide bombers, as they have come to be known. I don't know if my little homemade set of bibliotherapy readings, and our conversations about it, changed the suicidal intent of my fellow psychologist years ago, nor do I know if this current book might change future minds bent on suicide, or, worse, bent on murder-suicide, but we can hope it might, even if it can only provide the proverbial "food for thought," rather than any kind of solidly convincing argument or scientific evidence or proof. We do believe, however, that those reductionist materialists, who hypothesize that only nothingness awaits us after death, have no more certain evidence for their view than we have in this book for hypothesizing that there *is* meaningful existence following death.

A FEW WORDS ABOUT CHANNELING

One of us (Klimo) wrote what is generally considered the definitive book on the subject of channeling.[9] So, before continuing, it will be useful to provide some definition and context for this subject, since the process of channeling, or mediumship, is responsible for the otherworldly-afterlife perspectives that comprise most of this book.

For at least 2,500 years, and across virtually all countries, cultures, and peoples, one can find thousands of stories and reports of individuals who claim, or who have claims made of them, that they are receiving messages from spirits who exist on some other kind or level of reality than our own here on physical Earth.[10] Some of these communicating sources are said to be the spirits of human beings not currently possessing human bodies (said to be discarnate or disembodied), mainly those who have gone through the process of physical death and have survived with personal awareness in some kind of non- or trans-physical realm, called variously the afterlife, bardo, devachan, purgatory, heaven, paradise, or hell, the astral plane or etheric realm, Summerland, the happy hunting grounds, the abode of the ancestors, and so on.

Some of these nonphysically based beings are said to be nonhuman, ranging from angels and various other spiritual beings to nature spirits, from nonphysically embodied extraterrestrials to other-dimensional beings, from gods to demons. During the past forty years especially, we have an ever-growing published record of such beings communicating back to us using living, physically embodied humans called channels (or channelers) or mediums capable of this process.

In addition to such claims of people throughout history being passive, seeming accidental recipients of such apparently Earth-transcending communication, there have also been myriad accounts of individuals serving directly as active conduits for such information, purposefully allowing their bodies and minds to be used by someone or something nonphysical to communicate by means of them. This can occur through telepathic or clairaudient means, receiving it "within" and then saying or writing it down for the rest of us, or by usually willingly going into an altered state of consciousness or trance to allow such a nonphysically based being to temporarily use (co-opt, take over, possess) part or all of the physical body of the person in order to speak or write what it wishes to share with us on Earth.

People who are capable of having nonphysical spirits (beings or entities) communicate to or through them have gone by many names across different cultures and times, but the traditional term in the West, since the mid-nineteenth century, has been "medium," and more recently, in the past thirty-five years or so, "channel" has gained wide acceptance as well. We then speak of using a medium or a channel to seek contact with and communication from such non-earthly sources. The terms medium and channel, however, do not mean the same thing within and across the circles within which they are used. Mediumship is usually associated with communication only from human spirits who have survived physical death and exist in some kind of afterlife, while channeling can refer to receiving communication from such once-human sources, but, in addition, can also refer to communication from any nonphysically based source as well, including the non- or never-human.

As mentioned, the medium's or channel's method of reception may be through a voice within, hearing with the mind's ear (clairaudiently); through symbolic vision, seeing with the mind's eye (clairvoyantly); or by directly experiencing more abstract ideas, thought forms, or understanding (telepathically). Alternatively, one relinquishes the normal seat of control and awareness, stepping aside long enough to allow the nonphysically based being or information source to use the medium's or channel's body to directly communicate. Other methods have been used as well, but virtually all of them involve some kind and degree of temporary alteration of consciousness away from the normal waking state.

In addition, "automatic writing" and other kinds of automatisms are approaches where the individual's conscious awareness and control is bypassed and his or her own unconscious, or an external influence, controls the handwriting, typing, or other physical activity in order to communicate. Related is the use of the Ouija board, where a little platform, or planchette, under the fingertips of one or more participants, moves across a board pointing to letters of the alphabet to spell out messages either from the unconscious of the participant(s) or from outside spirits, depending on one's interpretation. Such modes are called automatisms because they involve relinquishing communication control to something or someone operating outside of the conscious awareness or control of the medium or channel. Channeling, mediumship, automatic writing, and the Ouija board, or something like it, have been in use for more than a century and a quarter in the West as well as in earlier cultures for thousands of years. Also, since the mid-twentieth century, what is called electronic voice phenomena (EVP) or instrumental transcommunication (ITC) has come into use as well. This approach involves the use of tape recorders, radios, video cameras, computers, televisions, and other electronic equipment to tune into and record the supposed presence of, and communication from, surviving human spirits.[11]

By this traditional definition of communication coming to or through an individual on Earth from some non-earthly someone or something, mediumship and channeling appear to have been part of, even at the root of, most of the world's major religions. Many of the Christian saints and prophets, for example, are depicted as channeling from the divine. A study of Christ's own words, and other biblical references to him, seem to portray him, when not appearing to be one and the same as God, as being a direct recipient of God's communication and will in a process of sacred channeling. At the same time, however, many, perhaps most, Christians, fundamentalist or born-again Christians in particular, greet any mention of mediumship or channeling, or communication with the dead, as biblically forbidden territory containing nothing but falsehood, deceit, possession, demons, or the devil. The entire religious-spiritual realm is a complex one with regard to the channeling process. It appears that, in a number of religious-spiritual establishment contexts, it is a real, known, and understood process, but only with regard to certain individuals where the practice is acceptable and considered genuine, while others are not allowed access to such practice, or, if it occurs, it is automatically considered inauthentic or as contact only with self-generated or undesirable or evil sources.

So the major religious-spiritually imbued cultures, and most smaller preliterate, aboriginal, Indian, and shamanistic cultures, throughout the world and throughout the ages generally accept the process of channeling, but tightly control who is allowed to do it or what sources are deemed to be acceptable, trustworthy, or real (i.e., not self-generated and not traceable to anywhere or anyone on physical Earth).

In contrast, the scientific community is quite another story altogether. With the exception of the still-controversial scientific discipline of parapsychology (since 1961, a member science of the American Academy for the Advancement of Science), almost no one trained and working in the scientific and academic mainstream "on the record" takes mediumship or channeling seriously. It is explained away in a variety of ways, including that it is the product of intentional conscious fraud or hoax, or that it is a case of less devious, manipulative forms of self-deception or operations of one's own unconscious activity. In the latter case, this can involve more psychopathological cases of "a house divided against itself" or of "the left hand not knowing what the right is doing," where supposed channels are consciously unaware that it is they themselves who are actually generating and responsible for whatever is supposedly being channeled from some entity beyond them; that, without awareness they are doing so, they are acting out from their own unconscious in a psychological condition or process involving one or more of the following: dissociation, delusion, thought disorder, hallucination, mania, schizophrenia, psychosis, or other psycho-emotional disorders.

Whenever one deals with channeled material, it is important, if possible, to get the information from more than one source. This is because the unconscious mind of the medium may act as a filter for, or color, the material that is received through psi (i.e., one's ostensible psychic ability or mode of anomalous cognition or channeling). Thus, unless mediums and channels have done a lot of work on themselves, odds are that they will each put their own spin on the raw material received. Furthermore, what sources they connect with and are able to channel, may be a function of not only their own talent, but their personality, which can adulterate things and affect where kind can call to kind across worlds.

SURVIVAL RESEARCH: A BRIEF OVERVIEW

Serious, organized attempts to study survival of physical death began in 1882 with the founding of the British Society for Psychical Research (SPR) in London and the founding of the American Society for Psychical Research (ASPR) in the United States in 1885. These organizations came into existence because a new, international, informal movement had arisen in the late nineteenth century called Spiritualism in England and the U.S. and Spiritism in France, Brazil, and elsewhere. Members of this movement believed in a form of Christianity that included a more metaphysical than biblical picture of survival of physical death and an afterlife we go to after death, and embraced practices whereby some of us—psychic mediums— can serve as connections for communication between those of us who have gone on beyond death and those of us still here on Earth.[12]

Spiritualism was characterized by a burgeoning of people practicing different forms of mediumship. The era gave rise to hundreds, eventually many thousands, of reports of communication from human spirits who had survived death and were communicating back from the afterlife through dozens, and then hundreds, of mediums. The mediumistically conveyed contact came in the form of spirits communicating to the medium, such as clairaudiently and telepathically, in a kind of anomalous information processing mode, or came directly through the medium, as through a possession-type process. While the medium would go into some form or degree of trance or altered state of consciousness, the discarnate spirit would then use the brain-mind, body, or speech production apparatus of the medium to speak directly to whomever was present. This activity was referred to as "mental mediumship."

Another very prevalent form of spirit contact and communication during that initial Spiritualist wave, a form extremely rare today, was "physical mediumship." In this process, the trance medium was said to lend his or her psychic energy so that discarnate, invisible spirits could directly interact with and affect our physical level of reality, such as by doing coded rappings on walls, tipping tables, levitating objects, even materializing objects. Physical mediumship also included spirits reported being able to temporarily manifest or partially materialize themselves so that whole rooms full of people at gatherings for this purpose, called séances, could see and sometimes also hear them, using their own, not the medium's, recognizable voices through a process called "direct voice."

The earlier-mentioned SPR included many notable researchers, such as F. W. H Meyers, Henry Sidgwick, Edmund Gurney, Richard Hodgson, Frank Podmore, Sir Oliver Lodge, and Sir Arthur Conan Doyle, the creator of Sherlock Holmes, to name just a few. The ASPR included, among others, the distinguished Harvard philosopher and psychologist William James. During this period, from the late 1800s through the end of World War I, France and Germany and other countries had many serious investigators as well. While a few of these researchers were beginning to study other anomalous phenomena besides mediumship and claims of survival of death, most were focused on the latter largely because of the worldwide prevalence of such activity under Spiritualism and Spiritism.

As time went on, psychical researchers began to look at other processes and phenomena in addition to mediumship and speculated survival, such as different forms of extrasensory perception (ESP), including telepathy, clairvoyance, clairaudience, and precognition, and varieties of psychokinesis (PK), or cases of seeming mind-over-matter capacity. Survival research meanwhile went beyond just studies of mediumship and attempts to verify that what was being studied actually pointed to survival of death, rather than to other causes, such as conscious fraud or telepathy. Such related survival fields included the study of reincarnation and the investigation of past lives, out-of-body experiences, near-death experiences, possession, ghosts, hauntings, poltergeists, and apparitions.

In the early part of the twentieth century, J. B. Rhine and his wife Louisa continued to carefully study what had been earlier called psychic phenomena, starting the fledgling field of parapsychology, initially as part of the psychology department at Duke University in Durham, North Carolina. Although J. B. focused primarily on laboratory-based, controlled experiments to study extrasensory perception and psychokinesis, Louisa specialized more in the area of what were called "spontaneous cases"—descriptive case studies of paranormal activities and capacities, which arose usually unbidden in the field of real life, rather than in a controlled laboratory setting. Many of the cases she gathered and studied involved deathbed apparitions, reported ghosts and hauntings, and poltergeists—cases of disturbances of unknown cause in the physical environments of some peoples' homes. Such poltergeist phenomena were speculated to be either a function of discarnate, surviving spirits able to affect our level of reality for whatever reason, or a function of the built-up, troubled, unconscious psycho-emotional energy of a physically very much alive member (usually an adolescent) in the household where the activity was taking place, through a kind of unconscious psychokinesis or "acting out" process.

Following the heyday of the Rhines at Duke around the middle of the twentieth century, a new generation of ever more scientifically trained and oriented parapsychologists continued the tradition of the prior late-nineteenth- and early-twentieth-century psychical researchers. The new scientific field of parapsychology was amassing many hundreds of journal-published and conference-presented controlled studies of various psychic-type phenomena and claims, using statistics, attempts to be objective and neutral in designing research and gathering and analyzing data, and making purposefully modest claims from the results. These parapsychologists brought their ever more rigorous scientific theory and practice to bear on the investigation of the three major domains studied by parapsychology: extrasensory perception, psychokinesis, and survival research, with the third of these including the study of mediumship and how, if at all, it can support the survival hypothesis, that we do meaningfully survive physical death. By the early 1960s, thanks to its disciplined attempts to do good science, parapsychology, as mentioned earlier, was accepted into the prestigious American Academy for the Advancement of Science (AAAS) as a member science, alongside all the other already traditionally accepted scientific disciplines such as physics, chemistry, astronomy, geology, and psychology.

In the most recent chapter in the story of survival research, electronic voice phenomena or instrumental transcommunication have been used to supplement mediumship and channeling to seek evidence that existence may continue beyond the death of the physical body.

Finally, we return to Gary E. Schwartz, professor of psychology, medicine, neurology, and psychiatry at the University of Arizona, Tucson. At his Human Energy Systems Laboratory, he has conducted some of the most recent, carefully designed, and evidence-rich research ever done to see if mediums can actually receive communication from what appear to be spirits in the afterlife, calling what he is studying "after-death communication," or ADC. He reports on these experiments in his 2002 book, *The Afterlife Experiments: Breakthrough Scientific Evidence of Life after Death*.

In stringently monitored experiments, under controlled laboratory conditions, leading mediums George Anderson, John Edward, Ann Gehman, Suzane Northrop, and Laurie Campbell were asked by Schwartz to each separately attempt contact with dead friends and relatives of a number of volunteer subjects, who served as "sitters." They were masked from the mediums' view and never spoke, so the mediums were unable to obtain any cues from them. The sitters then went over the material received by the mediums and rated it on a scale that reflected its accuracy, from a complete "miss" being not at all true of the source to a complete "hit" being information that was true about the source being contacted and that could not be known by the medium except through his or her mediumship.

Schwartz also made sure that his experimental research design took into consideration, and tried to control or rule out, an array of explanations to account for his results that were other than that his mediums were, in fact, receiving detailed, accurate information from departed spirits. Such alternative explanations that had to be constantly kept in mind included fraud, queuing, selective memory, vague information, lucky guesses, experimenter bias or mistakes, the motivation of the mediums, the mediums reading the minds of the sitters, and even that the information of all the decisive "hits" could be coming from some kind of universal memory bank contacted by the mediums and that there really was no individual survival of spirits involved.[13]

At the end of his series of experiments with the mediums, where their record of hits far exceeded chance, often with 100 percent accuracy recorded, Schwartz was led from his initial strongly skeptical stance of a seasoned scientist to eventually declare that, "according to the data collected in our laboratory, ... consciousness continues after physical death."[14] He found himself compelled by the success of his scrupulously conducted research to embrace a "model [that] says that mind is first. Consciousness exists independently of the brain. It does not depend upon the brain for its survival."[15] Schwartz concluded: "The challenge for contemporary psychology, neuroscience, and consciousness studies is to consider the implications of such findings for understanding mechanisms of consciousness and their implications for the continuance of consciousness hypothesis."[16]

It is not possible here to delve further into the history of the formal, organized psychical and parapsychological study of whether or not, or how, we survive physical death. Suffice it to say that in the past 120 years, thousands of investigations have been conducted, and hundreds of books and thousands of journal articles on the subject of death and survival have been published. Yet what can be said in the face of this more-than-a-century of purported evidence in support of confirming irrefutably the long-standing survival hypothesis that we survive death?

The most honest thing that can be said to date is that "the jury is still out." The field seems to provide a mixed bag of personal experiences, reports, and claims, and of evidence, or supposed evidence, that it is impossible to absolutely substantiate. In the case of mediumship, of supposedly discarnate, physically deceased human spirits communicating to or through currently physically alive mediums and channels, what can 120 years of research by hundreds of dedicated investigators truly prove regarding survival of death? It depends on whom you ask, across the spectrum—from true believers in survival, afterlife, and a range of other related nonordinary experiences, phenomena, and claims, on the one end, to those of different religious faiths and teachings of their faiths, somewhere in the middle, to the most hardened skeptics and physical-reductionist scientists, on the other end.

One thing is for certain: There is a range of what can be called competing or rival hypotheses that could be used to account for the kinds of seeming evidence that have accrued over the decades for the possibility of our survival of bodily death. There is, regarding the role played by mediums and channels and/or by those on their behalf, the possibility that it is conscious fraud and hoax that is responsible for what seems to be communication from the afterlife, or that there is unconscious motivation and behavior, including dissociation, delusion, hallucination, thought disorder, and various kinds of neuroses and psychoses at work.

Perhaps the most interesting hypothesis is that something truly unusual or paranormal is really going on in such cases of seeming nonphysically based spirit communication through a physically based person. In this hypothesis, competing with the survival hypothesis, something called "super-ESP" may be responsible for what is going on, not the fact that we survive death and that someone from the afterlife is communicating through the medium. Even when it appears that the information being communicated can only be accounted for as coming from some particular, identifiable once-living, now anomalous, transcendent source and not from the medium who would have no way of knowing the information involved, still something else may be going on instead of the speculation that we survive death and can communicate back. In this super-ESP hypothesis, what is shared by, or attributed to, a nonphysical, surviving spirit as its source, is said to be actually coming from someone's brain-mind still alive who knows that information or from somewhere on Earth where that information physically resides. The medium or channel, in his or her altered state of consciousness, and unconsciously desiring to please or be of service, telepathically connects to whoever on Earth has the information unconsciously in his or her brain-mind, or clairvoyantly, or in some other ESP "remote viewing," anomalous cognition, or out-of-body way goes to wherever the information is and sees or in other ways obtains access to it. Then, through a form of dissociation that could in such a case be considered as much functional, or even optimal performance, as psychopathological, the medium or channel then provides the information or message from his or her unconscious, where the telepathic or clairvoyantly derived information ended up. This information is often provided by means of a kind of dissociated subpersonality of the medium masquerading as an autonomous spirit separate from him or her. All of this rather complex anomalous information processing would be occurring outside of the conscious awareness or intention of the medium.

This rather convoluted super-ESP hypothesis still needs to admit to the reality of psychic goings-on, such as telepathy or clairvoyance, together with perhaps nonpathological forms of dissociation or psychodynamic intrapsychic unconscious processes operating outside of conscious awareness or control. One wonders, then, why we should want to embrace this kind of explanation, which has to include a component that is also paranormal, that goes beyond our current physical-reductionist-type scientific textbooks and understanding. Why would we accept an explanation that sounds so complicated, when it might just be easier to accept the no-less-, yet perhaps no-more-, paranormal-sounding survival hypothesis instead that says that the communication or information is really coming from a discarnate human spirit who has survived death, and that, in addition, we will survive our deaths as well?

This debate of super-ESP versus survival hypothesis brings to mind the old scientific adage of Occam's razor, that the best explanation is going to be the most parsimonious, least complicated one. Therefore, it is interesting to note that for so many of us today it seems to appear more palatable, less threatening, to accept the reality even of ESP and at the same time accept that death is the end of life, than to accept that death is not the end.

Whether or not we are going to meaningfully survive our own bodily deaths is one question that we will all eventually have to discover for ourselves at death, each alone. Until that time, one thing we can do is seek out potential hints of the truth from sources such as those that fill this book, that may turn out to be those who have passed beyond the veil before us and yet remain interested in, and capable of, communicating back. Or such sources may just be the skewed creativity or psychopathology of the dissociated unconscious of the all-too-earthly channel. Just because a self-identified source through a channel or medium may provide information that appears able to be known or provided only by that source itself may not mean for sure that that source really did survive death and is continuing to exist and communicate, for, according to the super-ESP hypothesis, the channel could unconsciously, telepathically, or clairvoyantly be picking up such information from someone else still physically alive or from some repository of the same information physically residing in some artifact or record somewhere on Earth.

The supposedly surviving spirit of the late American philosopher and psychologist William James, channeled by Jane Roberts, explained:

> In the universal drama, you might say that I am still in the same theater of events, but I have moved from life's stage to the balcony.... My status allows me a better view. I can look down, symbolically speaking, to see the actors coming in at one end of the stage, leaving at the other end, and I can also vaguely perceive other states, both above and below....
>
> While not presently involved in a physical drama, certain privileges are also allowed me in that I can shout out my comments and suggestions, urge certain actors on, applaud and boo as rambunctiously as I please. Not being personally involved, I follow the plots, characters, and themes, and because of my privileged viewpoint I can see where certain actions are leading, so that sometimes I call out in alarm, "Watch out," or "Don't you see what will happen if you don't do something quickly?" Or ... I

might feel at least like shouting out my irritation at poorly read lines or inept performances.[17]

So, if James and Roberts are to be believed, just because you're dead doesn't mean you're disinterested in what occurs on the physical plane. Furthermore, the dead may on occasion enjoy expressing an opinion about what they are able to still experience or know about that is occurring on Earth, including suicide, even their own.

One final note: Those who are knowledgeable about channeling recognize that one can never really prove to anyone where the seemingly evidential material truly is coming from. As mentioned, it could be the product of super-ESP, or it could be the unconscious creative mind of the person channeling the message that we are hearing from, which would simply be material being channeled from one portion of the psyche to another and then on to us. Or it could be one spirit masquerading as another (channeled messages often warn of tricksters); that is, it may be a case of genuine self-transcending channeling, but you are not getting the source you think you are or that it claims to be. You are getting another source or entity that for whatever reason—including its own ignorance, lost, damaged, or deluded condition—is misrepresenting itself to you as someone or something it is not. This perspective accounts for much of the biblical admonishments from the Christian Church, for example, to beware of and avoid "witches," "wizards," and the "familiar spirits" that may operate through them, and to interpret most mediumistically contacted sources as demons, demonic, evil, and the tempting work of the devil.

But why should we want to, have to, know the ultimate nature of the source of information, of the nature of someone or something anomalous or transcendent appearing to be communicating to us? At this point in the still-limited development of our scientific understanding, our only recourse may be to ignore the purported source, whose ultimate nature cannot yet be known or proven, and simply focus on the material itself. Is it any good? Is it helpful? Does it, so to speak, resonate with us? Does it feel right, think right, and/or intuit right to us? These questions must also be considered in addition to wanting to know for certain the ultimate cause or source of purported self-transcending information—a knowing for certain that at present, and due to the limits of current scientific capabilities, must remain unavailable to us unless we can find it through our own personal experience, belief, or faith alone.

Therefore, you are invited to read the material in this book with as open a mind as possible, to see what connects for you in whatever ways and at whatever levels, what can be meaningful and useful to you, given your own experiences and beliefs, and given the certainty of your own eventual death and the death of all those whom you hold dear, whether they have already died or will soon enough do so. Not all things are amenable to traditional scientific understanding and the demands for scientific evidence and proof. Some things must, for now at least, be left to the realms of personal opinion, belief, and faith.

THE APPROACH TAKEN IN THIS BOOK

First, in writing this book, our purpose is not to use the content of mediumistic/channeled communications to try to provide incontrovertible evidence that at least some of us do survive physical death and are able to communicate back to the physically living. As mentioned in the previous section, attempts to find irrefutable evidence either completely for or against the survival hypothesis are still indecisive and ongoing. Nor is it our purpose to try to make a case that mediumship/channeling actually involves mediating spirit communication from beings residing in an afterlife (or afterdeath) domain, rather than involving some kind of self-generated, dissociated brain-mind activity of the medium or channel, or, worse, being a function of intentional fraud or hoaxing. Again, attempts to completely prove or disprove the reality of mediumship or channeling are still in progress and any ultimate resolution of the matter still remains illusive. Rather, we choose to let the published, and séance-derived, material purported to derive from informants on the other side of physical death speak for itself and to let its themes and patterns emerge for you, however they may. Therefore, ours is simply descriptive research.

Second, we feel it is important, before turning to Part I of this book, to explain our approach to how we are presenting what is here. We realize the nature of our subject matter provides a kind of litmus test for most readers. There will be those of you who will be very accepting of what this book is about, because of your own pre-existing beliefs, faith, or personal experiences. Then there will be those of you who come to this book as yet undecided, as open-minded or agnostic, about what truth may be presented here. And, finally, there will be those of you who pick up this book predisposed to not believe a word of it because of your own training, preconceptions, and experiences (or lack of experiences). For us, as authors, this might seem to present a kind of no-win situation: If we come across like "true believers" about what we are presenting, we may alienate the more skeptical and scientifically trained readers, who we want to have hang in there and give the material a chance. At the same time, if we seem questioning and critical of what we are presenting at every turn, that could distract and turn off readers already accepting, or open to believing, what this book is about.

Let's use an analogy: When writing, most authors must decide on the manner in which they will consistently use either the singular pronoun "he/him" or "she/her," or use gender-neutral combinations like "him or her" or "he/she" throughout their writing. Constantly using "he/him" may give the reader the impression that the author wishes to give a bias to the dominance of the male gender, usually deemed politically incorrect, even if this is not the intention or value system of the author. On the other hand, constantly using only the combination of "he or she" or the construction "s/he" instead can become overly formal sounding, unwieldy, and tedious, and can break up the smoothness of the reading.

Such a decision about needing to choose how to handle pronoun use can serve as an analogy here for what lies at the heart of this book's writing style. The book's content heavily draws from and depends on what is called mediumistically conveyed, or channeled, information and messages. In the writing of it—similar to needing to take a stand on style of pronoun use—we as authors were faced throughout with a choice about how to present and refer to this kind of channeled/mediumistic material, to the sources from which it reportedly comes, to the reality of the process itself, and to the reality of survival of physical death and the presence of an afterlife.

On the one hand, we could use the style that constantly couches and qualifies every reference to each channeled source, to the nature of the channeled process, and to the notion of survival of death and of an afterlife, by over and over using conservative adjectives and defensively limiting phrases such as "supposed," "reported," "purported," "reputed," "ostensible," "hypothesized," "said to be," and so on. However, after just a few pages of this, such a practice can draw undue attention to itself as a kind of relentless self-monitoring, self-constraining editorial tone, and can be distracting to the reading process, regardless of the reader's point of view on the subject matter.

On the other hand, we could choose a kind of transparent, more direct style, by simply presenting to you what the sources we are using are presenting and in the manner in which they are presenting it. In virtually all of the cases of the published material and personal interviews and séances we used, the authors and interviewees do *not* use such self-conscious, hedging, conservatively qualifying modes of presentation and reference. Instead, they come across in a kind of straightforward, unapologetic manner true to their own experiences and beliefs, which then leaves it to readers to think and feel about what is being presented in whatever manner they wish, including in a way that may not be as accepting of the subject matter as are the authors or interviewees themselves.

Therefore, for the sake of transparency, ease of reading, and to avoid tedious repetition, we have chosen the latter approach, presenting things as clearly and simply as we can with as little continual self-editorializing as possible. Returning to the pronoun-use analogy, many authors at the beginning of a book may say something like: "Even though I will be using 'he/him' throughout instead of 'he or she,' this does not mean I support or wish to contribute to male-gender dominance. In fact, I do not. I embrace a gender-neutral or gender-equal viewpoint. I'm simply choosing the more familiar, straightforward route to provide a less encumbered text for the reader's sake." Similarly, in this book, we can now say at the outset: "Just because we are choosing to present references to channeled sources, the channeling process, and the existence of survival and an afterlife in an unadorned and unqualified manner similar to the way it was originally presented by the hundreds of sources from which we drew to create this book, it does not mean that we are 'true believers' who uncritically accept all these perspectives and claims as real and true."

As the authors of this book, we do not think that any one perspective about what is presented here can have the final say about the ultimate reality of what may be going on. There are those of us who are faithful to our beliefs even though we may lack what others would think of as sufficient empirical grounds for them. We have our own personal experiences and we are true believers as a result with regard to those experiences and perspectives. Still, in contrast, there are others of us who need more than personal experience, belief, or faith. We need solid, material evidence and proof, consensual validation, and sensate and instrumental verification, in order to determine whether we are to deem something believable, and this may then group us with hardened skeptics and physical-reductionist scientists in the eyes of others. As authors of this book, we want to reiterate our earlier refrain that we do not believe that adherents to either of these two basic orientations can presently provide irrefutable proof to the other's satisfaction of the correctness of their beliefs, cognitions, and claims. Once again, "the jury is still out" regarding the ultimate truth. At this developmental point for us as a species, there are deep-seated, heartfelt, even heated, perspectives being held both pro and con about whether we meaningfully survive physical death to experience some kind of afterlife that includes a continuation of consciousness and personal identity. All we can hope for, as authors, is that all of you, as readers coming from a variety of orientations, can find things in this book that are meaningful and useful to you.

PART I

Traditional and Assisted Suicide

Overview of Traditional Suicide

The taking of one's own life is the most drastic step one can imagine ever taking. It can be the result of a moment's impulse or deep and prolonged thought. Likewise, suicide can be completely conscious and well-planned or the result of unconscious, extreme risk-taking behavior. This book focuses on the conscious, intentional kind of suicide.

There are many reasons why people kill themselves. Regardless of their stated motive (real or imagined), they feel they have reached a point in their lives where they: (1) have no other options, (2) are exhausted from the constant pain and struggle of life, (3) believe it will garner them sympathy or emotion from those left behind, and/or (4) think they have nothing to live for. People may feel sad or hopeless or overwhelmed. Often there is a component of physical or emotional pain. This pain is so deep, so severe, that it simply becomes unbearable. However, even beyond this private suffering and the sometimes violent and painful method of their deaths, is the issue of the damage left in their wake. In addition to the usual sense of a hole being left in their lives, friends, co-workers, and family all have to wonder whether they are guilty for not having done enough. Psychiatrist Kay Jamison eloquently concludes, "Suicide carries in its aftermath a level of confusion and devastation that is, for the most part, beyond description."[1]

In this overview, we will first look at the history of traditional suicide, then at suicide in the present, including recent research findings and selected socio-cultural and psychological viewpoints, and we will end with the existential reality of death that looms for all of us, and the strange relationship that exists between life and death, especially, for the suicidal mind. Following this overview chapter, which admittedly takes a decidedly worldly, scientific, and scholarly look at the subject of traditional suicide, the remainder of Part I will turn its attention entirely to suicide from the perspective of purported spirits existing in the afterlife as received by mediums and channels. This overview can allow us to work with both worldly and otherworldly perspectives in order to develop our own views on the subject of suicide and what may follow it.

HISTORICAL OVERVIEW

An ancient Egyptian text, "Dispute Over Suicide," tells of the loneliness and social isolation fueling the author's suicidal thoughts as he looks to the attractiveness of death where "yonder" he shall stand in his "celestial bark" like a "living god." Only six suicides are recorded in the Old Testament. The most dramatic mass suicide of ancient times occurred at the fortress of Masada where the Hebrew forces, greatly outnumbered by the advancing Romans, followed their leader Eleazar, who led them to kill themselves rather than become Roman slaves.[2] In classical Greek times, suicide could stem from feeling dishonored or losing a loved one, and there was the "Orphic conception of death as fulfilling the immortal soul's innermost desire to free itself from the prison of the body and rejoin its divine source."[3] However:

> The suicide most highly regarded in Greek mythology as well as in Homer were the heroic suicides—the sacrifice of one's life for the benefit of another, and in particular for the defense of one's country. Such suicides were honored and admired. Society tacitly and sometimes alternately encouraged him [the one committing suicide].[4]

We shall revisit this type of supposedly heroic, sacrificial suicide in Part II of this book when we examine the present-day phenomenon of Islamic fundamentalist suicide bombers.

Almost 100 years ago, the great sociologist Emile Durkheim wrote what still remains one of the most influential books on suicide.[5] In it, he harkened back to ancient Greece, where those who wished to kill themselves were supposed to first seek permission from the proper authorities. Regarding someone preparing for suicide, Durkheim wrote: "At Athens, if he asked authority of the Senate before killing himself, stating the reasons which made life intolerable to him and his request was regularly granted, suicide was considered a legitimate act." He recounted the historian Libanius reporting the Greek law:

> Whoever no longer wishes to live shall state his reasons to the Senate, and after having received permission shall abandon the life. If your existence is hateful to you, die; if you are overwhelmed by fate, drink the hemlock. If you are bestowed with grief, abandon life. Let the unhappy man recount his fortune, let the magistrate supply him with the remedy, and his wretchedness will come to an end.[6]

During the Roman Empire, heroic suicides were still widely reported, as were honorably viewed suicides committed to avoid the indignity, disability, and suffering of disease and old age. Especially dramatic was the ongoing pattern of the deaths of Christian martyrs allowing themselves to be killed to enter the afterlife promised them by Christ and the other early Christian leaders. But although there was still a pull toward the spiritual afterlife in the face of increasing worldly deprivation and hardship during the Middle Ages, the Christian Church moved to reject suicide as an option. St. Augustine (354–430) pronounced suicide to be a crime, since it was killing oneself, and, as stated in the sixth commandment, "Thou shalt not kill" (including oneself). By 693, the Council of Toledo had proclaimed that an individual who attempted suicide was to be excommunicated.[7] St. Thomas Aquinas (1225–1274) saw suicide as flying in the face of the mandate to be charitable, including to oneself. Plus, committing suicide could harm one's community. But, especially, "it usurps God's power to dispose at his discretion of man's life, death, and resurrection."[8]

According to Corsini's *Encyclopedia of Psychology*, as time went on, society continued to create sanctions against suicide:

> From the 11th century on, whether or not the property of a deceased individual was to be kept by the heirs or had to be forfeited to the Crown depended on whether or not the death was judged (by the coroner) to be an act of God or a felony. Suicide was the latter, a felony against the self, *felo de se;* thus the way in which a death was certified was of enormous importance to the survivors.[9]

Then the Renaissance, with its renewed appreciation for earthly life and its beauties, and with new hope and vision for human possibilities, saw increased attention turned toward, not away from, this world, with suicide becoming less attractive. By the late eighteenth century, the Romantic Movement rekindled an attractive preoccupation with death and with a larger transcendental reality toward which the heart pines in the face of the less attractive insufficiencies and disappointments of life on Earth.[10]

Throughout history, many philosophers have focused on the topic of suicide: Pythagoras, Plato, Aristotle, Socrates, Epicurus, the Stoics, Seneca, Epictetus, Montaigne, Déscartes, Spinoza, Voltaire, Montesquieu, Rousseau, Hume, Kant, Schopenhauer, Nietzsche, Kierkegaard, and Camus.[11]

The essay "On Suicide" by philosopher David Hume, published in 1777, a year after his death, was promptly suppressed. The essay chose to refute the contention that suicide should be considered a crime. Opposed to the views of most of his contemporaries, Hume did not see suicide as a transgression of the responsibilities and duties we have to others, to ourselves, or to God, declaring: "Prudence and courage should engage us to rid ourselves at once of existence when it becomes a burden."[12]

SUICIDE TODAY

Jumping to the present, we can see a continuation of the social and legal sanctions against the strange form of murder that is suicide. *The Encyclopedia of Psychology* cites only two states, Alabama and Oklahoma, where the act of committing suicide is deemed a criminal offense, though, obviously, there can be no worldly punishment for the crime, given that the perpetrator is deceased. In some other states, suicide attempts are considered misdemeanors that are usually not enforced. Thirty states currently have no laws against suicide, attempted and failed, or successful. However, all states have laws against encouraging or helping someone else commit suicide.[13]

The current statistics on suicide are grim. Approximately 5–15 percent of American adults admit to having had suicidal thoughts at some point in their life and up to 50 percent of high school students have considered it.[14] Furthermore, according to Jamison, suicide has tripled in the last forty-five years, and is a major cause of death in college students and younger Americans. The National Center for Health Statistics reports that suicide was responsible for 31,655 deaths in 2002.[15]

Unfortunately, the United States is not alone in reporting such grim statistics. The University of Oxford Centre for Suicide Research reports that more than 5,000 people a year take their own lives in the United Kingdom.[16] In October 1999, the United Kingdom reported that the number of young males who had taken their own lives had doubled since 1989—a mere ten years.[17] France, too, has a high suicide rate.[18] China also appears to have a growing problem, with 287,000 known deaths a year due to suicide—and more that may not get reported.[19]

There are certainly plenty of statistics about suicide. Here are a few more examples: It is the tenth leading cause of death (at least 22,000 to 30,000 lives annually), with the actual number being as many as twice this because of suicides disguised as accidents and due to underreporting. Among causes of death, suicide ranks second for white males aged 15–19. For physicians under age 40, it ranks first. One out of nine attempted suicides is successful. "Those who are widowed, divorced, or single kill themselves significantly more often than married people."[20] The World Health Organization has seen a worldwide rise of 34 percent in suicide rates since it began keeping records in 1950. According to its estimates, by the year

2040, "approximately 1.53 million people will die from suicide, and 10–20 times more people will attempt suicide worldwide." This represents on average one death every 20 seconds and one attempt each 1–2 seconds.[21]

Adolescents and very young adults are particularly prone to suicide. Between 1960 and 1980, the suicide rate among adolescents in the United States increased by 150 percent. Following accidents and homicides, suicide is the third leading cause of death among American adolescents. "A recent study of high school and middle school students reported that 33 of every 100 had thought of suicide and six of every 100 had attempted suicide."[22]

From *The Harvard Guide to Psychiatry*, 3rd edition, we hear:

> Male suicidal behavior usually involves an inability to control angry impulse ... although adolescent men outnumber women in completed suicides by about 4 or 5 to 1, adolescent women outnumber men by about the same margin in numbers of attempts ... among children and adolescents who commit suicide, a statistically significant number come from fragmented homes with missing parents ... in a sample of 108 adolescents who attempted suicide, 49% came from homes with one parent missing.[23]

In looking over the data, it seems clear that some people are more at risk for suicide than others. These include those who have made prior attempts, suffer mental illness, young men in jail, gamblers, the police, those without jobs, teenagers, and certain ethnic groups such as Native Americans and African-Americans.[24] Which gender is most at risk for suicide can vary by age and country. But no matter how you break it down, we always have to come back to the fact that suicide rates are increasing. This is a growing problem. It desperately needs to be addressed by our society. With so many taking their own lives, it is critical to understand what motivates those who commit suicide, and what may become of their spirits or souls in the afterlife.

A great many reasons can lead a person to take the path of suicide, some of which may be inadvertent. Many threaten suicide as a cry for help or attention that is never intended to go that far, but is accidentally more effective than anticipated. It can be triggered by interpersonal differences, mental illness, and life stresses. Surprisingly, it is not particularly associated with health problems. However, mental illness is another story altogether. Furthermore, there may be a complex interplay of predisposing factors. Genes, personality, drugs (legal or otherwise), alcohol, mental illness, and the stresses of life may all work together to create a fatal cocktail. To fix only one of these problems, perhaps at the expense of the others, may not be enough to keep a person from taking his or her own life.

Kay Redfield Jamison, herself a psychiatrist, makes an important observation:

> Psychological pain or stress alone—however great the loss of disappointment, however profound the shame or rejection—is rarely sufficient cause for suicide. Much of the decision to die is in the construing of events, and most minds, when healthy, do not construe any event as devastating enough to warrant suicide....
>
> When the mind's flexibility and ability to adapt are undermined by mental illness, alcohol or drug abuse, or other psychiatric disorders, its defenses are put in jeopardy.[25]

This is important, suggesting that suicidal individuals may be thinking poorly and have clouded judgment at the time of their death.

SOCIO-CULTURAL PERSPECTIVES

The great French sociologist Emile Durkheim, in his landmark book (1897) *Le suicide*, described four kinds of suicide, all emphasizing the strengths or weaknesses of the person's relationships with society. He coined the term *altruistic suicide* to represent the kind that is expected and demanded by the rites and customs of the group. *Egotistic suicides* are carried out by individuals with too few connections to the community and too few demands from the community to continue living as part of it. *Anomic suicides* stem from the shattering of a relationship that the individual was accustomed to and valued, such as the loss of a job, close friend, or loved one, or loss of one's financial security and well-being. And *fatalistic suicides* come from excessive regulation, oppression, or denial of essential freedoms or birth-rites. All four are sociologically or psychosocially determined since they all involve in different ways the individual's interpersonal relation to others that has been changed in such a way as to lead him or her to choose suicide.[26]

Religious and cultural attitudes regarding suicide have run the gamut. Some, like the Japanese, may consider it the best, and sometimes only appropriate, behavior in response to a given situation. Nor are they alone in this. A number of cultures have accepted, or even encouraged, the elderly and sick to sacrifice their own lives for the greater good of the group.[27] Others, like the Stoics in ancient Greece, have felt everyone has the right to choose the time and place of his or her death, while still others, such as the ancient Romans and the Catholic Church, have taught that suicide is never appropriate.

Our own U.S. culture is divided on the issue, with some individuals advocating euthanasia and assisted suicide as an individual right, and others finding the whole idea of suicide as abhorrent as homicide.

Although the cultural discouragement of suicide has softened in recent times, there may have been good reason for it in the past. Suicide tends to be imitated by others. As Jamison explains:

> Society must deal with the potentially infectious repercussions of suicide, especially among the young, and must somehow try to keep a single tragedy from progressing to deaths of others. The contagious quality of suicide, or the tendency for suicides to occur in clusters, has been observed for centuries and is at least partially responsible for some of the ancient sanctions against the act.[28]

Historical methods of ending such suicide epidemics have often been brutal, if effective. Rome halted one by nailing the bodies of all suicides to crosses and putting them on public display, while in Greece the lifeless bodies of female suicides were at one point dragged naked through the streets.

This problem of one suicide leading to others is true even today, whether this deadly chain of events is started by a high school student or a high-profile idol. In the anthology *Straight to Hell: 20th Century Suicides*, Mikita Brottman points out:

> The suicide of a prominent youth icon is often followed by outbreaks of suicide by depressed and empathetic fans. This phenomenon is sometimes referred to as the "Werther syndrome," and was first witnessed in modern culture with the death of Rudolf Valentino, which sparked an epidemic of empathy suicides. In the days and weeks following the [suicidal] death of Kurt Cobain, a rash of fans from Seattle to Australia began killing themselves in empathy and tribute to the fallen grunge king.[29]

The publicity and romanticized nature of the act—especially when combined with the desire for attention or retaliation—appears to seduce many into following suit whether the individuals are friends or family of the person who committed suicide or are complete strangers.

One of the most notorious cases of mass suicide was that involving the Jonestown People's Temple. In 1978, 913 followers of the Reverend Jim Jones, members of the People's Temple, committed mass suicide in northern Guyana at a site called Jonestown. The People's Temple had been started by Jones in San Francisco; he moved it and its congregation to Guyana with the dream of setting up an autonomous communal utopia according to his vision. Initially he was reported to be a good minister and leader for his followers, but as time went on, he seemed to darken and his Temple became ever more a cult of personality that curtailed the freedoms and individuality of its followers.

In 1978, U.S. congressman Leo Ryan went to Guyana to investigate reported abuses by Jones of his members. When Ryan and his small investigative team tried to leave, along with four of the cult members who had decided to defect, Jones ordered them murdered by his own lieutenants. Some, including Ryan, died, while the rest got away in their small plane. Realizing that his People's Temple and the dream he had for it would now be ended once U.S. authorities found out about the murders, Jones ordered everyone at the Temple to take their own lives rather than wait to be subject to the repercussions of his homicides. If there was no longer a possibility of having his dream come true on Earth, then it was time to leave this Earth. Mass quantities of sweet punch laced with poison were prepared. First, the 267 children were given the poisoned drink, with some of the older ones taking it voluntarily. Then the adults took their turn.

When more investigators and law enforcement people arrived at Jonestown, they found the place strewn with the dead bodies of 913 People's Temple followers, along with Jones's own body. He had chosen to shoot himself in the head, rather than drink the potion. The question remains: How accurate is it to say that this was a mass suicide involving 914 people? Weren't the younger children simply murdered and the older children, who went along with drinking the poison, really too young to know what they were doing? The same could be asked for many of the adults. How much of this was a function of coercion, brainwashing, or mind control? How many of those 637 adults were "in their right minds" enough to purposefully take their own lives that way? Many probably did believe unquestioningly in Jones's vision.[30]

One key fact to note is that the violence—at least on a psychological level—is seldom isolated to the person committing the act of suicide, whether it takes place individually or in a group. Surviving friends, family, and acquaintances are all affected, and may end up performing suicide themselves. Perhaps what makes suicide so difficult to deal with is the fact that its consequences ripple out to affect so many. Friends and family are left in shock, always wondering whether they should have known or if they could have stopped it. Faith can be shaken, beliefs shattered. Emotions may be a confusing jumble of guilt, anger, grief, and—perhaps strangest of all—relief. And even once that is past, with all the questions within and without laid to rest, there is still that loss to come to terms with—the fact that someone you knew is no longer alive. Because of this, one cannot think of suicide as simply violence against the self. Not only can it lead strangers to copy the act, but it literally tears lives asunder. Those who survive it face a long, painful road to recovery.

PSYCHOLOGICAL PERSPECTIVES

How does present-day psychology view the nature of suicide? Edwin S. Shneidman, an eminent authority on suicide, added *suicidology* to our vocabulary as the term for its formal study. In 2001, the American Psychological Association published his milestone work,[31] an analysis of what he considered the thirteen leading books on the subject from the past century. Psychiatrist Bela Buda synopsizes Shneidman's findings:

> Suicide is always a consequence of "psychache," a strong psychic pain, tension, and suffering that makes life intolerable. Behind psychache lie four essential constellations: (1) thwarted love, acceptance, or belonging; (2) fractured control, excessive helplessness, and frustration; (3) assaulted self-image and avoidance of shame, defeat, humiliation, and disgrace; (4) ruptured key relationships and attendant grief and bereftness. Against the background of these elements a lot of other factors are active, such as biological vulnerability, social disorganization, cultural rules, isolation, etc.[32]

Shneidman noted four psychological features in those who successfully committed suicide, including: (1) "acute perturbation" [general upset]; (2) "heightened inimicality—an increase in self-hate, self-loathing, shame, guilt, and self-blame"; (3) "a sharp and almost sudden constriction of the person's intellectual focus ... a tunneling process, a narrowing of the mind's content"; and (4) "the idea of cessation—the coming into the person's awareness that it somehow possible to end this terrible and unbearable psychological pain."[33]

Based on his decades of research and clinical experience, Shneidman has developed what he calls "The Ten Commonalities of Suicide":

1. The common purpose of suicide is to seek a solution.
2. The common goal of suicide is the cessation of consciousness.
3. The common stimulus in suicide is intolerable psychological pain.
4. The common stressor in suicide is frustrated psychological needs.
5. The common emotion in suicide is hopelessness [or] helplessness.
6. The common cognitive state in suicide is ambivalence.
7. The common perceptual state in suicide is constriction.
8. The common action in suicide is egression.
9. The common interpersonal act in suicide is communication of intention.
10. The common consistency in suicide is with lifelong coping patterns.[34]

In her recent anthology, *Suicide Science: Expanding the Boundaries*, researcher Michelle M. Cornette and others present what they perceive to be the three leading theories of suicide held today. First is the *hopelessness theory*, in which there is "the expectation that highly desired outcomes will not occur or that highly aversive outcomes will occur and that there is nothing one can do to change this situation."[35]

Thus a kind of "hopelessness depression" sets in when there seems to be no prospect to either get what one really wants or to avoid what one really doesn't want. As part of this theory, negative events can serve as "occasion setters" for people to become hopeless, and there is a "cognitive vulnerability" for depressive thinking that accompanies the stress of such negative life events.

Second, the *self-discrepancy theory* draws on three different concepts of the self: the actual self, as one sees oneself; the ought self, which is the self one thinks one ought to be; and the ideal self, which is the self one would most like to be. Given these concepts, the theory states that "individuals are motivated to achieve a state in which there is consistency between their self-concept and these self-evaluative standards." Those "who possess discrepancies between their actual and ideal selves are relatively more prone to developing depression while those who possess discrepancies between their actual and ought selves are relatively more prone to developing anxiety." If one understands "depression as a consequence of psychological situations involving the absence of positive outcomes," then "failures to fulfill ideal standards ... are likely to become associated with experiences of depression."[36] Simply put, research has shown a strong correlation between negative evaluation of the self and suicidality.

Third, we have the *escape theory* of suicide. It states that "self-destructive behaviors can be explained in terms of motivation to escape from aversive self-awareness and negative affect."[37] An acute negative experience, calamity, or stressor can point up the large discrepancy that exists between what one wants or expects and what actually occurs and where what are often "unrealistically high expectations or standards" can be abruptly dashed. Then, "when setbacks or discrepancies occur, individuals can either blame external factors and absolve themselves of responsibility, or blame themselves and take on responsibility for the failure." Negative emotions, such as depression, anxiety, and anger, can arise from the resulting aversive, negative self-awareness. To screen out the negativity and damaged self-esteem, a kind of "mental narrowing" takes place, reducing one to the immediate present and blocking "meaningful higher-level thought," including anything that could compete with the overwhelming negative tone of the moment. A real recipe for suicide.

Still, it is not always so simple to get to the roots of suicide. For example, the depression theory of suicide, above, may give too much weight to depression as a contributing factor. Thomas Bronisch, Senior Psychiatrist at the Max Planck Institute of Psychiatry in Munich, Germany, believes there's more going on than this. He writes:

> There is no doubt that one can nearly always find depressive symptoms or a depressive syndrome accompanying suicidal behavior.... This is the one side of the coin. However, even severely depressed inpatients commit *suicide* in only 15% of the cases in long-term follow-up studies. Subjects with major depression report concomitant *suicide* ideas in 50% to 70% of cases, but report only 2%–4% *suicide* attempts in epidemiological studies.[38]

Bronisch also reports "an increase in rate of suicide in old age, whereas the diagnosis of major depression decreases after the age of sixty in both sexes."[39] In addition, vulnerability/resiliency to suicide may involve "factors including: family history of suicide, childhood sexual abuse, personality factors, peer affiliations, and school success." Also, "Comorbidity with anxiety and/or addiction is more important than a depressive disorder on its own for the development of suicidal behavior." And finally, he points out that the neurobiology of suicidal behavior, which can also include inward or outward aggressivity, "may be different than for depressive disorders or other psychiatric disorders without suicidality." As a result, Bronisch sees depression "to be rather a risk than a causal factor for the development of suicidal behavior."

Some additional perspectives on the roots of suicide include the fact that self-destructive behaviors can be traced to prior learning, including the social cognition view that we can learn indirectly by observing others' actions and their consequences, including in symbolic form, as through literature, film, or television. Contemporary psychiatrist Bruce Bongar points out in his book *The Suicide Patient: Clinical and Legal Standards of Care* that "suicidal individuals have unique cognitive characteristics, that is, cognitive rigidity, dichotomous thinking, impaired problem-solving ability, hopelessness, irrational beliefs, and dysfunctional attitudes."[40] The American researcher and clinician, Menninger, regarded suicide as including a "peculiar death that entails three internal elements: the element of dying, the element of killing, and the element of being killed."[41]

We turn now to some psychodynamic views on suicide. Sigmund Freud was a pioneer in developing psychological explanations for suicide, which he saw as essentially taking place within the mind and representing "unconscious hostility directed toward the introjected (ambivalently viewed) love object," which is the process of turning hostility originally intended for another toward oneself instead.[42] Bongar further characterizes fellow psychiatrist Sigmund Freud's interpretation of suicide:

> Suicide begins with a death wish that is directed toward others and then redirected toward an identification with the self. ... among the suicide mechanisms that Freud conceptualized as involving the breakdown of ego defenses and the release of increased destructive, instinctual energy were loss of love objects, aggression toward an introjected love object, narcissistic injury, overwhelming affect, and a setting of one part of the ego against the others.[43]

In Corsini's *Encyclopedia of Psychology,* Shneidman cites psychologist Gregory Zilboorg, who saw every suicidal case as involving a pronounced inability to love others and who also saw a relationship between the role of a broken home and suicide proneness.[44] Contributing to *The Harvard Guide to Psychiatry* (2nd ed.), Edwin H. Cassem also refers to Zilboorg's view that some suicidal patients believe they can escape the finality of death and achieve a kind of immortality.[45] He also refers to fellow psychologist S. Rado's view that suicide can atone for wrongs done in the past and can be a way of recapturing the love of someone or something earlier lost.[46]

Returning to Edwin Cassem, he points out that risk for suicide can occur when one experiences a loss of caring or support from another or others, especially when it happens suddenly, leaving one feeling rejected, alienated, and alone. Suicidal risk greatly increases at times of holidays and special times that remind the person of opportunities, friendships and loves, and sources of happiness and fulfillment that are no longer there. Such times can be marked with strong emotions that can move one toward suicide: loneliness and isolation, anger and guilt, feeling defective and hopeless.

Suicidal behavior is most likely when a person sees his or her situation as intolerable or hopeless. According to Cassem, suicide can stem from either a hateful, even murderous, impulse, or from an irrepressible need to escape one's own overpowering suffering.[47]

Robert E. Littman traced the development of Freud's thoughts on the subject of suicide from 1881 to 1939, and found a number of other factors besides hostility involved with suicide, including "rage, guilt, anxiety, dependency—as well as ... feelings of abandonment, and particularly of helplessness and hopelessness."[48]

Throughout reading these psychological perspectives on suicide, we may be moved to ask an obvious question. Bluntly put: *Are people who kill themselves crazy?* Is purposefully choosing to end one's own life, when it is otherwise physically healthy, always to be considered an act of someone who is mentally ill? We can readily agree that it is almost always a sign of mental health to choose to keep oneself alive in that it is eminently natural for life to want to perpetuate itself. But is it mentally healthy to choose to stay alive when experiencing an aching meaninglessness and purposelessness at the core of one's existence, or to want to stay alive when experiencing intolerable suffering and pain? Could choosing to end such a life ever be deemed an act of mental health, not mental illness? We will return to this theme in the chapter "Assisted Suicide" at the end of Part I of this book.

Many who study suicide make a distinction between suicide stemming from some form of mental illness and suicide that does not. For example, Dinesh Bhugra, head of the section of Cultural Psychiatry at the Institute of Psychiatry in London, has studied the Indian phenomenon known as sati, which she interprets as a kind of nonpsychiatric suicide.[49] The term *sati* is used to designate a woman who burns herself to death following the death of her husband, usually placing herself alongside his own funeral pyre. In India, this is seen as a noble deed done by a good woman selflessly devoted to her husband. Bhugra debates whether this form of suicide is done out of devotion, as one's dharma or sense of duty, or because the prospect of living as a widow on the charity of others might seem worse than death, or because, in her religious culture, she sees reincarnation awaiting her, or, finally, because it is a way she can independently assert her freedom and sense of self-worth in a patriarchal society. But whatever may lie behind this particular kind of suicidal self-sacrifice, Bhugra believes sati does not represent any kind of formal mental illness.

It is interesting to contemplate other examples of suicide that could also be deemed "nonpsychiatric." Faced with the impossibility of fighting effectively, let alone of winning, let alone of remaining alive, soldiers in wartime have chosen to throw themselves into certain death rather than run away or desert. Some people end their lives in order to save the life of another or in other ways act in an altruistic manner with nonselfish motives. And the list continues. While such individuals have intentionally killed themselves and in essentially the same ways that other traditional, probably mentally disturbed, suicides have, the state of mind underlying the act is decidedly different. The nonpsychiatric suicide has a reason for doing it other than to just end his or her own existence; it is, rather, done on *behalf* of existence, done in light of some code, obligation, duty, or principle, or done *for* another more than *against* oneself.[50]

Another example of this nonpsychiatric category could be hara-kiri. For the Japanese, the term *hara-kiri* is a vulgar version of *seppuka*, with seppuka meaning "stomach cutting" or "belly slicing," a centuries-old Japanese form of ritual suicide by disembowelment.[51] The phrase "to commit hara-kiri" has extended well beyond Japan. We in the U.S. know it through its many fictionalized film and television portrayals. Indeed, referring to committing hara-kiri has become for many simply a more colorful, cross-cultural way of saying "committing suicide." While there is little doubt that someone committing hara-kiri, or seppuka, is, by the traditional definition, committing suicide, the ritual context makes it somewhat different. The taking of one's own life in this way is following a prescribed formula: If such-and-such happens, you must then turn to hara-kiri. Obligation, lack of choice, and inevitability can characterize the act, along with honor, nobility, and heroism.

Here are some glimpses of the kinds of situations that can lead individuals to choose hara-kiri to end their lives. In 1895 a large group of Japanese military personnel committed hara-kiri together to protest against the return of a conquered territory to China. In 1912, a general and his wife killed themselves in response to the death of the Japanese emperor. And, at the end of World War II, many Japanese citizens and soldiers chose to commit seppuka rather than surrender to the Allied forces.[52]

One particular kind of seppuka, related to the Asian Indian practice of sati, is *oibara*, which is the historical Japanese practice of killing oneself at the death of one's master.[53]

ATTEMPTED SUICIDES AND NDEs

Richard Heckler, a counseling psychologist, social scientist, and faculty member at John F. Kennedy University in California and at the Union Graduate School in Ohio, wrote an influential book, *Waking Up, Alive: The Descent, the Suicide Attempt, and the Return to Life*. It is based on in-depth case studies of fifty individuals who survived their own suicide attempts. His study, and others like it, shed much-needed light on the experience and state of the mind of those who have tried to kill themselves. From such research, we can gain more insight into what may have lain behind those who were actually successful in ending their own lives, such as those throughout this book we will hear from, who are said to be in spirit form communicating back from the afterlife that supposedly follows physical death.

Those preparing to take their own lives, in Heckler's words, are confronted with "a frightening loss of their feelings of wholeness, order, and connection." They report that, leading up to the suicide attempts, "Faith dissolved, and their confidence in a gentle and nourishing world was shattered. An inner chaos unraveled the very fabric of their hearts and minds"[54] For them, "life begins to feel like a succession of insults, one after another, until a breaking point is reached."[55]

Speaking of the descent into suicide, Heckler reports on "that psychospiritual period during which the very fabric of one's world seems to stretch, tear, and break apart."[56] Others seem blind to one's suffering; the compassion that one is seeking is not there. One withdraws further from contact and connection, physically, emotionally, and spiritually.[57] Those attempting suicide say they had given up hope that there was anyone who could give them compassion and an understanding of their suffering.[58]

Heckler discovered in those who had attempted suicide what he called a consciousness-altering suicidal *trance state:*

> They no longer see or hear anything outside their own minds—the tight spiral of thought that tells them to die. ... the trance is a state of mind and body that receives only the kind of input that reinforces the pain and corroborates the person's conviction that the only way out is through death.[59]

This suicidal trance has its own logic. Abandoning hope of reclaiming their own lives, they now, instead, "apply their creativity to their own removal."[60] In this trance, "images of death as release and as an entry into a better world are so powerful and convincing" that they may be moved to try to take their own lives.[61] In the grip of this trance, one's mental and emotional perspective continues to narrow "until the only inner voices that can be heard are those that enjoin him or her to die"[62] One's romance is with death now, not life. Regarding one of his clients, Heckler remarks: "He wasn't afraid to die. ... [he] was afraid of living. Living seemed unfathomable."[63]

According to Heckler, a kind of dissociation can result, in which there are two parts of the suicidal person—one part experiencing intolerable suffering and the other part plotting death.[64] There can be a sense of freedom that comes from welcoming the prospect of suicide. As they near the moment, many report "there were sudden moments of stillness: feelings of acceptance, serenity, and peacefulness, and relief from pain."[65]

What lies at the heart of the suicide attempt? For Heckler, four of the biggest desires leading up to it are: escaping something in one's life, such as a dilemma, that feels inescapable; trying to gain control over something that may seem uncontrollable and confusing; sending a message by means of the suicidal act, a message that seemed earlier unable to be communicated in other ways; and, most obviously, desiring simply to kill the pain by killing oneself.[66] In addition, his research found that each of his subjects (also clients) had experienced one or more of the three main kinds of loss that he believes lead up to attempting suicide: (1) traumatic loss, (2) family loss that comes from extreme family dysfunction, and (3) loss that we can experience by way of our own growing sense of alienation.[67] Whatever may lie behind the act, choosing suicide flies in the face of all that our rational and scientific culture holds dear and totally undermines the normal, natural disposition to be healthy, functional, and relatively happy.[68]

Following a failed suicide attempt, Heckler found the following steps to recovery being taken by his clients: rebuilding the self; healing the past; taking responsibility for their actions; moving from isolation and alienation to reaching out, learning to ask for help, allowing others in, and letting others love them, and even being moved to give something back to the community.[69] These steps of recovering from a suicide attempt can provide ideas for those who work to help others turn away from moving toward taking their own lives. In the face of their failed suicides, some of Heckler's subjects also wondered if there were reasons, "existential or spiritual," for why they were unsuccessful in their attempts to end their lives.[70]

In contrast, among the hundreds of cases of completed suicides reported in this book, all said to be communicating in spirit form from the afterlife, we will hear from many voicing their own perspectives, existential or spiritual, regarding why their attempts at suicide, in fact, *succeeded*.

Of those who have been studied by Heckler and others, who attempted suicide, failed, and returned to describe their experience, some have also had as part of it what is called a near-death experience. Bruce Greyson is Carlson Professor of Psychiatry in the Department of Psychiatric Medicine in the University of Virginia Health System and a leading authority on the near-death experience (NDE). Most people who have experienced NDEs describe leaving their bodies, going through a tunnel toward a light, coming to the threshold of an afterlife hypothesized as the domain one may enter upon death, and being met there by someone known to them who has already died or by some other spirit. They also often report experiencing some kind of rapid review of their life. They are told it is not their time to leave life yet, and that they must return to physical reality for some further living. Most NDE experiencers (NDErs) are left very much changed by the experience. They feel they have been given a glimpse of a beautiful, spiritual realm of experience that awaits them when they actually die. Their fear of death dissipates and they have a renewed caring about life and themselves, imbued with new meaning and framed within a greater, deeper context.[71] According to Greyson, most who have experienced it report that "the NDE is an overwhelmingly positive, transcendentally beautiful experience. The view of death they come away with is a quite attractive one."[72]

One woman who attempted suicide in 1977 told NDE researcher Kenneth Ring, then Professor of Psychology at the University of Connecticut and President of the International Association for Near-Death Studies:

> I can't tell you what happened to me because I don't know, but something happened as I've never been the same since. People describe me as being "high on life." And they are right. I'm thankful for every new day God gives me and I never take one minute of my day for granted. I wish I could explain how very much that one experience changed me. But I just can't find words to express myself. But I'm sure of one thing: there is a peace that remains with me always now—it has the strangest calming effect on me.[73]

Many researchers, including those trained as physicians, such as psychiatrist Greyson, who have studied NDEs believe that they provide a genuine glimpse into some kind of spiritual-transcendental reality that seems to lie beyond the physical body and its senses and beyond physical earthly life. It is possible that the experiential realm briefly visited, and commonly described, by many NDErs may be the same as or similar to the realm that each of us will enter and then continue to exist within following our own physical deaths. Although there is no way to know this for certain, looking at the NDEs of attempted suicides may indirectly provide us with information about the experiences of those who have successfully committed suicide and are said to now reside in that Earth-transcending realm called the afterlife. Hearing the descriptions of NDEs can provide a potentially useful context for hearing the stories, conveyed by mediums and channels, that come from hundreds of spirits who, by their suicides, moved from near-death, into death, and through it to an afterlife from which they are now communicating to us. So, we invite you to compare the stories from suicidal NDErs with communications from the spirits of successful suicides.

In his chapter "Wish for Death, Wish for Life: The NDE and Suicide Attempts," published in a French anthology *Death Transformed*, Greyson reports on the initial three major studies done on the NDEs of attempted suicides. University of California at San Francisco psychiatrist David Rosen, the first to do this kind of research, interviewed eight people who had survived leaping from the Golden Gate Bridge in San Francisco. All eight reported having NDEs. The bridge has been a magnet for more than 1,200 successful suicides. Only 1 percent of those who make the attempt survive. University of Connecticut psychologists Kenneth Ring and Stephen Franklin did a larger-scale study of thirty-six suicide attempters, 47 percent of whom reported NDEs. This was followed by Greyson's own study, conducted at University of Michigan Hospitals, which involved interviewing sixty-one suicide attempters, 26 percent of whom reported NDEs.[74]

Based on his integration of the findings from these studies, Greyson notes a number of interesting patterns:

> The suicide attempters report the same kind of NDEs that other people report. They do not tend to have unpleasant or negative or hellish NDEs: in fact, people who want to die may have more positive NDEs than those who want to live. ... those who have NDEs become strongly opposed to suicide as a result of the experience. ... there is a "suicide-inhibiting" effect of NDEs.[75]

Greyson asked his attempted-suicide NDE subjects why they were less, or not at all, suicidal after their NDEs. Based on their descriptions, he found twelve categories of reasons why the NDE turned them away from any further thoughts of suicide. From most frequently to least frequently mentioned, these reasons are:

1. They experienced a "cosmic unity," a sense that they were now part of something larger than themselves.
2. Their NDE made the problems with which they were preoccupied prior to their suicide attempt less important now, putting them within a larger perspective.
3. The NDE enhanced their life, giving it more value and meaning, making it more precious.
4. The experience made their life seem more real than it had been before.
5. It enhanced their self-esteem.
6. It gave them a greater sense of bonding to other people.
7. It gave them a sense that their death by suicide was not meant to be.
8. It gave them an opportunity to reevaluate their life as a result of the life review they experienced as part of their NDE.
9. There was a secondary gain in the sense that their personal situation seemed enhanced as a result of the NDE.
10. They gained the conviction that suicide was ethically wrong.

11. Through their NDE, they experienced "a killing off of unwanted or offensive parts of the self so that the remainder can go on."
12. Least reported was that the NDE instilled in them a fear of going through the experience again.[76]

Studying these twelve categories, Greyson discovered that:

> The six *most* commonly offered reasons for not being suicidal after an NDE relate to transcendental matters, while the six *least* often mentioned reasons tend to be "reality-oriented." In other words, NDErs attribute their decreased suicidal thinking to a focus on transcendental issues.[77]

Finally, discovering that "although NDErs do romanticize death, they also romanticize life," Greyson concludes:

> If we can generalize from NDErs to others, then it would appear that the mundane crisis intervention practiced by most suicide prevention services, which focused on reality-oriented problem-solving and ego-strengthening, is not what makes people less suicidal. What makes people choose life is a transpersonal perspective on life and death.[78]

When we turn, following this chapter, to the rest of Part I, to hundreds of spirits of "successful" suicides reporting through channels and mediums from the afterlife about their experience, you will be able to compare both such *near-death* and *after-death* perspectives on life and death, on suicide and the larger transpersonal picture. Throughout this book, whether drawing from NDEs or from those who have passed beyond physical death, our overarching perspective will be transpersonal, transcendental, and spiritual.

TREATING THE SUICIDAL PERSON

Avery Weissman interpreted the wish to die as being an existential signal that the person's conviction "that his potential for being someone who matters has been exhausted."[79] Therefore, one of the things someone trying to help a suicidal person can do is try to make him feel he matters, that he matters to others, including to the clinician, and, above all, that he matters to himself.

Edwin Cassem refers to fellow psychologist Gregory Rochlin's theory that suicide, similar to other types of aggressive action, can serve to heighten damaged self-esteem; and that we can know the potential for suicide by the strong, dark feelings of hopelessness and helplessness that increasingly preoccupy the individual.[80]

Related to this, Cassem reports on research led by renowned cognitive psychotherapist Aron Beck: "In a rigorous investigation of 384 suicide attempters ... hopelessness is the key variable linking depression to suicidal behavior."[81]

So, it is important to try to strengthen the suicidal individual's critically damaged self-esteem and to provide resources to counter the feeling of helplessness and hopelessness.

Again, according to Cassem, the likelihood of developing major depression increases with the seriousness of the person's illness.[82] Therefore, highly important in helping the suicidal individual is combating the depression that is usually there, particularly by identifying, challenging, and trying to change or substitute for the beliefs, suppositions, and expectations that underlie and lead to the emotion of depression. In a predictable interrelation, researched and worked with by Aron Beck, Albert Ellis, and other cognitively oriented psychotherapists, self-destructive behavior, and ultimately suicide itself, arises from a negative emotional state, such as depression, and the emotion arose, in turn, from the beliefs underlying it.[83] So, one targets and works with the negative beliefs, the maladaptive statements and schemas about the self and the world that are carried within, to get to the negative emotion to abort the negative, even potentially self-murderous, behavior.

The Harvard Guide to Psychiatry (3rd ed.) provides guidelines for spotting and helping those who appear to be heading toward suicide. To protect life and its continuation, self-esteem and self-respect are the basic psychic conditions to be monitored and strengthened, and the individual's "narcissistic equilibrium"[84] should be restored and maintained. The therapist or other helper should act as "an ally for the life of the individual"; he or she should "have the capacity to hear out carefully and tolerate the feelings of despair, desperation, anguish, rage, loneliness, emptiness, and meaninglessness articulated by the suicidal person." The helper should give the suicidal person a sense that he or she is taken seriously and is being understood, and this may involve the therapist exploring the person's "darkest feelings of despair." The therapist should work to lessen social isolation and withdrawal on the part of the client, and help the client to initiate relationships, work, hobbies and other activities to enhance and maintain self-esteem. Any co-occurring psychological disorders should also be treated. And finally, the helper should be prepared to seek support or consultation for him- or herself if working with the suicidal person becomes especially depleting.[85]

In a similar vein, in *The Encyclopedia of Psychology* (2nd ed.), the eminent authority on suicide, E. S. Shneidman, lists a number of things to bear in mind for preventing suicide and working with the suicidal, including taking every incident pointing to possible suicide very seriously, weighing its degree of intensity and lethality, and continuing to assess for lethality throughout—knowing that those facing suicide are often ambivalent about carrying it out, torn between wanting to live and wanting to die, and thus may be crying out for help, and knowing that the person probably has a need for a "life-sustaining emotionally cemented relationship with the helper," which can provide "hope and succor." Schneidman continues that the therapist or helper needs to be willing to help and give with regard to the person's real-life problems; use community resources; as needed, seek consultation and support for oneself; consider hospitalization for the client, if deemed necessary; and involve those significant and close to the suicidal person who appear to be the best candidates to serve as a kind of "auxiliary therapist."[86]

EXISTENTIALISM AND DEATH

How we come to terms with our own inevitable death is one of the major themes dealt with by both existential philosophy and existential psychology and psychotherapy. Freud also wrote of death, claiming that the four most common fears associated with death are: (1) helplessness or loss of control, (2) being bad (guilt and punishment), (3) physical injury or symbolic injury (castration), and (4) abandonment.[87] He also posited that we each have a death instinct, which he called *thanatos*, that counterbalances our life and love instinct, which he called *eros*. In Freudian terms, then, it would seem that, in spite of whatever inbuilt fears we may have about death, and in spite of how present the eros instinct may be in us, when we are drawn toward suicide, we are definitely under the influence of thanatos, the death instinct. The existential struggle is to wrestle personal meaning and the will to live from the clutches of death that can mock us with its inevitability.

One definition of suicide, by Jean Baechler, emphasizes the functional nature of the act: "Suicide denotes any behavior that seeks and finds the solution to an existential problem by making an attempt on the life of the subject."[88]

There is the existentialist view of suicide presented by French philosopher Albert Camus in his book *The Myth of Sisyphus*, in which one is tempted, when life is experienced as not worth living because it is basically meaningless or absurd, to end one's life artificially, rather than wait for a natural death perhaps decades later. Anticipating the later Camus, the great American philosopher and psychologist William James endured relentless bouts of being pulled into the dark, depressive depths of what he termed his "melancholy" most of his life. In spite of his lifelong melancholy temperament, in an address entitled "Is Life Worth Living?" at the Harvard Young Men's Christian Association more than a century ago, James took a life-affirming, and an *afterlife-affirming,* stance:

> ... probably to every one of us here the most adverse life would seem well worth living, if we only could be certain that our bravery and patience with it were terminating and eventuating and bearing fruit somewhere in an unseen spiritual world.

James exhorted his audience: "Believe that life is worth living, and your belief will help to create the fact."[89]

Most existentialists do not entertain the vision of an afterlife to provide a larger meaning to either life or death. The existential challenge is to feel that life is worth living even if this physical life is all there is and nothing whatsoever follows death. An existentially oriented theory of suicide would explain self-inflicted deaths as stemming from the despair of those who see their lives as so lacking in meaning that they are no longer worth living.

From the existential point of view, we must each confront the fact that we are faced from birth with the inevitable fact that we must someday die. Our awareness of this fact, and acceptance of its truth, can lead to having a kind of "death anxiety."

Contemporary existential psychotherapist Irvin Yalom writes of the strange interpenetration of life and death and how they each give meaning to the other. Having a close brush with death, including the extreme case of having a NDE, can radically transform one's life. Yalom cites two fictional examples from the Russian writer Tolstoy. In *War and Peace,* the protagonist, Pierre, has led what for him is an empty, meaningless life until French troops capture him and prepare him for the firing squad. As he watches five others being shot before him, he prepares for his death. His life is spared, and for the rest of his life, he lives a rich life full of keen energy, perception, and purpose. Then, in Tolstoy's story "The Death of Ivan Illyich," the title character is a small-minded, insensitive, self-centered government worker who protracts a fatal illness and, while dying a painful death, comes to realize "he is dying badly because he has lived badly."[90] Once more, Yalom draws from Tolstoy, who asked:

> Is there meaning to my life which will not be destroyed by the inevitable death awaiting me? ... All my acts, whatever I do, will sooner or later be

forgotten and I myself be nowhere. Why, then, busy one's self with anything?[91]

Yalom points to six of ten people attempting suicide by jumping off the Golden Gate Bridge in San Francisco, who, upon their survival, went through a tremendous transition that changed their view of life in a deeply positive way.[92] There is a rich and growing literature on the near-death experience, including how powerfully it can change people's lives.[93] Throughout this book, in addition to hearing from purported spirits in the afterlife by way of mediums and channels, as mentioned earlier, we will also draw from the related experiences of attempted [unsuccessful] suicides and near-death experiencers, who claim to have had their own glimpse of a larger, transcendental reality that breathes new and lasting meaning into their mortal lives. Whether one has tasted death by suicidally seeking it, or life or the world has naturally pushed one to the very edge of life, death can revivify life. Agreeing with the philosopher Nietzsche, Yalom believes that only after we have fully considered suicide can we really take our lives seriously.[94]

Yalom notes: "The terror of death is ubiquitous and of such magnitude that a considerable portion of one's life energy is consumed in the denial of death. Death transcendence is a major motif in human experience."[95] According to Yalom, the presence of death in life and the choice of the living to leave life can give rise to some strange forms of reasoning. He writes of the parodoxical state of mind of some of his suicidal patients, who so fear death that they would consider taking their own lives just to escape the living terror of staying relentlessly confronted by death. Rather than feel a victim, passively at the mercy of the specter of death, perhaps better to actively take charge of the situation, controlling the manner, time, and place of one's own demise. He also points to what he calls the magical view of death held by some of his patients that somehow it may be only temporary and reversible. Also, to kill oneself in order to communicate anger, to punish, or create guilt in another implies that the person contemplating the act imagines that he or she will somehow be able after death to still experience the act's repercussions for others.[96]

Elsewhere, speaking of this "magical" view suicides often have, and the notion of a kind of immortality they may seek, Yalom tells of one patient who described why suicide was becoming more attractive to her:

> She believed that if she committed suicide, others would remember her for a very, very long time. This is an excellent example of suicide as a magical act.... There is in her view of suicide no idea of death; on the contrary,

she clasps suicide as a way to defeat death—as one may do provided one believes that one can continue to live if one exists in the consciousness of another.[97]

Yalom draws from the writing of Ernest Becker, who makes the case that our "universal ambition" is "prosperity" in the form of "continued existence." To follow this life-affirming, life-continuing "ambition," one must contend with death.[98] As Becker puts it:

> Man transcends death not only by continuing to feed his appetites [that is, in simple-minded blissful visions of heaven] *but especially by finding a meaning for his life,* some kind of larger scheme in which he fits.... It is an expression of the will to live, the burning desire of the creature to count, to make a difference on the planet because he has lived, has emerged on it, and has worked, suffered, and died.[99]

We may assume, then, that those who have taken their own lives apparently did not find such meaning for their lives, had not felt they counted or made a difference. At the same time, many may have felt that they *were* able to find meaning and count by the very act of their suicides.

In his book *Counseling the Terminally Ill: Sharing the Journey,* psychologist George Lair also addresses the topic of death anxiety. He sees both our problems and our hope for overcoming them as lying in our nature as creatures capable of learning. He reminds us that "Freud believed the fears surrounding death stemmed from unresolved psychological conflicts in childhood, meaning they [the fears of death] are not inherent, they are learned."[100] He points to the behavioral theory of psychology that sees that "The means of alleviating fear or anxiety surrounding death is through learning new, more appropriate responses."[101] Echoing Yalom, Lair draws on Ernest Becker's milestone book *The Denial of Death* and Weisman's *On Dying and Denying,* where, in Lair's words, the authors contend:

> Death anxiety is the most basic driving force for an individual ... that the fear of death is natural and present in everyone.... Shneidman (1973) said that death is universally feared: "Over the ages death has been the source of fear, the focus of taboos, the occasion for poetry, the stimulus for philosophy—and remains the ultimate mystery in the life of each man." Weisman (1974) pointed out ... "none of us is entirely free of a deep fear of death, or exempt from dread of annihilation." ... All of these add up to a continuing realization that at some point there will be no future, which leads to a natural state of anxiety. ... denial is a result of anxiety, an inability to face or accept the inevitable consequence of annihilation, or non-being. This is more than fear of alienation or separation, in which one would continue to exist as an individual being, albeit cut off from the

sources of emotional support. Annihilation means total absence of self or existence and is a concept that is difficult, if not impossible, for most of us to comprehend.[102]

James Hillman is considered one of the foremost interpreters of the writings of Carl Jung, and a leading twentieth-century psychologist and philosopher in his own right. He continues the themes of existentialism and introduces the concept of the soul, rarely done in modern psychology. In his important book *Suicide and the Soul,* Hillman offers some thought-provoking perspectives on the complexity of suicide. He writes:

> Under the pressure of "too late," knowing that life went wrong and there is no longer a way out, suicide offers itself. Then suicide is the urge for hasty transformation. This is not premature death, as medicine might say, but the late reaction of a delayed life which did not transform itself as it went along.[103]

Echoing the existential philosophers who preceded him, Hillman suggests that we cannot fully understand and appreciate our lives until we come to terms with our deaths; that the prospect of our inevitable deaths give meaning to our lives. Moreover, while most of us might associate suicide with escapism, irresponsibility, and cowardice, Hillman also sees it in relation to courage and truth-seeking. He writes:

> Until we can say no to life, we have not really said yes to it, but we have only been carried along by its collective stream. … the death experience is needed to separate from the collective flow of life and to discover individuality. Individuality requires courage. And courage has since classic times been linked with suicide arguments: it takes courage to choose the ordeal of life, and it takes courage to enter the unknown by one's own decision.[104]

For Hillman, "The impulse to death need not be conceived as an anti-life movement; it may be a demand for an encounter with absolute reality, a demand for a fuller life of the death experience."[105] He speaks of the Platonic idea of the soul being trapped in the body until death. Given this, "to encounter the realm of the soul as a reality equal to the usual view of reality,"[106] one must die to the world.

So often, we conceptualize suicide as a running *away* from reality. Hillman would have us stay open to the possibility of seeing suicide as a running *toward* something. What that something is—whether it will be better or worse than the world that drove us to suicide—we cannot know for certain. However, he does believe that "what comes next will for sure be something else, completely, the Wholly Other."[107] It would appear, then, that those who take their own life prefer this "something else," whatever it may be, to a life that is known and no longer desired.

In the remainder of this overview, we will shift our focus from a worldly scientific and scholarly view of suicide to a more otherworldly, afterlife-oriented view, which will set the tone for the remainder of Part I.

SUICIDE AND THE AFTERLIFE

In this section, we enter the frame of reference that we will maintain for the rest of this book. This frame asks us to entertain the possibility, even the actuality, that we will survive our physical deaths, whether they occurred naturally or by way of murder or the self-murder that is suicide. It asks us to be open to the view that after death we will continue to exist in a form that allows us to still consciously, meaningfully experience, and in a way that at least some of us are able to remember, aspects of our prior earthly lives, and, on occasion, even be able to communicate back to those still on Earth.

Some cultures and religions believe that a person's mental condition while dying has a tremendous impact on the soul's transition to the afterlife and beyond. For example, one Tibetan Buddhist comments: "The individual's state of mind is of paramount importance at the moment of death, and it is essential that he or she is not distraught or disturbed."[108] Ram Dass explains:

> It is said in Eastern spiritual traditions that the thought forms to which we are attached at the moment of death determine what happens next....
>
> This Eastern emphasis on the importance of thought forms at the moment of death is supported by evidence from shamanic studies and consciousness research. Shamans, for example, know that the nature of one's thoughts at the outset of the shamanic "journey" through altered states of consciousness is crucially important in determining the nature of that journey—whether the visions encountered will be heavenly or hellish.... Similarly, Western psychedelic researchers discovered early on that a person's mind-set at the beginning of the psychedelic experience is a key determinant of the quality of that experience. Thus, if the after-death states are indeed likely to be similar to altered states of consciousness, it seems probable that one's state of mind at the moment of death will strongly influence the nature of one's after-death experience.[109]

Thus, Tibetan Buddhists believe that:

> Those who have suffered *violent or sudden death* have a particularly urgent need for help. Victims of murder, suicide, accidents, or war can easily be trapped by their suffering, anguish, and fear, or may be imprisoned

in the actual experience of death and so be unable to move on through the process of rebirth.[110]

This concern over the suddenness of death is not unique to Tibetan Buddhism. Mertz and Smith mention this concern that a man who had died in a car accident might have trouble making his transition to the afterlife:

> A belief found in many shamanic societies is that people who die suddenly and violently need special help in crossing over to the other world.
> I did something ... showing him which way to go—because when you die that fast you're undecided.... You don't really know which way to go, because you're trying to figure out what happened to you. Maybe the last thing he knew he was driving and, all at once ... he just killed himself.[111]

Suicide is frequently chosen because people falsely believe it is a solution for them, perhaps the only solution, regardless of how it affects others. However, what parapsychologists know, and others need to understand if they are contemplating taking this action, is that suicide rarely, if ever, solves anything. Consciousness continues. Unfortunately, that includes a person's state of mind at the time of death. According to the channeled literature, if depressed, the person is still depressed following death. If angry, his or her spirit will remain angry. Sometimes, spirits can even continue to have the illusion of pain even though they no longer have a body. Suicide does not end problems; it only makes them worse because *now* there is no way to change things. As a result, the soul can end up stuck in a limbo between lives, unable to complete the transition to the afterlife or begin the process that may lead to another physical life.

In addition to traditional suicide, recent years have seen two other forms of suicide gain popularity—assisted suicide and suicide bombing. The individuals performing these latter acts are of differing ages, health conditions, and emotional states, and have varying purposes. The question arises whether they have the same problems in the afterlife as those who perform traditional suicide. Part II of this book will address this question, and we will see that these three types of suicide do indeed appear to have different consequences in the afterlife.

One cannot fully understand the ramifications of suicide unless one considers what those who have successfully committed it—and not just had a near-miss—say about their experiences. Parapsychology, as well as psychical research, is uniquely suited to this task, because its field of study includes the survival of bodily death. If there is some part of us—whether you call it a soul or something else—that continues to exist after the death of the body, it may be possible to speak to and hear from that part through psychic or anomalous means.

In this first part, we will talk mostly about traditional suicide—the killing of one's own healthy body without also taking the unwilling lives of others (as in the case of the so-called suicide bombers, which we will turn to in Part II).

There are countless ways to kill oneself, from the passive refusal of food, drink, or life-supporting measures to the active use of poison, hanging, drowning, jumping, gunshot, or other methods. The idea that the dead would not rest easily afterward has long held sway in a variety of cultures around the world. Practices used to keep those who have physically died through suicide from continuing to interact with us have included burying the corpses at a crossroads during the night, driving a stake through the heart, handling them as little as possible, refusing funeral services, and placing them in unconsecrated ground.[112] French, German, and Norwegian cultures have traditionally treated the bodies of suicides worse than those of criminals, generally refusing them burial, and taking steps to discourage their souls from returning home.

Viney observes that in parts of the subcontinent of India, "a woman who dies in her early years through suicide, accident or childbirth is believed more likely to become an active ghost or 'Mohani' than one who sees through her full life cycle."[113] Blavatsky reports that in the 1800s:

> Gorres, describing a conversation he had with some Hindus of the Malabar coast, reports that upon asking them whether they had ghosts among them, they replied, "Yes, but we know them to be bad spirits ... good ones can hardly ever appear at all. They are principally the spirits of suicides and murderers, or of those who die violent deaths. They constantly flutter about and appear as phantoms. Night-time is favorable to them, they seduce the feeble-minded and tempt others in a thousand different ways."[114]

The notion that the souls of suicides may be more apt to wander (or at least be seen doing so) might be supported by an unpublished study performed by Erlendur Haraldsson. He observes that, compared to the death rate, there was a higher proportion of contacts with those spirits who had killed themselves:

> Also of potential interest is my analysis of 449 Icelandic cases of apparitions/contact with the dead (unpublished). The cause of death for 5% of the identified apparitions is suicide (verified thru official records) whereas 1.5% of deaths in the population are due to suicide according to official statistics.[115]

Nationally recognized medium, best-selling author, and television personality John Edward writes of an accident victim who seemed to have a problem moving forward:

> In another reading, a spirit came through saying he had not completed his life lessons when he was in the physical body, and so his soul was not able to graduate to a higher level when it arrived on the Other Side. He had died young, at twenty-three, in an auto accident.[116]

Similarly, medium Kate Anders states: "My experience with people who die suddenly and violently is that they sometimes experience the same problem even though it was not their doing."[117] We will later note that a number of channeled messages suggest that all forms of sudden death are problematic, whether by suicide, murder, or accident.

One possible reason why the suddenness of death may be a problem is that there may not always be someone to meet the suicide on the other side. One spirit who died during war states:

> I can find no words to tell you the horror of sudden death. It is the one great tragedy. When thought returned, I was as one lost in a familiar, yet wholly strange world. Aimlessly I wandered, seeking what I knew not what, dazed, mystified. I did not know I was ... dead.
>
> When death comes naturally there are always those here to meet the voyagers. But there was no one to meet me, no one to explain that I had graduated into a new plane of consciousness.[118]

However, the ease of the transition may also vary based on how much spiritual development a person has when he or she crosses over. The spirit guide Silver Birch notes that how well a soul can adjust to the afterlife depends upon how evolved the soul is when the death has been sudden.[119] Thus, how easily a suicide adapts to his or her new environment after crossing over may be quite different depending on his or her intrinsic spiritual level—with more advanced souls doing quite well and poorly evolved ones badly.

Sometimes the medium has to pay attention to subtle clues to figure out whether the spirit they are channeling committed suicide. John Edward observes: "A suicide will come through to me with the feeling that a person brought about his own death. But this is tricky ground because I will get a similar feeling for someone who caused his own death unintentionally."[120] Other times, the manner of death may be all too obvious, and grisly, to the medium. Edward again:

> He showed me a pickup truck, then a wooded area, indicating the spot where he had ended his life. When I saw a tree I wondered if he had hanged

himself. But then he gave me a sense of his pain—thankfully, a relatively mild sense. I felt as though the skin on my arms and legs was being peeled off, and then I saw, incongruously, a cartoon of Bugs Bunny and Daffy Duck. The characters were trying to top each other and finally, Daffy set himself on fire with gasoline. I was nauseated when I realized what it meant. His family confirmed that this was how he had killed himself.[121]

However, suicide is more than just a death. It can bring up issues of shame and confusion in the survivors, which only adds to their difficulty of coping with the loss of a loved one. This can lead to unhelpful reactions. "Stephen" was channeled as saying:

> Suicide is still a taboo subject to talk about and people are ashamed to admit that one of their family members has taken his or her own life. Mostly, they just don't understand why, so they don't talk about it, as if that would make it go away. And there is such guilt carried on the shoulders of those left behind....
>
> Everyone feels partly to blame in some way. Or they get angry and try to blame the dead person, when inside they carry the secret guilt that maybe they did drive the person to their death. It is true that almost every person that knew the one who killed himself has contributed to the pattern of the soul who made that choice, but that soul is ultimately responsible for his or her choice.[122]

One of the earlier documented cases of the channeling of a suicide occurred in January 1885.[123] The spirit, Schura, had killed herself at the age of seventeen, after the death of a cousin. In this case, her motive for coming through the planchette[124] board was to try to help a cousin. Gauld describes Schura's message:

> Schura demanded, in no hesitant tone, that another cousin, Nikolaus, should be brought to a sitting. According to Schura, Nikolaus was in danger of compromising himself politically. Sophie hesitated for reasons of social propriety. Schura's demands became more and more vehement at successive sittings, until on 26 February 1885 she wrote, "It is too late ... expect his arrest." The von Wieslers then contacted Nikolaus's parents, who were, however, quite satisfied in respect of his conduct.
>
> Two years later Nikolaus was arrested and exiled because of political assemblies which he had attended in January and February 1885.[125]

Since then, there have been a number of other purported channeled messages from those who have committed suicide. Some are the products of physical or mental mediumship, some (as above) from Ouija boards, instrumental transcommunication (messages from discarnate sources obtained on audio, video, computer, or other equipment), and automatic writing. It should make sense that if these communiqués come from the dead, they can vary considerably in length and quality. Furthermore, these messages need not come days or years after the soul has crossed over. At least some suicides appear to be able to communicate within hours of their death. William Stainton Moses, one of the most well-known American mediums of the late nineteenth century, and author of the widely read *Spirit Teachings*, told this story where the message came through as automatic writing:

> As soon as we reached the drawing-room, he was impelled to sit down and write; and when a pencil and paper had been brought, his hand was moved backwards and forwards with great rapidity, and an object was roughly drawn on paper which resembled a horse fastened to a kind of cart or truck. Several attempts were made to depict it more clearly, and then the following sentences were written—"I killed myself—I killed myself to-day—Baker Street—medium passed." Here the writing became unintelligible, as the medium grew more and more agitated, until at length he rose from his seat in a state of trance, and exclaimed in broken sentences—"Yes! yes! Killed myself to-day, under a steam-roller. Yes! yes! Killed myself—blood, blood, blood!" The control then ceased, but the medium felt the same unpleasant influence for some hours afterward, and could not entirely shake it off for several days.
>
> In reference to the communication, I may state that, although the medium had passed through Baker Street in the afternoon, neither he nor any one present was aware that a man had committed suicide there in the morning by throwing himself under a steam-roller....
>
> In this case the unfortunate man was literally crushed to pieces, and yet a few hours afterwards his spirit could communicate in writing through the medium, and could also make use of his organs of speech.... Again, we may infer that spirits immediately after death are able to recognize a medium through whom they can communicate.[126]

We will later see that unexpected death by explosion may represent the one exception to Moses' first generalization. Some sources suggest that in cases where the soul does not have time to leave the physical body before it is blown to bits, that the astral body may require a significant recovery time before the soul can be active in the afterlife.

It should be noted that just because souls may be able to communicate soon after death, does not mean that they can do so *well*. As Noreen Renier puts it, the suicides she channeled "were not very good at communicating in this life and didn't seem to get much better on the other side."[127] Being dead doesn't add to your eloquence—it just changes your perspective a bit.

Another problem with these communications is the accuracy with which they are transmitted and/or received. A number of channeled sources suggest that it takes considerable practice for a spirit to learn how to send messages. Furthermore, from the early Spiritualist literature, entities have stated that the medium's belief system, language skills, level of education, and soul development can be factors that limit serious communication. For example, John Edmonds and George Dexter were told through automatic writing:

> There is one aspect of our meetings which has not been, before now, considered; as I have waited and watched to analyze your minds, and to test how far I might venture to avow opinions which I knew must conflict with all your preconceived notions ... and also to see how far you would permit your former belief to interfere with your judgment....
>
> If I could explain all the means that are used, and the various causes which retard or facilitate the flow of my thoughts, you would comprehend how much these manifestations are changed from their original form by the conditions of the minds to whom they are communicated, and you would realize that it is not faith alone that is required to enable us to teach you understandingly.[128]

The spirit, Silver Birch, has also pointed out, "I am limited, not only by my medium's vocabulary, but by the state of his soul evolution, because that limits the amount of myself that I can express."[129]

A medium's cultural bias could creep into the material channeled, either consciously or unconsciously, particularly in the case of hot-button issues like suicide. Consciously, the medium might not wish to say anything that could impel others toward suicide. Even more problematic is the way the unconscious mind can color or distort information to make it fit in with a medium's beliefs or personal issues.

Of course, the problem of receiving inaccurate or biased information is by no means limited to channeled material. It exists in every form of communication from the children's game of telephone on up to the mass media. As Heather Buckley once pointed out, there are probably as many, if not more, communication errors passed on through books, magazines, advertisements, newspapers, and everyday speech (which can be biased, illogical, and untrue) than occur in channeled messages.[130]

Not all of the incorrect material obtained through channeling may be due to problems on the medium's end of things—whether because of bias or lack of education or skill. Sometimes, it can be because the spirits transmit "wrong" information, either inadvertently or on purpose. Accidental or incomplete information is possible with an honest spirit who has limited knowledge or experience in the afterlife. In some cases, different answers may be true depending on the recipient's level of spiritual development. One way of looking at this is that the best answer for a two-year-old child would be quite different than what you might tell a graduate student. Hoodwin explains:

> Once in a while, information is withheld or given incorrectly because the person asking isn't ready to hear it. It might be too traumatic, or it would possibly interfere with completing a karma or lesson, or perhaps it is something best learned for himself. In cases like this, the greatest good may require sacrificing absolute accuracy per se.
>
> Wrong information may also be used as a teaching technique designed to trigger further questions, especially when it is obviously contradictory, or to remind a questioner to trust his own perceptions, no matter what anyone else says.[131]

Of course, deliberate misinformation is not always so altruistic. Many mediums have spoken of the existence of tricksters in the spirit realm. These beings actively try to pass on misinformation for their own entertainment. One channeled entity has warned of such discarnate mischief makers:

> The first class referred to are those who confuse these revelations most, particularly by misrepresentation and deceit. They are always on the alert to seize on impressible mediums, and through this channel to impart incorrect statements relative to "life in the spheres."
>
> Now, allow me to say ... that spirits (unprogressed ones) dare not assume the personality of any other spirit, so you demand of them the truth in the name of God. But they misdirect, bewilder, confuse, make false statements of the nature of these manifestations, and would willingly create doubt.... In short, they delight in inculcating error.[132]

Clearly, common sense needs to be used with any source of information. Facts do get distorted or may be accurate but misunderstood or limited in applicability. Together with the problem of poor communication, these are legitimate concerns and may explain part of why channeled messages vary in content. Nonetheless, there is a lot of data to look at. A great many individuals have taken their own lives, crossed over, and made an effort to talk to the living.

The communications reported in this book vary in terms of purpose and content, but certain overriding themes appear. These include such topics as why suicides kill themselves, what their initial experience of being dead is like, feelings of regret, problems with adjustment, self-judgment, moving forward, and what they would say to those who would follow in their footsteps, and to those left behind. We will look at each of these issues in turn after reviewing the general spirit attitudes toward suicide in the next chapter.

2

General Spirit Attitudes toward Suicide

Spirit attitudes expressed toward those who have committed traditional suicide vary considerably, perhaps in part due to the cultural values and/or beliefs of the one channeling as well as that of the soul communicating the messages and its level of knowledge and/or development. Nonetheless, a great many of the spirit comments lean toward compassionate disapproval. They understand why it was done, but point out that it was *not* a good idea. The spirit attitudes toward end-of-life euthanasia or assisted suicide tend more toward the neutral or accepting end of the spectrum, and will be discussed in detail in the chapter devoted to that topic.

The position a soul takes on suicide may not always be the same as that which the person espoused when living. It is difficult to assess whether this is due to a changed perspective from being in the afterlife or biases introduced by the medium bringing the messages through. This problem was recognized even in the 1800s. Emanuel Swedenborg's channeled spirit source purportedly said:

> In the earlier days of these manifestations, there were many forced interpretations given to statements made by spirits, which often assumed the color of the belief of the individual, not from design, but from impression, and consequently often a blending of truth with error was the result.[1]

The spirit self-identified as that of the writer Francis Bacon similarly noted that some differences in material could also relate to style:

> I do not differ from Swedenborg in his teachings, although he will explain my ideas in a different manner from myself. As he has said, though there may be apparent discrepancies, yet the germ of truth will be made plain when you arrive at the end.[2]

Of course, it is always hard to say how much of the material received through channeling is an accurate reflection of its source. Sometimes it is possible to compare the statements that were made by people when they were alive with what they purportedly said after their deaths. One might expect a certain amount of shift in opinion, perhaps even a more enlightened perspective, with greater compassion and forgiveness shown toward the suicide. However, in fact, the opposite has sometimes been true. For example, when the American medium Arthur Ford was alive, he tended to speak compassionately of those who had taken their own lives. He was often asked about what things were like for suicides in the afterlife. His attitude seemed to be one of understanding, while admitting that it could create a problematic situation for the newly dead.

After he died, Arthur Ford's attitude seemed to harden somewhat, if Ruth Montgomery's channeling is to be believed. Montgomery, a nationally syndicated political columnist and well-known Washington correspondent turned psychic and medium, wrote that the spirit of Ford told her:

> No person has the right to take the life within himself, any more than that of another person....
>
> [T]hey deliberately set out to destroy their own body, thinking that they were destroying their soul as well. Since they could not succeed in the latter, their problem is far greater here than there, because no problem has been solved, but only postponed until the next earth life, whenever that may be. Thus, they are what we refer to as suffering souls. They live hourly with the shame of self-destruction and rage within themselves for having failed to settle the problem while in the flesh, where it is much more easily faced than here.[3]

Since we rarely have the luxury of statements before and after death for comparison, it is impossible to say whether this shift in attitude truly reflects the soul's changed perspective (from being in the afterlife). Indeed, for the most part, we are limited to the attitudes expressed by either the living (which may have a wide play in the media) or the dead—not from a soul who has made comments from both states of existence.

So, what do spirits say about suicide? It seems to vary by era, or how old the data is—hinting strongly at some degree of filtering by the medium, perhaps coloring the words or meaning of the material spirits are trying to transmit. That this should be the case would seem to be acknowledged even by discarnate souls. The nineteenth-century French medium Allan Kardec (a pseudonym) questioned the spirit realm about this issue, and received the following explanation:

> They speak according to the comprehension of those who question them, when the latter are too fully imbued with preconceived ideas, in order to avoid any abrupt interference with their convictions. If a spirit should tell a Mussulman [Muslim], without proper precautions, that

Mahomet was not a true prophet, he would not be listened to with much cordiality....

Spirits of inferior advancement, who are not yet completely dematerialized, retain a portion of their earthly ideas, and describe their impressions by means of terms that are familiar to them. They are in a state that allows of their obtaining only a very imperfect foresight of the future. ... it often happens that spirits ... but recently freed from their earthly body, speak just as they would have done during their earthly life.[4]

Hence, there may be a combination of factors why channeled material does not reflect a single, unchanging viewpoint. Not only may the medium consciously or unconsciously bias the material, but the spirit sources of the information may have not yet let go of their old, outdated beliefs or have decided the recipient would not be able to accept the truth, causing them to tailor the material to be more palatable, in order to get other, perhaps more important, information across.

Regardless of the cause for the distortion of what is being channeled, there seems to be a considerable shift in attitude that has been expressed over time. Much of the material sounds suspiciously like it regurgitates the secular or religious views of the period verbatim, with no special insight or wisdom. Older channeled material, in particular, tends to reflect a harsher, more rigid, viewpoint. Although one would not expect such prejudice against suicide to carry over into the afterlife, some of the messages received almost make one wonder. For example, James E. Padgett's wife (who died in the early 1900s) made the blanket statement from the afterlife, "I think that the sin of suicide is the worst, and then the murderer."[5] Furthermore, Stewart Edward White quoted his deceased wife:

"Why," cried Betty, "the fact that you *are* a bit of individualized consciousness is itself a responsibility.... Consciousness is in evolution.... Each bit has to grow.... Consequently, the more quantity one attains in the obstructed universe [earthly life], the more beautifully he will be able to go on in the unobstructed universe [spiritual realm]. Indeed, just that accumulation of quantity is the reason a long life is desirable. That is why we have to look on suicide as cowardice. The suicide is the fellow who is not willing to accumulate as much as possible.[6]

These are strongly disapproving statements that smack of a rigid, intolerant outlook on the topic.

In some cases, the messages appear to be clearly imprinted with not only the cultural beliefs, but the language of the time. Stainton Moses channeled the following commentary through automatic writing in 1876 from a spirit who had not committed suicide discussing another spirit who had:

How should he be blest? He lifted sacrilegious hands against the shrine in which the All-wise had placed his spirit for its progress and development. He wasted opportunities, and destroyed, so far as he was able, the temple in which dwelt the divine spark, which was his portion. He sent forth his spirit alone and friendless into a strange world where no place was yet prepared for it.... Selfish in his life, and yet more selfish in bringing pain and sorrow on his earthly friends by his untimely death.... Miserable, blind, and undeveloped, there is no rest for such as he till repentance has had its place, and remorse leads to regeneration. He is outcast....

He fostered and encouraged morbid self-introspection. He brooded over self, not for the purpose of progress and development, not to eradicate faults and foster virtues, but in selfish exclusiveness. He was enwrapped in a cloud of distorted selfishness. This bred in him disease, and in the end he fell a prey to tempters in the spirit, who fastened on him and drove him to his ruin.... And now he throws the same influence around those whom he wounded in his death. A curse to himself, he becomes a curse to those he loves.[7]

Once we get past the archaic language, we can see a number of themes here, including: (1) the suicide's responsibility for his thoughts, (2) the suicide's selfishness and negative focus, and (3) the fact that his or her death may lead others to follow suit, whether in imitation of the suicide's deed or through a direct negative influence.

The issue of selfishness is an interesting one that will come up again. Perhaps the clearest spirit definition of this comes from a 1917 channeling session from Californian Nora Loder: "Anything which does not take the personal consequences to the other fellow first is selfish."[8] Another way of considering this is whether a person thinks about what would be the results of his or her actions on other people. To put it simply, selfishness involves not thinking as part of a collective whole, but only of yourself.

James Curtis compiled a host of Spiritualist readings and séance transcriptions in England in 1902, which included a message on suicide.[9] Again, we see an inflexible attitude toward those who take their own lives, even if the speaker appears to sorrow over their fate. He reported that a spirit said:

You have heard of the poor suicide who strives to rush away from the cares of life, and dreads to face the cares of to-morrow. Can he be welcome? No, dear, a thousand times no! He is shown his folly, the effects of his crime against nature, and against his Father, whose child he is. He is punished by remorse and the many other various phases and modes of punishment established by those divine laws which are set up in our midst;

laws which are not made for a time or an occasion, but are fixed on the same immutable principle which has established those other laws that so tend to increase our happiness and comfort.[10]

Silver Birch, the spirit guide communicating through British medium Maurice Barbanell during the 1930s, addressed the question of whether suicide is ever permissible by saying, "If you do you must pay the price for cutting yourself off."[11] This price is not so extreme as a soul being extinguished. The guide admitted that their light might die down to a flicker, but would never go out. This is because "the link which binds it to the Great Spirit is a link forged in eternity. No soul descends so low that it cannot rise."[12] Furthermore, Silver Birch reassured us that no spirit is so high that it will not descend in order to help those that are the lowest.

Like many other channeled entities, Silver Birch made an exception for suicide in cases where mental illness was involved. In these cases the consequences were not reported to be so severe. The guide stated:

> The soul is not judged from the standards of earth, but from the standards of eternal wisdom....
>
> It is the same with those, who, in moments of madness, as you call it, take others' lives or their own. They cannot be blamed because the machinery has gone wrong. In my world, the true standard is the standard of the soul's motive.[13]

Arthur Ford was said to have told Ruth Montgomery:

> These people, if suffering temporary insanity, are soon able to overcome the aberrations which provoked the attack on self, and as their awakening forces grasp the problem and come to understand the conditions which led to temporary insanity, they will adjust almost as rapidly as those who came here through accidental death.[14]

Sometimes the older channeled material also made special exceptions for certain other kinds of suicide—such as by captured soldiers who do not want to betray their comrades under torture. For example, Jean Marshall obtained the following passage through automatic writing:

> Suicide is not allowed by God. It is forbidden to take one's own life even in cases of extreme suffering; but he has mercy on those who are put to great pain and torture and who kill themselves in order not to betray others.[15]

Nineteenth-century Theosophist writer Annie Besant also felt the fate of a person who sacrifices his or her life to save others is completely different from that of suicide performed for selfish reasons. Furthermore, the messages she received suggested that such souls could find redemption. She stated:

> Let it not be supposed that there is no hope for this class—the sane deliberate suicide. If, bearing steadfastly his cross, he suffers patiently his punishment, striving against carnal appetites still alive in him, in all their intensity, though of course, each in proportion to the degree to which it had been indulged in earth-life—if, we say, he bears this humbly, never allowing himself to be tempted here or there into unlawful gratifications of unholy desires—then when his fated death-hour strikes ... it may well be that all may be well with him, and that he passes on to the gestation period and its subsequent developments.[16]

Allan Kardec made the same exception in his exposition on suicide.[17] He wrote that when a person gives up his or her life to save others, it would not be considered suicide, but instead a praiseworthy act. Kardec added, "It is the *useless* sacrifice that is displeasing to God, and also that which is tarnished by pride."[18]

Yet another example of the emphasis some sources place on the selfishness or otherwise of the motive for suicide comes to us from the teaching spirit calling himself Gildas, who communicated through Ruth White, a young British housewife in the 1960s and 1970s, stating, "Death by self-immolation, or suicide for some unselfish reason or cause, is always regarded differently from suicide which takes place for selfish reasons."[19]

When Western Edition (W. E.) discussed suicide in a channeling session, it also pointed out that since none of us live in isolation, suicide affects not only the person performing the act, but the lives of a great many others as well—which in some cases may even prevent them from completing their karma or chosen tasks. Hence, there is a certain amount of selfishness to killing yourself. Not only are you walking away from your own opportunities, but you may be preventing opportunities for others. As W. E. put it, "You are a part of the whole, and so you have to act as such, and not just for your own desires."[20]

Still, not all channeled material fully reflects the cultural values of its era. Allan Kardec collected a number of comments from spirits on the issue of suicide in Europe in the mid-1800s that, in addition to casual acceptance of reincarnation (unusual in that era) seemed to demonstrate more than the usual tolerance for those who take their own lives. For instance, he was told:

A spirit, when once incarnated, cannot regret a choice which he is not conscious of having made; but he may find the burden he has assumed too heavy, and, if he believes it to be beyond his strength, he may have recourse to suicide.[21]

Recent channels also talk about suicide as an attempt to escape the problems encountered in life. Contemporary British medium Sheila Jones passes on this message from the spirits:

> Those who take their own lives, often with the desire to end life completely receive a twofold shock when they come to this side of life; when they realize that the problems they sought to escape from are still there, still a burden to be borne.... One cannot escape by running away and suicide is just that, it is a running away.[22]

We shall later see that this insight—that one cannot escape one's problems through death—makes up a significant portion of what suicides tell us. If anything, taking your own life only makes things worse.

"Hilarion" is a self-identified nonphysical, advanced spiritual being, or "ascended master," who started transmitting telepathically through Toronto businessman Maurice B. Cooke in the 1970s. When asked about suicide, Hilarion said that suicide almost never has a positive impact. It is nearly always an act of desperation to end a life that just feels too painful, with the pain tending to be emotional or mental, not physical. Hilarion then made a very important point that applies to almost all the suicides reported in this book: "In most cases, the person attempting to take his own life does not understand the spiritual realities surrounding his earthly existence, else he would not allow such a temptation to sway him."[23]

When a person commits suicide for the selfish reason to end his own pain or to escape any more earthly existence, Hilarion refers to the universal or spiritual, rather than the earthly, law, when he tells us that "the law requires that the post-life experiences be somewhat more limited than is usually the case, and generally, the soul will be allowed less option in determining the nature and circumstances of the next incarnation."[24] In addition, according to Hilarion, in the incarnation to follow, the same basic test must be faced once more, "the same temptation to commit suicide." Next time, that temptation will be even more impelling and difficult to resist. However, "the incarnated personality who must endure this harder test will also be given more 'weapons' with which to fight the temptation, which usually means being on the receiving end of more love and support during the childhood phase."[25]

Hilarion claims that there is truth to the notion that the souls of suicides enter a kind of limbo following death; yet such a limbo is of the spirit's own making. The typical kind of fog experienced following death by suicide "arises simply from the *expectation* of the individual that, after death, there will be *nothing*." Upon realizing that one, in fact, continues to exist, albeit now in a nonphysical or astral embodiment, spirit helpers arrive to lead him or her out of the self-imposed limbo. As Hilarion puts it: "If only the person had realized before death that he would survive the killing of the body, such a limbo state would not arise. And in all probability, the person would not have taken his own life."[26] Unfortunately, however, most suicides do not possess this larger view at the time they choose to kill themselves. They simply believe that with their death comes the extinguishing of consciousness and the final end to their existence. From the hundreds of stories from the spirit realm that fill this book, we learn that suicide is an act of procrastination, not finality.

Many channeled souls make distinctions between suicides based on the underlying causes. Charles Leadbeater, noted nineteenth- and early twentieth-century British clairvoyant and Theosophist, wrote:

> It must be remembered that the guilt of suicide differs considerably according to its circumstances, from the morally blameless act of Seneca or Socrates through all degrees down to the heinous crime of the wretch who takes his own life in order to escape from the entanglements into which his villainy has brought him and of course the position after death varies accordingly.[27]

Madness would seem to be a case singled out for particular sympathy by the spirit realm. Allan Kardec was told that madness could lead to suicide: "In such cases, the spirit suffers from the constraint which he feels, and from his inability to manifest himself freely; and he therefore seeks death as a means of breaking his chains."[28] As with the previous statement, there does not appear to be particular blame attached to the soul for taking this course of action. However, it should be noted that this was not considered to be the case for all suicides. Over the years, Kardec sat with numerous mediums, questioning those in the spirit world:

> "He who voluntarily commits suicide contravenes the providential ordering which sent him into the earthly life."
> —*Is suicide always voluntary?*
> "The madman who kills himself does not know what he is doing."
> 945. *What is to be thought of those who commit suicide because they are sick of life?*

"Fools! why did they not employ themselves in some useful work? Had they done so, life would not have been a weariness to them."

946. What is to be thought of those who resort to suicide in order to escape from the troubles and disappointments of this world?

"They are weaklings who lack courage to bear the petty annoyances of existence.... The tribulations of life are trials or expiations; happy are those who bear them without murmuring, for great will be their reward!"[29]

The spirit Mentor, communicating through Meredith Lady Young, cofounder of New Hampshire's Still-Point Publishing, also spoke regarding the question of the taking of one's own life when insane. Mentor seemed to regard the issue with compassion, setting it apart from other causes of suicide:

> I can only speak here in general terms, but I can say to you this, that in a case such as this where a person is as you say mentally in [ill] and improperly balanced; they would be received with love and with sympathy. Remember there are many reasons for individuals bringing themselves to this side of life.... But a being who is ... not in control of themselves, would not be held to task.... They would be given love and help and sympathy.[30]

Madness as a nonculpable cause of suicide was also spoken of by Annie Besant in the late 1800s:

> Motive is everything, and man is punished in a case of direct responsibility, never otherwise. In the victim's case the natural hour was anticipated *accidentally,* while in that of the suicide death is brought on voluntarily and with a full and deliberate knowledge of its immediate consequences. Thus a man who causes his death in a fit of temporary insanity is *not* a *felo de se* [suicide].[31]

A similarly forgiving stance was reported when the topic of suicide came up during a channeling session in 1867:

> The soul that has committed suicide ... is very apt to learn that ... it would have been far easier to have gained the experience that was necessary for the soul in and through its own body, than in any other way; therefore it must, of necessity, drink more or less deeply of the cup of remorse. But, like all other mistakes in life, it always carries its own antidote. When a sufficient quantity has been ministered unto the spirit, it comes forth washed clean, regenerated and rejuvenated, and ready for the march of life.[32]

However, during a different session, Mrs. Conant reported:

> The suicide who seeks to escape the sorrows of earth, hoping to gain the joys of heaven, wakes from a mistaken dream, to find himself ofttimes

in deeper sorrow than when on earth. The shadow that belonged to him while here has followed him to the spirit-land, and by natural and perfect law he must outlive it.[33]

The spirits who spoke to Allan Kardec discussed a number of scenarios and variations not often brought up in channeled material—such as the karmic implications for those who drive another being to suicide, which, according to him, would be treated as murder, or when there are unusual circumstances. He wrote:

> *947. Can we consider as having committed suicide the man who, becoming disheartened ... allows himself to die of despair?*
> "Such self-abandonment is suicide; but those who had caused the crime, or might have prevented it, would be more to blame for it than the one by whom it had been committed, and the latter would therefore be judged leniently. But, nevertheless, you must not suppose that he would be entirely absolved if he had been wanting in firmness and perseverance, or had failed to make the best use of his intelligence to help himself out of his difficulties...."
>
> *948. Is suicide as blamable, when committed in order to escape the disgrace of having done wrong, as when it is prompted by despair?*
> "A fault is not effaced by suicide, which, on the contrary, is a second fault added to the first.... God is the sole judge, and sometimes diminishes the penalty of wrongdoing in consideration of the circumstances which led to it."
>
> *949. Is suicide excusable when committed in order to avoid bringing disgrace on one's children or family?*
> "He who has recourse to such an expedient does wrong; but, as he believes his action to be for the best, God takes note of his intention...."
>
> *950. What is to be thought of him who makes away with himself in the hope of arriving sooner at a happier state of existence?*
> "Another piece of folly.... His suicide will delay his entrance into a better world; for he himself will ask to be allowed to come back to the earth, in order to *complete the life* that he has cut short...."
>
> *952. Does he commit suicide who falls a victim to the excessive indulgence of passions ... which habit has converted into physical necessities that he is unable to control?*
> "He commits moral suicide. Do you not see that a man, in such a case, is trebly guilty? For he is guilty of a want of firmness, of the sin of bestiality, and of forgetfulness of God."
>
> —*Is such a man more or less guilty than he who kills himself from despair?*
> "He is more guilty, because he has had time to reflect on the suicidal nature of the course he was pursuing. In the case of him who commits suicide on the spur of the moment, there is sometimes a degree of

bewilderment not unallied to madness. The former will be punished much more severely than the latter; for the retributive penalties of crime are always proportioned to the consciousness of wrong-doing that accompanied its commission...."

955. *Are the women who ... burn themselves to death with the body of their husband, to be considered as committing suicide, and have they to undergo the punishment of that crime?*

"They obey the dictates of a superstitious prejudice, and, moreover, are often the victims of force rather than of their own free-will. They believe themselves to be accomplishing a duty, and such an act does not partake of the character of suicide...."

956. *Do those persons attain the end they have in view, who, unable to bear the loss of the objects of their affection, kill themselves in the hope of rejoining them in the other life?*

"In such cases the result of suicide is the opposite of what was hoped for. Instead of being reunited to the object of their affection, those who have made this sad mistake find themselves separated, and for a very long time, from the being they hoped to rejoin...."

957. *What are in general the effects of suicide on the state of the spirit by whom it has been committed?*

"The consequences of suicide vary in different cases, because the penalties it entails are always proportioned to the circumstances which, in each case, have led to its commission. The one punishment which none can escape who have committed suicide is disappointment; the rest of their punishment depends on circumstances. Some of those who have killed themselves expiate their fault at once; others do so in a new earthly life harder to bear than the one whose course they have interrupted."[34]

Franklin Loehr, founder of the Religious Research organization and press in Florida in the 1960s, put the situation more gently when he wrote of a soul in the afterlife that wondered why it couldn't have come sooner, since its last years of life had not seemed of much value.[35] The spirit was told:

> It was right for you to stay and wait for your time! There is a pattern for each of us. Some people take things into their own hands, and that isn't good because the general pattern which God has set up—which includes learning, and letting forces run out their energy, and lots of things—it's still best to follow along with the general pattern.[36]

Recent years have seen a continuation in this shift in attitude that purportedly comes to us from the afterlife—although it is unclear whether this is due to changes in the senders, the receivers, or both. Regardless, contemporary material comes across as far more sympathetic and tolerant toward the notion of suicide. Mediums may also speak of special circumstances and how all those who end their own lives suffer the same consequences—if there are any at all.

Medium Jeanne Walker channeled the surviving spirit of her daughter Karen, who died of cancer in Los Angeles in 1970.[37] Like many others, this soul made distinctions between different kinds of suicides. However, it also emphasized that suicide was not so much wrong, as it was not always a good idea. Karen stated, "It is not a crime, but generally a result of illness or error."[38] Karen explained the issue to her mother in terms of the importance for a soul to accumulate what she referred to as consciousness while alive. Such consciousness was said to be important for adjustment to the afterlife. Since those who are emotionally ill have trouble adjusting to problems, they are considered to be less apt to acquire consciousness and hence have a retarded progress in the afterlife. However, Karen said that for those trying to escape extreme pain or depression, the adjustment will completely depend on how much (and what quality of) consciousness had been obtained.

Perhaps even more interestingly, the spirit of Karen addressed the question of suicide in the elderly—a topic that seldom came up in the channeled literature.[39] In this case, Karen felt that society was at fault for not providing the elderly with meaningful work or companionship. Since human interchange and the ability to feel useful are necessary for the development of consciousness, such souls were felt to be better off making their transition to the afterlife, where they could advance. She stated, "'No blame.' This is the phrase I would apply to suicide. From our view there is never any blame, and there should not be from your side either.... Suicide is not a crime.[40]

In 1985, Tam Mossman, the original editor of the various Jane Roberts' channeled "Seth" books and author of *Answers from a Grander Self,* shared this communication from the spirit realm:

> Despairing of change within or without, the depressive may sometimes feel an impulse to suicide.... But such an event simply wastes valuable energy and intent....
>
> I am not saying that suicide is the worst of all unpardonable sins, because none is; or that you will burn in a hell of your own creation as a result of having committed it. I *am* saying that to *whatever* degree you evade the responsibilities and lessons that incarnate life has to grant you, to that degree you are wasting the advantages and opportunities inherent in consciousness itself.[41]

"Indira," self-identified as the spirit of a Hindu woman who died in

India in 1854 and communicated through Santa Barbara, California, channel Verna Yater, spoke of reincarnation and the fact that a soul sometimes plans to accomplish more than it can handle here:

> You don't by some strange accident fall into the circumstances of your life. You bring these circumstances into the incarnation which you, for the most part, have chosen....
> Sometimes ... once they arrive they ... fail their task. Well, it's not permanent failure. They have failed this time but there will be another opportunity given, and another, as needed.[42]

The source that identified itself to Jane Sherwood as the surviving spirit of T. E. Lawrence ("Lawrence of Arabia") also took a compassionate stance, noting through the medium's automatic writing that none of us has the right to judge others, and that because every person has a breaking point, it's just a matter of whether life tests us to that degree.[43]

Another recent communicator, the spirit of "Dr. John," working with Franklin Loehr, took a more rational (and less impassioned) approach, explaining:

> You see, the usual penalty of suicide is simply this: There is a pattern which has been established for this life. That pattern has its own ongoing momentum. If you commit suicide, you don't have the body in which to accomplish it. You are still on the job, but one of your major tools has been stolen or thrown away.[44]

As part of the development of this book, a number of séances and private channeling sessions were conducted. In one telephone session, a guide for a boy who had died through autoeroticism was contacted by channel Lauren Thibodeau:

> He's ... reminding me that all experience serves. *All* experience serves. And we're back to that whole "don't judge it." Learn from it. Examine it. Study it. Consider if you would do it differently. But don't judge it. I kind of like that idea. I mean, it makes sense to me. That's a good way to go through life. Just thinking carefully in advance, to the degree that you can, making your informed [decisions] but not judging either your choices or others. Just doing what you can to make them wisely. And carry them out well. No. Are there more enlightened ... ways to behave? Absolutely. But should it be judged? Never.[45]

The issue of a difference between enlightened behavior and what may be considered "good" or "bad" by those on the Earth has also been made by other spirits. This seems an important enough point to dwell on for a moment. The spirit through Thibodeau was not saying that taking one's own life, particularly in pursuit of sexual gratification, is a wise choice. Indeed, at one point she discussed the boy's actions in the following way:

> "It was selfish. It's okay to be self-focused," he's telling me.... "Look! Self-focused is appropriate. Self-focused is necessary because if you can't focus on the self you can't focus on the community. You have to know your place in the community first. And that's why self-focused is a good thing." Where these kids made the mistake—and he's claiming most humans make the mistake—is because they become self-focused in an unenlightened way. They elevate themselves out of community. They distance themselves. They feel "othered."[46]

Since reincarnation has become more accepted as a fact, some channeled entities started drawing a distinction between whether a soul had committed suicide for the first time (just for the experience of doing it) or is a repeat offender. Channel Arthur Fanning wrote that in the case of one person who killed himself, the entity "YHWH" stated:

> Well, we'll call it not good/wrong, good/bad again, good/bad this. Not great wisdom....
> In this particular case it is different, for she's never done it before. It was first time, so there be "oops!" Know you? And this thing called, "Well, I'm still here, still alive. Oops." But it was the opportunity to play this game to know what it felt like....
> That is the reason it was done. Anything leading up to it was the excuse to do it that way. You've all committed suicide before.[47]

It should be noted that on rare occasions a soul would claim to have committed suicide just for the novelty of the death. Again, the spirit channeled by Thibodeau, who had died during autoeroticism:

> He's kind of crude about it, but he says look, once you've died a thousand deaths we'll say—I don't know if he's being poetic here—once you've died a thousand deaths it's tough to come up with something new. And this was new.... Been there, done that. There's got to be another way to get out of this life, and this was one he hadn't tried.... It was a new experience and that's why for him, it was just part of the experience.[48]

Another spirit, through medium Suzane Northrop, also pointed out the importance of whether a soul had already accomplished all that it could—a subject that comes up frequently in spirit comments on assisted suicide. Northrop writes:

> The purpose of a soul is to continue to learn and grow. There can be learning in a physical body that cannot be learned here, in the spiritual realm. It is for this reason that a body is so important. However, if the body

cannot continue to be a vehicle for the soul to grow, then the soul will begin to pull away and leave. If the soul has completed all it has to learn, and the body can no longer be the vehicle for this learning, "pulling the plug," so to speak, is not considered suicide.

However, the soul, with full knowledge, must still carefully make this decision. It is not a decision to take lightly.[49]

In general, the afterlife does not appear to be a place where souls are judged by others for their acts in life. Instead, the focus is more on recovery. Best-selling author and psychic medium George Anderson reported that the spirit-realm attitude he has encountered toward suicide is one of complete understanding and forgiveness, explaining:

> I have come to understand over the years why the hereafter considers suicide a "murder"; it is a desperate act committed by desperate people. The souls who have passed by their own hand tell me that they were not in the right frame of mind prior to passing. This form of psychological turmoil is considered an illness by the hereafter, and those who pass by their own hand are victims of this illness. No one is to blame and no one is blamed....
>
> Those who have passed by their own hand have told me that the Infinite Light is at its most forgiving and compassionate, and these victims are helped to understand that whatever turmoil they endured on the earth, it is now over and they are in a peaceful and comforting environment.[50]

The viewpoint of the spirit Johannes, channeled by Hester Dowden, emphasized the self-inflicted nature of whatever problems may face a suicide in the afterlife.[51] Thus, it may not matter as much what others in the afterlife think of the soul who has killed itself, so much as what is its own attitude toward what it has done:

> Johannes regards the state of purgatory after death in this way. The soul must review its journey on earth, and make its own purgatory out of its regrets. It is not a place, for there are no places which bear any relation to the Christian conception of Purgatory or Hell. It is rather a state of mind and being, and our daemons and inspirers will shorten the duration of it as much as possible, for regret retards progress, except in so far as it is part of experience....
>
> "The act of suicide is not a simple one," he continued, "for there are many reasons which drive the soul to cast off the body before its time; some persons are severely punished for this act; some find no evil consequence in another world. If it is a deliberate act based on reason, no consequence awaits the soul which will delay its progress, except the shock of severing the thread of life too suddenly. But, if life has become too heavy a burden through weakness, or lack of wisdom, there is desperate confusion

in the soul which may continue for a long time on low planes where life is not progressive."[52]

Material purported to be channeled from extraterrestrial sources also indicates that taking your own life is not a good idea in terms of spiritual growth. Ashayana Deane, describing herself as a scribe for speakers of "The Guardian Alliance," members of pro-human higher intelligence, says:

> *Only natural, soul-orchestrated death transition will allow for the consciousness to ascend.* Suicide will not assist in this process, because, if the soul is ready to leave its manifest body, the death transition will occur naturally or through soul arranged events, and not at the hands of an unawakened personality. We heartily request, to those who may be thinking along such lines, do not use suicide as an attempt to release yourselves from the body, for this can actually stop the ascension process.... The soul uses the body as a means of assembling frequency patterns into the consciousness, and if the body is released prematurely, the consciousness of the individual may not have reached a high enough level.... Taking matters into the hands of the personality, such as is the case in suicide, usually botches the soul's ascension plan.... Under no circumstances do we endorse suicide as a way of making this transition. If you are still in a body, then that is where your greater soul identity wants you to be, in order to best facilitate your evolutionary process.[53]

We get yet a more neutral stance from the spirit realm when we look at messages from the group entity calling itself Michael, communicating through California psychic Jessica Lansing (pseudonym) in the 1970s (and later through a number of other channels as well):

> Each fragment must experience suicide, as it must experience ... all other forms of death....
> Sooner or later the soul learns that suicide is unprofitable....
> Death is a ghastly experience if you are depressed. You bring all your depression with you. That is why so many suicides must go back and finish that which they abdicated.[54]

Alexander, another group entity, or "pool of consciousness" as it refers to itself, working through the automatic typewriting of Ramón Stevens, took a slightly different tack on the matter.[55] As with Michael, it focused on whether a person had accomplished chosen tasks or learned his or her lessons. The difference lies in Alexander's assertion that the same soul might not have to be the one to return:

> If ... challenges were not surmounted effectively and the life ended with an overall cast of defeat and hopelessness, that particular slice must be recast into another lifetime before it can be reintegrated into the higher self. This does not mean that the same soul must reincarnate; it simply means the higher self sends down another shoot in another place and time but with life circumstances similar to those of the life just released, as another attempt at resolving the challenges to be resolved before reabsorption is possible.[56]

The issue of karma would seem to be an important one in determining the ultimate cost of suicide. Michael stated that fate does not exist—only karma—and emphasized that karma was not a bad thing in the way so many people tend to think of it, saying:

> Karma is a weaving together of life cycles. Karma is not fate.... Karma is law. There is a great danger in becoming fatalistic about karma. You must learn this about karma: that lessons learned in this way are eternally yours.[57]

In another place, Michael said, "There is no sin, only karma. There is no evil, only maya [illusion]. You will repay your karmic debts ... just by hard work. There is no one 'up there' to punish you."[58] Thus, karma is not about punishment, but about learning one's lessons.

We have seen in this chapter that spirit attitudes toward suicide seem to run the gamut, with answers ranging from rigid and monolithic, to flexible and complex. Furthermore, there appears to have been a general softening in stance over time, with recent material (which accepts reincarnation) placing the emphasis on compassionate understanding and forgiveness. Nonetheless, the spirit realm does appear to agree on one point—that suicide is not a good idea. It solves nothing. Furthermore, it may represent a setback to the soul, in opportunities lost and time wasted, if nothing else. They do not recommend it.

3

Why People Kill Themselves

One question that survivors always ask is why. Why did they do it? Why kill themselves? The spirits channeled come up with various answers. Some have the ring of truth while others sound more pat and rehearsed—after all, nothing says a soul has to tell the truth, even if it is the spirit actually communicating and not some part of the channel's unconscious mind. Furthermore, it is possible that what a suicide says may change over time as a soul gains more self-insight.

Anne Puryear states that, years after taking his own life at 15, her deceased son, Stephen, came back with a book's worth of messages "dictated to me by Stephen from the plane in which he now resides." He shared with her a concern for the growing problem of suicide.[1] His spirit felt that the family situation usually played a role when those under 18 commit suicide. However, Stephen also noted that past lives could also play a part, adding, "If they have chosen wrongly, and taken their lives in the past, they will often be in the rut of choosing wrongly in the present and future."[2]

Stephen observed that occasional suicidal thoughts are not unusual. What may shift the balance is whether people feel they have control over their lives. He explained:

> There is hardly a person who hasn't contemplated suicide at one time or another.... Thoughts of taking their own life can, at times, be enough of a temporary release to get their thinking back on track. The great majority of souls entertaining the notion also discard it as the rational mind and the law of self-preservation take over.
>
> All people ... need to feel some control over their lives. Most of them, if they feel they have some say about their lives, some control, are not going to kill themselves.[3]

A soul's underlying type or personality may influence how and why a soul takes its own life. Michael explains:

> We do not mean to imply that all romantic suicide pacts are the work of twin souls refusing to be separated. More likely, youthful romantic

suicides are indulging in high-flown theatrics. Depressed sages achieve the most flamboyant suicides, though most of them do not generally intend to kill themselves, only to reap the benefits and attentions of the attempt.[4]

Often, however, what drives the suicide to take the final step is simply a matter of pain. Suzane Northrop states:

> I've talked to many dead folks who consciously took their own lives feeling the other world had to be easier. At the time, they could no longer endure any more suffering—mentally or physically. They wanted to be out of pain and were willing to accept any consequence, including nonexistence or eternal damnation to achieve that goal.[5]

As we look over what mediums and channels tell us, we will see that what leads a person to take his or her own life may not be a single factor, but a combination of elements working together. Nonetheless, this chapter will separate out ten categories of reasons why suicides tell us that they take their own lives. These are: (1) as a pure accident, (2) to get attention, (3) to get even with someone, (4) acting in an irrational moment (which often involves extreme emotionality and drugs), (5) as a result of depression or lack of hope, (6) to provide relief to their families, (7) because they feel they have no other options, (8) as a result of possession, (9) a desire to return to the afterlife, and (10) due to karma. It should be recalled that one spirit, Arthur Fanning's YHWH, reported that some people kill themselves just for the experience of it.[6]

Finally, it is possible that suicide best be viewed as a spiritual problem. Michael Newton, who used hypnosis to regress people to the period between lives and then questioned them about their experiences (in essence, allowing them to channel another aspect of their current selves), observes:

> What I have found in my practice is that a soul's energy force may, during troubled times, dissociate from the body. There are those who feel they don't even belong to their bodies. If conditions are severe enough, these souls are prone to thoughts of suicide.[7]

It should also be noted that the manner of suicide may be highly significant. The spirit guide communicating to Lauren Thibodeau states that how a person takes his or her life is an indication of what level or kind of spiritual disconnection he or she was experiencing—whether generalized or specific to one area.[8] This entity also pointed out how different types of spiritual problems, as represented by what chakra (see the Glossary) is involved, will be reflected in not only how people live their lives, but how they end them:

He's claiming that ... people who have all-over problems, people who have like a blood disease where it flows all through you. People who have like Fibromyalgia and there's pain everywhere and there's no focused place. People who have autoimmune stuff, like Lupus. It tends to be first a spiritual disconnect and then the body organ it settles on the most is going to clue you into what chakra you're dealing with. But they kind of have a spiritual issue first.... Now in this case, the autoerotism wasn't a hanging [he had hanged himself]. He's pointing out that that's sexually focused, that's a chakra two thing.... If you choose to, through the temple, through the frontal lobe, shoot yourself, that's crown chakra stuff. If you choose to take a drug overdose, that was more of a spiritual [issue]. Overall malaise. Depression. Your whole life feels wrong....

The people who like to jump out of planes, people who jump, that's first chakra suicide....

Jump off a bridge, that's all about survival isn't it? You want to make it really short. You have disregard for the body entirely. You really don't want to be here. The autoeroticism and accidental stuff, sexual stuff, he's claiming people who have risky sexual behaviors, like could contract AIDS or other STDs [sexually transmitted diseases] that's not really suicide, but that's definitely second chakra stuff.[9]

Thibodeau's spirit guide continues, listing how other forms of suicide are associated with certain chakras:

Heath: What about third chakra?
Thibodeau: Evisceration. Hara-kiri....
Heath: Fourth chakra?
Thibodeau: That would be someone who shoots themselves in the heart. Fifth chakra, neck stuff. Sixth chakra sinuses and stuff, so asphyxiation. Taking it in through breath, my mistake. Fifth is hanging. Sixth is anything when you breathe gases. Okay? Breath of life or, in this case, death....
Heath: You said seventh was like shooting yourself in the head.
Thibodeau: Right. But he's pointing out either temple or above. If you shoot yourself in the mouth you're dealing with sixth, not seventh. The mouth is always sixth. It kind of makes sense, doesn't it?
Heath: Would drowning be like asphyxiation, the sixth chakra?
Thibodeau: Yes. But also that overall malaise. That's got overtones of birth and death, in water, and the meaning of being immersed.
Heath: What about the one-car accidents? The risky driving?
Thibodeau: He's showing me chakras one, two, and three, depending. Anything where you're doing death-defying stuff, it's one or two. If it's death defying, like how fast can I drive around this curve? That's a one thing. Two would be the autoeroticism—it's pushing the edge, isn't it? And you can die from it. Thrill-seeking stuff is always one or two, they're telling me. This is whether it's physical thrill-seeking or sexual-thrill-seeking.[10]

This notion that the form a suicide takes is meaningful is an interesting one and would seem to be significant. It is possible that this spiritual dis-ease may underlie many of the reasons why souls tell us they took their own lives.

A TRUE ACCIDENT

Sometimes a soul insists that what others claim is suicide is, in fact, an accident. The British medium Sylvia Barbanell spoke of one child who killed himself and vehemently denied it had been suicide as reported. During the séance:

> After several spirit voices had addressed relatives and friends, and some excellent evidence had been received, the luminous trumpet moved in the direction of Mrs. Donohoe's companion. We heard the voice of a boy say to him, "Dad, I want you to know I did *not* commit suicide...."
> "You know I had a gun, did you? But Mummy knew."
> "Yes," replied the sitter. "I've found that out since, but tell me how it occurred."
> Very pathetically, the spirit voice replied, "Well, Dad, I was only a boy like other boys, and I wanted to be a highwayman. I took the gun and went out on the by-pass road. Then I tried to shoot a bird and I stumbled and shot myself."[11]

Another example of this comes to us from W. Usborne Moore, in *The Voices: A Sequel to "Glimpses of the Next State,"* who describes this séance he attended:

> Mrs. Wriedt said there was a spirit present who had shot himself. He was for Mr. Robertson of Helensburgh. "Did he know a man like that?" Mr. Robertson: "Yes; he was thought to have committed suicide by shooting himself." Afterwards the voice addressed Mr. Robertson, and he, satisfied to the identity, asked, "Did the gun go off accidentally or intentionally?" The voice assured him it was an accident. "Man, I had nae need to do it" (commit suicide). Everyone seemed to think he had, but Mr. Robertson was always of the opinion it was an accident, and what the spirit said accorded with this belief. The man had been with him a night or so before his death, and told him, among other things, who [how] nicely everything was going on in business and other matters; he was in a cheery mood. The voice insisted that the story of his suicide was not true. "Man, I'd nae need tae destroy masel."[12]

British researcher F. W. H. Myers, author of the classic *Human Personality and Its Survival of Bodily Death* more than a hundred years ago, told a similar tale of a Scottish man:

> I dreamt ... that I was seated at a desk, engaged in a business conversation with an unknown gentleman, who stood at my right hand. Towards me, in front, advanced Robert Mackenzie.... "What is all this, Robert?" I asked somewhat angrily. "Did you not see I was engaged?" "Yes, sir," he replied; "but I must speak with you at once." "What about?" I said; "what is it that can be so important?" "I wish to tell you sir," he answered, "that I am accused of doing a thing I did not do, and that I want *you* to know it.... I am innocent." I then naturally asked, "But how can I forgive you if you do not tell me what you are accused of?" I can never forget the emphatic manner of his answer in the Scottish dialect, "Ye'll sune ken" (you'll soon know).... On that I awoke, and was in that state of surprise ... when my wife burst into my bedroom, much excited, and holding an open letter in her hand, exclaimed, "Oh, James, here's a terrible end to the workmen's ball—Robert Mackenzie has committed suicide!" With now a full conviction of the meaning of the vision, I at once quietly and firmly said, "No, he has not committed suicide." "How can you possibly know that?" "Because he has just been here to tell me."
>
> By the following post my manager informed me that he was wrong in writing me of suicide.[13]

As mentioned earlier, accidental suicides can also occur with autoeroticism. These individuals use partial asphyxiation while masturbating in order to try to get a stronger orgasm. Unfortunately, it is all too easy to cross the line and go too far. Lauren Thibodeau had three such spirits come through her.[14] It should be noted, however, that in at least one of the cases, the boy was suffering from undiagnosed depression and the death may not have been quite so accidental. She states:

> Yeah, this little fellow—and he was a little fellow—he's bringing through a very clear self-awareness (that I don't think the family had) that he was only fourteen and he was developing what you and I would consider a major depression. And that for him, the autoeroticism was a way to feel good. Feel better. Lend some joy. So, he's saying one thing that people need to look at is [depression]. And he says sometimes they are, but it's not the parents. Clinicians would. School people might. Anyone who's behaving this way, they should look for underlying depressive behaviors and treat the root cause essentially. Because he's claiming his life would not have been one of great joy anyway. He was okay with having not lived long. He's telling me that he didn't stand out at anything. So, he's actually happier....
>
> This for him was a way out of a life of depression. He's telling me, "I would have been one of those guys who never quite gets it together." And that this is better. He would have been an average Joe is the feeling I have. That could be a fine life if you weren't already depressed....

He would have been a depressive, someone who always struggles with major depression.... And he's claiming he really didn't want to play anymore. He says, "I know too much about what's possible to really want to live like that."[15]

Although the spirits could have lied about the true facts of their cases, it seems likely that some souls do take their own lives purely by accident. Our next category, involving an attempt to get attention that goes too far, is similar to accidental death in that suicide was never really intended, at least on a conscious level.

BIDS FOR ATTENTION

Many souls mention that their deaths came about as a bid for attention gone wrong. This certainly appears to have been the case in which a spirit stated, "I took my own life. I didn't mean to kill myself—I only meant to take enough cyanide of potassium to scare him."[16]

In communicating back to his mother, Stephen spoke at length about his own self-inflicted death at age 15 and what led up to it.[17] It reads, rather sadly, like the classic personal fable so many suicides have:

> I honestly didn't consider the finality of it all.... I imagined you'd all regret what you did, and I'd come back and you'd appreciate me more. After all, in the movies and on TV, people got killed one night and were on another program the next.... I didn't think how absolutely irreversible and final it would be.[18]

Although probably seldom seen as a single cause of suicide, the bid for attention may often be a contributing factor in suicide—particularly when an individual is extremely emotional or under the influence of drugs or alcohol.

GETTING EVEN

Strong emotions can lead to irrational actions. This can often be the case when love turns to anger. A number of souls described killing themselves in order to hurt another human being, using their own death as an ultimate tool to get even. Physician Carl Wickland, in his landmark *Thirty Years Among the Dead*, a compilation of his interchanges during the 1920s with spirits communicating through his wife acting as medium, reported that one spirit told him:

> I was in that state of anger and it was my death. What did I do? I killed myself. I did not mean to kill myself, but I did it in a mood of anger....

> I was swept by anger and what happened? I killed myself. Then when I woke up and saw what I had done, I was in anguish.[19]

Well-known contemporary medium and author George Anderson was put in the difficult position once of trying to explain why a mother had unexpectedly killed herself:

> "She says, 'I did it to get even.' I don't know what she means," George added apologetically....
>
> "Your mother is saying she was very depressed. She couldn't take any more. There seems to have been a great deal of friction with her husband—your father. There was a great amount of arguing, disagreement, shouting, and tension."[20]

The line clearly blurs somewhat between wanting attention, getting even, and acting in an irrational moment. Often these are combined elements, with drugs and alcohol playing a contributing role. Lysa Mateu has channeled many suicides over the years, and even devoted an entire book, *Conversations with the Spirit World: Souls Who Have Ended Their Lives Speak from Above,* to the topic. Her second book, *Psychic Diaries: Connecting with Who You Are, Why You're Here, and What Lies Beyond,* also includes some material on suicides. The following is such a message from a spirit, where anger and alcohol combined to create a lethal mix:

> We go to eat with a friend, and yes, I drink a lot. Husband gets angry, wants me to stop, I don't, he gets angrier, I storm into the ladies' room, call my girlfriend, crying. He comes after me, apologizes. At home, I'm a total wreck, drunker than I'd been in a while. As a "fuck you" to him, to myself, I grab the gun he'd taught me how to use, a bullet blasts through my head.[21]

In another case of Mateu's, a suicide was clearly executed in a manner planned for maximum effect:

> A son yells for his mother to come up to his room. Says he needs to see her right away.
>
> She walks up the stairs, feels weird in her stomach.... She opens the door. Sees her son in the closet, a rope tied around his neck, a chair beneath his feet. He kicks it out the moment he sees his mother's face—the ultimate fuck-you.[22]

Here, again, drugs were involved at the time the young man killed himself.

IRRATIONAL MOMENTS

Irrational moments can be due to a variety of factors, including extreme anger from a fight, mental illness, and mind- or mood-altering substances, including alcohol. In fact, it is common for spirits to mention drugs at the time of their deaths, whether or not they have a prior history of mental illness. Because of this, a suicide's mental state at the time of the crossover to death may be far from normal. George Anderson observes:

> Even the souls in the hereafter will admit that ending their existence here probably wasn't the best idea—that if they had allowed themselves more time to think or ask for help, a way around their problems could have been found. But ... they are not in a mental state where they are capable of making rational decisions. Many of those from the hereafter have also told me that ... there was an element of mental torture that could not be reconciled with.[23]

In one case Anderson channeled a young man who had shot himself:

> I'm not saying that he's going on a rampage, but he's not thinking clearly, 'cause he admits he's not in the right frame of mind. He is irrational prior to his passing....
> Had ... he been drinking or something ... doing a drug or something like this? Okay, 'cause there's something in my system that is making me not myself.[24]

James Pike Junior, son of Bishop James A. Pike, one of America's best-known clergymen, transmitted messages through a number of mediums after taking his own life. During a session with the English Ena Twigg, he was channeled saying, "I failed the test; I can't face you, can't face life. I'm confused.... God, I didn't know what I was doing."[25]

Arthur Ford felt that drugs were a major factor in the boy's suicide. He reported after a different session with Pike that:

> He'd been under stress at examination time, "said something about drugs" (Pierce-Higgins) and guess his mind had just cracked—couldn't face up to things all on his own....
> The younger Pike identified the drug he had previously mentioned as LSD—it had been another LSD tragedy. He had "got mixed up with the thing" in California, at college and had fallen in with some of the same crowd on his return to New York. The suicide had been the result of a "bad trip."[26]

When Montgomery inquired on behalf of a mother about a young girl who had killed herself through carbon monoxide poisoning, she was told,

"'Yes, she is here, Little Melissa, and so sorry for what she did,' the Guides responded. 'Teenagers have a hard time keeping balance in today's world, and she was emotionally unstrung, but should have thought more before acting.'"[27]

Because of his television appearances and best-selling books, James Van Praagh is one of America's most recognized mediums. Several souls who told him that they had killed themselves appeared to be suffering from a combination of bipolar disorder and the ingestion of drugs—not all of them legal. In one place he told a daughter, "I must tell you that I feel your mother was not mentally all there."[28]

Thus, we have seen that drugs and alcohol can be a major factor in why many people take their own lives. The violent mood swings often released by chemical agents have the potential to be particularly lethal when combined with mental illness. Furthermore, drugs may be particularly problematic in the afterlife, because in addition to whatever other problems they had, the suicide may have to deal with the psychological withdrawal from addiction.[29]

DEPRESSION AND LACK OF HOPE

Lysa Mateu has asked a number of spirits over the years why they committed suicide. She has received various answers—not all of which appear to be entirely truthful, as some spirits appeared to change their stories. One spirit, Charley, stated that for him, it was because "I felt hopeless when I saw the world the way it was, with all the harsh attitudes, intolerances, and pain."[30] However, it should be noted that he also suffered from bipolar disorder. For Kimberly it was more a case of depression. She explained, "I was feeling despondent and afraid.... I was begging someone to see the pain I was in."[31] Regardless of the predisposing factors, it seems worthwhile to consider what these discarnate souls say about what happened to them, and what they wish others would understand.

Sometimes the spirits channeled by George Anderson did not know why they killed themselves, but mentioned feeling down at the time. In one case of a teenage suicide, Anderson states of the boy: "He doesn't even know himself why he did it.... It's almost as if he were playing around and it went too far.... But he was in a slump, so to speak, a depression at the holidays."[32] With another case it appears to be even simpler: "He had taken his own life because he was so overwhelmed by this existence and was afraid all the time."[33]

The depression experienced by a person who takes his or her own life may continue after he or she has died. As recounted in her story of her own channeling experiences, *Epilogue: Souls Review Their Lives After Death*, a teenage suicide told Jean Foster, "I found no answers. That is why I emptied the bottle of pills into myself."[34] The soul then added that she felt nothing in life was of value, "and they either have to adjust to the emptiness or do what I did."[35] Unfortunately, this spirit felt things were no better in the afterlife. It was only after working with her guide for a period of time that the spirit began to view things differently. Foster writes of the spirit's communication:

> I see why I became hopeless in life....
> My truth then was, "Hate is all I see around me. Tenderness does not exist. Hopelessness is what everyone I know feels about life.... What's the use of growing up in a world like that?" Those were my thoughts.
> The weight of it ... was too much. Therefore, thoughts came to mind that if I killed myself, then all my heaviness would disappear![36]

Depression can take different forms. In one case, it appeared as a woman feeling utterly unworthy of her child. April Crawford channeled the following letter from a suicide to her daughter:

> I can now only remember the moment it all began to go wrong. My self doubt creeping in like a thief to steal our sunny days. Questions coming to the surface of my consciousness that clouded my judgment and made me feel unworthy. You see you were so worthy and I was not....
> The night it happened you were sleeping so peacefully. I cried in the moonlight admiring your innocence. My guilt over my unworthiness growing larger and larger until the bedroom suddenly disappeared from view. Who knows where I got the pistol.... Looking back I do not remember pulling the trigger.[37]

Depression is also seen as a cause of suicide reported during past-life regressions. One woman, who during an induced-trance session remembered killing herself by a drug overdose, shared her reason with Winfred Lucas, a psychologist who uses past-life hypnotic regression in her research:

> I feel so depressed! I don't want to live anymore. I don't want to hear the children crying, to see the dirt, to look at myself in the mirror, to wait for him to come home in a bad mood.[38]

Given the national statistics on suicide and depression, it is no surprise that many souls report it as a factor in their deaths. The problem becomes even worse when people self-medicate with drugs or alcohol in an effort to escape their problems, if only temporarily.

TO PROVIDE RELIEF TO THEIR FAMILY

Killing oneself in order to relieve one's family and friends of some burden, whether real or imagined, is most often reported with those who take their own lives when they have a terminal illness. However, it can also be seen in other cases. Suzane Northrop notes:

> One of the things that I've also learned is that a lot of times … people take their own lives not because they can't deal with their mental, emotional, or physical state of pain, but because they don't want to put their families through "it" anymore. This is a very key component in these cases.[39]

Although providing relief to the family is not a common element in traditional suicide—where there may be little, if any, thought ahead of time about how this action will affect the living—we will see this topic arise again in the chapter on assisted suicide.

THEY FEEL THERE ARE NO OTHER OPTIONS

Rarely, a person may be forced into the suicide against his or her will. Anderson channeled a teenager where this appeared to be the case, noting:

> It's strange. I feel he was forced to kill himself. He was drawn into something and he couldn't get out of it.… There's something very evil. His parents couldn't help him. There was nothing they could do. They can't blame themselves but they do.…
>
> He's saying he killed himself, but *they* pulled the trigger. It was more like murder than suicide in that this young boy was … forced to take his own life.…
>
> The boy is telling me this was his choice, but he was trying to protect other members of his family.[40]

James Padgett was a lawyer and medium who devoted more than a decade of his life to amassing spirit communications, eventually receiving more than 2,500 of them.[41] Many of these are collected as a series of letters in the book *What Happens After You Die*. In the case of a soul who came through Padgett, the reason appeared to be a case of seeing no other viable options:

> I thought that there was no reason why I should continue the life longer, which was one of monotony in a certain sense. Besides, I felt that I had arrived at the height of my mental powers and that they were on a decline.…
>
> Just before I fired the fatal shot, I thought intensely of all these things, and saw that what I supposed would be an end to everything was the true

solution of life's decay and mental as well as physical decrepitude. And when I prepared to do the deed, I was never more calm in all my life.[42]

W. Usborne Moore reported a séance where a suicide came through to explain why he had killed himself after his fiancée broke off their engagement. Moore wrote:

> After a few minutes the psychic said: "There is a man here who has been shot ... he shot himself. He appears to me to have committed suicide." A whisper through the trumpet: "George, I was with you in the *Penguin*." I at once said: "You are George; do you not regret your rash act?" Then came this remarkable answer: "No, I do not. I was ... impelled to do it" (a groan). "Admiral, she would not marry me, as I had not enough money; and there was a richer man than I in the background."[43]

Another soul explained:

> Suicide is not recommended because it ends any chance of becoming the truth of God in practice. But in my case, this truth was shut off, and I wanted release from my body. My true being, or spirit self, wanted to end the relationship which held me to wrong thoughts. There was no thought for others in my act.[44]

Thus, we see that many souls felt like they had no other choice at the time they took their own lives. Some later recognize that they were wrong, but others do not change their viewpoint while in the afterlife.

POSSESSION

Older writings frequently blamed suicide on madness caused by possessing spirits. John Ballou wrote the "Kosmon Bible," or *OAHSPE*, via automatic typewriting around 1880. He reported receiving information about earlier times and realms, including that during "the time of Thor" the spirits caused mass suicide of those on Earth. The book of Thor, chapter VI, verse 14 reads:

> And, save to the I'hins, the Light of Jehovih was shut out from men; thus ambition for improvement was at an end; they became as drones and vagabonds; and, when they died, their spirits continued to lie about in the places of their mortal life. And many of these spirits persuaded mortals to suicide, and they killed themselves by thousands and tens of thousands. Nor was there courage more amongst men to endure anything under the sun. They wanted to be with the spirits of the dead, to talk with them, to see them, and to be rid of earth trials.[45]

W. Stainton Moses channeled the following message in 1876:

> None lifts the hand of the suicide against himself save when the disordered mind has lost its power of judgment. The balance is destroyed, and the spirit has fallen a prey to the tempters which surround it.[46]

Psychiatrist Carl Wickland believed that possession by earthbound spirits was a common cause of suicide. A former friend was channeled by Wickland's wife. The soul was apparently stuck, tied to the Earth plane. According to her:

> As soon as I found myself out of my body, I saw at once the cause for my rash act. Evil spirits, who had been attracted to me by the jealous thoughts of other persons, were standing near, grinning with devilish satisfaction at their work.
>
> They had influenced me to end my life; I had no occasion to even think of such folly. An irresistible impulse had suddenly come over me—I fastened the rope around my neck, and only realized what I had done when it was too late.[47]

Many of the spirits of suicides that Wickland spoke to denied responsibility for their own deaths: "A big man with a black beard made me do it.... He met me in the barnyard and hypnotized me, and made me hang myself to a rafter."[48]

Wickland felt that mediums and those who attended séances were particularly vulnerable to becoming possessed, and could cause them to change in personality, becoming greedy.[49] Worse still, they could lose their spirit guides. Wickland remembered one such spirit who spoke from the afterlife after killing himself:

> He explained that while he had been honest in his early work, the woman whom he had married proved to be a dishonest and fraudulent medium, dominated by selfish, mischievous spirits. Her invisible forces had encroached upon his sensitive nature and, unaware of spirit obsession, he become overpowered by them, hence his fall and tragic ending.[50]

In another instance, Wickland described a woman who shot herself while purportedly under the influence of earthbound spirits:

> Sp: I didn't do it! I didn't do it! Those people around me made me do it.
> Dr: What did you do?
> Sp: I shot myself. (While controlled by earthbound spirits.)
> Dr: You are not dead; you are still alive. No one ever actually "dies." You only drove yourself out of your body.

Sp: They haunted me so!
Dr: Who?
Sp: All those people....
Dr: Look around you and you will find kindly spirits who will teach you how to overcome your present condition.
Sp: Will those people go away? (Earthbound spirits.)
Dr: They will not bother you any more....
Sp: I have suffered so. I have constantly seen my husband and mother, both very sad and crying. Oh, God help me.... Why should I be tormented so terribly?
Dr: You were evidently a psychic sensitive but did not know it.[51]

Evil spirits continue to be blamed as a contributing factor to suicide in the Philippines and Japan. The well-known contemporary Japanese medium Hiroshi Motoyama explains his thoughts on possession as follows:

> Attachment makes a spirit impure. This impurity has the power to exert a negative influence on the other beings with whom the spirit comes in contact. People who come from spiritual consultations often "carry" with them such suffering spirits. Sometimes I absorb the influence of the defiled spirits and feel temporarily ill myself.
>
> This phenomenon, commonly called possession, is much more common than most people realize. We "possess," or attach to, each other in an endless number of ways. This possession occurs both within and across the dimensions, and is positive or negative depending on the inherent relationship between the two beings.[52]

Another Japanese medium states, "People who commit suicide are usually possessed by evil spirits."[53]

Jaime Licauco, a Phillipino psychical researcher, wrote an article in the *Philippine Daily Inquirer* blaming the suicide of a young mother on a negative entity.[54] The woman apparently jumped from a building. Her family could not understand why she would have jumped from the top of a building and killed herself, because her health was good and they were not aware of any personal or economic problems that would lead to such a drastic solution. They contacted a channeled entity that claimed to be from the fifth dimension and were told:

> "Her suicide was caused by an external force, i.e., by a spirit," said the entity. "There was also a deep desire for Rose to end her life. This is the reason for the attraction of the black spirit in the form of a mental nagging thought to disrupt the flow of goodness in her life.
>
> "Rose was very discontented with the way her life turned out to be, though her physical form did not show it. Past life karmic appearances

contributed a lot. Her jumping, her suicide could not have been prevented by her husband."

The spirit of Rose came in at this point and continued the automatic writing. She explained that the negative spirit was controlling her. She could not do anything. She asked one of our companions to pray for her.[55]

Possession as a cause of depression was popular in the early Spiritualist era and is still accepted as factual by some cultures today. It should be noted that many feel that for possession or obsession to occur requires some degree of acceptance by people under this influence, or their temporary incapacitation through drugs (including alcohol). Furthermore, it is possible that being psychically sensitive could make one more vulnerable. As contemporary American parapsychologist and author Loyd Auerbach likes to say, he has never seen a skeptic successfully psychically attacked.[56] We will later see that the spirit realm often emphasizes a need for suicides to take responsibility for their actions, regardless of what impelled them to kill themselves. This would seem to suggest that whether possession is a factor or not, it is important for suicides to own up to their own role in what occurred.

DESIRE TO RETURN TO THE AFTERLIFE

Rarely, people will attempt suicide because they desire to return to the other side. This may be particularly true after a near-death experience. This may simply be due more to depression, which is quite common after the event, where returning to regular life can be difficult and even unwanted in light of the NDEs transcendental glimpse of what seems to be a wondrous otherworldly reality. However, there are other instances where there appears to be a genuine desire to return to the peace of the afterlife that does not involve such depression.

P. M. H. Atwater has discussed the fact that the depression NDErs exhibit as they struggle to come to terms with what happened to them may be made worse by the feelings that they were not good enough to stay in heaven or are incapable of meeting some unrealistic goal of perfection.[57] Such misplaced guilt combined with depression may even lead individuals to try to take their own lives again.

In her database of 3,000 adult NDEs, Atwater found approximately a 4 percent rate of attempted suicide within twelve years after their NDE.[58] When asked why, their response was that life was simply too hard. Knowing how much better the afterlife was than here, they decided to return to it. Atwater writes of one woman who twice attempted suicide after her NDE in an effort to return to what she thought of as a much better place, and of another woman who seriously considered suicide for the same reason.

The contrast of NDEs with physical life may be particularly tough on children. P. M. H. Atwater observed that 33 percent of them (compared to about 20 percent of adults) turn to alcohol within eight years of their NDE.[59] Furthermore, more than 50 percent of them had serious bouts of depression afterward and 21 percent attempted suicide within twelve years. Atwater reports:

> Numerous experiencers have admitted to me that they became alcoholics as children because they couldn't handle the aftermath of coming back from where they had been. Those who tried to kill themselves did so as a way to return "home." Kids who had their episodes while they were of school age were much more likely to be affected by such extremes than those who "died" in infancy or as a toddler.[60]

In discussing the use of suicide to return to the afterlife, Atwater has observed that children are more apt to act on impulse than adults.[61] Furthermore, because they do not think as much in terms of cause and effect, it seems reasonable to them to return to the light by dying. Interestingly enough, this is not considered to be self-destructive behavior by them.

Atwater talked about one child in particular, Debi, who seemed to exemplify this point.[62] This child had her first NDE at the age of eight, when the contrast between the awfulness of her physical life and the delightfulness of the afterlife made the return to existence seem harsh indeed. She told Atwater:

> The life I was leading at that time was so filled with abuse and negativity that I embraced being able to "leave." I went through the dark tunnel, found the "light." And tried to race into heaven. I was stopped by a very wise, older man. ... he looked at me with sadness ... and he said, "No, little girl, it is not time yet. You have to go back." I awoke coughing up blood in the ICU. From that moment until just this year I *hated* my life. I tried suicide at sixteen and when that didn't work, I went to great lengths to sabotage my life.[63]

Although much of the previous data involves failed suicide attempts, it would seem likely that in at least some cases, near-death experiencers succeed. In these cases, it might be said that the motivation is not simply an effort to escape life's problems, but also a genuine desire to return to the afterlife. The question is, which is more likely—that it is a running away from something unwanted (physical existence) or a running toward something wanted (the trans-physical afterlife existence)? One may feel that, no, I am not running just *away* from life—I am running *toward* even greater life.

KARMA

To speak of karma requires a certain acceptance of the idea of reincarnation, and the idea that past lives can affect what happens in the present, just as the present may influence the future. Since the early Spiritualist literature (Kardec excepted) was generally dismissive of this notion, it is only in more contemporary literature that we see karma mentioned as a possible cause of suicide. In these cases, souls are said to have apparently taken on more than they could handle in a given lifetime. Through British medium Ruth White, the spirit Gildas stated of a suicidal patient that:

> This girl carries an immense weight of karma; the roots of her problem do not lie in this life. There is very little which you can do, except let things take their course and give support on the personal, here-and-now level. It may be that the experience of suicide is necessary; perhaps she cannot at this time face that which was taken on by the higher self.[64]

In another case, Lauren Thibodeau found a karmic pattern when channeling the guide of a boy who had killed himself through autoeroticism. She reports:

> Thibodeau: I keep seeing an image ... of a man who looks like he has reddish-copper African skin. I see this guide with dark brown skin.... He was a ... shamanic practitioner in that culture. And this young boy was an apprentice to him. Actually, it was his nephew, he's telling me. So, they're well known to each other.
> Heath: In the previous life.
> Thibodeau: In previous lives, right. And that he's been helping him to understand a lot. And he's taking me to the lifetime they shared, and I want to go to the 1530s.... This is really karmic. He's showing me that the nephew that was his apprentice, was captured by slave traders and taken to the Caribbean. Not all the way to the U.S., but we're going way out to what today would be like Haiti. And then he was traded from there into the States.... Anyway, he's saying that he hung himself to escape it, and so this autoeroticism thing and all that stuff is all connected up.
> Heath: A kind of a karmic pattern?
> Thibodeau: Very karmic. Yes, very karmic.[65]

This completes our look at the different reasons that suicides tell us they were impelled to take their own lives. Sometimes what happens appears to be a true accident or there is a single cause. However, far more often there are a variety of elements—including a desire for attention, getting even, anger, drugs, and mental illness—that combine in an all-too-lethal mix. If there is a trend, it is that many suicides in the older literature blamed evil spirits and possession for what happened to them, denying any responsibility. Although some cultures continue to accept possession as a reality, many others do not. Rarely, traditional suicides speak of wanting to relieve their families of some burden, acting because they had no other options, or because of karma. Regardless of what leads a suicide to take his or her own life, many of them report similar experiences in the afterlife, particularly during the initial stages. Now it is time to shift our attention to how suicides describe their transition and what it is like in the so-called lower astral planes.

4

Transitioning to the Afterlife

A number of channels have spoken over the years about the newly dead. Some things appear to be true regardless of the manner of death. The consensus seems to be that people don't change just because they are dead. They are not instantly smarter or kinder or more honest. Nor do they instantly become enlightened. Indeed, according to the channeled literature, their status in the afterlife is determined for the most part by what kind of life they lived on Earth.[1]

The same basic truths hold for suicides in the afterlife. They are still people. They continue to have personalities (which often comes through rather strongly in the channeled material). And they are not necessarily any wiser or more enlightened than before they killed themselves, especially if they have recently crossed over. Nonetheless, the experience of dying can sometimes make them see things differently, which is even more true after they have gone through their life review. A life review is a stage widely reported across most survival reports, and even many NDEs, where one goes through a whirlwind, yet incredibly lucid and coherent, rapid review of one's entire life.

During a meeting of the Spiritualist Association of Great Britain, Sheila Jones received messages suggesting that a person's state of health and beliefs could affect the speed and ease of his or her transition to the afterlife.[2] Other mediums have been given similar information. For example, Suzane Northrop channeled the following message from a deceased psychiatrist:

> There are two important factors influencing us in our death transitions. The first factor is the circumstance of our death. Illness, accident ... war, or natural causes will all have individually specific side effects and influences on what happens at the immediate time of our death. The second and more important consideration is: Our beliefs, faith, thought processes, and state of mind immediately prior to and at the time of death. Any of these may ... influence the soul's consciousness at the time of death. If we're in a state of extreme emotionalism ... those emotions or states of mind will travel with us through our death.... If you believe in some form

of life after death ... your transition will be filled with love and guidance. However, the expectation of nothingness or ... fear of punishment—whatever terrifies you—may keep you in a state of semi-awareness until you are ready to see the light.[3]

Thus, we can see that a person's emotional state and system of beliefs may influence how smoothly the shift to the afterlife can be made. We will later note that suicide by blowing up your body may have an effect on the astral body, which causes it to need a longer period of sleep and recovery before the soul can function in the afterlife.

Another aspect that needs to be considered is how quickly the soul may be able to disengage itself from what is left of the physical remains. Much of the literature expresses the idea that many, if not all, souls need an adjustment period after they have crossed over, before they are fully separate from their bodies. Frequently, this is said to be three days. For example, Franklin Loehr was told by the spirit of Dr. John that the soul does not immediately separate from the body.[4] Instead, there can be a delay. How long that is can vary. With some, it can take a matter of hours, often only three, while with others it can take three days to complete.

Some of this period of adjustment may not be simply a matter of disengaging from what remains of the body, but due to the problem of orienting to one's new state of existence. There are no longer eyes to see with, or hands to touch with, and the world around the spirit is composed of energy, not mass. It may take time to understand a new way of making sense of one's surroundings. In a session done for this book, psychic and medium Johanna Carroll notes:

> As I said, it's almost like they have a recognition immediately, that something's wrong here and trying to find the body ... there's a little bit of a wandering of the spirit, trying to figure out what's going on. In terms of time lines, it's hard to measure. I really haven't been able to measure it to be honest with you.[5]

It should also be noted that this process of dropping the physical body may not be painless. Carroll states:

> The etheric body goes through a phenomenal amount of pain. It's like all the encoded information, documents, text, whatever you want to call it, that's in the etheric as far as the matrix.... When suicide occurs, it reminds me of a bunch of marbles, floating. And they get hit and everything gets shaken up. So, the matrix has difficulty realigning itself because it's a shock to the system—obviously the physical body, but it's also a shock to the entire matrix itself, which is another system.[6]

Although many channeled accounts speak of death as being painless, some Buddhist literature would seem to support the idea that the process of dying may involve discomfort. Sogyal Rinpoche states:

> The bardo of dying falls between the moment we contract a terminal illness or condition that will end in death and the ceasing of the "inner respiration." It is called "painful" because if we are not prepared for what will happen to us at death, it can be an experience of tremendous suffering.[7]

He later adds: "Kalu Rinpoche writes: 'For the individual dying, the inner experience is of being consumed in a flame, being in the middle of a roaring blaze, or perhaps the whole world being consumed in a holocaust of fire.'"[8]

It should be noted that a number of channeled messages from suicides specifically deny that they experience any discomfort in their crossing. Once more, returning to Lauren Thibodeau channeling a boy who had killed himself through autoeroticism gone too far:

> He's telling me that he appreciates the opportunity to try and explain that the trauma he's been through is not that bad really. He's claiming that it's harder on the survivors. That it wasn't a difficult passing. It wasn't planned, of course, but physiologically he didn't struggle. And that's something that he seems to feel is important for his family. They're still wondering. Was it painful? Did he struggle for air? All those things.[9]

Allan Kardec believed that the manner of death could affect the transition period:

> It is, in fact, only rational to suppose that the more closely a spirit has identified himself with matter, the greater will be his difficulty in separating himself from his material body.... The study of a great number of individuals after their death has shown that affinity which, in some cases, continues to exist between the soul and the body is sometimes extremely painful; for it causes the spirit to perceive all the horror of the decomposition of the latter. This experience is exceptional, and peculiar to certain kinds of life and to certain kinds of death. It sometimes occurs in the case of those who have committed suicide.[10]

And in another place, Kardec explains:

> Observation has shown us that the perispirit, at death, disengages itself more or less slowly from the body. During the first few moments which follow dissolution, a spirit does not clearly understand his own situation. He does not think himself dead, for he feels himself living. He sees his body beside him, he knows that it is his, and he does not understand that he is separated from it.[11]

Johanna Carroll also reports that many suicides do not initially realize that they succeeded:

> The very first thing I always see is them trying to touch the body, figure out not where they are, but where's the body....
> So, what happens on the other side is that the first experience is more of a "where am I," more of a "where's the body," because they are really attached to the body.... There's a lot of confusion.[12]

Once souls are able to separate from their bodies (which in some cases may occur very quickly), they are likely to experience what is commonly referred to as the "lower astral." This requires a certain amount of explanation. There is a consensus across many of those who for centuries have studied, speculated, and written on the nature of a larger reality that exists, only one subcomponent of which is physical reality as we know it and our current life here on Earth. This view involves a number of separate levels, planes, or densities of reality, of existence. We live within one, the physical, but there are a number of others and they are said to be inhabited as well, including the realm we are said to enter following the death of our physical bodies. In addition, many mediums, channels, psychics, and instrumental transcommunication sources (i.e., spirits said to be communicating the past few decades through radios, tape recorders, and so on, rather than through human channels or mediums) point to a number of dimensions or levels of existence that vary by vibratory frequency. Sources disagree to some extent about how many planes there are, but a common number found is seven. For example, "Technician," a being said to be communicating through instrumental transcommunication to a research team in Luxembourg, stated:

> The beyond [mid-astral planes] represents only one step of post-mortal existence. There are six other steps and the first one represents a huge nebulous region in which you wander about alone, should you have left the world by suicide or though other lowly motives. Those who believe in the theory of illusion, who claim mind and spirit totally dissolve when they leave your world, are wrong. Just the opposite.[13]

Others emphasize more how these levels vary by their degree of spirituality or closeness to the Source or the Light. George Anderson, who readily admits to a Catholic bias in his readings and interpretations, feels the afterlife has nine levels, seven of which are higher realms while two are darker dimensions.[14] According to Anderson, everyone (except for a special few, like Mother Teresa) begins in an introductory level, then moves their way up. The lower levels are dark ones, but as one advances to each higher level, there is a greater abundance of light.

Although other mediums list a different number of planes, most seem to agree that there are many dimensions in the afterlife, which vary in vibratory rate depending on how close they are to an ultimate higher deity or source of light. It is because of these variations in speed of vibration that one level may not be able to be aware of the next, rather like the different levels of sound frequency, like a dog whistle that cannot be heard by human ears. Thus, these dimensions exist simultaneously and interpenetrate each other, yet remain, in their own way, discrete.

The highest levels of frequency, which are said to be very fine and at an extremely high rate of vibration, exist at or near the Source. It is also said to be very bright or full of light there. The earth dimension would be on the opposite end of the spectrum, with the low frequency of vibration causing density of matter. Closest to the earthly plane in frequency, just enough faster in vibration that most people are unaware of it, is what is often referred to as the lower astral plane.

Most souls, including suicides, are said to initially pass through the lower astral after death. However, suicides are reported to often appear to get stuck there, in the lowest, darkest, levels of the astral, and have difficulty moving to a more pleasant, higher dimension. In the case of Bishop Pike's son, who committed suicide, the soul said, "I am not in purgatory—but something like hell here."[15]

George Anderson describes the transition process that souls experience in death as being initially similar to the typical near-death experience, with a tunnel that leads to the light.[16] He felt that one can go quickly through the first darker levels (his version of purgatory or hell) and pass into the third and fourth levels. There souls find others to greet them—friends and relatives who have already passed into the afterlife, and can act as guides, leading the way to the light. However, he adds this somewhat ominous comment:

> I've never really heard any complaints about the other side, unless the person has gone over there and into the darker levels, for committing some serious crime, hurting people, or committing suicide.[17]

Martinus Thomsen, studied by psychiatrist and survival researcher Nils Jacobson, was a Danish man who had what he called a "cosmic initiation" in 1920, after which he was able to gain insights into the nature of the larger reality. Martinus, who explored the spiritual realms in trance, felt differently than Anderson[18] about the initial afterlife experience. He believed that all souls, at least initially, spend some time in the first or lowest spiritual plane, "created totally by the being himself":[19]

> This consists of a personal mental universe, habitual conceptions and thoughts, which become materialized here as a very vivid outer reality. ... he is confined in a "mental prison" created of personal needs and ideas. He cannot make contact with other beings unless they are on the same wavelength, that is, have the same inclinations. As a result of the indefinite perception of time, the being may easily feel convinced that this state will continue for all eternity. All this contributes to a more or less intense experience of hell or purgatory....
>
> In purgatory the being experiences only his own thoughts, vividly materialized to constitute his entire surroundings, so that he may fully realize the extent of his development and the primitive qualities of his personality.[20]

This self-fulfilling prophecy may work to the detriment of souls who are in an extremely depressed state of mind or full of negative thinking when they pass over.

The lower levels of the astral plane are almost always described by mediums as dark and unpleasant. This was particularly true in older channeled material, which leaned toward the classic religious image of a hell within which there was everlasting torment and from which there was no escape. In line with religious dogma, the suicide was often thought to be condemned to these places in order to suffer.

Emanuel Swedenborg was a scientist, philosopher, theologian, and mystic who lived in the 1700s. He spent much of his final decades exploring the spiritual dimension, being taken there, he said, in visionary, seemingly out-of-body, experiences by angels and other spiritual beings serving as his guides and teachers. Swedenborg was shown that there were lots of hells, all of which were dark, unhappy places. He wrote:

> There are hells everywhere. They are under the mountains and hills and cliffs and under the plains and valleys. The openings or gates to the hells that are under the mountains and hills and cliffs look at first sight like crevices or fissures in the rocks. Some of them are quite broad and open, some narrow and confined, full of rough places. All of them seem dim and gloomy when you look in, although the hellish spirits who live there have the kind of illumination you get from glowing coals. Their eyes are adjusted to the reception of this kind of light. This is because when they were living in the world they were in darkness about divine truths owing to their denial of them. They were in a kind of light as to their false convictions because they affirmed them, which gave their eyesight the form it has. This

is also why heaven's light is darkness to them, so when they come out of their caves, they cannot see anything. This makes it abundantly clear that we come into heaven's light to the extent that we have acknowledged the Divine and affirmed within ourselves the values of heaven and the church. We come into the darkness of hell to the extent that we have denied the Divine and affirmed within ourselves values contrary to those of heaven and the church.[21]

Swedenborg went on to discuss how these places were run by angels, which were responsible for controlling the fighting and chaos. Furthermore, these hells seemed to be fearful places indeed, governed by punishment, with penalties ranging in severity depending on the nature of the crime:

> Most of the time, the relatively malevolent spirits are in power, having gained control by their experience and skill; and they are able to keep the rest in servile obedience by punishments and the fears that these give birth to....
>
> We do need to realize that the only way of controlling the violent rages of people in the hells is through fear of punishment. There are no other means."[22]

Thus, we see a lot of talk about punishment that corresponds with Swedenborg's emphasis on the bestiality of the inhabitants of hell.

It should be noted that Swedenborg's vision of the afterlife may have softened somewhat after he died. After death, his purported surviving spirit still saw evil spirits as living in like-minded communities in a variety of hells, but described them as follows:

> These places have their own fixed condition of darkness and of gloom, and many other attachments which increases the sufferings that spirits have to endure.
>
> There are, of course, no fires and brimstone lakes, and devils with pitchforks adding to the sufferings of the spirits, but yet, there are certain conditions and appearances which are outside of the spirits themselves, which ... work in a manner to produce a greater degree of suffering.
>
> These hells may be places of caverns and rocks and barren wastes and dark holes ... evil spirits do not live in pleasant places and suffer only from the punishments which their recollections bring to them.
>
> These hells are on the planes nearest the earth. ... they cannot escape from them, unless they accept the help from spirits who can instruct them.[23]

What brings hope to this vision is the suggestion that "they have to remain [in hell] until, by the operation of the law of compensation they are relieved from some of their evil tendencies and desires, when they are permitted to progress."[24] This is a shift from Swedenborg's position while alive that hell is a permanent state.

Gathering her information during the 1930s, Russian psychic Helena Roerich also tended toward a negative view of what would happen to one committing suicide. She wrote in a letter:

> Suicides usually stay in the strata that are closest to Earth, because the magnetic attraction of their energies to Earth has not yet been outlived. Their etheric ... body especially attaches them to earthly sensations.... If during life, their consciousness was clouded, then this haziness will be still more intensified after the separation from the physical body.[25]

Roerich also warned that such souls would remain "in a semi-somnolent state."[26]

Worse still, late-nineteenth- and early-twentieth-century British clairvoyant Charles Leadbeater stated that suicides tended to be particularly aware of their unpleasant surroundings in the lower astral:

> It will be readily understood that the man who is torn from physical life hurriedly while in full health and strength, whether by accident or suicide, finds himself upon the astral plane under conditions differing considerably from those which surround one who dies either from old age or from disease....
> In the case of accidental death or suicide ... a great deal of the grossest kind of astral matter still clings around the personality, which is consequently held in the seventh or lowest subdivision of the plane. This has already been described as anything but a pleasant abiding place.[27]

Some contemporary mediums take a similar stance, but admit to some variability in where a suicide may wind up. Furthermore, they recognize that spirit helpers exist whose function is to try to help these lost souls move forward spiritually to a better plane of existence. Suzane Northrop speaks of five levels of existence, the first being the astral place in relation to the Earth, and the second being the lower astral:

> I strongly believe that this level is the place the Bible refers to as Hell. Here is the gangrenous blob of all evil and negative energy, souls who have taken wrong turns in life.... Here are literally lost souls, who find themselves tangled in a web of their own emotional disturbance, trapped.... Some souls never leave. Souls may end up here temporarily for other reasons as well—due to suicide or having died from a deliberate drug or alcohol overdose. However, not all suicides, murderers, or willful deaths will end up here. Everyone's circumstance is different, creating completely different consequences.[28]

Elsie Sechrist, an international dream expert and friend of psychic Edgar Cayce, also believed that suicides can wind up in a terrible situation, far different than they had anticipated.[29] She knew of a man who had fallen in love with his secretary. The two had committed suicide, wanting to be together. However, after their deaths, Sechrist describes:

> One night as I was praying for them, I fell asleep and had a very vivid dream experience. In the dream it was nighttime. I saw the man standing alone by a large body of very dark water, surrounded by utter darkness. In the most pitiful human voice I have ever heard, he was calling out for his secretary—"Celia, Celia, Celia." Though they had committed suicide together, each was now completely alone.[30]

Sechrist comments that the entire scene was one of utter desolation—dark, gloomy, and depressing. Although it would be comforting to attribute the vision simply to her religious expectations, other sources suggest that suicides may indeed find themselves trapped in such situations, whether in part due to their psychological baggage or for other reasons.

George Meek, long-time survival researcher and founder of Metascience, used instrumental transcommunication to look at how long suicides might be stuck in the lower astral, and was told:

> The suicide has harmed only himself and his loved ones, if any. Usually he or she is immediately filled with remorse. When an offer of help and guidance is given, the suicide is likely to respond readily. *How* fast he absorbs the teachings offered will determine how rapidly he moves to a more hospitable level.[31]

This suggests that there is no fixed time a soul has to remain in the lower astral, and that it can vary depending on how quickly the spirit can be taught.

Suicide NDEs run the gamut from hellish to heavenly, and may include the usual meeting with higher beings and life review. Perhaps because of this, experiencers who triggered their NDE through a suicide attempt will show the same mixed reactions to what happened as those who triggered it through other means. Some benefit while others do not.

Let us look at some firsthand accounts. London NDE researcher and author Margot Grey chronicled the NDE of a woman who was in a coma for five days after trying to kill herself.[32] She appeared to go through a sequence of locations, initially finding herself in a world of silence, then in a dark room, and finally in a hospital-like chapel:

> Suddenly, she became aware of a dazzling light at her feet, which came from a beautiful gold lantern.... Presently, she saw a male figure, young,

pale, with dark eyes, which were fixed understandingly on her. She tried to communicate mentally with him and he answered in the same fashion. She called: "Help me, help me, whoever you are." He responded: "Be calm and have faith." She next became conscious of the sounds of voices which grew louder and louder.... Figures in dark cloaks were conversing—discussing her.... She knew that she was "being tried, accused of having transgressed and would have to pay." ... She was terrified, but says that the "being of light gave me courage and made me understand that it would be unjust if they condemned me and he would stop them if they did." ... The staircase creaked under the weight of a multitude who burst into the room. There were many dark figures who were old and bent. She continued: "They fell upon me. I hardly had time to throw a last entreating glance at the being of light. I felt the judgment was that they had condemned me." But when the crowd tried to seize her they were unable to advance. She said: "I escaped their hands because the light stopped them a few centimetres from me. They withdrew and I knew I was absolved." She ended her account by saying: "Was it judgment I feared? Or perhaps I feared not saving my soul. I saw that to cut oneself off from life was indeed a mortal sin."[33]

Another of Grey's NDE accounts is from a man who tried to kill himself and was even grimmer in nature:

At the last moment I suddenly felt an inner explosion and seemed to be enveloped in a blue flame which felt cold. At this point I found myself floating about six inches above my body. The next thing I remember is being sucked down a vast black vortex like a whirlpool and I found myself in a place that I can only describe as being like Dante's Inferno. I saw a lot of other people who seemed grey and dreary and there was an overwhelming feeling of loneliness about the place.[34]

Nor was this unpleasant account unique for Grey. Another comes from a woman who tried to kill herself with a drug overdose:

As I got drowsy, I remember going down this black hole, round and round. Then I saw a glowing red-hot spot getting bigger and bigger until I was able to stand up. It was all red and hot and on fire. The earth was like slimy mud that sank over my feet and it was hard to breathe. I cried out, "Oh Lord, give me another chance."[35]

As we have mentioned before, not all those who experienced an NDE changed their minds about life. Some failed suicides simply became more determined to take their own lives so that they could return to what they felt was a much better existence.

Finally, it should be noted that there are some differences between NDEs and the channeled messages of successful suicides. The former may report being turned back or seeing future events for their life—which do not seem to occur when a soul manages to terminate its incarnation.

In this chapter we have seen that the transition to the afterlife does not, by itself, change people for the better. They may hold on, at least initially, to all of their old feelings, attitudes, beliefs, and behavior patterns. Furthermore, their shift may be a small one in terms of vibratory frequency, in that many suicides appear to stay close to the earth plane in the lower astral. The lower astral is generally described as a very dark and disagreeable place, with older channeled material depicting it as hell at worst, or purgatory at best. Fortunately, this does not appear to be a permanent condition. We are told that spirit helpers may work to assist the souls stuck in this plane to move to a better place.

5

Afterlife Experiences

Afterlife experiences can vary considerably from one spirit to the next, especially early after their transition. A great many souls appear to be confused initially, as they first figure out that they are dead and try to orient to their new state of being. This period appears to go more smoothly if the soul is aware of being greeted by spirit guides or friends and family that made the crossing before them. Unfortunately, the suicide is depicted as not always being able to sense nearby helpers, either because the soul is still in a fog or the spirit realm has been caught by surprise and not had time to prepare the way. However, at least some channeled messages state that guides are always present; the newly dead simply cannot see or hear them without help from the living (such as psychic mediums) or the passage of time.

In his summary of channeled messages compiled in the mid-1900s in England, Robert Crookall reported that many beings experienced a lightning-fast life review as they shed their bodies.[1] This was spoken of as seeing a clear record of their life, often passing before their eyes as a procession of images, like a film. However, suicides more often mention watching their life unfold as part of the later phase of evaluation and self-judgment.

It is conjectured by those who have studied this, and from spirit reports relayed from psychics and channels, that the variability we see between initial experiences is due to a number of factors, including the level of soul development, personal beliefs about death, cultural expectations, and confusion or clouding of the mind at the moment of death due to emotion, illness, drugs, or alcohol. As we noted in the last chapter, most souls appear to find themselves, at least initially, stuck near the earth plane in what is often referred to as the lower astral. Psychiatrist Carl Wickland, working with his mediumistic wife, particularly describes suicides as being stuck in a very dark and dismal place—although some suicides seem to be able to bypass this plane completely or pass through it so quickly that they do not really notice it.[2]

When we look at the actual experiences that suicides return to tell us about, we see a number of common themes. Sometimes souls remember only a sense of peace. Other times, they report more frustration and anger at their situation. Frequently, they describe being greeted by people or animals in spirit. Some suicides also speak of going to their own funerals early after their transition to the afterlife. Although the initial adjustment phase can vary from one soul to the next, all of them seem to eventually advance to a subsequent phase of accessing their own life—the life review and self-judgment. It is reported that no spirit skips this step, which shows a soul not only what it has done wrong, but also what it has done well.

REACTIONS TO DEATH

Initial experiences in the afterlife are not the same for everyone. Some of this difference may result from variations in how well prepared spirits are for the afterlife (some having read about it in advance and believed in it) and whether there were guides present that could ease them through the transition. Reactions range from confusion to anger to peace. From Arthur Ford:

> The extreme negative, depressed mental state of the suicide at the time of his self-destructive act carries over into the afterlife, placing him at a great disadvantage in making his adjustment. Many times, upon awakening, he does not realise that he has passed over. He may go into an extreme panic upon discovering that he can no longer control his physical body.[3]

One of the commonest initial emotions reported by suicides is confusion, which then tends to lead to intense frustration. James Van Praagh speaks of a young man who had hanged himself:

> He can't believe he is dead because he feels so alive. He thinks he screwed something up and is trying very hard to get back into his body through his head. He can't do it, and he is getting very frustrated. He begins to cry![4]

Like many other successful suicides, Anne Puryear's son Stephen went through a phase of frustration that others could not see or hear him.[5] He tried repeatedly to get someone's attention, but only succeeded with his eight-year-old sister, whom no one believed. Stephen remembered, "It was getting more and more frustrating. I felt like crying, then I felt like yelling."[6]

Indeed, numerous such accounts suggest that this period of intense frustration is a common initial reaction. However, Stephen observed that this feeling is not limited to suicides, but may happen with all who die prematurely. He told his mother, "It's important to understand the unbelievable pain and frustration I felt. Most of us, no matter how we die, go through this agony."[7] However, Stephen added that a soul's emotional reaction may vary some, depending on the circumstances and how it died.

In some cases, the sadness and frustration of watching loved ones suffer, and not having any way to comfort them or communicate, may lead to psychokinetic (anomalous mind over matter) events. Lysa Mateu heard from a spirit identifying itself as Charley, who noted that after the life review, when he was with his still-living father:

> I sat beside him and bawled louder than he....
> I didn't see what happened next. My actions were so automatic, so blatantly carved from the pain of my soul that my energy caused a wooden dragon statue to come crashing to the floor. It tumbled on its side and its neck broke off. In that moment, I was transported upwards, in a spiraling, spinning motion, to the world in which I now live.[8]

The spirit of Jim Pike Junior also used psychokinesis as a way of getting his father's attention.[9] After a number of events, including clocks stopping and bangs of hair being inexplicably cut, Pike Senior reported:

> March 1, we found books which had been moved, windows opened which had been closed, safety pins lying open in several places, clothes misplaced, and a broken Marlboro cigarette (Jim's brand, not smoked by any of the three of us) in front of the nightstand between the twin beds. The culmination of that day came in two episodes.
> As we were examining a number of clothing items in Maren's bedroom which seemed to have been moved without our doing, we witnessed the first and only object in motion. Maren had reached into the closet for something when one of the four tissue-wrapped pieces of a silver dresser set ... began to move toward the edge of the shelf above the pole. As we watched in disbelief, the silver piece slowly slid off the shelf.[10]

These events continued to occur. That this was not a case of either pranksters or psychokinesis from living minds, stressed over the death of a loved one, became clear when the spirit of Jim came through British medium Ena Twigg, to state, "I came to your room, I moved books, I knocked on the door."[11] That the soul was frustrated in trying to communicate seems clear when he later added, "I've been so unhappy because I didn't have a voice and had to find a way to tell you."[12]

Of course, not all suicides recall frustration or the dark, unhappy lower astral realm. Some speak only of their sense of peace. For example, Arthur Ford channeled a mother who had taken her own life and stated:

> We are not sent either to heaven or to hell, we just continue to live. Some of us have to learn many lessons, but as soon as I got out of the body I had no more fear, resentment or hatred, for these are human limitations. I was met by my mother and Alexander (my brother, killed in the revolution). They let me sleep for a while, but not very long. Then I began to function in a perfectly free body.[13]

We will later note that the use of sleep is a common tool used for healing in the afterlife.

Although not all failed suicides (with NDEs) report having positive experiences, a surprising number of them do. For example, one near-suicide through drug overdose remembered of his NDE: "Suddenly without warning a bolt of light enveloped me and I was overpowered by feelings of such peace that there are no words to describe it."[14]

Still another man, reported by French researcher Jean-Baptiste Delacour, hanged himself in Red Square and was resuscitated many hours later, to report:

> I was in a country where I'd never been before.
> It was very big there, and so beautiful. I'd like to go back there again.
> I can still taste the sweet water that I drank there. For there was a fountain there and I drank out of it.
> I saw flowers that were three times as big as ours. They smelled sweeter than the prettiest flowers we have here at the height of summer.
> I saw a lot of people a great distance away. When I started to run toward them they moved away from me just as fast....
> How heavy my arms and legs are now ... in that other land where I was, everything was light as a feather....
> And then I started to run through all the beautiful greenness and call out loud for someone. Now I know it was my mother I was looking for. But she has been dead a long time. Anyway, I went looking for her and someone told me I'd find her soon. But it'll still take quite a while. It's always a long time before you find the one you're looking for.
> Then I fell asleep.[15]

This account has a number of interesting features. First, there appears to have been no one ready to greet him. Second, he felt a sense of peace. Like some other NDErs, when he awoke, he wished only to return to the idyllic setting that he had all-too-briefly glimpsed. Third, the sense of being very lightweight—something frequently mentioned in initial accounts of the afterlife. And finally, when upset, he fell asleep, which appears to be a common method of healing distressed souls.

This feeling of peace may be a temporary condition for some spirits. Canadian neuropsychiatrist and past-life researcher Joel Whitton joined with independent reincarnation researcher Joe Fisher to collaborate on a book about hypnotically regressed memories of experiences in the spirit realm between incarnations. In one case they describe the experience of a woman regressed to a lifetime in Spain, after she had thrown herself out of a window:

> The street rushed up to meet her and she felt its numbing impact followed by the wheels of a horse-drawn carriage crushing her chest. But she was also aware, from a higher perspective, of her body sprawled across the cobbles.... How inconsequential was this mortal husk now that the blinding light was forcing her attention upwards.... She had walked into the light, a light more lustrous and dazzling than the sun yet devoid of any sensation of heat. This absorbing brightness exuded peace and serenity and, utterly relaxed, she basked in its benevolence. There was also the impression of being enclosed in a tunnel or tube or cocoon. Words were quite unequal to the task of describing the magnificent environment through which she was drawn at incredible speed.[16]

The woman's diary continued to say that, after the shock of dying wore off, "The sadness was so intense I wanted to cry. Tears welled up."[17]

William Dudley Pelley gives the interesting account of a suicide's NDE, which seems worth mentioning because of its similarity to the channeled material—suggesting the latter may have basis in fact:

> A young man by the name of Charles Riley was a medical student who swallowed a large dose of cyanide because his fiancée had jilted him for another man. He was rushed to San Francisco's Emergency Hospital, and upon arrival his body showed no signs of life. He was, to all tests and appearance, as dead as he ever would be....
>
> Dr. Greiger injected a solution of a new preparation, Methylene Blue, and within fifteen minutes the would-be suicide was breathing almost normally....
>
> Charles Riley said, fully recovered: "I ... had no sensation except a numbness which started at the bodily extremities, and spread slowly throughout my physical system. There was no muscular rigidity in going under....
>
> "Even while supposedly dead, I had a distinct sensation of floating. There was none of the common blackness recognized as death. I felt as if I were coming out into the light—into a vast, glowing place of cool sunshine—like entering a new and mysterious world.... I didn't feel tragic about it, only tremendously surprised and happy to find myself still con-

scious.... I do remember a definite feeling of release, something like emerging from a dim room into sudden brightness."[18]

Thus, we see a variety of reactions occur when souls first cross over into the afterlife. Often, there is a feeling of being very lightweight or floating. Some feel frustration, which is exacerbated if they don't realize the reason others are ignoring them is because they are dead. Others experience great beauty and peace. NDEs appear to reflect the emotional variation that souls may feel when crossing over. One difference between the two groups is that the intense frustration experienced in their new state by many successful suicides may allow them to perform dramatic psychokinetic events as a way of communicating with those left behind.

BEING GREETED BY SPIRITS

Having died, many souls speak of being greeted by those already in spirit. Sometimes these may be friends or family. Other times they may appear as religious figures or simply friendly guides. Their purpose seems to be to smooth the soul's transition to its new state of existence. Unfortunately, not all souls appear to be capable of sensing those sent to help them. Being interviewed for this book, California medium Johanna Carroll explains what she has noted in her work with deceased suicides:

> The very first element was that their eyes were closed, so they weren't seeing. I don't know whether you want to call it psychically seeing, or spiritually seeing, or sensing. Because of the energy of the attachment and the energy of the confusion, it wasn't as if with other spirits that cross over immediately there's a recognition of familiar friends, family, loved ones. They kind of have to go through this cork pulling out of the bottle, and then it's like, "Okay, this is not where I normally am. Something's different here." When that awareness kicks in, in other words, when there's a shift in the awareness in a consciousness, then there's a revealing of familiar people.[19]

Stephen (who hung himself at age 15) observed that the experiences of suicides are not much different from those of people who die in accidents or by old age.[20] He claimed that spirit guides are with people at the time they die and help the newly dead let go of their body and move to where they can be met by various friends and loved ones. In his own experience, Stephen recalled floating out of his body and watching it hanging from a tree. After he figured out that it was his body, he panicked and began to cry. However, it was at that point that he became aware of others, who comforted him. Stephen said:

And as I looked around, the forms around me began to become clearer. I saw Grandfather H. I didn't even remember him except from his pictures, and there he was. I saw your grandfathers. I saw a lot of people that I'd only seen pictures of in the albums. I saw a couple of ... acquaintances that I had known, and I remembered that they were dead. I saw a whole lot of people I didn't know, but I felt like I knew them from somewhere. I was confused and didn't know what to think.... Some of them came up to me and hugged me. Others said, "Hi, Steve." All I could see were the people. I felt so much better.[21]

Some spirits are distrustful of others when they cross over. In these cases, the greeters may be children, animals, or others who appear to be carefully chosen so as to be acceptable to the newly dead. George Anderson alludes to this in the following passage:

She says she greeted him when he came over because he wouldn't trust adults. It was as if he were afraid of being tricked. So there must have been some sort of experience here on earth in which he felt tricked by an adult....

This girl came forward, and he had more trust in her because he remembered her. She led him through and helped him out.[22]

For the most part, guides seem to be around even when a death is sudden or unexpected (at least by those on Earth). George Anderson channeled a young man who shot himself in the head without warning. The medium reassured the family, "He didn't die alone because there was somebody here to help welcome him over."[23]

Of course, such guides need not appear in human form. In some cases, an animal or family pet may serve as the greeter. Anderson describes one case:

He says actually the pet welcomes him over first, because it's something he knows, something he trusts, something he loves, knows loves him—there's a sense of safety and a comfort level with it....

So, this is something he would have trusted and would have followed into the Light thinking, "Okay, everything's all right." Because ... there was like, "What happened? Where am I? I'm in this, you know, dark vortex—what's going on?" And then he goes toward the Light, and then the animal comes forward, then he realizes, "Well, I must have passed on if I'm here," and he followed it, where it crossed him over, so to speak.[24]

In yet another case, Anderson told a daughter: "She says the dog was there to greet her when she arrived on the other side. That was a comfort to her."[25] Anderson has stated that he thinks animals are frequently used to help suicides make the transition to the afterlife because people think of animals as loving and nonjudgmental.[26] He felt this was true even for those who never had a pet. Puppies and kittens just seem safe to follow.

In some cases, spirit guides appear to be the first ones to greet a soul. Jean Foster channeled one suicide who stated, "My guide came to me immediately after I entered here to reassure me and to help me to overcome my first great fear of wrongdoing."[27] This particular soul was interesting, because it did not meet up with loved ones for quite a long period in the afterlife. It told Foster that it had been unable to have any such reunions because of its inability to feel what it called tenderness. As it was, this spirit noted it needed to learn, not spend time with family and friends, because it would not be able to advance any further until it had mastered the ability to feel this warm emotion.

Foster continued to follow the progress of this spirit over time.[28] At a later channeling session, it noted that because it had begun to learn how to love, it was finally beginning to meet up with other souls it had known in previous lifetimes, as well as those who had been its parents on Earth. This case would seem to suggest that the ability (or lack thereof) to feel tenderness toward others may act as a factor that determines when and what you will meet in the afterlife.

We have seen that many, though not all, souls report being greeted by others in spirit, whether guides, deceased friends or relatives, family pets, or even previously unknown kittens and puppies. These welcomers can often greatly smooth a soul's transition to the afterlife, providing reassurance and a helpful orientation to the suicide's new state. It is possible that some of the increase in problems reported with sudden death, whether due to suicide, murder, or an accident, is due to the fact that there is not always a spirit ready to greet the newly dead.

FUNERALS

One might think that most spirits would attend their own funerals. It would be an easy way for them to recognize an end of their old way of "life" and say good-bye to those left, if temporarily, behind. However, it may not be so simple, and some mediums suggest that it can even be hazardous for those recently crossed over. Franklin Loehr was informed:

> Not everybody attends his own funeral.... With some, death is such a wonderful release from such very unhappy conditions and circumstances in their Earth lives that they go as far away as they can and just don't ever come back. But for most people, your funeral can be something like your high school commencement.... We all have something nice we haven't

yet said or done about nearly everyone we know, and that person's funeral seems our last chance to say it or do it or think it.

But then he warned me of the dangers that could develop at the funeral itself. It seems as though I am not yet as solid over here as I seem to be, and if there's any strong emotion or grieving down there, I should keep away from it, or it could suck me in and down to the earthplane I had left.... I was warned not to get pulled back to the level I had now left behind.[29]

Anne Puryear reports that her son Stephen told her, "Many souls are encouraged to attend their funerals or memorial services, if there is one. Most want to. It can be a very difficult time emotionally, or a very healing time."[30] This comment about souls being encouraged to go to their own funerals was contradicted by a few older messages. Beginning in the 1920s, "Darby and Joan" recorded many visits from the spirit realm as Joan, usually blindfolded, would go into a mild trance, attended by Darby, and various spirits would speak through her. On one occasion, addressing the topic of whether the dead attend their own funerals, they received the following answer through Joan's automatic typewriting:

> Surely I have already indicated to you ... that we do not let newcomers do that. We take them away from it all. They are still pretty human, pretty close still to the earth consciousness. Sometimes, though, when there is great love, we do let them go back, and ... comfort those who are left behind.[31]

Another spirit, "Hiram," communicating through medium Jean Foster, stated that he had not attended his funeral service because it would have been an unwanted distraction and possibly harmful to his development.[32] The risk appears to be one of whether a soul gets pulled back into old thought and habit patterns. Foster reports this communication:

> The truth is what I must work on, not the notion of what others there open their minds to. The one who helps me here would not enter me into the earth bound stream anyway. The reason, this one says, is that I must be single minded here or else I could fall back into the earth truths.[33]

Nonetheless, the majority of channeled material suggests that spirits do attend their own funerals. Franklin Loehr emphasizes that the souls themselves may decide this on an individual basis, noting:

> Some souls are very much involved with the life of the body, and will stay close to that body until it is laid to rest after the funeral, to make sure the body is taken care of. Then there are those souls who just as soon as

the body is dead and the "silver cord" is cut, go on without a backward look....

Some deceased persons will attend their own funeral service, some will not.[34]

Either the spirit realm has lightened up about this attitude since the early 1900s or the material was inaccurate, due to biases and limitations on the part of the sender or the receiver.

Even the surviving spirit of suicide Stephen Puryear had things to say on this issue. He noted that personalities don't change just because a soul has crossed over into the afterlife, noting:

> Your consciousness, your state of mind, determines the course the next days and weeks take. Most souls want to see loved ones left behind to see how they are, to see how they are taking the death and to tell their families and friends they are OK.[35]

In at least one case, the inability to have a funeral appeared to upset a spirit. Carl Wickland had worked hard to convince an entity that it was in the afterlife and sent it on with spirit friends. However, the problems were not over. She returned to them, grieving, because:

> The girl had been a devout member of the German Lutheran Church, but because she had died a suicide the pastor had refused to allow the funeral service to be held in the church, nor would the congregation permit the body to be buried in the consecrated ground of the churchyard....
> I had so much suffering afterward and was very, very miserable.[36]

Psychic Johanna Carroll has experienced spirits always going to their memorial services, as long as one is performed:

> They're always present. They're still very attached to the Earth. So, in my personal opinion, based on my own experience, they're still very attached to that Earth experience and the physical body and the people they left behind. ... there's definitely a very strong presence at any kind of a ceremony that's attached to the physical body.[37]

Lauren Thibodeau also suggests that many suicides attend their funerals. This came up in a discussion on the three boys who had accidentally killed themselves doing autoeroticism:

> I've never been through a situation where the person was not at their own service except, of course, in cases where—the 9/11 people come to mind—there was no formal service, they come around but obviously not in that structured way. But if there's a structured remembrance service, they're always there....

I did Hospice volunteer work for four years. And I wasn't "out" about being a medium, but I attended a lot of funerals. And it was interesting to me to kind of test it out. Will they come? Are they here? They're always there.[38]

Funerals often seem to provide closure to both the living and the dead. Some earlier channeled material claimed that spirits were either not allowed to go to them, or at the least discouraged from it. However, many contemporary mediums state that souls often attend their own memorial services. Whether or not they are present at these events appears to be a matter of choice. Occasionally, souls may report disinterest in their funerals or a belief that it will be an unwanted distraction from their new existences.

LIFE REVIEW AND SELF-JUDGMENT

One of the most consistent and universal themes that spirits speak of is that of the life review. This comes up in essentially all channeled material. Even the *Islamic Book of the Dead* describes a version of this after a person has died:

Then the Noble Scribes enter on his right and on his left. The one on his right says: "As-salamu 'alaykum. I am entrusted with your right actions." So he brings out a white page and spreads it before him and says: "Look at your deeds." So he is happy and rejoices.

The one on his left says: "As-salamu 'alaykum. I am entrusted with your wrong actions." So he brings out a black page and spreads it before him and says: "Look at it." So his sweat pours down, and he looks right and left for fear of reading the page. The angel insists and puts it down on his pillow and goes.[39]

Furthermore, the life review is one of the more common features of NDEs. Well-known NDE researcher and author P. M. H. Atwater notes:

Fewer than half of the people I interviewed encountered a tunnel, yet the majority described a life review that was facilitated either by a tribunal or some sort or self-judgment. This life review, by the way, was in some cases so profound that it included the consequences of the individual's actions on others.[40]

In his summary of psychic and mediumistic communication until 1970, Robert Crookall indicates that the life review typically occurred at the moment of death. However, few suicides mentioned it at this time. One that did was Charley, who noted:

When I first died, I felt I wasn't dead. No way I could be dead with all the vivid images and pictures of those I loved racing before me in a sudden burst of memory. I saw everyone ... everything.... Every feeling, thought, and experience I had ever felt in my entire life, I saw in one fell swoop ... a flash of light before my eyes. It was an awesome display of the love I had shared and the people I had touched ... and the pain I had caused.[41]

The life review for suicides was reported more often as part of the judgment phase—a chance to see, understand, and integrate in the triumphs and mistakes of the past lifetime in order to determine how they need to work toward mastering their problems in the spirit realm and often their next life.

One of the earlier documented descriptions of the life review comes to us from Emanuel Swedenborg, who wrote in the eighteenth century:

> [8] In a word, all their evils, crimes, thefts, wiles, and deceptions are made clear to every evil spirit. They are drawn from their own memories and exposed. There is no room for denial because all the circumstances are presented together.
>
> I also heard that angels have seen and displayed from the memory of one individual everything he had thought one day after another over the course of a month, with never an error, recalled as though he himself were back in those very days.
>
> [9] We may gather from these instances that we take our whole memory with us, and that nothing is so concealed in this world that it will not be made known after death, made known in public, according to the Lord's words, "Nothing is hidden that will not be uncovered, and nothing concealed that will not be known. So what you have said in darkness will be heard in the light, and what you have spoken in the ear will be proclaimed from the rooftops" (Luke 12:2–3).[42]

According to *Spirit Teachings* author Stainton Moses, who did automatic writing in the 1800s, the judgment phase all spirits go through may not be limited to the single life review, but be repeated as the soul continues to make spiritual progress:

> The judgment is complete when the spirit gravitates to the home which it has made for itself. There can be no error. It is placed by the eternal law of fitness. That judgment is complete, until the spirit is fitted to pass to a higher sphere, when the same process is repeated, and so on and on until the purgatorial spheres of work are done with, and the soul passes within the inner heaven of contemplation....
>
> Judgment is ceaseless, for the soul is ever fitting itself for its change. No such arraignment before the assembled universe as is in your mind. That is an allegory....

The soul is the arbiter of its own destiny; its own judge.[43]

We will later see that at least one channeled message from the guides who specialize in dealing with suicide bombers also indicated that the life review may be repeated until it is felt everything has been fully learned from it.

Some channeled sources have suggested that souls are eased into this process in stages. The first stage involves letting the newly dead see precisely what they expected to find. Medium Arthur Ford, once dead and in spirit, explained through another medium:

> I have watched faithful churchgoers who believed they would pass through the gates and be judged worthy. They passed through the gates to the heavenly state they had been told about, and imagined this to be their new home in heaven. What they didn't know was that it was not their new space, but rather, the first state of the transition bridge.[44]

Ford added that once these souls realized they wouldn't be staying there, they were moved to what he called the second stage. This involved recalling important thoughts and feelings from the past, which could make up new thought forms. Thus, according to Ford, the life review begins soon after an effective transition to the afterlife.

It should be noted that this period of memory and self-assessment seems to apply to all spirits—not just those who have committed suicide. Well-known American medium John Edward states:

> When you get to the Other Side, you must review your life and incorporate it into your plan for your existence on the Other Side and maybe for the next incarnation. We are not punished on the Other Side, except by ourselves. We ask ourselves why we did what we did, and seek to improve.[45]

This self-judgment is not a light matter. Souls take their shortcomings very seriously and often deal harshly with themselves. As George Anderson notes:

> What he and so many of us don't understand is that there is judgment there, but it is not done by God on a throne. Judgment rests basically with yourself. And we all know that the greatest enemy we can face is ourselves.[46]

Even those who pass of normal causes speak of this, as in the following passage involving a spirit who had sexually molested his nephew:

Your uncle said that when he went to the other side he had to face and judge himself. That's what they call the judgment after you die. He had to follow his life and had to watch his life and see the humiliation and horror he caused his nephew. Plus, he sees from the other side what he's going through. So he put himself into a hell-like state more or less of his own free will because of what he did.[47]

Turning our attention specifically to suicides, "between-lives" hypnotherapist Michael Newton observes, "While all suicide cases are treated with kindness and understanding, people who killed themselves with a healthy body do have a reckoning."[48] Lysa Mateu channeled Alexy, who pointed out that this self-judgment can be severe:

One of the things with suicide is that we have to pay the price for our faulty deed. We have broken our agreement.

We have not been faithful to our word and must be punished, not punished in the way you know punished to be, punished as in feeling and seeing the consequences of our actions and the impact those actions had on those still living.[49]

The acceptance by others in the spirit realm and focus on self-judgment as a means toward spiritual growth are common themes. Indeed, channeled messages say repeatedly that there is no punishment or censure, only acceptance. The spirit of James Pike Junior stated simply, "nobody blames me here."[50] In fact, sometimes the opposite may be true, where guides actively help suicides remember the positive things they had done in their lives. As the spirit of Hiram, speaking through Jean Foster, put it:

There is no condemnation here. The one who came to help me pictured all that I had done which was good. That way these things can be made permanent within my being and there is growth. The rest of it falls away.[51]

The old adage "If at once you don't succeed, try, try, again" appears to come into effect as Hiram stated that souls will repeat their lives as often as needed to master this task—but only after a thorough life review:

Now I must go back over my lifetime step by step to eternalize the good. By this I mean that I must wrest the bad out of the experience until I hold only the good within me. In that way I can grow in spite of the recent way I left that lifetime.[52]

Jean Foster continued to follow and channel this same soul for several months, which allowed her to watch Hiram's spiritual progress during the life-review process. Perhaps surprising for some, is the fact that the life review may not be limited to the most recent lifetime, but include a number of past lives, as well. Months after he was originally contacted, Hiram spoke of how difficult this process was for him:

> I am sure there is more to learn about this matter. I touch the surface, as it were. The cracks go deep into the experience, and I am only at the top part.
>
> The truth that I get here exists to help me, but it can penetrate only as far as I allow it. Of course I do the best I can, but it is very hard, and I inch along in the process much as the caterpillar who sets out to encircle the world.[53]

Some of the spirits channeled by Lysa Mateu had a slightly different perspective on what goes on in the life review. Joseph stated:

> At the end of your life, everything is reflected back to you. All the love you have given. All the pain you have caused yourself and others. You get to reexperience the love AND you get to step into the other's shoes and experience the pain and hurt your actions caused them.
>
> If you really felt what it felt like to hurt another, you wouldn't do it....
>
> That's why there's no punishment from others up here. No damning God to blame us for our sins. We are our own judge and jury. Self-punishment and regret is worse than any punishment from the outside.[54]

After he had taken his own life, the surviving spirit of Stephen Puryear spoke of the life review in this way:

> We do this in stages for no one could handle it all at once. We begin to look at specific things honestly and clearly ... and we see what we did correctly and incorrectly. No one sits in judgment on us. Though we judge ourselves very harshly at first, we soon begin to ease up and see what we can learn from reviewing our mistakes and our strengths....
>
> At first, it's very emotional because you see all the people you have interacted with, helped, hurt, and forgotten. Unfortunately, everyone around you sees them too. Soon, what others see about you is unimportant. What you see about yourself, how you fell short, and what golden opportunities you failed to use, is heartbreaking. You feel such shame, other times anger. Later, there is a little more detachment.... All of it is something you know must be worked with and understood before you can advance further. Or before you can again claim a physical body to return and get about what you have left undone.[55]

In the case of the child who had died through autoeroticism, the help of a healing center appeared to be necessary for the life-review process. Lauren Thibodeau states that the spirit had been in a healing center for two and a half years because of a lack of "readiness."[56] When asked what this meant, she explains:

> Emotions don't really count after you don't have a body in a way. But he's still dealing with ... the waves of [energy]. It's as if everything that people respond to about his death has to be felt by him. Meaning, he has to take it on a spiritual level and then somehow release. Take it on. Sit with it. Address it. Heal it. And release it. Four steps there. He has to do all that for the anger from everybody. And the judgment of all the people who read accounts like this in the paper and say, "Well, he should have known." And all of that has to be processed. And that's what takes the time and adjustment.... He's saying that every feeling someone has about him has to be felt and processed. And when you leave in this kind of a fashion, traumatic and painful, most of that expression is going to be angry, bitter, judgmental, and so on. That's what slows it down. Eventually there's the loving thought, all that kind of stuff is there, too. But there's a lot of muck ... to wade through. And ... he's showing me like a vision of slogging through a river. And there's sort of a flat rock in the middle. And he can climb on that rock and raise his arms to the sun. But he's gotta get through. He's got to do the hard slog first.[57]

When questioned, a guide later described the life-review process further:

> Heath: Will one of the things this guide will be doing is showing him other possibilities of how this situation could have been handled?
>
> Thibodeau: Oh, absolutely. Yes! "Oh, we've gone over that!" is what I'm hearing. And another thing the guides do in a situation like this is to help talk about the ripples in the pond. "If you toss a stone over this way," he says, "this is the way the ripples would have gone, and the things that would have arisen from that. And if you toss it over here, the patterns of the ripples would go in a different direction. But either choice has ramifications. Either choice makes ripples in the field, in the energy of both you and others. Because of interconnection. We are one in the end. So, everything you do affects the specific pond we share. Because of that, we have to look at what might have happened if he had tossed the stones this way."
>
> Heath: So they show simply all possibilities?
>
> Thibodeau: All possibilities.
>
> Heath: In a neutral way?
>
> Thibodeau: Very neutral. There's no good choice.
>
> Heath: And not necessarily which would be more enlightened?
>
> Thibodeau: Right.
>
> Heath: Because each individual has to decide for him- or herself which is the best action at the moment in time?

Thibodeau: Right. And you do the best you can. Hopefully you do it consciously, and the guide is claiming that is the *one* thing we can alter—how much of our conscious intention we put to these decisions. And now he wants to embrace all three boys. He's widening his arms and showing me all three, and saying, "They may not have made the wisest choices, and yet they've all found a way to embrace the learning from those choices. And that is something to celebrate.... They have learned and continue to learn."[58]

Psychologist and hypnotherapist Michael Newton also found people reported remembering experiencing life reviews when regressed to the period between lives. In one case, he was told:

S[pirit]: I ... am going to have to make some kind of ... accounting ... of myself. We go through this after all my lives, but this time I'm really in the soup.
Dr. N: Why?
S: Because I killed myself.
Dr. N: When a person kills himself on Earth does this mean they will receive some sort of punishment as a spirit?
S: No, no, there is no such thing here as punishment—that's an Earth condition. Clodees will be disappointed that I bailed out early and didn't have the courage to face my difficulties. By choosing to die as I did means I have to come back later and deal with the same thing all over again in a different life. I just wasted a lot of time by checking out early.
Dr. N: So, no one will condemn you for committing suicide?
S: (reflects for a moment) Well, my friends won't give me any pats on the back either—I feel sadness at what I did.[59]

We have seen that initial experiences in the afterlife can vary considerably. Souls may remember great frustration or feelings of peace. Most suicides appear to eventually become aware of being greeted by spirits who try to help them move on from the lower astral. Sometimes, souls also report returning to watch their own funerals—although this is by no means a universal phenomenon. However, every spirit seems to go through its own debriefing—a combination of life review with self-judgment. This may include an evaluation of past lives and can be repeated as often as spiritually needed to advance in the afterlife. It is during this phase that the most learning can occur, and new insights can be gained. Because of this, it should be no wonder that self-judgment is such a consistent and integral part of every spirit's time in the afterlife. Life review and self-judgment, then, are seen as part of the overall, seemingly unending, process of the growth and development of the individual soul. The spirit world emphasizes learning from prior existence to improve in the future, whether this process is placed within a one-chance perspective of having just a single life followed by an afterlife of continued nonphysical existence, or within a scenario of cyclic reincarnational lives. There is even the rather mind-boggling contention on the part of some that all of the lives of the individual are occurring not sequentially in time but interactively all at once in a superimposed, multi-dimensional universe.

6

Adjustment Problems

Some spirits appear to have great difficulty acclimating to the afterlife. In a way, it can be looked upon as a similar process to that of grieving. Denial, bargaining, anger, and depression or regret can all occur before acceptance. John Edward has noted that souls can vary considerably in terms of how well they adjust.[1] One of the sticking points can be whether they feel their life tasks are completed or remain attached to their old life on Earth. Perhaps hardest for many to deal with is the recognition that they can no longer interact with the living in the same way as they were used to doing. The spirit of Stephen told his mother that souls may have to reach this point before they can move forward:

> After a short while, most of your friends who still have bodies forget about you.... When you try to impress on them you're still alive, they don't even hear, or they ignore you. You feel crazy, tormented, wasted. That's when the helpers on this place take over and you start getting on with your life here, if you will allow it. Some won't.[2]

On the other hand, some spirits actually seem to adjust rather easily to the afterlife. This may be partly due to not having enjoyed their physical life. George Anderson reported on one young man in the afterlife:

> He says it's easier there, because you're accepted by your value ... not that he's begrudging his existence on the earth, but he says he feels more at home there.... He just admits that he really didn't like it here too much.... So, he just wants you to know that he's much happier there and that he's doing all right.[3]

However, it should be noted that this spirit was stuck in its attitude, because it was unable to forgive those it blamed for having contributed to its suicide. This soul admitted that it would need to work on this before it could progress. Anderson reported:

> So he ... knows that he's going to have to work this out. But he really doesn't want to right now.... Not that it's upsetting him over there, where he can't function and be happy, but he admits—right now he holds a

grudge.... This is the first time I've heard this, but he says he cannot in his heart and soul over there honestly ask you to forgive them, he says, "Because I haven't."[4]

Another reason that some spirits may do better than others after taking their own lives relates to their general knowledge base and expectations. Peter and Jane Boulton had many sessions with spirits as they sat with psychic sensitive Lenora Huett. On one occasion they were told that after suicide:

> The spirit ... does, in time, reach forward.
> One who has been spiritually enlightened accepts suicide in a better manner, for if he takes his own life he is aware that he needs to look for light helpers. However, one who is spiritually enlightened seldom does commit this type of action, except in cases where he would relieve a physical burden on others.[5]

We will look at a number of adjustment problems, including the problem of left-over psychological baggage, the refusal of some spirits to accept that they are really dead, and why they can sometimes fail to sense those trying to help them. Finally, we will consider how suicides may deliberately, or inadvertently, cause harm to the living.

PSYCHOLOGICAL BAGGAGE

Whoever said "you can't take it with you" unfortunately did not mean your personality, with all of its attitudes and issues, good and bad. One of the bigger problems with adjustment may be that suicides bring all of their psychological baggage with them to the afterlife. After countless experiences with spirit communication in the first half of the twentieth century, Stewart Edward White wrote:

> Suicide ... is no solution to anything. The very act of suicide cuts one off, for a long period, from normal participation in life. One does not, as in normal death, go on at once there from where he left off here. He is not "punished," but he must first get back to normal, so to speak. Like getting over a shock; and it is most uneasy and uncomfortable. He is not escaping one bit from anything. There is no possible gain from a mere shift of environment.[6]

Based on his many sessions during the 1920s talking with spirits, using his wife as a medium, Psychiatrist Carl Wickland noted more gloomily:

> The "death ends all" doctrine encourages many perturbed persons to conclude that the easiest way out of their difficulties is to plunge over

the brink of the supposed "unknown" by committing suicide with the idea that by this act their troubles will be ended forever. But suicide does not do this; it only plunges the person from light into darkness.... The suicide merely shuts himself out from contact with the external; his mind is more disturbed than before.

Many remain in this condition for years, ignorant of spiritual laws and even unaware of being spirits, since they find themselves in possession of a spirit body which they mistake for a physical one. Nor does this free the spirit from an accusing conscience, if his life has not been right; the new conditions only add to his mental torment.[7]

Some spirits spoke of running into whole groups of others that appeared to be stuck, unable to progress. Through Jean Foster, a soul known as Penny described briefly hooking up with such spirits after entering the afterlife:

The weird teammates I had there wanted me to enact my whole last lifetime for their entertainment....

Never could I have believed anyone would be that gauche! They had no life other than going over one another's lifetimes, living it with them, having the miseries, the awfulness that led them all to do what I did—kill myself. But they had no ideas of anything better because they closed themselves in. That existence wasn't for me, I'll tell you![8]

A different spirit told Foster:

There are those ... who want me to join them, but I recognize them as people who also had problems in the earth plane. They reject a guide and want to cling together to have whatever it is that such clinging brings them. But not for me! Entering here as I did, I want to open myself to a better life, not the same or worse.[9]

Clearly, the case of like calling to like can be either good or bad, depending on one's mood and how evolved one is as a spirit. Hells of a spirit's own making need not be solitary affairs.

Drugs may compound the problem some suicides face on the other side. This may be a combination of dealing with increased confusion from the drugged state and psychological withdrawal from the addiction. The spirit James stated that those who were hooked on alcohol or drugs during life, may also have a very hard time learning how to cope without them.[10] James explained that, at least initially, rather than try to do without:

They attempt vicariously to continue to enjoy their vices by sharing those of earth addicts. An earthbound alcoholic will remain with a hard drinker, inciting him to further imbibing. If he took heroin on earth, he still thinks of himself as a "user," and he will stay with addicts and urge them on to additional excesses.[11]

Even once the body is gone, breaking a psychological addiction is no easy task. George Meek notes:

> A person addicted to hard drugs is in the deepest possible trouble. He will be resistant to any offer of help and will persist in his craving. He will experience torments which equal anything pictured in the old ideas of hell. He may remain in this dreadful condition for what would be centuries of earth time.[12]

In one specific case, Ruth Montgomery was told:

> Yes, Marilyn Monroe is slowly getting back some of her strength, so to speak, after a torpor which lasted some time because of the drugs and the suicide. She will be all right eventually. Has lots of friends and admirers on this side to help her, and she is repentant for taking a life that was housed in such exquisite form and rare beauty.[13]

The well-known medium Arthur Ford discussed the topic a number of times, both while alive (acting as a channel or writing about the material channeled by others) and after his own death (when being channeled). As quoted earlier, he observed that the problems suicides face in the afterlife may relate more to their state of mind than for any moralistic reason, stating:

> The extreme negative, depressed mental state of the suicide at the time of his self-destructive act carries over into the afterlife, placing him at a great disadvantage in making his adjustment. Many times, upon awakening, he does not realise that he has passed over.[14]

Another spirit was channeled by Ford saying:

> The mood that drives the suicide to self-slaughter ... will envelop him like a cloud from which we may not for a long time be able to give him release. His emotional thoughts, his whole attitude of mind sets up a barrier which can only be broken down by his own strenuous efforts ... and above all by the call ... to higher beings to bestow succor.[15]

This emotional baggage appears to have been the problem in a case where a woman (remembering a past life) knew that she had died, but was so torn by regret that she was unable to fully make the transition. Using an out-of-body (OBE) technique earlier perfected by OBE pioneer Robert

Monroe, Bruce Moen described being able to journey into the afterlife realm to contact spirits, instead of remaining here in the body and channeling messages from them. He recalls one situation:

> We arrived at the bedside near a young mother grieving over her own death. She was locked in grief and shame at having left her three young children to fend for themselves. She was painfully aware of her own death. She had suicided out of her life and was locked in regret, grief, and guilt over abandoning her children. She was so overcome with these feelings that she was unable to leave the scene of her suicide and break free of them.[16]

Following his brother's death in World War II, Peter Richelieu was visited by an Eastern-type adept who then took him on a series of out-of-body experiences, or "astral voyages," to the afterlife realm where he continued to have experiences with his brother now in spirit form. At one point, Acharya, Richelieu's guide, described somewhat differently the problem earlier addressed by fellow OBE traveler Bruce Moen:

> Because the man suffers so much remorse and because he would give anything to get back into his physical body ... he often refuses to make the effort of will necessary for him to get rid of his etheric vehicle.... Being a suicide he does not get the same sympathetic help from the astral helpers as you have seen is selflessly given to all who pass to the next world in the normal way; thus he may remain "earthbound" through ignorance, being unable to function properly either in the physical or the astral world, feeling the extreme loneliness that exists under these circumstances.[17]

Thus, we have seen that one of the major problems suicides have with adjusting to the afterlife can be their own personalities and issues. This is particularly problematic when the situation is complicated by addiction, with needs and cravings for substance involved clouding the soul's judgment and encouraging it to remain earthbound.

REFUSAL TO BELIEVE THEY ARE DEAD

Denial appears to be a frequent issue with suicides. Sometimes this can be simply a problem of confusion about whether they are really dead, since they still feel alive. This can be a major obstacle, completely halting any further progress. Franklin Loehr was told that:

> To recognize and accept the fact that you have died is very important. That is sort of your passport, your ticket to the new world. Until you know you have died to Earth, you can't really find yourself anywhere else.[18]

Of course, the problem of a soul being unaware that he or she has died is by no means unique to those who have committed suicide. The *Islamic Book of the Dead* notes the value of reciting the Sura Ya-Sin because "It is not unusual for the newly dead person to fail to grasp that they have in fact passed from the body-stage."[19] Haunting investigators also frequently discover that ghosts involved have not quite managed to figure out what has happened to them. This difficulty can occur even with those who passed on through natural causes, such as old age. Furthermore, it can be a considerable shock to the spirits to discover the reason they are being ignored is because they have passed to the other side. Loehr wrote that the living may be required to rescue lost spirits who, for whatever reason, don't know they were dead:

> Actually, the best way to reach most of these—about the only way, it seems—is by a person still in the body. These lost ones don't recognize the reality of their death, you see. So they are closed to us. But they recognize the realness of persons still living in the physical body. So these lost people can be reached by living people on Earth, if the living person can reach out and make contact with the realm of The Lost. Psychic rescue work, it's called.[20]

Sometimes the spirits don't realize that they have passed on because their preconceived notions do not fit the reality of their situation (see the later chapters on suicide bombers). As the spirit of Stephen explained the problem: "You find it kind of hard to believe you're dead because you feel so alive, so free, so light, and away."[21] He added: "Some do not know they are dead. Others will not accept that they are dead for a long time."[22]

Nineteenth-century British medium Robert James Lees, using the process of automatic writing to receive messages from a spirit calling itself "APHRAAR," noted that one spirit blamed this lack of understanding about the new state on the "nebulous confusion and ignorance existing on the other side [earth plane] concerning death."[23] He wrote:

> Now, when these ideas are accepted, and have the sanction of constituted authority before death, why should it be thought incredible, when, having made the transition, the souls find nothing even remotely associated with any one of the expectations, it fails to understand what has actually occurred?
>
> Still one can scarcely believe it possible....
>
> The confusion of the transit is not so dependent upon its suddenness as upon the erroneous ideas as to what it will reveal. Ignorance produces ignorance.[24]

This explanation makes a lot of sense. When there is misinformation about what a person will find on the other side, or, worse still, he or she is convinced that nothing exists after the death of the body, the soul is likely to be seriously confused by the transition, and may well be unable to comprehend, or accept, that he or she has died.

Allan Kardec also reported this phenomena as being a common one with various forms of violent death, including suicide:

> In all cases of violent or sudden death, by suicide, by capital punishment, accident, apoplexy, etc., the spirit is surprised, astounded, and does not believe himself to be dead. He obstinately persists in asserting the contrary; and, nevertheless, he sees the body he has quitted as something apart from himself; he knows that body to be his own, and he cannot make out how it should be separated from him. He goes about among the persons with whom he is united by the ties of affection, speaks to them, and cannot conceive why they do not hear him.... Death having come upon him by surprise, the spirit is stunned by the suddenness of the change that has taken place in him. For him, death is still synonymous with destruction, annihilation; and as he thinks, sees, hears, it seems to him that he cannot be dead. And this illusion is still further strengthened by his seeing himself with a body similar in form to the one he has quitted; for he does not at first perceive its ethereal nature.[25]

Contemporary Japanese researcher Hiroshi Motoyama also found the dead are often ignorant of their condition:

> Just as most spirits are unaware in life, they are unaware of what is going on in the death process. I will go into the mechanism of dying later on, but for now suffice it to say that most people are not immediately aware that they are "dead," even after their soul has left their body. The spirit continues to contain and feed on a certain amount of energy it carries over from the physical dimension, and it continues to direct itself toward this plane. This energy dissipates in a week or two and then a difficult period sets in....
>
> The spirit may find itself alone in a kind of deep dark pit and cannot figure out where it is or what it is doing there. I have seen this painful condition continue for two or three weeks in some cases, one to two months in others. The individual spirit eventually comes to realize what has happened and to accept the fact of his or her death. Then he or she is ready to move on to the next karmically determined place of existence.[26]

Franklin Loehr also pointed out the problem of spirits stuck in limbo, unable to complete their transition to the afterlife. Here he channeled Dr. John's explanation:

> Well, some who die suddenly do find it difficult to realize they are dead. If they are not caught in consciousness, and if they are not acceptive of their new estate, if they rather egotistically insist on being in their old estate or on limiting their knowledge in the new estate to their own knowledge, then they can cause more concern and be in the borderline state, the borderland of just coming over, for a longer time.[27]

In other cases, spirits may have observed their bodies and yet have trouble understanding that they are dead because they feel alive. Carl Wickland quoted one disconsolate spirit:

> My brother John found me and cut me down, and my parents were almost beside themselves. But I am not dead. I am at home all the time and I talk to my mother and father. I try to comfort them and make them know that I am not dead, but they do not notice me and do not answer me. My folks all sit around the table crying, and there is my empty chair, but no one answers me. Why don't they answer me?[28]

Lysa Mateu mentioned that one suicide she channeled, called Nancy, initially appeared to be in complete denial about her death.[29] Later on, Nancy admitted that it was only the fact that she was unable to comfort her grieving parents that finally drove home just what she had done.

Filipino parapsychologist Jaime Licauco reported an even more dramatic case of a suicide who couldn't figure out after cutting his wrists that he was already dead, and kept trying to kill himself over and over:[30]

> A clairvoyant saw what he did. His spirit kept on slashing his wrist, although his physical body was already dead. He could not understand why he wouldn't die. He continued to slash his phantom wrist thinking he was still in the flesh.
>
> Such a spirit will remain earthbound until he begins to realize he is already dead and accepts it.[31]

We have seen that many suicides have difficulty understanding that they are dead. This can often be due to the fact that they still "feel" alive and have an astral body. The problem can be particularly exacerbated by false expectations and cultural beliefs, such as that there is no such thing as a life after death or that they are supposed to be asleep until judgment day (see the later chapters on suicide bombers). Regardless, understanding and accepting that they are truly dead can be the first step toward souls' integration and advancement in the spirit realm.

FAILURE TO RECOGNIZE HELPERS

Adjustment problems can occur when the newly dead fail to recognize or accept guidance from those sent to greet them. Franklin Loehr tells the following amusing tale of how the spirit realm may sometimes work to get around this issue:

> Our teacher says there are some literal-minded people who are looking for angels playing harps ... and won't believe they're dead until something like that happens to them. Would you believe it, there's actually a group here—sort of a Little Theatre group; mostly they were actors and the like on Earth—who have worked up a six-angels-with-harps act? There they are, six very lovely female "angels" with big white wings. ... all to catch the attention of the new arrival and convince him he is really over here. Then from a corner at the back of the stage a very impressive-looking male "angel" walks out, blows a blast on a long trumpet, and announces something like this: "Welcome to Heaven, in the name of God. I am Gabriel. And now may I introduce you to the Committee which God has asked to take charge of you and prepare you for your new life here." Then the curtain dramatically opens and out step those who have been selected as most likely to get through to that person—relatives, friends, a teacher, etc. It's quite effective, too. I've seen it used several times.
>
> And there are other acts, of course, to suit the other Earth-ideas of what Heaven should be like. But it still leaves a lot of explaining and teaching of the newcomer before he understands things as they really are here and settles down.[32]

Unfortunately, this problem may be much worse for those who have taken their own lives. Some channeled messages (particularly older ones) emphasize the fact that suicides are frequently completely unaware of those from the spirit realm desiring to help them. In these cases, intervention may be necessary from the living, whether through prayers or direct contact via a medium. Through mediumship, Stewart Edward White reported the following commentary on suicide:

> Those, however, who deliberately ... take into their own hands the termination of prescribed experience are in a different class. ... in place of the impulse forward toward onward progress, the soul is bound, by an urge which it cannot overcome, to the backward view. Do not confuse this with the conventional picture of the "earthbound" spirit. The longing of regret for opportunities now seen to have been thrown away—the opportunities for certain fulfillments—blinds the entity to the possibility of those same fulfillments, with greater labor and lesser opportunity to be sure, in

another state of being. Until that fixation is resolved, the entity is static and impervious to the helpful influences that so quickly heal the victims of a purely accidental passing.

To that extent, and to that extent only, is he cut off from those who would help him on this side. His help must come from that toward which his attention is thus drawn.[33]

Carl Wickland described a case where the soul of a suicide, unwittingly attached to, and causing depression for, a man, was helped to "see" those trying to help it. Wickland wrote:

Mr. A: Now there will be others (intelligent spirits) with a much brighter light to help you.
Sp[irit]: Did I do much detriment to you?
Mr. A: Yes, you did.
(The spirit was then made to understand that he was a spirit.... His attention was also called to the presence of invisible friends whom he could discern if he would look around carefully. He remained quiet for a moment.)
Sp: Oh, look there! There's my dear old mother! She says, "Phillip, your father and I have been trying to find you but you were too clouded in earthly conditions. You were lost in a cloud of ignorance; you did not pass to the spirit world but stayed near the earth." My mother thanks you for having helped me.... I thank you and I am sorry I bothered you.[34]

Carl Wickland was not the only one to describe rescue circles for suicides, a rescue circle being get-togethers of living helpers, including one or more mediums, often working with one or more spirit guides in the afterlife, to communicate with, guide, and counsel relatively lost newcomers to the afterlife realm. In addition to records from such rescue groups, a number of other sources mention these newly arrived souls as being confused and unable to contact those in the spirit realm that would assist them. In the 1920s, British medium Charlotte Dresser described the following interchange:

"We have one who needs help whom we think is a suicide. She has been wandering long in darkness, and cannot see nor hear us. Can you speak to her?"
"I hear you are lost. I am a friend who would like to help you."
"Well, I am lost, all right. Who are you?"
"I am a friend, as I said. Can you tell us where you are?"
"I am where it is cold and dark and dreary. Why did I come."
"I suspect you came of your own accord by committing suicide."

"Yes, I did. I had dreadful trouble over there. But I don't want to remember it now. It was all a foolish love affair.... Why didn't I know better? I thought death ended all, and I looked forward to forgetfulness and rest. But here I am with keen remembrance, and so far from rest that I am wandering ... in the dark, and alone."

"How do you know you are alone?"

"I know I am alone because no one speaks to me."

"Can you see?"

"I see nothing...."

"Did you know that friends near you have been trying to talk to you?"

"No, I never hear them."[35]

The lost soul was then encouraged to say repeatedly, and with as much earnestness as it could muster, that it could hear. It was only then that the suicide was able to make contact with helpers from the other side.

The spirit identifying itself to medium Jane Sherwood as the late Lawrence of Arabia described a similar problem from the viewpoint of the afterlife of getting the soul of an old friend that had committed suicide to recognize him.[36] He stated, "I hailed him and he let me come up but it was hard to make him see or hear me. In fact, his body was so ill-developed that his new senses were as yet of little use to him."[37]

We have seen in this section that suicides in the afterlife may often have problems sensing helpers in the spirit realm. Because of this, it is thought that rescue circles by living mediums may be required to help some souls successfully leave the lower astral and finish their transition to the afterlife with the life review and self-judgment.

HARM CAUSED TO THE LIVING

Some sources state that the unhappy souls of those who have taken their own lives can harm the living, sometimes even causing others to follow in their footsteps and commit suicide. As already mentioned earlier in this chapter, psychic researcher and author Suzy Smith reported that the spirit James warned her that the souls of those who were addicted to drugs or alcohol while alive can have great difficulty breaking that habit in the afterlife.[38] The addiction may only be psychological, but it is nonetheless quite potent, and, as mentioned before, may lead them to encourage others to indulge in order to vicariously participate. James warned that this could be a real danger to the living; unless addicts remained strong-willed the insidious voice of an attached earthbound[39] might lead them not into crime or self-destructive behavior, but suicide. He added, "Many have committed crimes or have taken their own lives because a voice, or even a mere strong impulse, continually pressured them."[40]

George Meek also came to the conclusion that the dead could cause problems for the living:

> For example, an alcoholic, being on the lowest astral plane, is in close touch with the physical or earth plane. Often he is not truly aware that he is "dead." He may seek out his old haunts and get a vicarious thrill from visiting a bar. In fact, if he finds a person who is depressed, muddled and psychically sensitive, he may obsess that person. By this merging of their respective energy fields the dead person may become more directly locked into the physical aura of the bar patron and experience more directly the feelings to which he had become accustomed. If the possession of the patron continues, it may completely wreck his life, and in some cases may even cause the patron to commit suicide.[41]

Franklin Loehr echoed this concern that problems could be caused by those whose bodies are gone, but whose physical appetites seem to remain:[42]

> Alcoholics, dope addicts, sex maniacs, gluttons of all sorts, executed criminals and others filled with hatred and revenge, walking the very streets of Earth, sometimes attaching themselves if they can to living people there with similar weaknesses, pushing these poor weak ones ever further into temptation and wrongdoing.[43]

Richelieu's guide Acharya noted that it could take a long time for suicides to adjust, and that during this time they may try to cause others who are still living to follow their path:

> The exceedingly unpleasant conditions ruling in that "no-man's land" sometimes make a man so bitter ... that he wanders about the place where he took his life, trying to influence other people to do the same thing. The reason for this is the awful loneliness of his present condition, and he feels that if he can persuade other to do what he has done, he will not be entirely alone in his misery. On very rare occasions he succeeds in his efforts and the karmic result of such a deed means he must suffer greatly in the life that is to come.[44]

Russian psychic Helena Roerich also alluded to the potential for suicides to harm others after they had crossed to the other side: "Certainly, the low entities among suicides can practice all sorts of excesses. Vampirism is not a rare occurrence; their not yet outlived, not yet transmuted energies drag them with special power toward earthly sensations."[45]

In his work as a psychiatrist, Carl Wickland felt that the spirits of suicides were responsible, if unknowingly, for a number of problems:

> Such spirits, hovering about the earthplane, may often be the indirect cause of unpremeditated suicides, for, not realizing that they have already succeeded in separating themselves from their physical bodies, they persist in striving to "end their lives" and becoming enmeshed in the auras of mortal sensitives, they convey to the latter their own gloomy thoughts and sudden impulse to "end it all." Many a person who suffers from such strange impressions ... concludes he is going insane and determines to commit suicide.[46]

The harm done by suicides to others may not always be deliberate or intentional on their part. Wickland described a case where the soul of a suicide became attached to a man with negative consequences:

> Mr. A., an elderly gentleman, was well situated financially and had everything to live for but subsequent to his attendance at Spiritualistic dark circles he became afflicted with insomnia, melancholia and an indefinable depression for which there was no assignable reason.... Static electricity was applied to the gentleman in the presence of Mrs. Wickland who became entranced by a foreign entity....
>
> Dr. Wickland: Where did you meet this man?
>
> Spirit: I found him at a meeting. (Mr. A. had attended a trumpet séance.) I was so depressed. (Coughing and choking, evidently repeating his death struggle.) I took something. (Committed suicide.) Then I slept for awhile and after that I walked a long time in the twilight. It seemed like the desert. Then I came to a meeting; it was dark and they were singing all kinds of hymns....
>
> Sp: I made my money in the wheat pit.... I won money in the market and wanted more. Then the crash came and down I went. Then I began to worry and was always depressed.
>
> Mr. A: Now all that depression of yours you bring to me.
>
> Sp: I do? I'm sorry. When I come close to you I can have a little peace. But I always feel as if my hands are tied and I get down-hearted and think there is no use to anything. Did I make you feel that way?
>
> Mr. A: Yes you did.
>
> Sp: (Emphatically) Well, I wouldn't do that for the world.... When you went home I followed you because you had such a bright light around you.... The others (sitters at circle) at that meeting were gray and muddy; don't ever go there again.[47]

Wickland noted: "The spirit departed and the gentleman afterward declared himself relieved of the depression."[48] Thus, his mood disorder would appear to have been due to the unwitting spirit attachment of the suicide.

In other cases, suicide appeared to be the root cause of a person's physical symptoms.[49] That this was not a case of fantasy or pure imagination on the part of the living, would seem to be bolstered by the later corroboration of another. Physician Wickland wrote:

> A young girl suffered from attacks which had been diagnosed by physicians as epilepsy. At times she complained of pains in the stomach or dryness of the throat and alternately had paroxysms of choking and spells simulating paralysis. The patient had been under our observation for some weeks, receiving electrical treatments and medical attention, when one morning Mrs. Wickland became controlled by the spirit of a woman that had been dislodged from the girl.
>
> The spirit gave her name as Frances Dickinson and was very despondent. She said she had had severe stomach trouble and when she became paralyzed her husband had left her. Discouraged, desperate and unable to make a living for herself, she had committed suicide by turning on the gas in her room.
>
> When her true situation had been explained, spirit kindred appeared to her and she was taken away to receive further enlightenment.
>
> The father of the patient was greatly interested in the statements made by the spirit and decided to verify them if possible. Accordingly he made inquiries at the Coroner's office in Los Angeles and looked up records of the Bureau of Vital Statistics, where he found the following entry:
>
> "Frances Dickinson, age 71, native of Canada, committed suicide by turning on the gas in her room at Number South G—Avenue, Los Angeles, June 13, 1922."
>
> Obtaining the address of the undertakers in the case, he found their records showed Frances Dickinson had died from gas, and the body had been cremated June 20, 1922.
>
> Further verification was received from the woman's place of residence and the added information given that she had suffered considerably from stomach trouble.[50]

On the cusp of the nineteenth and twentieth centuries, British clairvoyant and author Charles Leadbeater expressed the Theosophist view that suicides and other souls stuck in the lower astral planes could drain energy from the living—a belief still held by some cultures around the world, such as the Maori of New Zealand. Leadbeater stated:

> It should be noted that this class [of suicides], as well as the shades and the vitalized shells, are all what may be called minor vampires; that is to

say, whenever they have the opportunity they prolong their existence by draining away the vitality from human beings whom they find themselves able to influence.[51]

Later he added:

> The lost entity would very soon after death find himself unable to stay in the astral world, and would be irresistibly drawn in full consciousness in "his own place," the mysterious eighth sphere, there slowly to disintegrate after experiences best left undescribed. If, however, he perishes by suicide or sudden death, he may under certain circumstances, especially if he knows something of black magic, hold himself back from that awful fate by a death in life scarcely less awful—the ghastly existence of the vampire.
>
> Since the eighth sphere cannot claim him until after the death of the body, he preserves it in a kind of cataleptic trance by the horrible expedient of the transfusion into it of blood drawn from other human beings by his semi-materialized astral, and thus postpones his final destiny by the commission of wholesale murder.[52]

Such ideas as vampirism seem far-fetched to the modern mind. However, there may be some grain of truth to it, in that present-day psychics and channels sometimes speak of "psychic vampires"—people who drain energy from the living.[53] It could be possible that spirits can do the same, if only on an energetic level.

Suicides frequently have reported trouble adjusting to the afterlife. Causes for this include their psychological baggage, difficulty understanding and accepting that they are really dead, and a frequent failure to sense help. Rescue circles made up of incarnate humans may sometimes have to intervene to help these souls onward. If not, their presence can sometimes harm the living, whether through a deliberate attempt to induce others to follow their footsteps or as an inadvertent effect of their attachment to the living.

Fortunately, most suicides have spirit guides devoted to helping them leave the lower astral plane and grow spiritually. The goal is for these unfortunate souls to advance to higher levels of existence, receive training, and hopefully have better results in their next incarnation. Next, we will look at some of the inherent problems of moving on, and review some of the techniques used to assist in the upward progress of suicides, including the use of prayer, sleep, and various forms of spiritual therapy.

7

Moving On

It should be noted that in older channeled material, perhaps in keeping with the culture of the time, it was said that reincarnation did not occur and spirits were stuck at whatever level they were at when they first arrived in the afterlife. Emanuel Swedenborg stated in the 1700s that:

> ... *after death we remain the same forever in regard to our volition or dominant love.* I have been allowed to talk with some people who lived more than two thousand years ago, people whose lives are described in history books and are therefore familiar. I discovered that they were still the same, just as described, including the love that was the source and determinant of their lives....
>
> Angels have told me that the life of our dominant love never changes for anyone to all eternity....
>
> They have also told me that this is because after death we can no longer be reformed by being taught the way we could in this world.[1]

According to Swedenborg, only those dwelling in heaven receive instruction by angels, and the resulting enlightenment does not particularly change their state.

It is reassuring to note that this attitude appeared to shift with time, softening as the notions of a loving God and spiritual growth gradually gained acceptance among Spiritualist mediums. The spirit of Bacon was channeled to say about all Earth-bound spirits:

> It is this ... principle of good, this germ of truth, which is breathed on them as it were by the Spirit of God, and impels them to seek for happiness in progression through the higher spheres.
>
> They say, who are opposed to these revelations, we teach doctrines contrary to the Bible.
>
> They believe in a hell, in a place of punishment where spirits are tortured either by other spirits more evil or by their own thoughts. But even were this so ... can you imagine a portion of that germ, pure and self-existent, could be confined in a place where there is no hope, where the spirit could not progress? No; even were this so, were even the hell existing

as it is said, no spirit could remain there; for the impelling force of that power which is of God would send it self-seeking the universe through, to seek that food which its nature so much craves....

To this source do we all tend, some in one position, some in another, but all arriving at last at the point at which his nature can be most developed.[2]

In the mid-1800s, L. Alph Cahagnet addressed the issue of suicide directly:

"What is the punishment that God reserves for suicide?" "That which he inflicts on all those who do evil, a public reprimand; after that, God renders it impossible for them to do evil, by consigning them to a place apart."—"What sort of place is it? Is it the hell of which men speak?" "There is no such hell as is depicted on earth; there are places of purification, which are termed places of punishment, because one is there deprived of the sight of God and his divine light; but those who are there are happy."[3]

Issues of moving forward for those who have committed suicide seem to vary from one medium to the next, suggesting possible cultural bias may have crept into what was received. Reincarnation, in particular, was often hotly debated in the early Spiritualist literature. Early twentieth-century medium Frances Bird questioned spirits and received answers through automatic writing. When she asked about those who had committed suicide, she was told:

When a spirit enters this sphere, his condition is the same, as when he left the earth. Nothing can be done, except to change what he brings with him, if it is wrong. The conditions were, at the last, of his own making and must be removed by him. There can be no condemnation of wrong. That is not punishment for what he has done, but a removal of seeds of evil he brings with him.... The work is his to do, alone, for it is done within himself. He has much to overcome....

He has a very heavy burden to life; and he'll be long in freeing himself from his earth-bound [condition]. But, with a spirit of love, his progress will be helped.[4]

Carl Wickland was far less optimistic, saying, "The fate of a suicide is invariably one of the deepest misery, his rash act holding him in the earth sphere until such time as his physical life would have had a natural ending."[5] Based upon her long experience working with the spirit world, noted British medium Geraldine Cummins also felt that suicide had harsh consequences. She tells of one such soul: "His suicide led to his being plunged into darkness and isolation here for a very long time."[6]

A spirit channeled by William Stainton Moses was another that tended toward a gloomy outlook of what a soul who had committed suicide needed to do to move on:

> For long their efforts availed little; but by degrees they succeeded in awakening some measure of consciousness of sin, and the spirit began to grope blindly for some means of escape from a state which had become loathsome to it. Frequent relapses dragged it back....
>
> The hope for the spirit is that it may be nerved to occupy itself with some beneficent work, and so to work out its own salvation. To this end it must journey on through remorse and uncongenial labour: for by no other means can it be purified. Selfishness must be eradicated by self-sacrifice.... The spirit much be purified by suffering....
>
> This is the inevitable penalty of a wasted life. It may be that the half-quenched spark may be quickened again, and be fanned into a flame strong enough to light the spirit onward. It may be that the spirit may wander in gloom and desolation, deaf to the voice of the ministers, and groaning in lonely unrest, nerveless for the struggle, till the sin through cycles of purgatorial suffering has eaten out its own virulence.[7]

Contemporary Japanese Medium Yuko Chino also felt that most suicides are doomed to an unpleasant time, at least initially, in the afterlife:

> If they give in to the impulse to kill themselves, they become locked in a dark place after they die. Furthermore, some people repeat the same suicidal behavior over and over again after they go to hell. ... members of the Kamikaze suicide missions have this tendency. However, the majority of war victims and those who committed suicide because of it were people who had a tendency of being almost too good. When these people died, the spirits working under high level beings in heaven went right down to raise these souls up.... The self indulgent types and those trying to run away from themselves invariably have to go underground to await their salvation. There are cases there souls are raised to heaven after being granted a special pardon, but suicide cases are most often found under the ground clinging in some dark corner or otherwise sleeping. These dead souls and lost wandering souls and souls trapped underground are being raised up to heaven regularly.[8]

Some messages focus not so much on the unpleasant fate of suicides, as on their need for healing or recovery. Charlotte Dresser was told through automatic writing that:

> When a human life is broken by the owner of that life, there is a long period of unconsciousness before any reconstruction can take place. Years may elapse before they are ready to begin any advancement. The suicide

takes his own way instead of God's way; and the result is, to paralyze the finer spiritual qualities, and prevent entrance into the joy of this life for a long time.[9]

Later, Dresser was informed:

> Those who come over mentally unbalanced, those needing kind and wise treatment to bring them out of sin or out of selfishness, and those who are projected into this world by accident or suicide or other sudden ways, all need spiritual physicians.[10]

Hence, suicides may face a prolonged recovery phase, commonly marked by long periods of sleep.

Stewart Edward White, who received messages from his deceased wife, Betty, said:

> In general principle nothing one has earned spiritually is ever lost; and one must go on in the evolution of spiritual development. One can do things to retard or make difficult that progress, but can do nothing to lose it or stop it. Suicide is one of those things that make it difficult. Very difficult, perhaps....
> Of course they [suicides] are helped and instructed.[11]

This stance has continued to shift in a positive direction. American trance medium Kate Anders points out that, if present, this problem of being stuck can sometimes be overcome through help from the living:

> My experience is that the person committing the suicide is always regretful. The idea to use suicide as an escape does not work. The lessons we have to learn continue with us and have to be worked though sooner or later. In fact, if anything, the suicide slows down the process. In all cases with suicide, the person who has killed him/herself seems to need help from this side to become 'untrapped' and move on. One case comes to mind where a woman's brother had killed himself. The picture I saw was of him in a cylindrical building at night where the only thing he could see was his reflection. He couldn't extricate himself from the building to move on. He was very regretful and sad. With his sister's help and her forgiveness (along with his own forgiveness of himself) he could move on.[12]

Sometimes the spiritual growth work is done with groups of souls, as in the case of one guide that Lauren Thibodeau channeled:

> Heath: So, he works with groups of kids?
> Thibodeau: Right.... He's telling me it's not really about the type of death so much as it's efficient this way.... The guides themselves can allow a lot of the learning to happen from others who share their experience.

And at this one thing he's laughing and pointing at me and saying, "We've heard it from you too. You don't live on Earth. What could you possibly get about life in the body? And even if you did live in a body, it's been awhile. And it's easier for you." So, they've found that working with groups who share common themes—often the common theme is the way we die—can come together for healing. He's claiming—he's using the phrase "accelerated time"—that we need to get as much accelerated in terms of the enlightenment as possible.[13]

Contemporary literature addresses the issue of spiritual advancement with considerable optimism, although noting that a soul who has taken its own life may face two problems—completing what should have been his or her expected lifespan and the potential increased difficulty of making spiritual progress. While the former issue would always solve itself with time, the latter may call for special measures—from prayer, to increased sleep in the afterlife (which appears in this realm to be the general cure for all ills), to actual spiritual therapy and therapeutic assignments. Let us look at each of these issues in turn.

PROBLEMS DUE TO LIFESPAN

The first problem is that a soul needs to have completed its expected lifespan in the lower astral before it can move to a higher, more spiritual, dimension. A number of sources suggest that this can be a real stumbling block, particularly if the soul's blueprint called for a long lifetime. The spirit of Alvin Daniel Mattson communicated through Margaret Flavell:

> Persons who commit suicide before the time they are meant to die find themselves in a state of heavier vibrations and closer to the earth than those of us who died natural deaths. They remain in this state of density until the time when they would have died naturally. They then pass into the planes of finer vibration. There are those from the higher planes who dedicate themselves to helping these people grow spiritually during the period of waiting.[14]

Other mediums have also expressed the idea of suicides having to remain close to the earth plane until their time is done. L. Alph Cahagnet described the following exchange during a sitting in the mid-1800s:

> Adèle says: "I see a man, about thirty-six years of age, of middling stature; black hair, rather long, coming down to the bottom of the ear, but not as is worn in the present day ... air sad and downcast.... He has blown out his brains! Oh, the wretch! I can understand his sorrowfulness. ... those who commit suicide enter not forthwith—they wander around

the earth!"—"What, then, is their suffering?" "That of being unable to enjoy light as the rest."—"When does he hope to enjoy it?" "When the time that he should have accomplished on earth is terminated."—"That is to say that he will wander to the age of sixty, were he to have lived to that age materially?" "Yes.... This man, without being positively wretched, is not happy: his ideas have suffered—they are still agitated, under the influence of those that drove him to suicide."[15]

In the late 1800s, Annie Besant stated that taking one's life before its anointed time would cause a soul to be stuck until its planned years on Earth were completed. She said of the suicide:

> It had an appointed life-term determined by an intricate web of prior causes, which its own willful sudden act cannot shorten. That term must run out its appointed sands....
>
> So you may destroy the body, but not the appointed period of sentient existence. ... this must run on for its appointed period.[16]

Another time Besant said, "Suicides, although ... quite potent in the séance room, nonetheless, to the day when they would have died a natural death, are separated from their higher principles by a gulf."[17] Later, she wrote:

> The rule is that a person who dies a natural death will remain from "a few hours to several short years" within the earth's attraction, i.e., the Kamaloka. But exceptions are the cases of suicides and those who die a violent death in general. Hence, one of such Egos who was destined to live, say, eighty or ninety years—but who either killed himself or was killed by some accident, Id [let] us suppose at the age of twenty—would have to pass in the Kamaloka not "a few years," but in this case sixty or seventy years, as an Elementary, or rather an "earth-walker."[18]

Moving to the early 1900s, we see that suicides may not be the only spirits unable to move forward until their planned years on Earth were completed. California minister and medium Nora Loder received the following message as automatic writing from a spirit who had passed from tuberculosis:

> I am only too thankful I came when I did, though it was long before I was needed here, and so I must remain a student until my life clock should have run down of its own accord. I came here for a fault of my own, and for that mistake I must pay the price.[19]

In Russia, Helena Roerich also believed that suicides had to wait until their natural time was up before they could hope to advance. She felt they were trapped, rather like objects without enough energy to reach escape velocity and make orbit. However, she noted that while difficult, with prayer and a desire for help it was possible for them to move forward spiritually:

> The despair that drives them to commit this act of madness causes the complete ebbing of the psychic energy and thus they are left in the power of earthly attraction. Their anguish and sufferings will last until the very day of their natural death. In exceptional cases when consciousness has been obscured only temporarily ... these unfortunate ones may remember about Light and ... strive for redemption. Therefore, a sincere prayer of the heart to the forces of Light, asking for help for these unfortunate ones, is not left without an answer, provided of course, that these unfortunate ones shall themselves strive to rise in spirit.[20]

The purported surviving spirit of Lawrence of Arabia was channeled by Jane Sherwood, saying, "I am told that there is a belief that suicides remain in coma until the time when they would normally have died."[21] However, this same spirit noted that this kind of thing is impossible to prove, since there was no way to know when their lifespan would have ended. Lawrence stated that he could only attest to the fact that spirits exhibit comas of varying length, and that other spirits who made their transition because of violent deaths also may remain unconscious for a time.

Some modern mediums agree. James Van Praagh explains that, "when someone commits suicide, he is still tied to earth until it is his natural time to die."[22] This may not always be a significant problem. In the case of a father who killed himself after his wife's suicide, Van Praagh notes, "Your dad is saying he didn't have to wait around too long over there because his life was close to an end anyway."[23]

Suzane Northrop also feels that souls have an expected (or predetermined) length of life. She states that souls of people who have taken their own lives have told her:

> Yes, there is "an allotted time."
> They have also stressed that suicide is not the only manner in which we can go before our time. Overindulgence, misuse of drugs, alcohol, or food, may affect our physical bodies to the point that they no longer can endure the abuse. This is a suicide of another sense and can also result in our transition before the allowed time.[24]

Even NDErs have suggested that there can be a long period before suicides are capable of moving on. Psychiatrist and pioneering NDE authority Raymond Moody states:

Others who experience this unpleasant "limbo" state have remarked that they had the feeling they would be there for a long time. This was their penalty for "breaking the rules" by trying to release themselves prematurely from what was, in effect, an "assignment"—to fulfill a certain purpose in life.[25]

Although a number of mediums have reported that suicides remain near the earthly plane until their expected lifespan is completed—which could vary in length depending on their advance blueprint or plans—not all suicides appear to be stuck in this manner. It is unclear whether this is due to the soul simply having been expected to die young. Lauren Thibodeau states that, in the case of a young boy who had accidentally taken his life, he had stayed by his own choice:

> Thibodeau: By choice. Not stuck....
> Heath: And what made him choose that?
> Thibodeau: The grieving family and friends he wanted to be near energetically. And again, the more you feel and process their grief and pain and sadness and anger and all that stuff, the easier and more quickly you make the adjustment to the spiritual side of life. Therefore it's in his better interest, too, to stay close. It helps him. It helps them. But it does take a lot of spiritual strength, which is why he shows me coming in what I always think of as the attended mode. There's two or three others with him every time. They come with guides.
> Heath: So, that's not really stuck. That's just returning.
> Thibodeau: No. That's not stuck. I've never seen anybody stuck. I really haven't. They're not stuck. Perhaps over time an unwillingness to allow oneself be guided. But they're not stuck. If they're stuck it's by choice. And illusion on top of it.[26]

We have seen in this section that quite a few mediums (but not all) have felt that those who take their own lives early may have to spend the remaining period that they would have lived near the Earth plane. This was particularly true of the older channeled material, but even many modern channels have stated this is true. Nonetheless, there are exceptions. As Lauren Thibodeau notes, it may be that spirits are stuck by choice, wanting to remain near grieving loved ones, or because they mistakenly believe they cannot move on.

SPECIAL ASSISTANCE

Many suicides are said to need extra help to move forward spiritually. Sometimes this appears to come from the earth plane, while at other times there seem to be special guides in the spirit plane, often ex-suicides, who work to help those beings stuck in the lower astral. In 1876, William Stainton Moses channeled the following story about a soul who had taken its own life:

> When the cord of earth-life was severed, the spirit found itself in darkness and distress. For long it was unable to sever itself from the body. It hovered round it even after the grave had closed over the shrine which it had violated. It was unconscious, without power of movement, weak, wounded, and distressed. It found no rest, no welcome in the world to which it had come unbidden. Darkness surrounded it....
>
> It was not till the first shudder of awakening conscience attracted the ministering spirits that anything could be done to palliate the misery, not yet half felt or acknowledged, or to minister healing to the soul. When it stirred amid the darkness, the ministers drew near and strove to quicken the seared conscience and to awaken remorse. In seeming cruelty they strove to bring home a knowledge of its state, and to paint before it a picture of its sin....
>
> For long their efforts availed little; but by degrees they succeeded in awakening some measure of consciousness of sin, and the spirit began to grope blindly for some means of escape from a state which had become loathsome to it.[27]

This passage, despite a certain amount of apparent cultural bias, suggests that adjusting to death may be a problem if the soul is either unaware of those in spirit trying to help it or, due to the suddenness of the event, there has been no preparation on the other side to receive the soul. Special assistance may need to be provided for those lost in the lower astral planes—whether from the living or from those in spirit.

It should be noted that even if help is offered to a suicide, he or she may have trouble benefiting from it. James E. Padgett states that a suicide told him, "I am in a condition of great darkness and suffering and I am not able to find a way out of the darkness or to relieve myself from my tortures."[28] In this case, the soul admitted that it had been offered help by another, but was unable to accept it:

> I know that you may think it strange that I did not listen to Mr. Riddle when you brought him in contact with me a short time ago, but I could not believe what he told me or understand in what way the darkness would leave me by merely praying to God, and trying to believe that there is such a thing as Divine Love which I might obtain by letting my belief in what he said become sufficiently strong to cause me to forget the recollections of my awful deed.[29]

Thus, although help had been offered, the spirit had trouble accepting it and remained stuck in the lower astral.

A soul having difficulty moving on need not be a lost cause. The literature describes a number of ways in which these souls can be helped to move forward spiritually, including through the use of prayer, sleep, and various forms of therapy. We will discuss each of these in turn.

The Value of Prayer

A number of channels talk about the value of prayer in helping spirits move forward spiritually, especially if they have been hampered by having killed themselves. These messages have been common since the 1800s. F. W. H. Myers reported the following eyewitness account of a séance, where the details of the woman's death were later confirmed:

> At the sitting held at M. Nartzeff's house, November 18, 1887, we received a communication from an intelligence giving the name of Anastasie Péréliguine. She asked us to pray for her; and said that she had poisoned herself with Lucifer matches, and had died on the 17th of that month.[30]

This request for prayer was by no means rare. Robert Crookall analyzed a number of messages from the dead, and states, "Suicides who communicated typically plead, '*Pray for me.*'"[31] This still appears to be the case. In a recent news report from the Philippines, the spirit of a suicide came through in automatic writing asking that a companion pray for her.[32]

Other cultures also speak about the value of prayer. Although the cross-cultural nature of this has already been hinted at by the above case from the Philippines, others in Asia have endorsed the usefulness of praying. Japanese medium Hiroshi Motoyama writes:

> During the difficult period before the soul becomes aware of its new situation, it is a tremendous help if relatives and friends are praying and making offerings on the deceased's behalf. Mourning rituals have a real purpose.... Intercessionary prayers, particularly those of spiritually evolved people, can be a great help in facilitating any suffering spirit's passage to the next stage.[33]

Motoyama believed that prayer could help a suicide even if it was performed by nonrelatives, as in the following instance:

> Mr. K took time out from his hectic schedule to come and see me the other day; he had just found out that there was a huge well on the building

site and that a woman had drowned herself in it fifty years ago after a fight with her elder brother. He wanted to know if it was okay to demolish the well or if he should leave it alone. I advised him to pray that the spirit of the woman be freed from her pain and to offer ritual thanks to the Water Spirit who sustained the people of the area.[34]

George Anderson also feels prayer can be helpful to those in the afterlife. When asked once about what can be done to aid a suicide's advancement through the afterlife, he states:

> He is not on any dark plane; no suicides are. The Infinite Light is compassionate and understanding when it comes to people who have passed by their own hand, and will do whatever the soul needs to recover and learn from the mistake. You are already helping your friend more than you know by praying or thinking about him, which sends spiritual "hugs" to the hereafter.[35]

Anderson has received a number of messages from the souls of suicides and accidents over the years that have stated that the prayers of the living seem to help them progress in the afterlife. During readings for family members, he often makes statements like, "He certainly thanks you for your prayer and asks that it please continue"[36] and "You obviously pray for him, because he certainly thanks you for prayer and asks that it please continue."[37] Anderson notes that this was true of all spirits, not just those that had taken their own lives. He explains:

> The souls in the hereafter always ask during a reading that we pray for them or even talk to them out loud. They still consider themselves part of our family and are always listening, and they appreciate being thought of.[38]

Afterlife researcher Elsie Sechrist also comments that prayers could be helpful for all souls, not just suicides:

> I have heard of a great many instances in which the departed have plainly asked the living for prayer. Each of these cases demonstrates that the deceased want to progress. The souls who request aid know they need help.... Perhaps most significant, they recognize the value of our prayers and their power to give them what they need.[39]

Sechrist recalled being how she was told at a dinner party by psychic Olga Worrell that her prayers were appreciated:

> Olga said to me, "I see a large number of people from the other side standing around you. They want to thank you for your constant prayers for them."

When I asked her who was there, I was astonished to hear her identify nine people—each of whom was on my daily prayer list! Even the name Tante Bartetzko was given correctly. No one could guess that!

Then Olga said, "And your brother is here." I was truly amazed. My brother had committed suicide some years before. I had been praying for him nightly but had told no one outside the home about it.

Olga added, as if to console me, "He says to tell you it's all right. He is now with your grandmother, in the light."[40]

Thus, it appeared that prayers may indeed be able to help the dead, particularly those in trouble. Sechrist concluded after this experience that, "there are no problems in the afterlife without solutions; even a soul's stay in outer darkness is not permanent. It may take time, but liberation is possible."[41]

When speaking of the experiences she had had with the souls of suicides and their families, contemporary channel Johanna Carroll states, "And there's some kind of special prayer or releasing, the more they can release through love, the more that spirit will really evolve on the other side."[42] Later, she notes of the souls, "they always ask the basic things. Pray. Send love."[43]

Finally, the general importance of prayers for the dead would also seem to be supported by electronic voice phenomena messages that request it. Latvian instrumental transcommunication researcher Konstantin Raudive obtained a number of statements on tape, such as "Please, pray for Margarete's soul,"[44] "Don't talk, that doesn't help, pray!"[45] and "pray for me."[46]

It is possible that prayer may manifest far more strongly in the afterlife than we realize. NDE authority P. M. H. Atwater mentions:

> During my research with child experiencers of near-death states, I was continually surprised by the number of kids who saw the actual prayers being said for them, while they were out of their bodies.... They described how the power of those prayers turned into beams of radiant golden or rainbow light.... They showed me with gestures how that beam of light arced over from the one saying the prayer, no matter how many miles away, to where they themselves were hovering....
> Once a prayer beam reached them, some said it felt like a splash of love. Others said it felt warm and tickly. Because they saw prayer as real energy that did real things and had a real effect, these youngsters went on to pray easily and often.[47]

Thus, we have seen that a number of sources speak of the fact that prayers are heard by those in spirit and can be of great value in helping souls to advance, whether they are stuck or not. Furthermore, these prayers need not be performed by a priest, but appear to be beneficial regardless of who says them.

The Use of Sleep

Sleep appears to be nearly a panacea in the afterlife, able to cure all ills. The reader will notice that a number of stories told by suicides, or about those who are troubled for other reasons, mention its use. In his book *The Supreme Adventure: Analysis of Psychic Communications,* Robert Crookall reports that sleep is a common feature of the afterlife, particularly when one dies in old age. He writes, "Transition must involve some shock, due to the changed 'vibration-rate.' The 'sleep' stage aids adjustment."[48] Sleep also appears to be a commonly used tool to help distressed souls adjust to their new state. The spirit of suicide Stephen Puryear spoke to his mother of waking up and falling back to sleep again several times when adjusting to being newly dead.[49] This sleep appeared to help him as a form of therapy:

> The next thing I knew, I woke up and it was daylight, and I felt so good.... I was lying down on my bed, and there was a window. I could see the sun outside.... I couldn't remember where I was. I had some vague thought come to me that I had seen somebody hanging on a tree, and I fell back asleep....
>
> I kept waking up and getting afraid and then very gently going back to sleep. Someone came and sat by me. I could hear them talking to me, then I'd go back to sleep. I didn't really want to hear what they were saying to me.[50]

Other suicides also have mentioned waking up and falling back to sleep again after their transition, often in a peaceful hospital-like setting.

Another way that sleep can be seen is as a prolonged coma immediately after death. Lawrence of Arabia wrote, through Jane Sherwood from the afterlife, of his experience finding a friend who had committed suicide in the lower astral, which he called a "misty half-region":

> He was in a kind of stupor and I was told that he might remain in this state for a long time and that nothing could be done about it.... Until he regained consciousness there he had to remain; had we forcibly removed him his poor body would not have been able to stand the conditions of our plane....
>
> Suicides often show this long-lasting coma. It is really a merciful pause during which some of the damage to their emotional bodies is quietly made good. Much always remains for them to do when they come to themselves.[51]

In this case, spirit helpers had to watch and wait for the suicide to come out of his coma on his own, before any further spiritual assistance could be provided.

Spiritual Therapy

Most modern channels agree that suicides are not condemned to the lower levels, but are capable of moving forward spiritually. Santa Barbara, California, paranormal researcher Kit Tremaine was told by one of the channels she studied that, not only are these souls not condemned, but that they are afforded extra help in their transitions.[52] Tremaine worked with medium Verna Yater, whose spiritual contact, Indira, explained to her that souls are always given assistance and an opportunity to learn after making their transition to the afterlife, and that this is even more true with those who died quickly, had mental illness, or committed suicide. One thus chooses "what would be the greatest benefit in form of study, in the consideration and preparation for a return to the physical form."[53]

James Van Praagh had a young man who committed suicide state to his mother, who had come to Van Praagh for help, "I'm getting help here, Mom. They have some nice people who have seen to it that I get back to myself again."[54] Also through Van Praagh, a different soul explained her situation after taking her own life while mentally ill:

> Your mother wants me to tell you that she has received help from another lady. Sort of a counselor. Your mother stopped her own life but not consciously. She really was mentally out of it. Since passing, she has been working to change her mental condition and to learn how to bring her own love back into her heart. To recognize love in herself.... She says that even though she is dead, she is not resting. Far from it. She is trying in her own way to make up for lost time.[55]

Psychic and channel Johanna Carroll notes that she feels many (if not all) suicides spend some time in a special healing center. She describes it in the following passage:

> Just for purposes of making it simple, I've been told it's called the Healing Room. And it's like this place, and in terms of a vision, it feels very cool. It feels very calm. I always see this person still in their body, lying down, as if they're sleeping. I see them being attended to by members of the spiritual family on the other side, which to me is always like the guides and the teachers. I feel that that is a positioning of the spiritual body connection that allows them to separate so that they can rise up in spirit, fully aware that "I am not alive in the body anymore." And then, they're really

moving on to more of an interaction of this core group of family, friends, people who are familiar, which allows the transition to take another step. Now, the Healing Room is very key in suicides. I have also seen this in someone who has died a very painful death, say they've really suffered through cancer—something like that. It's a real healing. I feel that the spirits who are working with an individual are working with the energetics of the system and the etheric body, as well.[56]

Suzane Northrop has also said that souls have told her that they receive education in the afterlife that helps them to advance spiritually. Mention of this occurs in the following conversation between a living mother and her discarnate daughter, as channeled by Northrop:

Eleanor, Jennifer's mother, asked her directly, "Was this your destiny, were you supposed to end your own life by suicide?"

"No. We don't have the right to take our own or anybody else's life," Jennifer responded. "I ended my life before the right time. These and other things are what I'm now learning and confronting in the spiritual realm. I can do this in nonphysical spiritual school or in another life-time."[57]

Bishop Pike's son was channeled saying, "I'm not being blamed.... I've been met with compassion and understanding."[58] He admitted being confused and distrustful immediately after his transition to the afterlife, but then was gently taught by guides to understand things differently. He described his lessons as follows:

We tried to find out what are the things that really matter—to have compassion and understanding and to be kind.... You have to put them into operation. You have to relearn how to think, how to really put yourself in the other guy's place to see how you would work out in the same circumstances.... They show you things that are essential and they put the things that are not essential on one side.[59]

Later the spirit of Jim Pike Junior added:

You see, we have to be selfless. This creates freedom ... by loving, one gets a return of love.... This is man cleansing himself, gradually and continuously, and he evolves and becomes more enlightened. He throws away his props and his shackles, and he works to what is essential.[60]

Such spiritual advancement sounds wonderful. However, it may not be an easy task for the suicide. George Anderson notes:

Through their own free will, they can progress. This is why it's so important that people, no matter what your religious belief or persuasion, even if you're an atheist, remember to pray for those who have passed on.

Because that embraces them in love and encourages them to progress. The problem that the suicide faces in the next dimension is that ... they cannot forgive themselves....

And it's very important that those coming through acknowledge what they've done.... A friend of mine who had recently taken his life came through and did not know how to go into the light. I kept telling him to go forward to the light, but he was afraid of judgment. He couldn't forgive himself. Also, he was having a problem with the fact that after he had taken his own life, his spirit had obviously lingered around the scene of the act. He could not overcome the memory of his father's discovering him, and that was haunting him emotionally to a tremendous degree in the next dimension....

It can take eons of time as we understand it before they go into the light. It depends on the person.... Those who've come through those darker levels have said that they've had to face themselves and realize that if they don't shape up, in other words, learn more about themselves, they're not getting anywhere.[61]

Jean Foster was told by a young girl who had killed herself that spirits may have to reach a point where they are willing to open themselves up to help.[62] Suicides, in particular, bring their problems with them into the afterlife, and may need help working things through. Her spirit contact Hiram explained to her:

Those whom I have not understood come toward me, those whose lives touched me in one way or another. I must enter into dialog with them, apply my new tenderness.... This is the way I must proceed....

I rest a lot. This rest is to give me a chance to meditate within on the truth I am trying to make my own.... Never think that it is easy here when you once enter with the externalization of the wrong truth.[63]

Later on, Hiram told Foster:

The emptiness that my son feels over my death is hard to enter into, but enter into it I must until everything that he feels is my gentle truth. What tenderness opens itself to me! This tenderness is not even close to what I imagined! It helps me in one way, but it hurts me in another. But because I entered into this plane by my own hand, this kind of work is mine.... This entire process, this examination of those who were my family, will not be necessary for everyone, I am told, but it is needed by those who enter this plane as I did—if they want to make progress.[64]

After more time had passed, Jean Foster reported that Hiram had moved past this phase to another, involving different spiritual work. Some of this involved his communicating his truths with her. Hiram stated, "Helping others ... helps me. And telling you, the readers of this book, the way it really is here when you enter by your own hand, helps me too."[65] Later, this soul indicated that it had begun working as a guide to greet other suicides. This appeared to be done as a form of spiritual work that would help it to evolve and progress.

A number of sources emphasize the help provided suicides by spirit doctors and other healers. Highly esteemed veteran British medium Harry Edwards received this message through automatic writing:

> More tragic could be those who were driven to suicide. They would not be damned to all eternity as some religions would have us believe. They would be treated with special loving care, knowing how mentally ill their tortured minds had suffered from troubles that were so real to them, so fearful, that in panic they ended their earthly lives by their own hand. Just as a normal person possesses his character and memory at the passing, so it may be that unfortunate one on coming into the new life could still have the fears and reasons for upset, possibly deep grief.
>
> A feeling mind will be able to create a picture of the treatment the spirit doctors and nurses would give to them; the kind soothing voice, the giving of love to wipe away the effects of cruelties and indignities, the giving of flowers, granting sleep, restoring the strength of personality and confidence, rebuilding their perspective, and providing them with a new avenue of service, possibly nursing or some other form of rendering help.[66]

George Anderson, who has channeled a great many suicides during his career, takes a similar stance, commenting:

> I will state simply and emphatically that according to the souls in the hereafter, no one who commits suicide goes to Hell.... The wisdom of the Infinite Light understands the reasons behind every action taken against oneself or another. The souls in the hereafter who have passed by their own hand tell me time and time again that they were not in the correct frame of mind to consider the gravity of their actions. This in itself is a form of mental illness, which the hereafter would try to reconcile—not punish.[67]

His view is both similar to, and different from, that of Harry Edwards. Anderson explains:

> When souls arrive in the hereafter after having taken their lives, they are immediately taken to a "hospital of reflection" to begin the process of unwinding the turmoil that brought them there. What is interesting about this place is that there are no other humans with whom to create confrontation. It is a place with serene beauty filled with fields and grass. The only beings there are small creatures, like rabbits and fawns, kittens

and puppies. Animals are greatly known both here and hereafter for their ability to heal and their unconditional love. They are used as a kind of therapy for the souls there. When the suicide victims are strong enough, they begin the slow process of understanding and learning with the help of friends, relatives and guides.[68]

Anderson once told a grieving family:

> He says that your husband was sent to what we would consider a very exclusive rest home where he was only around animals for a period of time. There were fawns, dogs, cats and things that he wouldn't feel threatened by, until he basically calmed down, and then Uncle Mike came and visited him again, and asked him if he wanted him to be there to try to work him "out of himself."[69]

John Edward also does not believe that spirits are stuck after suicide. Instead, they continue to grow and move forward with their spiritual state after death. He writes:

> I've had people come through who have ended their own lives, and in some cases they have given me the feeling that they have a spiritual type of therapy going on around them. Even though they are all right—they are not in any kind of limbo, as some might believe—they are trying to understand why they did what they did, and using it in learning their spiritual lessons.... Someone with minimal human success—spiritual, not material, of course—will have to work on his lessons on the Other Side. Our physical lives are analogous to formal schooling. You're better off doing well in school—you'll have a leg up when you graduate—but even if you don't do well, or you drop out (suicide) you can still become a success story. It depends on what you do after you leave school.[70]

It is possible that the circumstances surrounding the suicide can influence how easy it is for the soul to move on and incarnate again. Ruth Montgomery wrote that the spirit of medium Arthur Ford told her from the afterlife:

> Bishop Pike and son, yes. Have seen them both.... They will, of course, review their past lives before becoming eligible for a choice in the matter of environment and parents. The boy will probably get a chance before his father, for although he took his own life he was so doped that he had not intended to, and therefore it is viewed more as an accident than as a deed requiring great penance.[71]

Several spirits have spoken of performing missionary work helping others who have died the same way they did. Carl Wickland and Anne Puryear both describe spirits who volunteered to perform these tasks as part of their spiritual work, helping them to move forward. George Anderson referred to this process in the following:

> Well, everybody has their own specific jobs, but at this point, like in Geoff's case, he's still, it seems, studying himself, like going through a state of reflection and understanding of self, coming to grips with himself and then from then on, he can move on to something else or whatever he wants, helping other people that are in emotional distress over here or over there. It's like in Alcoholics Anonymous, getting help from somebody who's been through it before.[72]

We will later see that this type of spiritual work is not limited to any one form of suicide.

In addition to their "missionary work" with others who are at risk for killing themselves or newly dead by their own hand, suicide souls will sometimes act as guardian angels for loved ones still living. To some extent, this appears to be the role Stephen Puryear played for his mother, Anne.[73] George Anderson also mentions this situation:

> Hindsight being 20/20, these souls who enter the hereafter and have had time to rest and reflect come to the conclusion that their intention was never to hurt those they left on the earth. Although it is only of small consolation to their loved ones still here, they tell me that they will continue as "guardian angels" from their unique vantage point in the hereafter.[74]

In conclusion, contemporary channeled messages make it pretty clear that suicides are not permanently stuck in some unpleasant hell dimension. They may be in limbo for a time, but eventually are able to leave the lower astral plane and advance spiritually—although this may require more help for them to do so than that which is needed by those who have died from other causes. Prayer appears to be a universal method of assistance that can be used by the living or those already in spirit. Sleep, on the other hand, seems to be a common tool for healing by discarnate entities. Although it is a common factor in all transitions, it may be used more extensively, and repeated, for those who have a rough time adjusting to their new state of existence. Finally, spiritual therapy can involve either special tasks assigned to suicides or spirit healing centers, doctors, and other helpers. These methods are often combined to aid a soul in learning those lessons that, from a reincarnation perspective, are needed before they can consider taking on a new life.

THE IMPACT OF SUICIDE ON FUTURE LIVES

The impact of having taken your own life appears to have the potential to carry on into other, future lives. Although some of the earlier Spiritualist literature had real trouble accepting the idea of reincarnation, generally casting aspersions on it, the vast bulk of writings on the afterlife talks about reincarnation quite matter-of-factly. Sources have assorted answers regarding how many lives a soul might have or need—with most saying simply that it varies from one spirit to the next—and whether or not it is possible to incarnate as a plant or animal—with the general consensus indicating this is unlikely, if not impossible.

Some suicides have spoken openly about reincarnation and their hopes for their next lives. The spirit originally identified by medium Jean Foster as Hiram explained at one point that most of the spiritual therapy in the afterlife is oriented toward one goal—"getting ready to return again to earth life.... I know that I must return, and I do not mind that. In fact, I welcome it."[75] Hiram explained:

> Reincarnation gives me hope to overcome my problems. And it gives me hope that those who hurt because of me will also overcome their pain and have more lifetimes that will be happy. Reincarnation is the better outlook, the more hopeful and optimistic outlook.
>
> Yes, I was surprised, but when I get to the point of putting my recent lifetime in perspective, I am told I will remember my other lives, and that it will be more natural to express myself as the sum total of all my lifetimes.[76]

The time suicides spend in the afterlife before incarnating again can apparently differ, but is typically not right away. From his position in the afterlife following his suicide, the spirit of Stephen Puryear noted that most children would not, for example, reincarnate while their families were still alive, because it took too long for them to prepare for a new lifetime.[77]

Between-lives hypnotherapy researcher Michael Newton also speaks of the length of time between incarnations varying based on how often a soul has committed suicide:

> In suicide cases involving healthy bodies, one of two things generally happens to these souls. If they are not a repeat offender, the soul is frequently sent back to a new life rather quickly, at their own request, to make up for lost time. This could be within five years of their death on Earth....
>
> For those who display a pattern of bailing out when things get rough there are places of repentance for a good purpose. These places do not contain a pantheon of horrors in some dark, lower spirit region reserved

for sinners. Rather than being punished in some sort of bleak purgatory, these souls may volunteer to go to a beautiful planetary world with water, trees and mountains but no other life. They have no contact with other souls in these places of seclusion except for sporadic visits by a guide to assist them in their reflections and self-evaluation.[78]

Newton also mentions that souls are sometimes placed in isolation as part of their therapy: "In suicide cases, the soul's guide might offer seclusion, aggressive energy regeneration, a quick return, or some combination of these things."[79] We will later see that energy treatment and placing a soul by itself is also often used with suicide bombers (they do not seem to make the fast transitions that would be needed to rapidly incarnate again).

Of all the books speaking of suicides reincarnating, only one indicates the possibility that repeated suicides, if combined with evil, could eventually lead to a soul being dismantled:[80]

> Dr. John: The soul that ultimately, irretrievably chooses darkness instead of light, that soul shall be taken apart. The energies within it can be used elsewhere, but that soul in its own individual beingness shall be no more. And the Father will weep for every one such....
>
> The question was asked if a series of suicides, lifetime after lifetime, and a soul constantly refusing to live within the light, would cause that one to be recycled. The answer given:
>
> Dr. John: Yes, but I think the key factor perhaps should be viewed a little differently, understood a little differently. It would be the infusion of a soul by evil, by darkness, to the extent where that soul could not be reclaimed by light.[81]

It should be noted that this work (unlike others) also seems to suggest a limit to God's patience, even with souls who had not committed suicide. Loehr states:

> The soul does not continue indefinitely to have incarnations. As. Dr. John has observed, God is frugal in all He does, including bestowing incarnations upon His children. A child which does not learn what earth has to teach it, in perhaps a maximum of 100 incarnations, just isn't going to learn it and gets recycled along with other souls which more deliberately "miss the mark."[82]

This writing, originally published in Florida by "Religious Research Press," seems reminiscent of the older, punitive, biblical approach to spirituality. It is, perhaps, reassuring to realize that other channeled material tends to emphatically disagree with Loehr's "Dr. John," instead emphasizing the Ultimate Source's infinite patience and love.

Considered the leading researcher on reincarnation, University of

Virginia psychiatrist Ian Stevenson's investigative work with children supports the idea that eventually suicides do indeed move on and return to have other lives on Earth.[83] Unfortunately, the suicides' problems may not end when they are born again. Stevenson pointed out a potentially disturbing fact:

> I have often suggested that special interests—for example, in particular foods or activities—may be carried over from one life to another. I think that this may be true also of attitudes toward more important matters such as suicide. If a person thinks he can remedy his difficulties by killing himself, he is not necessarily going to rid himself of this opinion by doing so. If he should survive death and should reincarnate, he is likely to bring that belief with him.[84]

Japanese karmic researcher Hiroshi Motoyama notes that "most children are born ... with a full karmic package."[85] He encountered individuals for whom the seeds of their psychological problems lay in their earlier lives. Motoyama describes the past-life reading of a depressed woman:

> As his daughter she had fallen passionately in love with a young man who was not considered suitable for her station and whom she was not allowed to marry. Her sorrow was so great that it killed her—she committed suicide in her early twenties....
>
> Her tragedy became the basis for her reincarnation in this body.... When she reached the same age now as when the incident had occurred in the former life, her strong affection for her lover and her subsequent sorrow rose to the surface and she became ill.
>
> To dispel her depression, Ms. Y needed to detach from the long-held emotion. She had to recognize that its source was deep in the mind belonging to her past life.[86]

However, Motoyama saw these negative emotional manifestations as being potentially positive events, explaining:

> In Ms. Y's case, the actual experience of the results of the attachment and sorrow which she experienced in her previous life manifests as depression and emotional instability. When karma manifests in this world, when it is functioning, it is in the process of being fulfilled.
>
> The fulfilment [sic] of karma brings the opportunity for one to dissolve it. If one attaches to the results of the present circumstance and tries to suppress its expression, the karma will continue. But if one simply lives out the manifestation without attachment, while making one's best efforts for others for society in whatever position one finds oneself in, the manifest karma will eventually dissolve and be gone. To cite a previous metaphor, it's like opening a bottle of soda. At first there is a lot of

carbonation, but after a few minutes the fizz decreases and finally disappears. If one is alarmed at the explosiveness of the fizz and tries to put the cap back on the bottle, it is like forcing the karma which is on its way to dissolution through manifestation back into its original latent condition. Such repression means one will continue to experience the results of the karma for more lifetimes instead of just getting rid of it.[87]

Interviewed for this book, California psychic and medium Johanna Carroll states that many suicides recognize the need to reincarnate again:

> Many, many times, the suicides choose to reincarnate. And they get really clear on that right away. "I've got to go back. I've got to balance this out." It's sort of a rectification of their mission, in terms of the theme of their life. As a result of that, they'll tell the family member, "This is what I'm going to do right now. I'm probably going to come back, and in order to do that I have to go back to school, whatever. I need to relearn certain things." And a lot of times they will reincarnate within the same family unit so that the family karma can be healed, as well.[88]

When asked to explain the issue of how suicide affects family karma, Carroll explains:

> It's a break in the contract. You know, we have these sacred contacts as individuals and then collectively, based on past life or whatever the intention of the reincarnation is. I mean, we're all part of a whole. And so, we have the family karma contract that collectively we all agree to do our part. The suicide creates what's called a tear in the contract. So that part of it, as the collective energy, needs to be healed. Generally what I found is that suicides really do take ownership for that. They take responsibility for that. And as a result, they realize the importance of the family karma contract, that they do need to come back to heal that in another timeline. Sometimes, depending upon the family member, if there are certain things on the family karma level that this individual did not complete, depending upon how evolved the remaining family member is, they can take on that karma of unfinished business for the suicide that has crossed. It would take a very highly evolved person spiritually to understand that, in my opinion.[89]

The issue of wanting to stay within the same family also came up in a channeling session conducted for this book when an accidental suicide in contact with Lauren Thibodeau was asked about reincarnating:

> Heath: Yes. Is he planning to incarnate again? Has he looked at that?
> Thibodeau: Someday. He's telling me someday. He says he's considering reappearing as his brother's child, it would be his mother's grandson— I'm sorry, granddaughter. He says to see a baby boy would be too much

for her. But he's considering that whole idea of being a granddaughter to his mother.

Heath: Anything special he'd try to accomplish that lifetime, then?

Thibodeau: That way for her. He's claiming people talk about looking into the eyes, the windows of the soul. She'll be able to look into this future baby's eyes and know it's him on a deep, deep level. And this will give her comfort that he lives on. Because her big thing is that he never got to finish out his life. Well, then again, that's kind of judgmental review. He did finish his life. Just not in the way she had hoped. So, he wants to bring her some comfort by doing it that way.[90]

A number of investigations have been done with children who reportedly have spontaneous past-life memories. Some of these may involve individuals who committed suicide during that prior life. For example, Icelandic parapsychologist Erlendur Haraldsson and Lebanese parapsychologist Majd Abu-Izzeddin looked into the story of one Lebanese child who at age 4 began making what appeared to be accurate statements about a former name and life, although he did not describe having hung himself (he said he was shot).[91] This is a bit unusual, as Haraldsson and Abu-Izzeddin pointed out: "It seems common among children who claim to remember a previous life that the imagery of the death scene lasts longer than other memories."[92] They speculate whether the boy (or his soul) could have felt guilt over the fact he had taken his own life and did not wish his family to know about it.

Ian Stevenson notes that of the two thousand participants questioned, twenty-three remembered killing themselves in their former life—four accidentally, two when about to be captured, and seventeen because of social situations.[93] He concludes:

> If we regard reincarnation as the best interpretation for these cases, they disprove the belief expounded in some religions that persons who commit suicide live in Hell for centuries or even for eternity. They also offer for a person considering suicide the thought that it would not end his troubles but only change the location of their occurrence.
>
> Several of the subjects of this group of cases had phobias of the instrument of the suicide, such as guns or poison. The memory of the suicide did not necessarily extinguish the inclination to suicide. For example, three of the subjects, when frustrated as children, made threats of committing suicide to their parents; a fourth actually killed himself in middle life; and a fifth told me that he would probably commit suicide if he found himself in a situation he judged intolerable. On the other hand, another subject (of an unverified case) told me that the memories of a suicide in a previous life had deterred her from killing herself.[94]

More recent data from parapsychologist and psychiatrist Jim Tucker involving the University of Virginia database he has worked on also suggests that these individuals may indeed reincarnate, and some have apparently attended their funerals. He writes:

> I thought I would let you know what we have in our files of cases of children who claim to remember previous lives here at the University of Virginia. We now have 1200 out of 2500 cases logged into the computer database. They are generally being put in by country, so the cases in the computer are not necessarily representative of the whole set, but of the 1200 in there, we have information on the mode of death of the previous personality (the PP) in 996 of them. In 29 of the 996 (2.9%), the PP committed suicide.
>
> In general, these cases seem similar to cases where the PP died by other means. When combining variables, some cases drop out due to lack of information, but here are some stats for you. The suicide subjects made an average of 7.24 verified statements about the previous life compared to 6.39 in the other cases. They began talking about the previous life at an average age of 40.83 months compared to 35.87 months in the other cases. I developed a strength-of-case scale, and the suicides scored 12.89 compared to 11.80 in the others (a higher score indicated a stronger case, but this difference is insignificant).
>
> Seven of the suicide subjects described the life of a deceased family member; 10 described the life of a stranger, and the others described the life of an individual with a connection somewhere in-between. Of the 10 cases where the subject described the life of a stranger, a PP was identified in five of them, and in four of the five, the suicide was independently verified.
>
> Three of the 29 suicide cases reported recalling the PP's funeral or disposition of the body, and details were verified in two of those. Five claimed to remember other events that happened during the interval between the death of the PP and their own birth, and five claimed to remember an existence in another realm. Reports of interval memories are uncommon in all of our cases, so 66 out of 371 cases with other modes of death recalled the funeral, 114 out of 519 recalled other events, and 117 out of 521 recalled an existence in another realm.
>
> To summarize, a quick glance at the database indicates that the suicide cases are essentially indistinguishable from other cases. What this database cannot answer is whether an individual who commits suicide is as likely to be the PP of a future case as other individuals are. They represent 2.9% of our cases, but we don't know the suicide rates in the various regions where these cases occur. Even if we did, we couldn't draw any firm

conclusions since a number of factors may affect whether we learn about and investigate a case.[95]

Past-life regression therapy under hypnosis would seem to support the notion that suicide can affect future lives in more ways than simply through a carry-over of depression.[96] In the case of a woman who had been a Dutch painter in an earlier life, California psychiatrist Roger Woolger notes how the death of a child, which led to a marital breakup and suicide, caused the soul to choose rebirth near the reincarnation of that child:

> P[atient]: Oh, God! I hanged myself. (Sobs deeply.)
> When asked to move forward she spontaneously found herself re-experiencing her birth in this life with the cord wrapped around her neck.
> Full understanding came moments later when, as a baby, she looked up to her mother, having survived the second trauma.
> P: I know why I'm here.
> T[herapist]: Why are you here?
> P: To be close to my mother (sobs). I know who she is now.
> T: Tell me who she is.
> P: She's the baby who died. I see that I've been trying to make it up to her all these years.
> The guilt about the neglect and the death of the baby had been lodged, as an imaginal imprint, at the moment of the Dutch painter's remorseful suicide.[97]

In another case, hypnotic regression to a death involving suicide appeared to give a patient a much greater understanding of her situation, and a chance to do things differently. Contributors Rob Bontenbal and Tineke Noordegraaf transcribed a woman's insight during such a session:

> C[lient]: Oh my God. This is really the worst thing you can do. Killing yourself. It does not solve anything. I know now. I am still having these feelings. Lately even more. With my boyfriend in this life it's almost the same. It started out all right, we had a good time together, but not the relationship has grown distant, cold, like all positive feelings have gone, I am just repeating it....
> T[herapist]: Knowing all that, what does it mean for your present situation?
> C: First of all: never, never commit suicide again. And second: talk to my boyfriend about ending the relationship or give it a new try. It makes me feel better to say that. Like a new start.[98]

Michael Newton reports that during the evaluation phase after a life, suicides are sometimes shown alternative possible outcomes—what could have happened had they not taken their own lives. After one such session, a man who recalled killing himself in a previous lifetime stated:

> It was a waste to kill myself. I know it now. I think I knew it all along. Right after I died I said to myself, "God, that was a stupid thing to do, now I'm going to have to do it all over again!" When I went before my council they asked if I would like to be retested soon. I said, "Let me think about it awhile."[99]

Hickman writes of a similar case she had involving a depressed widow, where dredging up a past life memory of suicide seemed to mark a therapeutic turning point:

> After all the old former-life emotions had been dredged up, fully expressed, and the old pressures relieved, she became able to see why the former pattern was repeating. She had given herself a failing grade for her reaction to her earlier widowhood and had chosen to repeat the course. Now she was almost failing again. Through regression she came to a new awareness that she had to learn the lesson of acceptance of loss and that her earlier non-acceptance and suicide had been for selfish reasons. "I don't want to hurt!"
>
> Having gained this insight, she became able to accept and live creatively and contentedly.... I followed her progress for several years and was gratified to watch her life becoming full and more joyous.[100]

Thus, we have seen that most channeled material seems to take reincarnation for granted. This can be a positive thing, as it tells us that we have more than one chance to succeed at life. This becomes even more important when a person "fails" by taking his or her own life. Unfortunately, suicide sometimes appears to have a detrimental effect on future lives. Souls may carry with them the habit pattern of wanting to opt out of life. In recent years, some past-life therapists have been able to turn this around, bringing up memories what happened before in order to help their clients let go of negative behavior patterns and ways of thinking. In these cases, the previous suicide can actually become a positive impetus for doing things differently this time around. However, it should also be noted that many who have taken their own lives are reluctant to return again, and once again have to face the situation that they failed at before.

8

Messages of Regret

We know that society discourages suicide. But what do the people who have been successful say about it? The paranormal channeling of such information may give us a unique perspective on the situation. Not all mediums say the same thing. But certain types of messages appear repeatedly, and frequently involve regrets. As one spirit put it, referring to another that had committed suicide, "He has been in hell, not a hell of fire, but a hell of ignorance."[1] Another soul commented, "I'm tied to my regrets. Yet they are showing me the way out."[2] The spirit, Acharya, summed up the problem in the following passage:

> The taking of one's own life is not only a crime, but is also an extremely foolish act. You do not solve your difficulties by running away from them, but merely postpone their solution for a future life. ... he is merely delaying his own evolution, and until he has faced and overcome these obstacles and thus learned the lessons they were meant to teach him, he cannot advance any further on the journey toward perfection. Extreme remorse usually follows an act of suicide, and within a very short time of their arrival in the astral world, the majority of suicides would give anything to undo their action. Unfortunately, they cannot go back, but must wait until the time arrives for their next incarnation, and they are left in no doubt whatever that in their next life they will have to face the same difficulties.[3]

Although regret is not unique to the communications from suicides, it is seen far more commonly than in messages from souls who passed on from other causes.[4]

It should be noted that one thing some suicides do not always regret is the fact they are dead. As Johanna Carroll notes:

> In some cases, they'll say it was the only solution because they feel, once they've crossed over, that they lived with a limited vision. That their vision on their life was limited. Whenever I get into that, and I can feel it now, it's like heavy, heavy boulders weighing down on the shoulders, like life is really oppressive, just pushing them down. And whenever that memory or that picture of life comes up ... there's so much energy focused on

everything being wrong, that life is just so incredibly heavy. Like it hurts to even wake up in the morning.[5]

There are a number of types of regret expressed by these souls, including for those left behind, being dead, wasted potential, karmic backsliding, and the manner of their death. Furthermore, we will see the issue of regret again in a later chapter, as it makes up a large part of what suicides would tell others who want to follow in their footsteps.

REGRET FOR WHAT HAPPENS TO THOSE LEFT BEHIND

A common regret expressed by suicides is for the harm done to those left behind and the grief this action causes for the living. It should be noted that this may not be unique to suicides. John Edward comments that he sees this kind of regret with other forms of sudden death:

> There is also a sense of sorrow for the people they left behind. This is not to say such feelings are unique to those who have committed suicide. I have had many spirits who passed from the physical state in "natural" ways, or in accidents, come through conveying to me that they are working on those same kinds of lessons.[6]

Nonetheless, regret would appear to be even more prominent after suicide, compounded by the guilt of knowing that they had only themselves to blame. A typical comment comes from a woman who hung herself, who said through a medium:

> I would have given the world to have been able to regain possession of my body. Oh, what horrors of despair and remorse I have gone through! My home shattered, my husband broken-hearted and discouraged, and my little ones needing my care!
> They do not know that I come to them and try to comfort them, and I have seen nothing but gloom and darkness until now.[7]

Another example of this remorse was channeled by Lysa Mateu:

> The moment I put the gun to my temple, the moment I pressed my finger against the trigger, I forgot ... how much I love my son—how much life is worth living—how tomorrow could have been better. If the image of my son had entered my mind, even for a moment, I could not have killed myself. I had to completely block what was good, and focus solely on my pain....
> The moment I died—the light came on, and I remembered....
> I'm sorry ... so sorry, for the pain I've caused.[8]

As noted in the chapter Overview of Traditional Suicide, suicide can sometimes have a domino effect. In these cases, there may be regret for the fact that their suicide led another person to take his or her own life. One case of this involves a daughter whose mother, first, and then her father, committed suicide. James Van Praagh notes, for the daughter, "Your mother felt awful about your dad. She is going on about how she felt responsible."[9] Of the father, Van Praagh notes, "He is going on about how stupid he was."[10] Later, the soul became more specific:

> "Your dad shot himself through his left temple. He says you know this. Is that right?"
> "Yes, I was the one who found him...."
> "Oh, I'm so sorry. That is awful. Your dad says to tell you that he was wrong. He didn't know how to go on without your mother. He said he also didn't want to be a burden to you and John. You had your own lives.... Your dad is saying he didn't have to wait around too long over there because his life was close to an end anyway."[11]

Rarely, regrets may involve legal trouble that the suicide inadvertently causes for the living. In a bid for attention gone wrong, where a young man was inappropriately accused of murder, the spirit stated:

> "I did it! I did it! Nobody can help me now. If I only could tell them and make them understand—but they will not listen. I am in the dark and can see only the past and everything foolish I have done. Oh, what a foolish girl I was!"
> "What is your name?"
> "Marion Lambert."
> "Where do you think you are?"
> "I do not know. I am not acquainted with any one here. (Crying.) They talk of hell, but that could not be as bad as what I have gone through, just because of my foolishness. I would like very much to get out of all this trouble...."
> "I'm half crazy with trouble and worry...."
> "I am in such agony, I don't know what to do...."
> "Everything is so dark and I am in such trouble."[12]

In a similar case, the spirit stated to Carl Wickland:

> I didn't mean to do anything. I was just going to frighten him. It was just foolishness, foolishness, foolishness....
> I don't know anything, except that I go to mother and Harry, and all over, and no one pays any attention to me. I want to tell them how things happened, but no one will listen to me, not any one. I am so distressed, and I don't know why I cannot be heard when I talk. I am so unhappy....

> Oh, how I suffered! I do not see how I could be dead, because when you die you never suffer any more, and I have suffered.[13]

In another instance, Wickland describes the emotional regret of a woman who shot herself:

> Dr: How long have you been dead?
> Sp: (Hysterically.) Forgive me, A! Oh, forgive me!
> Dr: Calm yourself and we will help you understand your condition.
> Sp: Oh, I didn't mean to kill myself!
> Dr: Did you take your own life?
> Sp: Yes. (Crying distractedly.)
> Dr: You did not destroy your spirit, you only destroyed your body....
> Sp: Forgive me, forgive me, oh, A....
> Dr: You are in the dark.
> Sp: I can see my mother crying all the time....
> Dr: Try to collect yourself and listen to me. We can help you if you will become quiet.
> Sp: Poor A!
> Dr: Who is A?
> Sp: He's my husband. I love him so. If only I could get to him....
> Dr: What did you do?
> Sp: I was so sick. My poor husband and mother! They are mourning and mourning. I got free, and now I can't tell them I am free. I am so sick and worried.[14]

James Van Praagh says of a young man who hanged himself:

> Andy says he waited around not sure of what to do. He saw his dad find him, and he was so upset. Andy realized immediately that what he did was wrong. He felt badly for you and his father. He watched his father tell you and saw you break down. He heard your thoughts about how you always knew this was going to happen. He also felt your feelings of love. He felt quite horrible about the way he made you feel.[15]

Physical pain may vanish when the body is dead, but the spirit can be left with a mental anguish that is far worse, and not so easily assuaged. A spirit known as Jay said:

> I just made the biggest mistake of my life.
> That's what caused me pain....
> Watching Ben, my friend's face as it came through the bathroom door. That's what caused me pain.
> For the first time in my life, I truly knew what it felt like to be in another's shoes....
> Regret cannot even describe the immensity of what I felt.[16]

Anne Puryear writes that her dead son Stephen told her:

> I could feel your hurting inside, your heart inside my heart. I had never hurt so bad, *ever*....
>
> I wished I could go back and not jump....
>
> I felt sick. I wished I could kill myself to stop hurting.... I hated what I had done to you. I never realized how much I loved my home and the girls and Bob. I wanted to be back....
>
> I began to cry. I couldn't stop.... I cried and cried. It hurt so bad.[17]

He later described how he felt the pain and sorrow of those left behind:

> My grief was like the combination of the grief of everybody in the family. I felt it all. I hadn't meant to hurt anyone.... When I felt and saw each of you grieving, it was as if I were a sponge—I soaked it all up. I wanted to console each of you, but there was absolutely nothing I could do. Your grief and lack of attunement kept you from hearing me....
>
> There is nothing we can do. Nothing! It's the most awful feeling because you would give *anything* if you could go back and undo your death and you can't, ever. There is no place which is hell as such, but the pain we feel creates our own hell emotionally, for a long time.[18]

George Anderson describes a case where, "he admits he commits suicide. Now he realizes that is the worst thing he could have done, not that he's in agony or suffering over there, but he realized that it caused more harm."[19] A milder comment comes from Arthur Ford: "James, Jr., through the medium, expressed regret for his suicidal act. He didn't mean to hurt anybody and wished he hadn't done it."[20]

Ruth Taylor gives an example where one spirit communicated to a daughter that her father "had been deeply grieved over his suicide and its effects on your family. He was so remorseful that he had great difficulty adjusting to these spiritual realms."[21] Suzane Northrop similarly speaks of another young suicide:

> Jennifer repeated throughout the session her regret for not having the strength to confront and deal with her pain and her shame for the suffering she caused her family. She hadn't realized, she said, that this was one mistake you can't undo.[22]

In some cases, the sorrow is more for who found them and how that experience is going to affect that person's life. Lauren Thibodeau reports such a feeling for a soul who had died through autoeroticism:

> Now I'm with the one who had the six-year-old find him. That young man is not as well adjusted. And it's because of his little brother, he says.

"He needs me. He needs me." He keeps saying, "He needs me." And real weighty kind of sorrow about this, that his brother found him. Because that is a traumatic experience that will shape his brother, he says, forevermore. And it does. And he will. That's the thing that he didn't want to use the word regrets exactly, but that he's really sad about. Not having foreseen that particular consequence....

He's not sorry he's dead. ... he regrets the effects of the ramifications but not the act. He's sorry people are hurting, but not sorry for the act. And he's kind of giving this sigh of relief feeling. It's nice to be able to say that. Because it's true. I try to convey that kind of thing sometimes in my work and people don't want to hear it. They want to hear "I'm sorry." But often times, more often than not, the people aren't sorry. They're regretful of the consequences of their free will choice but not regretful of the choice.[23]

Remorse is not always expressed through a medium. Sometimes the message can be passed on during altered states of consciousness, such as dreaming. In one case, a woman spoke of her brother Chet:

His suicide was so sudden! It was awful. My parents just couldn't bear it. I was the oldest child and had to handle his funeral and everything.

Maybe six months later, he came to me in a dream and we talked face to face. He was extremely sad because of what he had done to his family.

I remember Chet had a melancholy and confused look on his face. He was very sorry because we were all hurting—because we were all going through this pain. He didn't want to put us through that. He seemed remorseful and bewildered. He hung his head and shook it, like he just couldn't believe what he had done.[24]

There are also cases of expression in the hypnogogic and hypnopompic states—psi-conducive states that occur between being wide awake and asleep. Guggenheim and Guggenheim report the following story, which also points out the gulf that can sometimes exist between making an apology and receiving forgiveness:

This was the first Christmas Eve after my brother killed himself. I had gone to bed and had been asleep maybe three or four hours. I remember being awakened, and I knew Kirk was in the room—I could physically feel it.

I was really scared for a couple of seconds, and then I could see Kirk, peripherally, off to my left. I knew it was him! His face was dark and shadowed, but he looked as solid and real as could be.

I said I was glad to see him and wanted to talk to him. But all Kirk said was, "I'm sorry. I'm sorry I did that. I didn't want to hurt anybody. I'm sorry." I started to get panicky because I didn't want him to leave me again after such a short, quick visit. Then he was gone....

Kirk could apologize a thousand times for putting us through hell, and it still wouldn't make it any better.[25]

Another interesting way that people can learn of the regret a suicide experiences after having performed an irrevocable act is through past-life recall. Winifred Lucas reported that individuals undergoing hypnotherapy sessions for past lives involving suicide sometimes expressed regrets centering around those left behind. In the case of one soul who had overdosed, the person remembered the children: "I can't move anymore. They are crying. I feel terrible. I have let them down. I want to stop it. But I can't, I can't anymore!"[26]

In another case, a woman undergoing hypnotherapy screamed and moaned for several minutes before stating:

> I see my body hanging by a rope from the rafters. I see my baby crawling across the floor and reaching up toward the body. I see my real self over in the corner observing the scene and helpless to do anything about it.[27]

As the therapist noted, "When her real self saw what she had done, that she had not really died but had merely deserted her helpless child, the guilt became even more overpowering."[28]

Regret over what will happen to those left behind appears to be a large part of what suicides would communicate to others. Not only is remorse mentioned frequently in the channeling literature, but may also appear in dreams sent to the living or as past-life memories. The regrets themselves can center around a variety of issues, including the grief, guilt, sadness, legal troubles (being blamed for the death of the person who committed suicide), or abandonment of those left behind. Unfortunately, most souls only seem to realize their mistake when it is too late to undo it—often mere moments after they have taken their own lives.

REGRET OVER BEING DISCARNATE

The regret expressed by a suicide may be simply that he or she no longer has a body. Many spirits report that as soon as they've crossed over and realize what has happened to them, they regret being dead. It is almost as if they didn't quite realize the permanence of their actions. Ena Twigg channeled a girl who had killed herself at age 17 by using gas; the girl is reported saying, "I didn't want to die. I wanted to live. I wanted to get married and I found I had killed my body and I couldn't get back."[29]

Michael Newton notes: "When I work with clients who have committed suicide in former lives, the first thing most exclaim right after the moment of death is, 'Oh, my God, how could I have been so stupid!'"[30] This seems indeed to be a common reaction.

Many of the souls of suicides Lysa Mateu channeled have been eloquent when speaking of their regrets. One spirit, called Jess, explained:

> The pain I feel at not being able to let them know I am there ... torments my soul even more than when I was alive.
> When I was alive, I wanted to be invisible.
> Now that I am dead, I feel more visible than ever and just when I want people to see me—They cannot.[31]

Thus, what the suicide thought it wanted was not what the soul had truly wished for after all. These sad realizations are a common thread in many of the expressions of regret we see.

Another spirit, known as Charley, stated through Lysa:

> I wanted to go back to the life I had chosen to leave.
> But I could not.
> I was stuck with my decision.
> I had thought that life on the other side would be free from life as it were on earth. I now know that life is life, no matter where it occurs. And what better place to play it out than on earth, where I could have materialized the visions I had in my mind and impacted the world in a way that now, I cannot.[32]

Arthur Ford felt suicides often deeply regretted their act as soon as they realized they were successful.[33] Sometimes this regret and panic over being dead could spill over into dramatic psychokinetic events. In one case:

> On discovering his plight, he was desperate. He produced every kind of poltergeist effect within his power—smashing things, disarranging clothing, moving objects, bending and distributing safety pins, moving books that would call attention to his memory—all to attract help in his plight.[34]

One might also recall the earlier mentioned story of Charley, who had a similar kind of psychokinetic event, and said:

> My actions were so automatic, so blatantly carved from the pain of my soul that my energy caused a wooden dragon statue to come crashing to the floor. It tumbled on its side and its neck broke off.[35]

Another case of accidental suicide involved a 14-year-old boy named Nicholas.[36] He, too, was scared and apologetic. Although we will later see a number of instances where the dead return to comfort the living, in this case, it was the living who reassured the dead. Bill and Judy Guggenheim were told the following story:

> My son, Nicholas, was afraid of going to a big high school. He told a friend he was going to take some pills, just enough to make himself sick, so he wouldn't have to go to that school. But he went too far and died.
> The night after Nicholas died, I went to bed and heard noises in his room. I felt pulled to go there, so I got up and went to his room and sat on his bed. I said, "Okay, here I am. What is it that you want from me?" I was so angry with him!
> It was like Nicholas's very soul was there—his presence dominated the whole room. He said, "Mom, I'm so sorry for what I did. I didn't mean to do it. I'm so frightened!"
> I said, "Nicholas, go find Grandpa. He'll take care of you. It will be all right. Just find him."[37]

We have seen that sometimes the thoughts expressed by suicides may be a simple message, that they were sorry they did it and regret no longer having a body. Many of them do not seem to have understood the permanence of their actions, or considered that they might soon long for the very thing that they had thrown away—their body.

REGRET FOR WASTED POTENTIAL

Another kind of remorse spoken of by suicides is for that which did not get completed in life—in essence, their wasted potential. This does not come up as frequently as sorrow for those left behind or regret that they no long have a physical body. Nonetheless, it does come up. An example of this kind of thought was purportedly communicated in the early 1900s from a poet, long dead, who had committed suicide:

> My only regret, which is useless, is that I played the Judas to my quality, that I failed to contribute to the common whole of my degree here the gift of quantity. The potentiality of my quality would have made it possible for me to have offered something not unworthy.[38]

Lysa Mateu quotes Charley as saying:

> You have a mission that was created especially for you.... We failed that mission by cutting our lives short.
> Don't you see, we cannot get out of what is ours to fulfill. Now we have the double task of finishing our mission through someone on earth and of learning the lessons we thought we had left behind.[39]

Hiram expressed remorse for the fact that he had not demonstrated lovingness during his lifetime. The spirit noted sadly:

> Thoughts that gave me pain showed me that the people I had thought did not care really entered into the purest kind of caring for me. That was the truth that was hardest to bear.... Would I ever want to repeat this misadventure? No! The next lifetime experience must be one of demonstrating tenderness.[40]

Johanna Carroll also speaks of suicides having regret for their unfinished business:

> Well, they regret that they weren't able to complete their life cycle. They really regret holding onto so much pain and not seeing their life in a larger context. Again, it gets back to the karma of the family. It's really not "I'm sorry I hurt you." It's like "I'm sorry I didn't accomplish what I really originally intended to accomplish."[41]

Regret for that which was not completed in life was not particularly mentioned in older channeled material, suggesting there may be greater awareness of, or belief in, the idea that lives are chosen as a way of learning certain lessons. This tends to go along with an acceptance of reincarnation and karma, and may overlap with our next topic—regret for karmic backsliding.

REGRET FOR KARMIC BACKSLIDING

Souls who accept karma and reincarnation as a fact may talk about regretting the effect their suicide has had on their spiritual progress. They indicate that performing suicide represents a setback in karmic progress, and can undo whatever good work they had performed prior to that point, making their life a wasted one. A spirit going by the name of Moses stated through his receiver, Glenn Johnson, that:

> A physical body is a gift from God to a spirit being. In accepting a physical body a spirit has a responsibility to protect the functions of that body.... Therefore, when the intent of a spirit being is to protect its physical body, or the environment needed for its body to function in, these acts would carry less negative karma than not protecting its body....
>
> To us on this side of the veil the physical body is of little value, but to the spirit being that is in a physical body on Earth, that body is of the utmost importance. It is through the functions of its physical body that a spirit being can proceed with the missions of that lifetime. It is true that a spirit being can be given another body and start a new incarnation, but it cannot be given more time....
>
> The spirit beings who do not progress within the required time will become nothing.[42]

This passage suggests that killing oneself has negative karmic implications and that there can sometimes be a time limit on advancement. It should be noted that the latter issue is fairly unique to Moses, and does not come up in most channeled material.

Other mediums have also spoken of the fact that suicide can have bad spiritual consequences. James Van Praagh notes:

> To this day, I have not had one spirit come through and tell me it is happy with its decision, nor would it commit such an act again. Quite the contrary. All suicide victims share a sense of regret for the crime committed against their soul. I can say all of those who have come back have warned others not to repeat their mistakes. The suicide act slowed their spiritual progress, and they had a very difficult time forgiving themselves.[43]

Sometimes this karmic backsliding may be related to the purported spiritual benefits of suffering, which has possible implications for those who would perform assisted suicide, as well. The spirit guide Silver Birch also explained that life's trials serve a crucial role—they help the soul to evolve to a stronger, higher quality of existence. Without such trials, the soul would stagnate or decay. Thus, Silver Birch noted:

> Every experience is part of the pattern of your life....
> The events in your lives, sometimes of bitterness and despair, of pain and misery, all play their part in preparing the soul....
> There is no experience that comes to the human soul, which, rightly understood and rightly faced, does not leave you better for it.[44]

Silver Birch also stated that suicide is not without cost for the soul. It requires a longer period to adjust and creates a gulf that separates the soul from its loved ones.

In a few cases, we are given specific examples of how taking their own life has set souls back, undoing any prior spiritual progress that they had made. Arthur Ford, as a discarnate spirit, explained:

> Hemingway made great progress as Ernest Hemingway the writer, even though there was still some remaining thirst for brutality and excitement for the sake of exciting passions. But the unfortunate method by which his life ended, has somewhat undone the tremendous advance that he had made. He will be working on this for some time yet. He had everything: fame, friends, wealth, talent. But he took his own life. Must never do it![45]

Thus, karmic backsliding has the potential to affect what choices a suicide may have for future lives. When souls speak about how death was not a solution (see the next chapter), they often mention sadly that they will have to repeat the same course over again, as many times as needed until they have mastered it. Spirits do not look forward to again facing such difficult lifetimes. Joel Whitton and Joe Fisher state, "People who commit suicide are frequently seized with a feeling of dread in the interlife; they know they must return to cope with the level of difficulty that led to their premature departure from the Earth plane."[46]

Michael Newton observes of the souls he hypnotically regressed to the period between lives:

> I never cease to admire the brutal honesty of souls. When a soul has led a productive life beneficial to themselves and those around them, I notice they return to the spirit world with enthusiasm. However, when subjects like Case 13 report they wasted a past life, especially from early suicide, then they describe going back rather dejected.[47]

Furthermore, this dread that souls may feel toward their next life may be with good cause. Whitton and Fisher note that in the case of one woman who had viewed several past lives through hypnosis she had a "penchant for suicide, which, as reincarnation investigators such as Dr. Ian Stevenson have shown, can exert a domino effect from life to life."[48]

Jane and Peter Boulton report the following channeled conversation, which seems to indicate that suicide may not always have the same consequences:

> BH [the authors' adopted daughter]: Is suicide ever justified or forgiven without paying a heavy karmic debt?
>
> S: This again depends upon the motive. There can be times when suicide is necessary for that particular entity to leave the earth plane., for the problems have become so overwhelming that he would do nothing but deteriorate from that point on.
>
> In this case, it is possible that the body be released. The spirit, however, does remain near the earth for a time, and it causes that one to have more difficulty in trying to work out those problems given to it. However, it does, in time, reach forward.[49]

It should be noted that not all channeled material supports the idea that suicide is a form of karmic backsliding. When asked about whether death by self-immolation carries the same penalties as suicide or earns a reward because of its selfless (if sometimes mistaken) motive, the spirit of Gildas said:

> Even such apparent "crimes" as suicide can be seen as part of the learning process, motive being all-important....

Death by burning always causes difficulties in the transition period between one plane and another, but there is usually a karmic factor involved.[50]

This is interesting because it suggests that some forms of suicide are due to karma, instead of leading to greater problems in future lives.

Channeled messages sometimes discuss how suicide can affect karma (or rarely, be a result of it). Where future karma is concerned, the reasons leading up to the taking of one's own life appear to be important, with unselfish reasons having possibly a lesser impact. Nonetheless, the majority of souls recognize that their suicide represented a form a failure, and they do not look forward to having to face the same challenges again in their next life.

REGRET FOR THEIR MANNER OF DEATH

Not all suicides express the previous regrets. Some are glad that they are dead and do not mind that they have left others behind. Nor do they feel bad about unfinished business or karmic backsliding—they just wanted out. However, even these souls sometimes speak of a wish that they had departed in a different way.

One of the earlier of these messages comes to us from F. W. H. Myers.[51] This involved a message received through a planchette on June 26th, 1889. The spirit, an ex-soldier, stated:

> I killed myself on Christmas Day, years ago. I wish I had died fighting.... I did not fail. I was not slandered. Too much for me after ... pen was too much for me after the wound. I was wounded in the head in Peninsula. It will be forty-four years next Christmas Day since I killed myself. Oh, my head.... I killed myself. John Gurwood.[52]

Myers later confirmed that a Colonel Gurwood, who had successfully led the storming of Ciudad Rodrigo in 1812, had killed himself on Christmas Day in 1845. It was thought that his job editing dispatches had led to a fatal depression. One of the more notable features of this account is that the spirit's sorrow for the manner of his death would seem to have lasted for over four decades.

There have been a number of similar messages of regret in the years since that time. James Van Praagh channeled a woman who shot herself and notes the soul "mentioned to her friend that the memory of her death still haunted her but that she was getting help from people in spirit."[53]

Finally, souls may have some regret for the way they died because it leads to a loss of face in the afterlife. Michael Newton reports of traditional suicides:

> These souls tell me they feel somewhat diminished in the eyes of their guides and group peers because they broke their covenant.... There is a loss of pride from a wasted opportunity.... Particularly when a young, healthy person commits suicide, our teachers consider this an act of gross immaturity and the abrogation of responsibility.... They have infinite patience with us, but with repeated suicide offenders their forgiveness takes on another tone.
>
> I worked with a young client who had tried to commit suicide a year before I saw him. During our hypnosis session we found evidence of a pattern of self-destruction in former lives. Facing his master teachers at a council meeting following his last life, this client was told by an Elder:
>
> Once again you are here early and we are disappointed. Have you not learned the same test grows more difficult with each new life you terminate? Your behavior is selfish for many reasons, not the least of which is the sorrow you caused to those left behind who loved you. How much longer will you continue to just throw away the perfectly good bodies we give you? Tell us when you are ready to stop engaging in self-pity and underestimating your capabilities.[54]

Accidental suicide while performing autoeroticism seemed to be another common (although not universal) cause for regretting the manner of their death. This may in part be due to the impact it has on the survivors. As Lauren Thibodeau notes:

> I'm used to the anger of suicide, the strong emotions—the grief and pain and sorrow and loss, and all of it—but [for] this group there is an even bigger piece of it. They ache in a way that I don't see survivors of suicides generally aching, which is tough.[55]

Thibodeau has channeled a number of these souls. With one 14-year-old who had killed himself in this manner, she reports he was "incredibly sorrowful.... I shouldn't say more than usual, but it *feels* like that. Deep, deep regret here."[56] She touched on the subject again when discussing what the guides do after greeting those who have taken their lives accidentally during autoeroticism: "It's healing and energizing and helping them, I want to say, 'stop the sobbing.' Because there's real, real sadness and grief. These people, this was never their intention. Even remotely. It was supposed to be a joyful thrill."[57]

Hence, we see that even if suicides have no other regrets, they may feel bad about the way in which they died.

REGRET FOR THEIR CONTINUED EXISTENCE

One of the rarer forms of regret expressed by souls is that for their continued consciousness. They wish death had been the permanent oblivion and nonexistence that they had longed for when they took their own life. James Padgett recounts what he was told by the soul of an old friend, Perry, who had killed himself:

> I want to tell you that if I only again could shoot myself and by that means end my existence—I mean annihilate my spirit and soul so they would go into nothingness—I would gladly and quickly pull the trigger and send the bullet into that spot which would bring about the desired effect. But I realize now I must continue to exist and suffer—for how long I don't know, but it seems to me forever and ever. Oh, why did I do such a thing? I had no occasion to take my life....
>
> I thought that death was an end of all, and that in the grave I would know nothing and sleep in utter oblivion.[58]

Another soul, Hiram, also regretted his continued consciousness—at least at first—but for several months denied sorrow that he had killed himself. He stated:

> The body is now dead, thank God! The body enters into dust. Death opened the door for me to enter this new, this most real and eternal life here. Get this thought straight.
>
> There is no regret for what I did. There is only tenderness for those who grieve so bitterly....
>
> There is not regret.... This is where I belong.[59]

Hiram admitted that at the time of his death he was unhappy to realize that it had not accomplished what he had intended—a cessation of consciousness. He remembered:

> What a disappointment.... Nothing had changed! This thing called "death" had not brought me the expected peace of mind.
>
> Nothing had changed. Think of that! Nothing had changed. "Betrayed by my own hand," I thought. Tormented by my own inability to function in earth life, the entity who entered this plane tried to enter into thoughts of temporary peace, but nothing worked.[60]

Even this soul, after several months of working with his guides, later admitted that what he had done was probably not a good idea. He said:

> My way is now lighter and brighter than it was in the beginning. But I see for a fact that it is not as easy to start over as I thought it was the last time I reported on my life here....

No use in glossing over the life here. No use in giving false hope to others.[61]

This chapter has looked at the various messages of remorse which suicides come back to express to the living. These tend to fall in a variety of categories, including regret for: (1) what happens to those left behind, (2) no longer having a body, (3) their wasted potential—all the things they might have done in life but did not do, (4) karmic backsliding, (5) the manner of their deaths, and (6) their continued existence. Traditional suicides typically report at least one, and sometimes a mixture of, these regrets. Furthermore, we will see next that they make up a large part of what suicides want to get across to those still living who want to kill themselves.

9

Messages to the Suicidal

Suicides often have a lot to say about whether others should follow in their footsteps. The most frequently repeated theme is simply "Don't do it!" They tell us that suicide is a very bad idea, and one they regret having acted upon. This sentiment is often combined with other messages, such as that life is worthwhile, death is not a solution, the importance of love, accepting responsibility for your choices, and being aware that there is help available. We will look at each of these topics in turn. However, it should be noted that because they tend to be combined in messages, there will be a certain amount of overlap.

SUICIDE IS A BAD IDEA

The simplest message received from one suicide to another thinking about it is not to do it. Taking your own life is a very bad idea, and one that spirits do not recommend to others. One woman reported a dream message that said just that:

> My sister, Peggy, had been treated for depression since she was sixteen. She was an alcoholic and died of an overdose of prescription drugs when she was twenty-one. My mother, who was a recovering alcoholic, had been extremely depressed her whole life. And finally, at age fifty, she committed suicide, too.
> After breaking up with my boyfriend, I was overwhelmed and couldn't continue with the pain I was feeling. I was in a deep depression and decided that I wanted to die. So I drank a whole bunch of alcohol, told my cats good-bye, and wrote a note to my family before I fell asleep.
> Just before waking up in the morning, I had a dream that I got a phone call from my mom. I recognized her voice as she said, "Sally, don't do it! Don't do it!" She was loving, but pleading. That was all she said to me, but it was really powerful!
> I used this experience to turn my life around.[1]

D. D. Home recounted an incident in the mid-1800s, when the spirit of a child managed to stop her still-living father from taking his own life:[2]

I well remember a poor man being present one evening, and the spirit of a little girl coming with the following message. "Father, dear, your little Mary was present last Wednesday, and God gave her power to prevent you from doing what you wished. If you were ever to do that, you could not come where your own Mary and her mother are. Promise me you will never think of such an awful thing again." We all looked astonished, but could not understand to what she alluded. Still it was evident the poor father knew too well, for throwing himself on his knees, he said, as the tears rolled down his cheeks, "Indeed, it is but too true, that on Wednesday last I decided to cut my throat; but as I took the razor to do it, I felt that had my child been alive, she would have shrunk from me with horror, and this very thought was the saving of me."[3]

The spirit of a daughter who had killed herself stated through a medium at a séance:

"Do not let any influences whisper to you to commit such an act. Be strong and overcome."

"Do you know the consequences of taking your own life? I wish I could impress them firmly on your minds." "When you have committed suicide, you stand there, looking at your own body and you cannot, cannot, control it again. You thought you were in trouble before, but now—!"

"What misery to see your body lying there and realize that because of your own deed you can never control it again!"

"You see people in great distress standing around your body; your relatives are crying and you are helpless. You are left alone, in darkness, because you took your own life. You are alone with your thoughts."

"There is no death; the spirit lives on after dissolution takes place."

"I wish to emphasize that if troubles come to you, do not shun them; face them. Be brave and do all you can to meet them. Do not destroy your physical body. Do not be a coward and run away from trouble."

"Learn to live rightly. Your sorrow is only a phase through which your [sic] are passing."[4]

The idea that it's not worth it to take the risk of killing yourself through autoeroticism also came up in the interview with medium Thibodeau about a child who died during an autoerotic event:

Heath: Okay. And if he could come back and talk to other kids, what would he tell them?

Thibodeau: The first thing I hear is "Listen to my mother. Listen to the pain of a mother." And that no sexual gratification—he's giving me the word "high"—no high is worth that.[5]

A different child who had died the same way had specifically mentioned that he did not regret being dead, but he had a surprisingly similar message:

Heath: Well, what would he tell other kids who are thinking about exercising their free will?

Thibodeau: "Think about your mom. Think about your little brother. What if your little brother were to find you? That's what I would tell them," he tells me. "Think about what that would do, even if you think you hate your little brother or your little sister. Think about what would happen."

Heath: And what would happen?

Thibodeau: The pain it would cause them. Think about the emotional pain. The grief. Think about the consequences of having to live every day of your life saying "I used to have a brother." And then I just feel this deep sorrow again, like he really, really, *really* aches for his little brother.[6]

If there is one common theme among the messages that come to us from suicides, it is simply to tell others not to do what they did, that taking your own life is a bad idea and one they will regret. We will see this thought come up repeatedly in the next sections, combined with other sentiments.

LIFE IS WORTH LIVING

The message not to commit suicide can sometimes be accompanied by a reminder that life is worth living. A hint of this comes to us from Carl Wickland, where a spirit stated, "There is beauty around you if you will only look for it."[7] Another such message was passed from a soul who had committed suicide to her grandson in the following dream:

My girlfriend had left me, and I was extremely depressed for three weeks. I contemplated suicide and was at the end of my rope....

That night, I had this dream right before I woke up. I was all alone in a very empty place. It was like a great hall that had no beginning and no end, no doorways and no windows. It was total emptiness.

My grandmother came up to me. She put her arms around me and kissed me on the cheek. She told me, "Your life is worthwhile. Don't give up your life because of someone else. You have everything to live for and many things to do. Go out and be yourself. You'll love again, so live and enjoy yourself!"

I woke up and I felt better than I had in three weeks. This experience did me a world of good. I no longer felt the pain inside.

I had never met my grandmother before. I had only seen two pictures of her in my life. But I knew of her accomplishments and I knew how she had died. She had committed suicide about forty years earlier!

Taking my own life was not worth the pain and suffering I would have put myself through and everybody else around me. My grandmother came because I needed somebody to tell me that. She knew what her death had done to my mother and father.

In a way she was saying, "Don't do what I did. Live your life because it's worth it. Take the chances while you have them here. If I had the opportunity to do it over again, I wouldn't have committed suicide."[8]

Lysa Mateu makes the important observation that:

> Spirits who've committed suicide tell me there is a difference between preventing someone from killing themselves (suicide prevention) and helping them find a powerful enough reason to live. Stopping them from dying doesn't change the quality of their life.[9]

Later, it was a deceased wife who found the answer for her husband who was contemplating suicide after losing his wife and children. When he asked how he could even want to live after what had happened, his wife responded through Mateu:

> He cannot kill himself. He won't be with us if he does. There are rules. He must face the pain where he is. He must go through it on his own. We will be with him. We will lead the way. There is another life awaiting him. A wife. A child. Tell him this is my promise. He will fall in love again. He needs to know this, and to wait, and see.[10]

In some cases, the message that one's life has been chosen (and hence has a purpose) is more oblique. One spirit told Jean Foster that if it could pass on any messages to those left behind, it would be not only that suicide was wrong, but perhaps more important that "they enter life to be in the body, and the great news is that their reality is spirit."[11]

The notion that life is worth living would seem to be a natural accompaniment to the one that suicide is a bad idea. The reader has probably noted that it is sometimes stated in indirect terms or a circuitous manner. Perhaps part of the reason for this is that, having taken their own life, suicides understand that the idea that life is precious may be a tough sell to those who want to kill themselves. It is therefore the next message, that death is not a solution, that suicides speak of the most.

DEATH IS NOT A SOLUTION

One of the commonest themes in the channeled messages of those who have taken their own lives is that death does not make anything better. This is one of the most consistent comments seen in the literature, regardless of the era in which it was channeled.

It should be noted that a person's problems may carry over into the afterlife regardless of the manner of his or her death. Thus, suicides may not be unique in this. One woman remembered a dream experience involving her father who had passed to the other side through cancer two years beforehand:

> My father came to my kitchen door.... It was like real life. Everything was very vivid, very sharp, and very clear.
>
> He was dressed casually in slacks and a dress shirt. He looked well, like he did before he got sick.... But he looked distressed. So I opened the door and my father walked in. He was carrying some papers under his arm. He began to discuss with me some problems I was then having with my business. I said to him, "Well, since you're dead, I guess I can ask you this. What is it like over there?" My father's answer surprised me. "Well, if you think that it's hard over here on earth, it's *twice* as hard over there." He seemed very angry and upset as he spoke to me.
>
> It seemed that he could not get past whatever problems he'd left on earth.... It's been very, very hard for him, I felt. It seemed like he was blaming everyone but himself for his problems....
>
> I think that whatever personal and family problems my father did not resolve in life, he's working through now in the afterlife. My father was always the type of person who would never blame himself. Things were always somebody else's fault. I suppose that now he has to face that, and it hasn't been easy.[12]

This gets back to the issue mentioned before that we take all of our psychological baggage with us to the afterlife. Death only eliminates physical problems—such as cancer—not what led up to them.

Needless to say, the issue of problems not being left behind with the body appears to be even more true for those who take their own life. Acharya stated it well: "Suicide is *never* a release, only a postponement, and no circumstances in the world are so bad that a man should resort to such methods for evading them."[13] Dr. Peebles was channeled as noting:

> The person who absolutely can no longer tolerate being in the physical body and chooses, on his own, to end the physical life, will cut short the learning process, will incarnate again rather soon, and with very much the same challenges. Your religions of your world teach that suicide is a sin. It is not; it is the epitomy *[sic]* of frustration.[14]

Similarly, Claude told his mother from the spirit realm that:

> Nothing can kill the soul, not even man himself; though sometimes, if before the final separation of body and soul the illness has been very severe, there has been brain disease, or the end has been violent and sudden, the shock to the soul is very great, and it may remain in a state of unconsciousness for many days or weeks, till it is recovered sufficiently to awake in its new conditions. You see, therefore, a suicide, far from escaping

trouble, only goes from one form of misery to another; he cannot annihilate himself and pass to nothingness.[15]

Robert Crookall also reflected the thought of older channeled messages when he stated:

> Although special arrangements may be made to compensate those few suicides who willingly sacrificed their lives for others, those who cast off the body deliberately in an endeavour to escape the trials, tribulation and duties (which, properly viewed, are inestimable opportunities) of earth-life are "earthbound." One reason for this is that the vehicle of vitality is charged with energy that has to be dissipated. Another, is the mental factor—namely the rejection of opportunity, of life itself. The deliberate suicide has not "ended it all": he survives the death of the body and takes his problems with him but into harder conditions.[16]

Contemporary messages reflect the same thought as the earliest ones recorded—that suicide is no solution. Suzane Northrop comments:

> DPs [dead people] who have committed suicide discover a hard-core truth; you cannot kill yourself. Your essence, your state of mind, and consciousness remain, with full knowledge of why you took your life in the first place. Suicide won't solve any of the problems, it only eliminates the body as place or means in which to work them out. And the concept of curtailing one's own lifespan "before the allotted time" is very real. There is a blueprint.[17]

Her words are backed up by the spirits of many suicides. Bishop Pike's son was channeled stating, "I thought there was a way out ... I've found there is no way out. I wish I'd stayed to work out my problems."[18]

Toward the end of Jean Foster's work with Hiram, the spirit told her:

> Entering into this plane provides no reasonable answer to any problems. If the problems would disappear, then the matter would be closed, and then suicide would be a good thing. But ... I know that I have left the problems on one plane but recreated them here. They will stay with me until I team up with the truth of how to disperse them—every last one of them.[19]

Western Edition (W. E.) agreed that suicide is not a solution. Instead, it compared them to being like an abortion, and noted that such souls would almost immediately be reincarnated to finish what they had not completed. In this sense, it is like failing a grade in school—you are forced to repeat it over and over again until the lessons you were supposed to get from it are learned.[20]

Often, taking one's own life seems to only makes a bad situation worse. Speaking from the afterlife, Ford said more than once through Ruth Montgomery that is was much easier for a soul to solve its problems while still in the body than in the afterlife:

> If a person takes his own life in a fit of despondency or frustration ... the solution will not easily be found here, for we have no right to extinguish that which God has lighted; and the privilege of a physical body in order to work off karma is not to be dismissed lightly. Others await their turn to try for spiritual advancement there, and if we angrily snuff out the life in physical wrappings bestowed upon us by our Creator, we will have to pay and pay for that in this phase [the afterlife], as well as in delayed opportunity to return to the body to work on karma which has now increased tenfold.[21]

Lysa Mateu puts it simply:

> I've had many people come through who, right after pulling the trigger or swallowing pills, wish they hadn't. They were so damn angry they didn't stick around to handle what they falsely believed dying would erase. Then, they crossed over and had to deal with it anyhow.
>
> You can't kill your spirit, put a gun to your problems, or swallow pills to erase your pain. You must go through your situation and deal with it in order to move past it.
>
> There are no shortcuts.[22]

Another spirit told Jasper Swain that it was foolish to think of suicide as an easy out or a way of punishing others, because as soon as the soul has finished resting long enough to recover from its act, it immediately reincarnates, remembering nothing of its previous life, and has to face the whole thing over again. The soul added:

> What is more ... he is going to be confronted by exactly the same problems. If he fails a second time, the process will occur and continue to occur until he learns to face his problems rather than escape them....
>
> So, if you want a frustrating round-trip ticket up to our world and right back down to yours again, Dad, commit suicide! It will get you nowhere fast![23]

Such sentiments have been echoed in the channeled messages of those who took their own lives for more than a century. Fourteen years after her death in 1904, the spirit Minnie stated:

> Do not think that by taking your own life you can bury yourself in the hereafter.... I am suffering because my father and mother are still

> mourning for me. Very often, I go to see my poor old mother, and she is very old now....
>
> If one takes his own life he goes through a bitter experience and suffers greatly—yes, suffers greatly.[24]

Clearly, though a great many years had passed, the family still hurt, and the spirit was suffering because of it.

Spirit attitudes toward the appropriateness of suicide as a choice have not changed in the decades since Minnie died. The spirit Alexy stated:

> I want you to know that just because I no longer have a body in which to deal with my pain doesn't mean I am without my pain. I still have to deal with why I CHOSE TO END MY LIFE.
>
> The problems didn't just go away when I died.
>
> My body did.
>
> The problems did not.
>
> Now I must deal with them from another realm, without the support and love of my family on earth....
>
> It is difficult to watch those on earth hurting themselves in the way we once did.[25]

This sentiment appears to be echoed by messages channeled through instrumental transcommunication. Pat Kubis and Mark Macy state:

> As George Richie saw, suicides roam the lower places, too. There is no "escape" from life. You cannot escape your life or your problems by death. When you die, you still have a body, an astral body, and you still are confronted by your same problems and emotions.
>
> The [entity] Technician says:
>
> Avoiding work and responsibility in this world is only delaying the learning process. This is also true for those who are tempted to escape to a nicer world by taking their own life.
>
> He says again and again that there is no escaping any personal problems. If you don't solve them now on Earth, they will be waiting for you on the next plane. Merely dying doesn't solve mental anguish and pain.[26]

Yet another warning comes from James, a spirit channeled by Suzy Smith:

> No man escapes his problems by killing himself. He only magnifies them. He has to make amends not only to those whom he would have been able to help while on earth, but he has to assist many others to make up for all those he had not yet met who might have been influenced for the better had he continued to live....

Make no mistake, nothing good can ever come of suicide, and a terrible amount of unhappiness, misery, and misfortune is always caused by it....

And the extra problems that you place on others by your suicide are your responsibility. You have to find ways to make amends for them, even though it might take you hundreds of years.[27]

An even longer, and more clear-cut, message was channeled in 1917 from one suicide (who claimed to have been possessed at the time) to a woman tempted to follow her path:

I should like to say a few words to this young lady who is contemplating suicide.

Many years ago I was a happy wife, with two dear children and a very kind husband....

One day, when my husband went to work, I kissed him goodby [sic] and was very happy, but after he was gone, all in a moment, something got hold of me. I remember feeling very strange, as if somebody had taken complete hold of me, and I did not realize what was taking place.

After awhile everything changed. I saw my husband in terrible mental agony, and he was crying very bitterly. When things became a little clearer to me, I saw my body hanging there!

Oh, if you could only realize what a condition I was in! My husband stood there in the shed, looking at my hanging body; he was crying heartbrokenly but I could do nothing to help him. There I stood at his side, wishing with all my power that I could have that body again, but I could not. There were my two little children weeping for me, and I could not help them....

[F]or ten long years I could see nothing before me but what I had done. I could see how much the children needed me, but I could do nothing for them....

I want to warn anybody who is thinking of trying to get out of the physical body.

Do not do it under any circumstances.

You do not know, you cannot realize, what a hell you will find yourself in.[28]

Messages from the dead can affect the living in a positive way. This is seen nowhere more clearly than when people teetering on the edge of taking their own life receive a communication from a suicide that convinces them not to do it. An example of this occurs in the following story, involving the spirit of a woman with cancer who had died by suicide six months earlier:

> I became very depressed about my relationship with my boyfriend, Terry....
>
> I was at my lowest. I cried uncontrollably for a while, thinking about terminating myself. I just cried and cried until I couldn't cry anymore.
>
> About 5:00 in the morning a baby-blue misty light appeared in the hallway and moved into my bedroom. It was oval shaped, about three feet high and a foot wide, and was three feet off the ground.
>
> I closed my eyes, and Terry's grandmother started talking to me in my mind. It was just like the conversations we used to have when she was alive.
>
> She said that my family and Terry's family would not understand why I had terminated my life. And that life was too precious to give up. She reassured me that I was loved and would truly be missed. She told me that suicide was not the answer. She had made that mistake herself, but I should not make that mistake too.
>
> It was like she encompassed me and surrounded me. I felt a warmth inside of me that I had never felt before. She gave me an inner strength, and I felt that I could do anything that I wanted to do at the point. Then the light was gone.[29]

In this case, the mental communication that life is worth living and death is not a solution appears to have worked, providing needed comfort and renewed strength to someone in dire need of it.

George Anderson has channeled a great many messages from suicides over the years. He summarized what he has been told in this passage, which includes the idea that suicide is not a solution:

> They also do not recommend suicide as a quick ticket to the Other Side. They realize that theirs is a long road to understanding and healing, and that so much more can be accomplished by working out problems on the earth. They insist that any lessons cut short on the earth *must* be continued in the hereafter and that there are no shortcuts. Since time here is finite, it takes much less time to learn and understand here than in the hereafter, where time is infinite.
>
> If there is any lesson to be learned by those who pass by their own hand it is that our experience on this earth, no matter how privileged, will be fraught with experiences where we will have to make decisions critical to our existence on this earth. These souls encourage us to continue understanding that everything we must go through in this existence is of benefit to us in the hereafter, and that there is no easy way out of the lessons we must learn.[30]

In another case, Anderson was even more succinct as he channeled a father who had killed himself:

> He knows that on certain days you just wish you would die, and then you wouldn't have to deal with this anymore, but he says, "Trust me—don't take the way out that I did because it's not going to solve the problem. ... unfortunately, when you get very depressed and feel a state of desolation you don't think rationally....
>
> Have you at times been suicidal? Because he's telling you, "Don't do the same thing I've done, don't," he says, and he's right. It will not solve the problem; you will only bring more unhappiness to yourself.... he knows you are like a time bomb that could go off at any time. He says again, "Don't do the same thing that I've done, it's not going to solve your problems, it's only going to make matters worse."[31]

From his place in the afterlife, Stephen expressed concern over the growing numbers of people taking their own lives. However, he also made this distinction between suicide in the young and that of the elderly:

> Some of the elderly suicides aren't always wrong. It can be a more correct decision if it's handled correctly, or at least it's an option. This is not true of adolescents.
>
> I can't say it strongly enough—it is never correct for a young person to commit suicide, there is always a way they can be helped, there is always someone who cares. It isn't always easy, and it will take a lot of work, but there is always a way.[32]

Of course, it is obvious that if these messages truly come from the dead, then consciousness survives. Furthermore, being dead only makes what a soul needs to accomplish that much harder. A number of spirits have suggested that if people could only recognize the golden opportunities inherent in life, and the choice we have in how we live it, that they would never throw it away. The spirit of Joseph explained that the living don't appreciate what a wonderful gift they have in the body.[33] You have complete freedom to be however you want, in whatever way you wish. Joseph pointed out that sometimes it's a matter of unrealistic expectation—that we should always be happy—or whether we focus on positive or negative aspects of life.

A similar message was passed through a dream reported by Bill and Judy Guggenheim, who recount the following tale of a woman who had a dream experience involving an ex-boyfriend who had committed suicide:

> Wes came to me in a dream that was totally vivid. But it wasn't just a dream—it was a real experience.
>
> He was surrounded by a fog in a desert wasteland. It was a lonely place that was mostly dark and bleak. He was wearing a tattered T-shirt and shorts.

> Wes was despondent and resigned. He was definitely not at peace. He said, "I've been sentenced." I asked, "To what?" He said, "I've been sentenced to eternal life!"
>
> Wes was a lost person, and I understood. He didn't find the peace he was looking for, and I felt immense sadness and pain. I told him I would pray for him.
>
> I woke up realizing it doesn't do any good to commit suicide because you're still going to be alive. You can't escape. It's not going to be any better after death. You have to live though this life and take responsibility for it.
>
> You are always responsible for your actions, whether you're here or there. If you abdicate your lessons by taking your own life, you can't expect that death is going to take away the pain or change the lessons you have to learn.[34]

George Anderson channeled a message from a woman to her daughter. The passage below repeats the theme that suicide is not a good solution:

> "Does she call out to my father?"
>
> "Well, just to say that she should not have done this as a way to even the score, so to speak. She understands the burden he and the family carry now because of this...."
>
> "Your mother is calling out to a daughter. Younger than you. She's concerned for her, especially...."
>
> "She's sending your sister the same message: 'This was not the way, suicide was not the answer.'"[35]

Jean Foster was told by a teenage suicide from the other side:

> Therefore, without much more thought, I simply ended my life. Then the other two, those guys who thought similar thoughts, they did the same. When we met here, guess what? Nothing was different! Our bodies were gone, of course, but not the problems, not the heaviness![36]

Given all the direct messages that suicide is not a solution, it should be no surprise that suicides who have NDEs have said the same thing to researchers. Raymond Moody noted that such NDEs were generally unpleasant, and was told by one woman, "If you leave here a tormented soul, you will be a tormented soul over there, too."[37] In another case he was told, "I didn't go where [my dead wife] was. I went to an awful place.... I immediately saw the mistake I had made.... I thought, I wish I hadn't done it."[38] Moody felt that it was clear from the reports he heard that the suicide doesn't escape his or her problems—instead, they only get worse. Suicides are helpless to do anything but watch as the consequences of their action play out, including its impact on loved ones.

Margot Grey pointed out more recently:

> What suicide-related NDEs revealed was that the conflicts that these people had attempted to escape from by this method were still present when they died. They further differed from the experiences of others whose NDEs had been brought about through illness or accident, in that they found their complications had the added disadvantage that in their disembodied state they were unable to do anything about their problems and were obliged to view "the unfortunate consequences which result from their acts."
>
> This sentiment [that suicide is a mistake] has also been expressed by a number of people who had "core experiences" who said that while they were near death it was communicated to them that suicide is an act against God, that all life is sacred, that to take the life of oneself or another is attended with very severe penalties.[39]

P. M. H. Atwater has also noted that NDEs resulting from suicide attempts frequently (but not always) cause experiencers to change their minds about whether death really is a solution:

> Contrary to popular notions, most suicide near-death scenarios are positive, or at least illustrative of the importance of life and its living.... Near-death survivors from suicide attempts can and often do return with the same sense of mission that any other experiencer of the phenomenon reports. And that mission is usually to tell other potential victims that suicide is not the answer. For example, this young man (he asked not to be identified):
>
> "Since then, suicide has never crossed my mind as a way out. It's a copout to me and not the way to heaven. I ... hope my experience will help stop someone from taking his own life. It is a terrible waste."
>
> Suicide near-death episodes can lay to rest problems and conflicts, explain away confusions, and emphasize the need to remain embodied. Experiencers usually return with a feeling that suicide solves nothing.[40]

Spirits, regardless of their manner of death, appear to be united on two issues. First, that, as George Meek observed, "it is not possible for you to die, even if you commit suicide."[41] And second, that dying not only doesn't solve problems, it tends to make them worse. After performing research involving laboratory-based communications with recently deceased souls, Meek reported that when he asked whether a suicide could escape his or her troubles, he was told:

> No, he only compounds them. There is no escape for any individual from the requirement that each one *must* evolve mentally, emotionally, and spiritually. A person who fails to cope with everyday problems does

not escape by suicide. He cannot "kill" himself. He is just as alive after destroying his physical body as he was before he pulled the trigger, jumped out the window, or took an overdose of sleeping pills.

He finds himself in the darkest, most dismal and frightening level of the astral plane. A long, hard and lonely struggle lies ahead before this soul achieves the level on which it would have arrived by natural death.[42]

If there is one thing that suicides and most attempted suicides (who come back after NDEs) agree upon, it is the fact that suicide is not a solution to life's problems. One man who had triggered his NDE through a drug overdose had a peaceful, loving experience.[43] Afterward he never reconsidered taking his own life, and shared his experience with others in the hope that it would discourage them from doing what he had attempted.

THE IMPORTANCE OF LOVE

A number of themes recur in the channeled messages of the dead. A central one is the importance of love. Lysa Mateu writes that the spirit Charley would tell others in pain about the importance of love:

> Snap out of it....
> [I]n the long run, what you don't take with you to heaven, you don't need to spend all of your time focusing on down there.
> The same things you need on earth are the same things you need in heaven—love, connection, compassion, passion, you know, whatever.[44]

The same spirit also stated, "Love is all there is.... What I learned ... is that love never dies. People never die. Their bodies die. But they ... do not."[45] Charley later observed that the problem seems to be a widespread one, noting, "It is this generation of denial, this avoidance of intimacy at all costs, which is killing us."[46]

The spirit known as Jay repeated this theme, saying, "Love, that's what scores points. Self-love, first, and from that flows love for all living things."[47] It is interesting to note that after NDEs many people report returning to life with a greater sense of the importance of love.[48]

Carl Wickland reported the words of a woman who had killed herself that came through a medium at a séance as:

> Mother, I wanted to come to you today to let you know I am with you to help and guide you. I can help you so much better now than I could when I was here with you because I have learned the lesson of overcoming selfishness and jealousy.
> Those were my worst faults but now I have learned to understand what love, true love, which each one should have, means. But I had to go through trouble and sorrow to understand that.[49]

Love was the only emotion that suicides returned to talk about, suggesting that greater emphasis may be placed on it in the spirit realm than the earth plane. No one spoke of how we should hate our neighbors more—a fact that many might do well to take note of.

RESPONSIBILITY FOR YOUR CHOICES

A second issue revolves around choice—the fact that every individual chooses how he or she perceives the world. Because of this, happiness or its lack are, to a large degree, a matter of how you elect to go through life and what you focus on. The spirit Joseph stated:

> Lightness and darkness do not coexist....
> It's all a matter of focus, of finding those things that bring light into our lives. They're always there. Life is forever handing you a million miracles, a million reasons to feel happy, but we often deny that beauty and instead, choose to reflect on what is not working in our lives, what is not beautiful, precious, and loved.[50]

Later on, the same entity explained how we create our own realities and self-fulfilling prophecies during life. Psychologists know well that individuals tend to gravitate toward those people and experiences that will reflect back to them their worldview, reinforcing their self-image, whether good or bad. In the case of suicides, this can mean avoiding situations that might conflict with low self-esteem.

A related theme that came up is the issue of responsibility for one's actions while alive. Jeffrey stated simply, "There is no one to blame,"[51] while Charley observed:

> Lysa, there are no victims out there. Although I know lots of people who would win an Academy Award for the best portrayal of one, you each have a choice in how you live your life, in how you perceive others' words and make meaning of your world, including the world of what happens to you, around you, in you, and outside of you.[52]

A third spirit channeled by Mateu reiterated this theme, stating, "We alone must take personal responsibility for what we choose to believe and for the impact those beliefs have on the quality of our world,"[53] and later, "It really comes down to responsibility, for our thoughts, our actions, our words, and our lives."[54]

Considering how often people try to blame their problems on others—whether their parents, ex-lovers, or someone else—it seems significant that the spirit realm wants us to acknowledge our own responsibility for what we have made of our lives. It is only when we shoulder that responsibility that we can make changes in ourselves and how we go through life.

HELP IS AVAILABLE

One of the messages that comes through from some suicides is that, although they did not realize it at the time, there were people around them—both in the flesh and the spirit realm—who were trying to help. A teenage suicide stated that she was told by her guides in the afterlife, "Those in this plane who work with people who would end their own lives tried to reach through to me."[55] The same spirit later lamented:

> There are helpers who will come to anyone in earth life. ... if a person thinks it is possible, then enters the request for help, advanced spirits enter immediately to help one get the great truth of God.
>
> Why work alone? Entirely foolish! The tender presences here who will help anyone who wants this help know how to work through the great problems of earth life, and they will lead anyone into the positive truth by helping to build a channel straight from your mind to God-mind. I have seen this work from this side.[56]

A different soul went into more detail about the aid available to anyone who asks for it:

> The teamwork here on this plane includes those who turn to help you each minute of every day. They, this special group of advanced spirits ... wait for your request. They stand ready to help you with every problem, every tender point of your life.[57]

The spirit Indira spoke generally about how those in spirit are always present and try to help people who are struggling in life.[58] However:

> The teachers cannot take away your individual free will....
>
> They don't abandon a person, and they do try to reach them. They try, incidentally, in many ingenious ways, but unless the person is open once the veil has been drawn, they may not be able to reach them.[59]

Sometimes suicides suggest that those who are thinking of taking their own lives should seek out help. This came up in a session with Johanna Carroll. When asked what these souls would like to tell others who want to take their own lives, the medium channeled:

> "Review your options"—and I think I'm just getting this now—"Seek counsel of one wiser." Obviously if you can. Some of them are paralyzed with pain and not able to do that.... "Sometimes"—this is what I'm hearing now—"the pain of remembering, when you've first crossed over, is

greater than the pain of the actual experience." The pain of remembering that you've committed suicide. So, in this whole healing process that occurs so that the spirit can move on, they have to come to peace with that.[60]

We have seen that suicides often have a lot to say to those who would follow in their footsteps. Perhaps the most important message is not to do it. Spirits tell us repeatedly that suicide is not a good idea, that it solves nothing and, if anything, will only make things worse for the soul. Sometimes, they also talk of the importance of love, and that life is worth living. But even as they remind us that help is available, they also warn us that we must accept responsibility for ourselves. Next, we will look at what suicides return to tell those who have been left behind.

10

Messages to Those Left Behind

All spirits seem to want to talk to those left behind, regardless of the spirits' cause of death. George Viney observes that, in most cases, "phantoms return for a variety of reasons: to deliver messages, to honour death compacts, to seek justice and, most commonly, to reassure loved ones of their continued existence."[1] For the most part, the messages of suicides fall into the latter category.

So what do suicides come back to tell us? Frequently they seem to want to reassure those left behind that they are okay on the other side. They pass on expressions of love. Often, words are used to comfort the living or relieve them of guilt. As George Anderson observes:

> The souls will appear to us, not because they need anything, but just to let us know that they have reached their destination and are trying to help us cope. They do this because they care a great deal about us and don't want us to get bogged down in the circumstance of passing, but rather that the transition was made and completed.[2]

Although love, reassurance, and guilt issues are the most prevalent messages, we will also see that some suicides want to apologize or beg for forgiveness. Rarely, one finds the spirit giving advice or warnings. This would include the earlier mentioned example of the spirit who John Edward channeled, pointing out a woman should not repeat the mistakes of the past.[3] In fact, one of the few differences with suicide messages and those who have died from other violent causes, such as accidents or murder, is that you rarely see messages that focus on taking care of unfinished business or seeking justice. Perhaps, for the suicide, they typically conclude such business before killing themselves.

REASSURANCE

Possibly the simplest form of reassurance provided by the dead is that they are, in fact, still "alive." Indeed, spirits almost invariably want to reassure loved ones that they are well—which is part of the reason for their extreme frustration when they first try to talk to family members and realize no one can see or hear them. This reassurance can sometimes also include specific statements that the living will be okay without them.

Some beings appear to work very hard to come across in dreams or through mediums in order to comfort those left behind. Hans Holtzer notes that there seem to be two very compelling reasons why the dead come back to talk to the living.[4] First, they want to reassure others that they are okay and death is simply a change in dimension, not the end of existence. Second, they want their loved ones to know that they are still around, so they can continue to be a part of their lives.

These messages of reassurance can sometimes be passed along nonverbally. An example of this was when a young man who committed suicide by inhaling carbon monoxide later appeared to his mother and sister:

> All of a sudden, they noticed a bright light to their left, moving toward them....
>
> Sandra heard herself cry out: "It's Neal!" At the moment she called out her late brother's name, the light blew up to its brightest glare. With that, a feeling of great peace and relief came over the two women.
>
> Mrs. R, still unable to move her body, asked: "What do you want? Why did you do it?"
>
> With that, she started to cry. At that moment waves of light in the form of fingers appeared inside the bright light as if someone were waving goodbye. Then the light gradually dimmed until it vanished completely.[5]

Yet another case of nonverbal reassurance came during a funeral service. A man, Donald, who had committed suicide, was seen by his sister and a witness:

> During his memorial service, I looked out the window and saw Donald walking toward the church! His body was not solid, and I could see the trees behind him. He looked a bit younger and seemed to be whole—and he didn't have his limp anymore!
>
> He was wearing a plaid shirt that he liked and a pair of trousers. He looked very peaceful and happy, like he was out for a stroll. Donald walked up to the window as if to beckon me to come with him. Then he just disappeared.
>
> After the service my sister-in-law, Joyce, said, "Did you see Donald?" I was quite surprised and said, "Yes!" She said, "I saw him too!"
>
> This was probably my brother's way of saying goodbye. It was an impactful experience that brought a natural kind of closure to my grief.[6]

A third case combines nonverbal reassurance to a daughter after her mother committed suicide with later verbal reassurances after her son-in-law passed. A daughter had the following vision in a funeral home of her mother, who had committed suicide:

> I looked up to my right, and way up toward the ceiling was a vision of my mother and Christ, walking hand in hand away from me. It was in full color and just as natural as life. They both looked over their shoulders, and then they smiled at me and disappeared.[7]

Her husband of ten years, Bill, died a year later. The woman decided to try contacting him through a psychomanteum.[8] She had this experience:

> I saw my mom.
> First I saw her a long distance away, and it was just her face. Then, as she came closer and closer, she was more ghostly, but not in a haunting way....
> She smiled and ... said, "I have come to see you because Bill is not able to come. I am a little farther along than he is, and he still has a lot to learn. He is studying. But he's all right and he loves you very much and he's fine."[9]

After this experience, the daughter was able to access her mother at will through meditation. She stated, "I usually see Mom during times of difficult problems. She comforts me by saying 'It's okay,' or 'You'll be all right.' It's good to have her around."[10] Thus, a positive bond was able to be continued after death, with the mother a welcome part of her daughter's life.

Occasionally the reassurance provided is that it is okay for those left behind to continue their lives and remarry. In the mid-1800s, L. Alph Cahagnet reported that a sitter received the following message from the spirit of a man who had shot himself:

> Madame D—inquires whether this gentleman knows her. "Yes; she is related to him by marriage." ... Tell him she has married the baron D—: and ask him if she has acted agreeably to his wishes! "Oh, my poor wife!" exclaimed he; "may you be happy—it is the sole wish of my heart.... He says that he applauds this union; but, at the same time, he seems pained at it, for he was very fond of madame.[11]

Another topic that can come up is whether suicides go to hell and suffer eternal damnation—that this does not happen. Those who kill themselves sometimes make a point of reassuring their family that they have not been condemned by God. Suzane Northrop tells of a session involving the parents of an 18-year-old suicide:

They were deeply religious Catholics, believing that suicide was inevitably punished by damnation in Hell. While trying to cope with Jennifer's loss, they also had the agony of questioning themselves, "Will our beautiful daughter be welcome in Heaven or go to Hell or worse?" Jennifer, clearly and articulately, in the witty manner of the "old" Jennifer declared, "No, there is no fire and brimstone, and God didn't punish me. I punished myself and, worse, I punished the ones I loved, my family."[12]

In another case, the spirit of a brother made a series of dream visitations to his sisters after he had died of a deliberate drug overdose.[13] In them, he seemed to be trying to convey loving reassurance to his family that he was okay. These visits began a month after his death, in the following manner:

> David appeared dressed casually in a blue sports shirt and neatly pressed new jeans. He was perched on a barstool.... David was pointing above his head to what Darcy describes as "pictures and images" of people he and Darcy had known. Each image appeared to be bathed in light, although each was otherwise surrounded by darkness.
>
> Then suddenly from David's right and above him, a bright white light began glowing. Gradually, the light grew larger and intensified until it consumed the entire scene. Then, Darcy recalls, "I could see every line on David's face. He looked tired and aged, and there were tears in his eyes." Glancing up, Darcy saw that the images over his head had vanished. Then David turned to her and hugged her. They embraced tightly, and Darcy remembers not wanting to let him go, although, "I just knew he had to go back. I could feel it, although nothing was said."
>
> When Darcy awoke, she was crying but felt comforted and reassured....
>
> A month or so later David returned in another dream. This time Darcy found herself at a funeral.... David was there, but this time he looked younger. His eyes were much brighter, his skin was vibrant and smooth....
>
> Suddenly, Darcy saw her late paternal grandmother, Angelina, who had died more than a decade before. David was sitting next to her, but they were not speaking to each other. As in the first dream, David turned to face Darcy. She knelt by his chair and he embraced her. Again, Darcy experienced a sense of physical warmth and a feeling of love....
>
> Other members of Darcy's family have encountered David, and through all the direct after-death contacts runs one undeniably clear thread: that David was growing and finding contentment on the other side. In one, Darcy's sister Dale dreamed of David as a young, carefree boy. Then several months after David's passing, Darcy and her sister Dina both had similar dreams of David—the same night. In both dreams David was sitting on the edge of Dina's bed in her house. "It was as if we were just hanging

out like we normally did after David would come home from work in the evening," Darcy says.[14]

Another case involving a suicide returning to comfort a family member involved a father who returned five years after he had killed himself.[15] His daughter recalled:

> I was going through a really hard time emotionally. I was very, very depressed. I was down and out, probably like my dad had been before he took his life. I felt so totally alone and just wanted to be with him.
> One day, I was sitting on the floor crying uncontrollably. Suddenly I felt as if someone hugged me, but no one else was in the room. Then I heard a "clink" on the hardwood floor. I went over and picked up a penny that had the Lord's Prayer on it.
> I smiled and said, "Thank you, Dad." I had given that same penny to my father before he died to keep in his pocket.[16]

There have also been incidents when children's voices have been said to come through with similar messages through trumpets during séances. In one case, it said, "Don't cry Dad.... I'm all right now."[17] Other cases can involve hearing the voice of a dead person outside of the séance parlor. Elsie Sechrist reports the following story about a woman who was suspected of killing herself:

> About three weeks after Ann died, I was washing dishes and thinking of her. Suddenly I heard her voice saying, "I'm O.K." In my mind I expressed my sorrow at missing her funeral. She said, "Don't worry about it. I'm O.K."
> Then, mentally, I asked her, "Was it an accident or not?"
> Her answer was, "I'm where I want to be. I'm O.K. Don't worry about me. I'm happy." And abruptly she was out of my presence as fast as she'd entered. I believed her and quit worrying.
> The following year I met someone who had been living across the street from Ann when she died.... One of the firemen, who had been inside the apartment, had said to him that Ann's body looked as though she had knelt down and stuck her head in the gas oven. The firemen were sure it was suicide.... They had called it an accident to spare the family's feelings.[18]

Sometimes these messages of reassurance are simple ones, like when George Anderson channeled, "he keeps saying that he's fine, that he's all right."[19] Other times the spirits come across as being more interested in letting the living know that things will be okay without them. Hans Holtzer writes:

> Her sleep was interrupted in the middle of the night by the feeling of a presence in the room. ... she discerned at the foot of her bed the form of her husband, and all at once she realized that he had gone across to the hereafter.
>
> "You are not to worry," the husband spoke; "everything will be all right. Wally will take care of you and the children." The apparition vanished.
>
> Early the next morning she was notified that he had fatally shot himself, evidently overcome by a fit of depression.[20]

Many messages channeled from suicides focus on how life continues after death, reassuring those left behind that they need not fear it. Anne Puryear's dead son, Stephen, told her:

> Mom, I can't say enough times—I'm here! I am not dead. I'm alive. More free and alive than when I had a body. Only my physical body is gone.... Death is not the end, it is simply walking out of the physical form and into the spirit realm, which is our true home.[21]

Raymond Moody and Paul Perry describe the channeling of suicides through psychomanteums.[22] Once again we see the spirit demonstrating an interest in putting to rest the minds of the living. A West Coast physician felt like he made contact with his nephew, who had committed suicide. He stated, "There was this very strong sense of his presence, and I heard his voice very clearly.... He said, 'Let my mother know that I am fine and that I love her very much.'"[23]

The spirit Stephen summed up the situation nicely:

> Almost everyone without exception wants to tell someone remaining behind that they aren't dead and that dead doesn't mean what they think. They want to talk to their loved ones or friends, to give them a message. They want to let them know that they are really alive—more alive than ever.[24]

Sylvia Barbanell also reported countless channeled messages that indicated deceased children—regardless of their form of death—appeared to visit their loved ones through mediums and dreams.[25]

It is interesting that suicide performed when one has a terminal illness may be like assisted suicides in that there appears to be less regret in the messages to the living, and more of simple reassurance and messages of love. One such communication occurred during a dream state:

> The night before Hank died, he got his family and my family together. I was the only one who wasn't there. He told them about his terminal cancer—no one knew of this before. He told them he planned to take his own life, and the next day he committed suicide.

> Four days later, Hank came to me in a dream. There was a knock on the door, and when I opened it, he was standing there. He was very healthy, not sick at all. He looked completely normal....
>
> Hank had a happy expression on his face and said, "It's okay. I did this because I was dying and couldn't live with the pain anymore. You and your family will be fine. Everything will be okay for all of you. Go on with your life. I love you." That was the end of the dream.[26]

In another case, a man who had shot himself in the heart appeared to return to speak with his mother while her body was under anesthesia. Suzane Northrop writes:

> A few weeks after the surgery, Susan's mother told her that while she was on the operating table Andrew came to her. "It was so incredible, he put his arms around me and told me he was never going to leave my side again."
>
> Susan's mother continued, "I know this may be hard for you to believe, you probably think your old mama is senile, but I feel closer to Andrew now than I did the last few years of his life. Each morning he comes and is there while I'm having my coffee. I know now he's fine and God didn't punish him."[27]

Messages of reassurance appear to be important to the dead. They work very hard to get them across to the living, whether through mediums, dreams, or psychokinetic events. These messages can be as simple as that they are okay or that life continues after death. Other times more specific reassurance may be provided, such as that they are not stuck in hell or that the living will be okay without them. It makes sense that this would make up a large portion of afterlife communications, as the dead are still aware of those left behind and, as we shall see next, still care for them.

THOSE LEFT BEHIND ARE STILL LOVED

One message that is often combined with others is that transitioning to the afterlife does not diminish the ties of love between family members. The reader will have already noticed that many suicides speak of love when reassuring their friends and family that they are okay. However, there are other times when it appears to be the main point a spirit is trying to get across. George Anderson passed on many such statements such as this one: "He certainly wants you to know that he does love you and knows how much you love him."[28]

This is a common message. Medium Laurie Campbell channeled, "He just keeps saying, 'Mom, I love you.'"[29] James Van Praagh also had the soul of a suicide state, "Forgive me. I love you very much and I love my dad too."[30] Another time Van Praagh passed on the following message to a daughter:

> She is trying to let you know that she loves you very much and is sorry about not being able to tell you this when she was alive. I think your mother didn't understand love and wasn't sure how to give it.[31]

Bishop Pike's son took desperate psychokinetic steps to get his message across to his father—moving books, burning off the secretary's bangs, messing up closets, turning milk sour, and scattering about safety pins that appeared to be opened up like the hands of a clock set at 8:15—the hour of Jim's death.[32] Ena Twigg channeled Jim's admission of responsibility for the acts and why he had caused so much chaos:

> "I was worried about you, Dad...." Jim, Jr., was saying through Ena.
> "I came to your room, I moved books, I knocked on the door—came to your bedside—you dreamt about me and spoke to me....
> "I love you very much," Jim went on. "So much love and no means of giving it."[33]

Suzane Northrop reports a case involving a precognitive dream of suicide followed by a dream from that suicide providing reassurance and a message of love:

> Donna had a dream about her son, Greg. In the dream her son appears to her drinking and doing drugs. At the time she found this odd: Greg was very much alive and well, and not doing those things. Or so she thought.
> Three days after the dream Greg died from suicide, through an overdose of alcohol and sleeping pills. After his death he came to his best friend in a dream to tell him he was fine and well. Greg also asked his friend to please tell his mother he loved her and was sorry.[34]

The previously mentioned suicide channeled by April Crawford told her daughter, "Please take my love with you from this life to the next. ... remember my love."[35] And in the opposite situation, a teenage suicide communicated love for her parents:

> She loves her mother dearly and worships both her mother and father. She is saying: "Why, why, why was I such a fool? Oh, Mother, please don't blame yourself or Daddy. It was a crazy kid thing to do, and I love you all so much. Forgive me."[36]

This statement is reflective of many in that it combines the sentiments of love, regret, and desire that those left behind forgive her and not feel guilty.

Similar feelings were expressed by another woman who killed herself to her teenage daughter in a dream:

> Weeks after the suicide, Sandra collapsed into the bed one night and cried hysterically until she fell into a deep sleep. Within minutes, she was overwhelmed by what she describes as "a beautiful aroma," the fragrance of "a beautiful garden of all different kinds of flowers." Then she saw her mother surrounded by flowers. Stepping forward, she said to her daughter, "I love you, baby. I'm sorry. Don't blame yourself for anything. Mommy loves you. Forgive me. I'm fine now. Go on and be happy." After repeating the message twice, Sandra's mother walked back into the garden. Sandra continued to smell flowers for several more minutes.
>
> Sandra awoke feeling "very peaceful" for the first time in her life.[37]

Again we see a mixture of sentiments, including love, reassurance, an effort to eradicate guilt, and a request for forgiveness. This, as in many messages from the dead, seemed to be successful in comforting the person who had been left behind.

THE NEED FOR LOVED ONES TO LET GO OF GRIEF

The grief of the living sometimes seems to have a detrimental effect on the dead. Because of this, it may be in everyone's best interest to let go of sorrow. It should be noted again that this is not limited to spirits who passed on through suicide. Spirits of all ages can run into difficulty if those who are left behind long for them. Heather Buckley speaks of how grief can trap the souls of babies:

> Deep loss is normally dimmed by time and other events but some people carry on their emotional grief so extensively they prevent the little soul from going on. They keep it earth-bound. It can neither rise and go on to the next plane to learn and be happy ... nor can it return to its earth body. It is held in a limbo of cold and darkness, on a shelf where it can go neither up nor down because its loving parents ... keep drawing it back by their grief.[38]

One spirit who claimed to have been trapped for fifty years told her:

> I could not go on. I was neither here nor there. My parents ... have held me to them from the time I left.... They kept me like a ball bouncing up and down. Sometimes they would release me and I would nearly touch the finger tips of those reaching down for me and then my mother would pull me back.... They wouldn't let me go. They would not send me up to God and let me be.[39]

Nor is this problem limited to babies. Buckley was told stories of children having been trapped until their parents either died, accepted the death, or underwent shock therapy. When the spirit of a 9-year-old boy who had died in 1898 and been stuck until his mother's death was asked where he had been during that time, he replied:

> Caught.... By my mom.... Evertime [sic] I'd try to get away she'd pull me back.... She left that room just like it was when I was there. ... she still kept my toys and stuff.[40]

Sylvia Barbanell also reports a number of messages purported to come from deceased children to their parents, combining reassurance with a desire that their loved ones let go of their grief.[41] Jasper Swain received similar comments from a spirit who had died suddenly in a car accident:

> Perhaps the most important message we can send you from here ... is that grieving, weeping, and wishing for the soul of the departed to return, are the worst things that you can do to someone who has just died.
> You see, wherever there is a bond of love, there is an unbroken line of communication.
> When you grieve for someone you love, your sorrow is immediately transmitted to him in his new world ... but he cannot come back to the earth plane. ... he is torn between a desire to comfort his loved ones, knowing it to be impossible, and a need to adjust himself to his bright new surroundings.
> So please, Dad, tell those who are still on earth not to grieve for those of us who have come over here.[42]

The American and U.K. television medium, Chris Fleming, who is from Chicago, believes that deceased celebrities can similarly become trapped by their adoring fans:

> James Dean was harshly mad at a woman at the séance table who stated with a slight ignorance that spirits should be happy that fan clubs keep their image alive. ... he shouted through me "You don't understand. Let us go. Let us go! Let us GO!" in her direction....
> Marilyn Monroe stated that, "I just want to be free. Please, I just want to go home."[43]

Fleming concludes:

> The energy sent out to icons and celebrities can be incredibly strong when it is being done by a lot of people at the same time. It's like a chain that keeps the spirits shackled to our plane. They can't cross over unless we all release them. Thought on the other side is so powerful for them that we have to be careful for the messages we send.[44]

Ralph Knight channeled a message from his deceased mother, who suggested that ongoing grief can hamper even those souls who have successfully made their transition to the afterlife:

> Tell him ... that earth people impose a drag on natural forward progress of dear ones here through the vagueness of their immortality sense and the resulting acuteness of sorrow about being separated from them. Your yearning for heaven people and their inability to reach through to comfort you, may tarnish somewhat the luster of their enthusiasm for the celestial work they have chosen.[45]

Lysa Mateu received messages that addressed why the heartache of those left behind could be detrimental to the souls of suicides. The spirit, Alexy, stated through her:

> We suffer when you do, but not in the same way. We don't feel actual pain, like physical pain, we just find it difficult to move on when you're in pain....
>
> It's like if a child is crying and you reach out to help them, but you're behind a wall, so they do not see you there. You're knocking and yelling real loud, but they cannot hear you.
>
> How do you walk away from that?
>
> The answer is, you don't. But in staying beside you as you grieve for many years, we are putting off the growth of our souls. We have things to do up here as well. So the best thing you can do to assist us in getting to where we need to go is by you moving forward with what happened so we can do so as well.[46]

Many people who grieve have trouble letting go of not only the memory of those they lost, but also their artifacts. Stephen communicated through the Reverend Daisy this message asking his mother to let go of his old things:

> He wants you to know he's fine. You're such a worrier.... He wants to thank you for talking out loud to him when you sit on the bed in your room. But he wants you to open the drawer in the bottom of the bedside stand and get rid of all the things of his you have stored there. He doesn't need those things anymore and neither do you. Give them away.[47]

Later, Stephen warned that continued sorrow, and longing to be with the dead child, may lead a family member to make the mistake of consciously or unconsciously committing suicide.[48] He warned that this was not a good idea because not only will this family member miss the ones left behind, but s/he will not be able to see the deceased child as much as if s/he were still alive, seeing the children during dreams, meditation, and other times. He concluded, "Better to live fully and help others as a gift to the dead child, and know with a certainty that you are meeting them and can begin to remember those meetings."[49]

A spirit who came through George Anderson combined reassurance with a desire that the family move on from their sorrow:

> He certainly knows that you love him and you miss him, and the terrible tragedy that you had to go through, but he says that he is coming along—that he is all right and at peace. And continue to pray for him, but certainly he'll feel much better if all of you put yourselves at peace as well.[50]

Some spirits seemed less affected by the grief of those left behind, taking a more philosophic approach. Jean Foster was informed:

> It would not do any good to tell those who tenderly regarded me as the husband or the father or the friend that I live and work with you. Those who regarded me thus enter into grief, and that is the way they will work through the earthly problems of how to dispose of me. But if they could only remember the good things, they would shortcut this grief process by eternal time.[51]

One of the entities that Lysa Mateu channeled was a higher being named Vertitude. It worked with souls who had committed suicide and explained the problem of grief for the dead here:

> If you suffer, day after day, replaying the gruesome details of their death, who suffers?
>
> You do.
>
> Why?
>
> Because you think that it's going to eventually bring you some relief. It's like, if you suffer enough, you will someday be cleansed of all your self-created sins....
>
> Suffering does not change what we did. It only brings more pain to the future of our existence....
>
> They would be freed more quickly if you healed your pain, rather than relived it year after year....
>
> Why do you not think your pain and suffering is any different than theirs? They ended their life. You are refusing to live yours by remaining in regret and pain. So what can you do?
>
> You can understand what has transpired by understanding that your life can be the continuation of theirs. Your progress can lead them forth.[52]

Although many may find this concept hard to accept, the dead frequently ask that we let go of our grief for them. When we suffer, they suffer. And their suffering may be even more intense than ours. Furthermore, it may hold souls back from progressing, tying them to the lower astral or earth plane, and making it hard for them to focus on that which they need to be working on or dealing with. Thus, it may be not only helpful, but important, to accept their reassurances that they are okay, come to terms with their absence, and move on. Since grief can often be exacerbated by feelings of guilt, it should be no surprise that our next topic arises—messages that try to relieve the family from self-blame.

RELIEVING THE FAMILY OF A SENSE OF GUILT

Messages from suicides often ask those left behind not to feel guilty for what happened. Many spirits speak of accepting full responsibility for their actions and resulting death. They repeatedly point out that the living should in no way feel responsible.

Stephen told his incarnate mother, "You're not to blame for the choice I exercised in taking my life. It was my decision, right or wrong. I know it was a totally wrong decision. I have to accept the responsibility for what I did."[53] George Anderson also reported a desire in suicides to assuage guilt with comments like, "He states that it's no one's fault"[54] and "He keeps saying 'You didn't fail me. You didn't fail me.' And he just wants *that* to be understood."[55]

A related issue involved suicide notes, and whether they should be taken to heart by the survivors. After dying, Stephen worked with other children who had committed suicide.[56] He reflected:

> I'm working a lot now with kids who take their lives, and a lot of them leave horrible blaming notes to hurt someone, when they didn't feel that way most of the time. The people reading them are devastated, sometimes for the rest of their lives, and carry terrible guilt. Most of these notes are written in a very unclear, emotional, and fragile state of mind.[57]

Regardless of the notes left behind, many spirits feel guilty for the burden of having their bodies found by a relative. In one case, the spirit of a teenager who had hung himself passed these messages on to his family through the mediumship of George Anderson:

> "He says, 'Please don't think you've failed me. I don't want you to feel guilty.'" Neither parent responds. A few seconds go by....
>
> "Wait." George pauses, then looks at the girl. "He's apologizing to you. Did you find him? Because he says you did."
>
> "Yes...."
>
> "He's saying to you"—George indicates the girl—"that he's appearing to you in your dreams. You've been restless in your sleep."

"Yes," she acknowledges, stunned.

"He says that he's disappointed in himself. He's hard on himself on the other side, too.... He apologizes to you and asks for prayers.... He doesn't want you to be guilty, angry or carry bitterness....

"He says his biggest problem in life was himself. But he's coming along, and don't feel you've failed or have let him down." ...

Again he focuses on the sister. "He says you feel bad because you didn't keep an eye on him. But he says, 'I want my sister to know that she's not to blame. I made the decision of my own free will.'"[58]

In a different reading, involving a teenager who shot himself, Anderson stated, "This boy says his sister is being accused of this, but she had nothing to do with it."[59] Later, the same spirit was channeled with a more specific message:

He also says, "Don't go on any guilt trips because this happened." Sometimes you might have felt this wouldn't have happened if you hadn't moved there. It happened. There's nothing you can do about it.... There's nothing to reproach yourselves about.[60]

In a third case, Anderson received a similar message from a dead father to his family:

"He leaves in turmoil? He admits not being the happiest person here—true?"

"Not in the end."

"'And that's nobody's fault,' he says.... He just states that he wants his sons to know that it's not their fault, that he was so unhappy when he was here toward the end of his life. He admits being in turmoil.... Were you guys afraid that he was mad at you or something? Because he keeps saying that he's not mad at you. Things just started to go downhill for him, so he felt. But he admits being his own worst enemy.... He apologizes to you."[61]

In another place, the same spirit combined this message that the family was not at fault with one of responsibility for his own actions:

He just wants all of you, especially the three of you, to know he is not mad at you, nor did you do anything to add to his anxiety of frustration, nor did you do anything to fail him. He just cut off his nose to spite his face. Unfortunately, he says, I have no one to blame but myself. ... he's looking himself straight in the eye and saying there's no one to blame but me. As he says ... you can easily cheat others but you can never fool yourself or the Infinite Light—you have to face up to yourself.[62]

James Van Praagh also reports suicides coming through him to apologize to those left behind and ask them to let go of their sense of guilt. He recounts the following session:

> "I'm sorry, but I feel as though she killed herself with a gun in her mouth. Is that correct?"
>
> The woman gasped and answered, "Yes."
>
> "You know, I feel that before she died she was screaming and yelling. Was there a big fight that she was in?"
>
> "Yes."
>
> "She said she was very confused and locked herself in the bedroom for a couple of hours."
>
> "Yes. We fought. That's right. Please tell her I'm so sorry, and I love her very much."
>
> "Yes, she knows this," I replied.
>
> "Your friend is telling me that it was her decision to kill herself. At the time she wanted you to feel guilty and knows now this was not right and asks your forgiveness for the pain she has caused you. She wants you to know she didn't have the courage to end the relationship with you, and the thought of someone else was too hard for her to deal with. Does this make sense to you?"
>
> "Yes, that's it. I understand, but I will never forgive myself."
>
> "You have to. You didn't pull the trigger. You tried to talk to her, but she wouldn't listen.... She came back to tell you it was not your fault."[63]

Suzane Northrop writes of two suicide souls she had known early in life, one of whom came back to reassure her that she should not feel guilty over the other's suicide:

> Also, long after my friend, Bobby, had died and I was finally learning to let the DPs [dead people] through fully, Peter (the friend who had committed suicide in New York) came to me and told me to be at peace, that I had had no share in Bobby's death.[64]

In some cases, psychologists have used mediums to help their clients deal with guilt. Pyschotherapist Brenda Lukeman, appearing on the television program *Psychic Channels* with medium George Anderson, reports:

> I did have a patient who came to me. Her sister had committed suicide quite a few years back.... The sister was fine one moment, the next moment she went over to the balcony, jumped off the balcony, that was it. She hit the ground and died immediately.
>
> The suicide's sister came to me. We were working on guilt.... It was as if she were living under a blanket of sorrow and guilt.... I sent her to see George....

George said, "I feel someone here," and he knew her name, he knew details about her relationship with her sister that she had not even told me.... Her sister said, "I love you, I beg you to forgive me for doing this. I'm here with Father. I'm working through my painful karma that I've created as a result of doing this. It wasn't your fault."

It had such a profound effect ... she was so deeply moved on many levels. First of all, it just lifted years of guilt and sorrow from her.[65]

April Crawford channeled this comment as a letter from a suicide to her daughter:

My last thought was the realization that you would blame yourself. But then of course it was too late.

So now I write you from another place.... My friends here have helped me regain my worth. I am whole. And this opportunity to write to you has been a blessing. Please take my love with you from this life to the next. Do not blame yourself for my fears. They had nothing to do with you.[66]

In yet another case, Lysa Mateu channeled a son who hung himself in front of his mother; he explains that he wants her to forgive herself for what happened:

"Mom tells people I died in my sleep," he tells me. "Lying is destroying her, breaking her spirit. I was drunk. Drugged. Angry. Stupid. Selfish. I admit it. I don't want her to forgive me, only herself. It's not her fault."[67]

Like regret, the need to absolve those left behind of responsibility is a frequent theme. Guilt is a powerful emotion—one that can easily destroy lives. Given what we know about souls gaining greater insight into themselves and their newly finished lifetime, it makes sense that many should return to relieve the living of any residual feelings of self-blame. Instead, in essence, they ask friends and family to forgive themselves. Along with a need to reassure those left behind, reminders of love, and encouraging them to let go of their grief, it appears to be a key reason many suicides return to communicate with those left behind. We will see next that some suicides also ask for forgiveness for themselves.

FORGIVENESS

Forgiveness is a potent topic. Together with guilt and regret, it can transform a life or, if withheld, destroy it. Although most suicides have spoken of their regrets and apologized for their actions, often hoping for forgiveness, in a few cases they bestow it on those left behind. Anderson channeled:

> "No, he keeps apologizing—"
> "... Well...."
> "—for distancing himself. It's almost as if—because he says to you, 'I forgive you and I hope you do, because ...'"
> (In tears) "Instantly."
> "He's telling me.... 'It takes two to tango.'"
> (In tears) "He really does forgive us?"
> (Long pause) "Yeah, he knows—he knows you are in a very delicate frame of mind, so he's trying to be very careful how he expresses himself—but was there a point when he felt banished?"
> "It could have happened. (crying) Oh, yeah—"
> "Yeah—he admits, again he's not blaming, so don't, 'cause he knows the two of you....
> "But the one thing he keeps telling me to tell you is that you have to relieve yourselves and forgive yourselves for thinking, 'Did we play a role in his killing himself ...?' and he says you have to let go of that. He just doesn't want you to feel that."[68]

A spirit told Carl Wickland through the mediumship of his wife: "My conscience hurts me so much. See the sorrow I have caused. I go home but they cannot understand that I am suffering.... Will you ask my husband and mother to forgive me?"[69]

James Van Praagh has also had suicides come through him asking for forgiveness. In the case of a mentally ill mother speaking to her incarnate daughter, he said, "Your mom is feeling very sorry. She is asking for your forgiveness. She says she didn't mean to cause you such upset."[70]

J. Bernard Hutton describes a dinner party séance that turned grim when a woman at the time of committing suicide (or very shortly thereafter) asked forgiveness through a medium:

> Very soon her expression changed—it seemed as if she was experiencing something terrible.... Suddenly, the medium uttered in a strange, tearful, trembling voice:
> "Please forgive me that I had to choose this particular day for my plan....
> "I don't want to hurt you, my darling—you know I've never hurt you—but I must do it.... Please forgive me and remember me as your loving mother...."
> I sat between Dr. Keppler and Uncle Siegmund, and heard the latter stammer: "Mother! It's my mother's voice!"
> At this moment, the medium gasped out in a choked voice:
> "No! ... Help...."

> On sudden impulse, Uncle Siegmund rushed to the telephone and dialed his mother's number.
> There was no reply.
> "Must have got a wrong number," he uttered as if speaking to himself while he dialed the number again....
> Again there was only the ringing tone.
> By now, Uncle Siegmund was greatly alarmed. He ... ran to his car. I followed....
> No word was spoken while Uncle Siegmund drove ... at break-neck speed to his mother's home....
> His mother's body was hanging from the window frame....
> The body was still warm.[71]

In this case, her pleas for forgiveness were also in a suicide letter left at the scene. Hutton notes: "It was medically established that Uncle Siegmund's mother died at approximately the time Ruth Bomke had been in trance."[72]

Souls sometimes communicate in order to ask for forgiveness. Several mediums have mentioned that this can be an important task that must be accomplished (and not just by suicides) before the spirit can advance. The living cannot always find it in their hearts to forgive those who have crossed over. Nonetheless, forgiveness is a powerful emotion, which when given, can heal the wounds on both sides of death.

ADVICE

Some channeled messages seem to relate to general comments or spiritual advice. Trust is one issue that comes up. Lysa Mateu reports that the spirit Angie told her:

> Trust in that which could not readily be seen. Trust in the oasis of love that you have called your home. Trust in the creator called life. Trust in your soul who knows exactly what to do....
> Trust from the innermost recess of your soul that you are cared for, taken care of, looked after, and well. Trust that the purpose of your life is that which brings you the most joy.
> Ask not what your next move shall be. Ask not what you shall *do*. Instead, be calm and quiet and one with the force of life that has created you, that cares for you, and watches over you, from the day you were born, until always.[73]

Sometimes the messages focus more on personal relationships. Lysa Mateu channeled the following statement from Charley:

> This is why relationships fail, why we get bored with one another and with life. It's because we think we know what everything is.
>
> We do not *listen* to each other. We already always listen to what they said a week ago, a moment ago, last month, last year, ten years ago.
>
> When was the last time you listened for the first time? Listened in the moment, that moment, to what was actually being said?[74]

Angie spoke of this in-the-moment beingness, too:

> What I didn't know then is that there is a reason we are called human beings, not human doings. Being is essential to living.
>
> If you cannot be with yourself exactly as you are, not in some future date when you get better, but right here, right now, then how can you do anything worthwhile with your life? And how can you be with another? You cannot.[75]

Miriam Jacobs tells how her father returned to visit her after his death in order to give advice.[76] He had suffered from congestive heart failure, colon cancer, bipolar disorder, and renal failure for months before he decided to refuse dialysis treatment, knowing that it was sure death. It took two weeks for him to die. Within a few weeks, Jacobs remembered seeing her father appear on the edge of her bed in the early morning, giving her business advice. This continued for months, until one night when he said, "I'm going to leave you alone now." Jacobs noted wryly that her father had taught all these things to her brother, but never felt it important, when alive, to teach her, a girl. She supposed his attitude had changed once he crossed over, and he returned in order to correct his mistake. Once her father had given her all the advice he felt was needed, he disappeared, never to return.

Thus, we see that sometimes suicides come back to give specific advice to the living. This advice may be about trust, personal relationships, how to live life, or even business.

WARNINGS

On rare occasions, a spirit may return to pass on a warning to those left behind. Emma Hardinge told the following story:

> In the year 1826, at Bishopville, South Carolina, Captain William Sumpter, a grandson of General Thomas Sumpter, committed suicide, and was buried at the Baptist churchyard. His grave is about ten steps from the public road, leading from Bishopville to Sumpterville. In a few weeks after this, William Bateman … was riding from Bishopville to his home, about three miles off, and as he passed by Captain Sumpter's grave, at about

twelve or one o'clock in the night, the moon shone brightly; he informed me the next morning that Captain Sumpter arose from his grave and came to him, and placed his hand on his stirrup, and just before he disappeared, he informed Bateman it was his time next. In a few days after this, a man by the name of James B. Reaves shot Bateman, giving him a mortal wound, which did not terminate fatally for two or three weeks. … a few hours before his death, I took down his statement … and he said it was as he stated before, and that he was not mistaken. He observed to me that it was not imagination, and said, "Don't you see it has happened as he told me?"[77]

George Anderson received the following message from a suicide:

There was also someone who wanted to use him sexually. There's pornography involved. There's a cover-up. The young boy is warning his family to be careful. If they try to investigate this privately, be very careful. If they expose it, they'll be in danger. In fact, the boy is saying the family should move.[78]

Later, he repeated the warning while combining it with reassurance:

He puts his finger to his lips to remind you that silence is golden. You'd better keep silent….
He says, at any time if you feel any threat of being pulled into this again, definitely move.[79]

Warnings are not common messages from suicides. It is possible that this could be because those left behind are seldom in grave danger.

ONGOING ISSUES

In cases of accidental suicide during autoeroticism, sometimes the spirits ask their families to speak out about the subject to prevent other deaths. Lauren Thibodeau states:

A lot of times they encourage for the family advocacy and awareness-building activities. Which, for a lot of the parents, is just too much. But occasionally—I did have one woman who had gone to school to speak about it. More than once. It wasn't just a one-time thing. And it was within a few months of her son's death. I mean she was really courageous.[80]

Spirits may also indicate a desire for ongoing continued dialogue with the family they left behind. Thibodeau explains how she sometimes sees and facilitates this communication:

The usual messages tend to follow pretty much the same format of I'm around, I'm here, you're seeing signs of me, have seen signs of me, or soon will. What the medium often does, I do my best to do, is to help the person see the ways in which that will be coming to them. Because what mediums can offer as a service isn't always understood by the people coming to see us. The energy balancing that we bring to it. We sort of smooth the way for the pathway of connection from the loved one on the other side and the loved one here to connect. We're sort of training wheels, or a blueprint, or a map to get here. And that energy trail is left behind. So, it tends to enhance the experience of after-death communication without a medium by seeing a medium. So that's what I get a lot of from these people. These folks often have a real, real visceral need to have communication. And the kids who have passed will give me information for how to look for that. So, it tends to be a bit of confirmation, some validating detail. Right? You left the CD, my favorite CD, in the casket with me, I appreciate it. Something that the family can know and verify—that's passed. Then, they'll talk about—once the families have accepted that, wow, they understand at that point that there's a connection and that even though that person had died, they were around, say at the funeral or something. Something that happened fairly recently. Other confirming detail I think that goes back to during when they were alive, and can share memories, that helps I think, too. But in a case like this the most helpful stuff I have found over the years is the validation that happens in that early grief period. And then taking it forward a little bit into "plus look for this. Here's how I came to you and know what you've done for me." Right? "I am very aware of the scholarship. I'm very aware of how you went to see Mister so-and-so at the school and arranged to speak to the assembly about autoeroticism." And then it will move into, "Here's how you'll know my ongoing presence in your life." I think that's a big part. At least for me as a medium that's how I like to work it. It's not just about the past, but what are we going to do to continue this communication into the future.[81]

Not all spirits adjust well to the afterlife and speak only of love. Some continue to hold onto their grievances. George Anderson, who seems to have channeled as many suicides as anyone, observes:

> In some rare instances during discernments, souls have come across to me from the hereafter that they are not quite ready to reconcile the circumstances that brought them to end their life on the earth. Although they are now in a place free of pain and torment, they might, at least for a brief time, harbor some resentment about the circumstances of their passing. It is a rare occurrence, happening perhaps three or four times in the thousands of discernments I have done, but they are still there.... It is rather like having your face slapped, and then after the pain is gone, you still resent having been slapped. They do understand in the hereafter that their pain is gone, but they still must reconcile their feelings. This is only a temporary feeling for them in the hereafter, however, since everything from

the moment of their passing becomes easier as time passes. Some wounds take longer to heal than others, but all wounds heal, especially in the hereafter.[82]

John Edward also describes an incident in which he felt the spirit was trying to help the living, but that could also represent difficulty letting go of past issues:

> In another case, a young woman came to me hoping to connect with her fiancé, who had recently committed suicide. And he did come through, but it wasn't just love and peace. He came through talking about the jealousy and contentiousness that apparently marked their relationship. I felt bad for her, and saw that when we were done she didn't want to leave. I asked her if she wanted to talk about what she had heard.
> "You focused on all the negatives," she said.
> "I didn't—he did," I said. "And that's probably because it's something that's not finished between the two of you. And that's what he felt was important. Maybe so you don't repeat the same pattern with someone else."
> "But he didn't tell me he loved me."
> "If he didn't love you, he wouldn't have shown up in the first place. This whole thing is born of love."[83]

It is rare that suicides come back to talk about issues they had when alive. This may be due to their changed perspective or the fact that they receive teaching in the spirit realm to help them let go of the past and move forward. Nonetheless, a few souls do communicate somewhat hostile messages, whether intended that way or not. It is likely that this is simply a reminder of the fact that being dead by itself doesn't make you smarter, and your psychological baggage follows you (at least initially) into the afterlife.

CONTROVERSIAL STATEMENTS

Some channeled messages are controversial. One of these came through Anne Puryear and relates to mortal illness. Stephen stated:

> The truth is, most deaths are some form of suicide, either conscious or subconscious.... For instance, cancer is an acceptable form of death, whereas oftentimes it has been created or activated by the individual as a way to get out of circumstances they cannot tolerate, or because they have lost hope. This is not true for every case of cancer, of course, but for a great many. This is also often true for those with the major terminal diseases. The diseases are not visited upon people by some unloving god. They enter bodies where choices are being made many times as to whether to live or

die. The person would never overtly take his own life.... But they are responsible. Emotions and stress left unattended, unhealed, open the door to disease entering and viruses being activated, when the door could be shut.[84]

It should be noted that there is at least some medical evidence to back up these comments. Physicians know that bodies are constantly creating and destroying cancer cells. The immune system normally keeps this in a state of balance. A variety of factors—including stress, nutrition, and mood—affect how well the immune system can do its job. It is typically when the immune system is overwhelmed that illness results. Also, the type of cancer individuals acquire often seems to have a meaningful relationship to underlying psychological issues. For example, it is well known that breast cancer is strongly associated with nurturing issues, and that if those issues are dealt with through psychotherapy, then survival rates improve and there is a greater incidence of cure. Other forms of cancer also appear to be oddly appropriate to what a person is struggling with psychologically.

Stephen also made another controversial statement, this time regarding the death of children:

I've told you that there is a gift that each child who commits suicide leaves. These is a gift to be found in every death if you'll look for it. This is too difficult to hear when a young person first dies, but it is true and should be sought later. They didn't take their lives to leave this gift, but out of their death and your struggle, a gift can be discovered. This applies to the death of all children.[85]

Controversial statements have always been a part of channeled messages. In the Spiritualist era, comments about reincarnation and other "nonChristian" messages were considered to be extremely inflammatory, and caused a storm of disagreement. As accepted cultural values change, so does what is considered contentious. Only time may separate that which is true wisdom from that which is false.

11

Assisted Suicide

In an April 2005 *Time* magazine article, "Choosing Their Time," Margot Roosevelt presents what could be considered the classic right-to-die assisted-suicide scenario:

> Steve Mason is ready for death. Since last December, the 65-year-old writer has kept four small bottles of clear liquid Nembutal—a lethal dose of barbiturates—in his Ashland, Ore., condominium. And at some point in the next few months, when terminal lung cancer has spread to his liver or brain, when his breath is short and he feels too sick to eat or sleep, he will pick a day to gather close friends and family about him. He will give away his belongings and say his goodbyes.
>
> "It will be a celebration of life," Mason predicts. "I'd like to hear Satchmo singing What a Wonderful World." When he actually swallows the potion, he expects to slip into unconsciousness and die within minutes. "I've lived my life with dignity," he says. "I want to go out the same way."[1]

Diagnosed as having terminal cancer a few months earlier by one physician, in order to seek euthanasia, Mason, a retired Army captain and Vietnam veteran, had to go through the legal process of procuring both oral and written requests in the presence of at least two witnesses, then wait a minimum of fifteen days to get a second physician's terminal diagnosis. Only then would his original physician write a prescription for the drug which he could use to end his own life.

Referring to his plan, Mason says, "This isn't suicide. Suicide means a needless taking of life. When five doctors tell you nothing can be done, you are merely ensuring your life ends at the proper time. I don't want my daughters to see me wither away to 80 lbs. and have some night nurse shave my beard and get some feeding tube into my mouth."[2]

Still, who is to say if taking one's own life is needless or needed? As long as one purposefully ends one's own life, does this make it, as Mason puts it, "the proper time," when proper to him appears to mean according to his own personal will and schedule? Many today believe that intentionally ending one's own life, or having someone else help one do so, is by definition always an improper time, since a truly "proper time" would be decided from a spiritual frame of reference transcending the human. As sociologist Emile Durkheim found in the Koran, "Man dies only by the will of God, according to the book which fixes the term of his life."[3] That is, we are to be authors of our own lives on one level, but not on another.

Assisted suicide is a controversial issue. It is legal in one country, the Netherlands, perhaps not surprising given their cultural attitude toward death. In the United States, the state of Oregon has approved a "right-to-die" law and a dozen other states are considering similar legislation, with most proposals allowing physicians to assist in a patient's suicide only when the patient is deemed to be in a terminal condition with less than six months to live.[4] As of 2005, a *Time* magazine poll found 52 percent of Americans agreeing with Oregon's Death with Dignity Act allowing assisted suicide and 41 percent disagreeing.[5]

Approximately 57 percent of all physicians in the Netherlands have performed euthanasia or assisted suicide at some point in their careers. The number of reported cases has stabilized during the period 1995–2001 as physicians have increasingly needed to hear their patient's unequivocal desire for help in their own termination.[6]

Passed twice by the state's voters, in 1994 and 1997, Oregon's unique right-to-die law:

> allows a doctor to prescribe lifesaving drugs to a terminally ill, mentally competent adult whose doctors have forecast death within six months. According to state records, slightly more than 200 patients, most of them suffering from cancer and undergoing pain treatment at hospices, have taken their lives since the law took effect in 1990.[7]

California voters rejected a similar measure in 1992. In 2001, John Ashcroft, then U.S. Attorney General, moved to nullify the Oregon law, threatening that doctors who prescribed federally regulated barbiturates used to end patients' lives would lose their federal prescription licenses. But two federal judges, one in Oregon and one in San Francisco, ruled that Ashcroft had overstepped his authority since he was inappropriately trying to apply a law intended for narcotics trafficking to medical practice, and, in the process, was confusing state and federal provinces of legal application.[8]

The Harvard Guide to Psychiatry reports that the numbers of those siding for and against legalization of physician-assisted suicide in the U.S. are about equal, and that ten of twelve experts cited in a recent report say they "believe that it is not immoral for a physician to assist in the rational suicide of a terminally ill person."[9]

University of New Mexico researchers Tony DiPasquale and John Gluck concur with a great many others today: "In recent years, the relative explosion in awareness and debate over physician-assisted suicide (PAS) has elevated the topic to perhaps the most controversial and widely debated medical-ethical-legal issue since abortion."[10]

They point to the New Mexico Assisted-Suicide Project, "[which] sought to identify attitudes toward legalization and participation in PAS among mental health professionals.... When asked if PAS should be legalized for certain types of cases, three fourths (75 percent) of the respondents said 'yes.'" Reflecting on this finding, they write, "The broad unison supporting the patient's right to autonomy and a merciful end to unbearable suffering likely reflects compassionate recognition of the human condition in complex end-of-life situations."[11]

However, DiPasquale and Gluck point out that such matters may lead to a struggle between the values of the two parties:

> A patient should never be able to get us to do things we don't believe in....
>
> Human beings, mental health providers included, are not automatons and cannot be expected or required to act outside of their personal values. On the other hand, we don't want our personal morality to interfere with well-established rights of patients.[12]

In a 1991 Dutch study, patients requesting euthanasia cited their reasons for wishing to choose death: loss of dignity (57 percent); pain (46 percent); pain, when it is the only reason given (5 percent); when the nature of one's dying seems unworthy (46 percent); having to be dependent on others (33 percent); and being tired of life (23 percent).[13]

In *The Harvard Guide to Psychiatry,* suicide and assisted-suicide authority Edwin Cassem recommends to his fellow clinicians, who are being asked by their clients for prescriptions strong enough to potentially be used to take their own lives, or are being asked to help them hasten death, that they first ask themselves:

> What is it that now makes death seem a better option than life? What was the last straw? What is it that must be avoided or escaped? Is the patient depressed? At what specific point does he believe that his potential for being someone who matters has been exhausted? These questions are critical when a non-terminal patient asks for pills to commit suicide.[14]

So, the questions remains: Just how much can or should physicians do for their patients before resigning themselves to agreeing to help end their lives? To what degree can medicine make assisted suicide unnecessary? In 1991, the World Health Organization defined palliative or hospice care as "the active total care of patients whose disease is not responsive to curative treatments."[15] Cassem points out:

> Legal and ethical sanctions have rarely if ever been imposed in circumstances where the physician acts to provide palliative measures to hasten death when the patient is suffering, his condition is hopeless, and death is imminent ... [and] which allows physicians to ease pain even when it may hasten death.[16]

Cassem's own reservations regarding assisting with a patient's death at his or her request are based on what he calls "religious tenets" and on the professional ethics issue that if a doctor is legally able to cause his or her patient's death, it damages the traditional, life-preserving covenant held between doctor and patient.[17]

One final perspective on the relation between life-ending assisted suicide and life-prolonging palliative care: Herbert Hendin, Medical Director of the American Foundation for Suicide Prevention and Professor of Psychiatry at New York Medical College, writes that "patients requesting a physician's assistance in suicide are usually telling us as strongly as they know how that they are desperate in their need for relief from their suffering, and that without such relief they would rather die."[18] In light of this, Hendin feels that "compassion for suffering patients and respect for patient autonomy serve as the basis for the strongest arguments in favor of legalization" of physician-assisted suicide.[19] Nonetheless, for Hendin the key issue is how knowledgeable physicians are with regard to the best, most advanced medical means of reducing or relieving the kind of unbearable pain and suffering that has driven people to approach them for helping them end their lives as the only way they can see to relieve their suffering. He believes that the more physicians know about palliative care, the less they favor assisted suicide, while the less they know, the more they favor it. In relation to this, he has found that "opposition to legalization [of PAS] in the United States is strongest among physicians who know the most about caring for terminally ill patients, i.e., palliative care specialists."[20] From this perspective: "Under the Oregon law, when a terminally ill patient makes a request for assisted suicide, physicians are required to point out that palliative care and hospice care are feasible alternatives."[21]

Finally, we consider "suicide-by-cop," a relatively recent phenomenon that could be seen to fall under the category of assisted suicide. One person who has specialized in this area and created the definitive website for it is Rebecca Stincelli, who worked for twenty years with the Sacramento (California) County Sheriff's Office as a crisis interventionist and post-trauma liaison for victims of violent crime. On her website,[22] she writes that its goal is to develop and present a more clear understanding of citizens apparently purposefully ending their own lives by threatening the life of police officers in order to provoke the officers to do the dirty work of killing them so they don't have to kill themselves. The website is intended for law enforcement personnel as well as for the general public.

Stincelli provides three interrelated terms and their definitions: *Suicide-by-cop* is defined as "a colloquial term used to describe a suicidal incident whereby the suicidal subject engages in a consciously, life-threatening behavior to the degree that it compels a police officer to respond with deadly force." *Police-assisted suicide* is used to describe a suicide "whereby the suicidal subject completes the act with the assistance of a police officer." And a third term, *victim-precipitated homicide*, implies "a shared responsibility between two (or more) parties whereby a suicidal subject provokes his or her own death by means of another."[23]

The following are excerpts from one officer's description of such an occurrence. Answering a call with his partner, they see a white male come out of a house, saying his uncle, drunk, has been pointing a rifle at his family throughout the night, threatening to kill both them and himself.

> We take our guns out and I knock on the door.... The uncle is laying down ... he sits up ... stares at me for a couple of seconds ... picks up the rifle and I remember thinking I can't believe he is doing this.... He starts to swing the rifle toward me and I tell him drop the gun, drop the gun, drop the gun. He swings the rifle almost to his shoulder and I fire one shot....
>
> I held his left hand while his cousin held his right hand. We prayed.... Mr. Knuckles then looked at me and said "why did you shoot me?" I told you to drop the gun. "I wouldn't have shot you!" How was I supposed to know that? The man I killed that night pointed an unloaded 30.06 at my partner and I. Why?[24]

One answer to the officer's "why?" was that "Mr. Knuckles" wanted to die and preferred to have his unwanted life ended by someone other than himself.

We do not want to conclude this overview without consideration of a religious-spiritual view of assisted suicide. In the introduction to Part II, Murder-Suicide and Suicide Bombers, we will have an opportunity to consider the traditional Islamic spiritual perspectives on death, suicide, murder, and the afterlife, as well as the contemporary extremist Islamic perspectives that lie behind the suicide bombings. But for now, and given that Christianity is the dominant religion in the United States, it is useful to consider here the Christian perspective on assisted suicide.

Physician H. Tristram Engelhardt, Jr., of Rice University, and Ana Smith Iltis of St. Louis University, writing in the prestigious British medical journal *The Lancet* as part of its series on end-of-life issues for different religions, present the traditional Christian view: "Traditional Christian moral prohibitions such as those against suicide and euthanasia should not be interpreted as independent moral constraints, but as flowing from an all-encompassing way of living and dying aimed at union with God."[25] In light of this, they see "the U.S. Supreme Court's upholding a prohibition of physician-assisted suicide because of a traditional prohibition in Anglo-American law, which was grounded in Christian moral understandings."[26]

So, what are some of these Christian understandings? They write: "The Christian pursuit of holiness through humble submission to God excludes intentionally bringing about death through either commission or omission."[27] An example of a life-ending act of omission might be withholding food or treatment from a terminally ill patient making such a request, while an example of an act of commission would be a physician prescribing or providing lethal amounts of life-ending drugs, again at the patient's request. Further, they say:

> Traditional Christianity regards suicide as self-murder, and therefore physician-assisted suicide and euthanasia as forms of assisted self-murder or direct murder. Consent of the patient does not defeat the evil, although it is recognized that those who are insane can take their lives without true consent and culpability.[28]

This view leaves the question of what constitutes the grounds for judging whether someone was insane at the time of death. It appears we have here a kind of religious "insanity plea." How do we objectively evaluate the mental state and competence of those choosing to take their own lives, or asking another to help them do so, if such might have some bearing on the future of their "immortal souls?" It would appear that deciding to hasten one's own death while in the throes of unrelenting physical pain and suffering accompanying the final period of terminal illness could be judged a rational act stemming from sanity, not insanity, while it might be considered a form of insanity to unnecessarily prolong extreme suffering where all quality and meaning of physically embodied human existence has disappeared.

According to Engelhardt and Iltis, the traditional Christian view does allow some forms of medically assisted, "easier" death when death is soon inevitable anyway. But it emphasizes allowing the patient enough clarity for as long as possible so that he or she is capable of consciously carrying out appropriate Christian end-of-life choices and rites. They write: "Christianity also accepts the appropriateness of analgesia and sedation to avoid terminal suffering and despair if this does not, by obtunding [i.e., reducing, dulling, or blunting] consciousness, take away a final opportunity for repentance."[29] That is: "Knowledge of one's impending death offers a final chance to become reconciled with those whom one has harmed and to ask God's forgiveness," thus choosing for oneself "death with repentance."[30]

Dominant across the hundreds of spirit communications in this book is the presentation of a transcendental, spiritual context for understanding life, death, and what comes after death, including the transcendental, spiritual meanings and repercussions of taking one's own life. One's state of mind at the time of suicide, what was being avoided in life, what had not yet been learned from life that needed to be learned at the time of death, and the peace one had, or had not, made with oneself and with the larger spiritual reality and with God—these are all essential themes we find recurring throughout the afterlife spirit stories in this book.

Concluding this focus on assisted suicide, one can find situations where an entire country (the Netherlands) or state (Oregon) has agreed to physician-assisted suicide, and yet in most of the country and the world there is still strong feeling against this practice, no matter how much someone may be unavoidably, consciously suffering in spite of the best palliative care that can be found. This polarization of attitudes toward assisted suicide and euthanasia tends to be reflected as well in the channeled material, with different eras espousing different views on how it affects the soul—suggesting that cultural bias, operating within the mediums and channels, may have crept into the material. Indeed, unlike traditional suicide, commentary purporting to come from the afterlife appears to cover the entire spectrum of possibilities, from absolute rejection of the concept of assisted suicide to enthusiastic endorsement.

SPIRIT ATTITUDES

Let us now turn our attention to this topic from the perspective of selected afterlife communications, much of which takes a rather dim view of assisted suicide and euthanasia. Allan Kardec, for example, received the following channeled answers to his questions about suicide when a person finds him- or herself terminally ill:

> 953. Is it wrong on the part of him who finds himself exposed to some terrible and inevitable death to shorten his sufferings by killing himself?
>
> "It is always wrong not to await the moment of dissolution appointed by God. Besides, how can a man tell whether the end of his life has really come, or whether some unexpected help may not reach him at what he supposes to be his last moment?"
>
> —We admit that suicide is reprehensible under ordinary circumstances, but we are supposing a case in which death is inevitable, and in which life is only shortened by a few instants?
>
> "There is always in such a case a want of resignation and of submission to the will of the Creator."
>
> —What in such a case are the consequences of suicide?
>
> "The same as in all other cases: an expiation proportioned to the gravity of the fault, according to the circumstances under which it was committed."[31]

In the early 1900s, W. Usborne Moore asked the spirits at a séance what their opinion was on the fate of a suicide, and was told, "That is a fate no one would court—groping in the dark to pick up the dropped stitches that fell from knitting needles."[32] When pressed whether the situation was the same for someone who was terminally ill, Moore was told, "Their fate must be worked out in this phase or the next. Trouble can only be overcome by endurance. You can never escape the law of consequences."[33]

As early as 1938, Silver Birch discussed whether doctors should provide euthanasia (which appears pertinent to assisted suicide) to those in pain.[34] The guide noted that it was okay for life to be prolonged even if that meant the individual was suffering, for in Silver Birch's view, "When it is time for the soul to be released it goes, and there is nothing that you can do in your world of matter to alter that law."[35] The guide further notes that the euthanasia of terminally ill patients may be a shock to the system, which causes the soul to have to adjust a great deal more than would otherwise be necessary.

Other views on euthanasia expressed through automatic writing are equally negative, sometimes sounding almost suspiciously like they may have come straight from the unconscious mind of the receiver. Jean Marshall writes:

> It is always difficult to see the ones one loves being put to pain and suffering and dying slowly. But one must not be tempted to hasten their end by any form of euthanasia. It is not according to God's Laws, and he will not forgive it.[36]

A channeled message from the spirit of Rahman on euthanasia appears to be similar:

> The span of human life is the prerogative of the Godhead alone, and no other must intervene. Know this: Mankind is born to live a life to a set pattern.
> It is definitely decided when he will die at the onset.... There are certain markers or sign posts in his life at which he must arrive....
> On the other hand, we often see that by abuses of the physical body you may be incapable of living long enough to complete all your tasks.... We must then make hurried preparations for your reception and cut short our plans.[37]

This passage would seem to indicate that a person should not take either his or her own life or that of another because it cuts short a person's life plan. However, it also suggests that the spirit realm can be flexible when necessary.

Not all material channeled from the early- to mid-1900s was so negative toward assisted suicide. Some messages take a softer stance. Arthur Ford states that the channeled spirit of Myers felt there was nothing wrong with using medications to aid the passing of terminally ill individuals.[38] However, Myers qualified that by stating that "he thought several days should be allowed for the transition."[39] He also indirectly addressed the question of how those who assist in euthanasia are viewed by the spirit realm, adding, "Under these conditions the merciful physician is entirely justified in committing what the law still holds to be murder."[40]

Aaron was channeled through Barbara Brodsky as saying that those who leave life through assisted suicide have similar experiences to those who took their own life while in a healthy body. In both cases:

> First of all, when they first begin to open to the light, however long that takes, they will experience some sadness that they let go of the opportunity for learning.... There is an acceptance. ... there's not a condemnation anymore, but a growing compassion which helps the being move off further into the light and, eventually, into a new incarnation....
> There can be profound learning on the astral plane, sometimes learning that was not possible during the incarnation because you were so blind and caught in your own misery. But, of course, there is still the loss of that opportunity.... And that learning that occurred on the astral plane still must be carried into the incarnation. With few exceptions, only in the incarnation is karma resolved.[41]

With assisted suicide, Aaron added:

> Perhaps learning was possible. Perhaps if one could have tolerated that state, made more space for one's pain, a certain opening of the heart would have been possible that was not permitted. On the other hand, there is a kindness and sense of compassion toward the being, the human who found its situation intolerable. So, there may be a sadness, but, also ... a resolve to look with compassion at the being that it was.[42]

James Van Praagh has voiced concern over the fact that one never really knows until after the fact (when the soul learns the truth of the situation in the afterlife) whether something valuable was lost with cutting your suffering short. He states:

> In the case of terminally ill or elderly persons, some are sick and want to save their families time, money, and heartache by committing suicide. These persons are unaware of the spiritual side of their actions. Perhaps before coming into the physical plane, family members set up certain conditions and situations in order to work out their group karma. Or they needed to experience being of service to the one who is ill. Furthermore, some argue that assisted suicide is best—it stops suffering and gives death some dignity. But who can play God? How do we know that a soul didn't choose to go through an experience of a fatal illness in order to burn away karma? If we cut short someone's natural time on earth, we never know whether something valuable could have been learned or whether such an experience was necessary to reach a new spiritual plateau.[43]

Western Edition was also channeled expressing concern over what might happen if a lot of people opted out of any illness they felt it might not be in their personal best interest to suffer through.[44] It stated that should this happen, one consequence might be that they would lose the opportunity to practice the suffering that is needed for them to develop greater compassion for others.[45]

The entity, Dr. John, channeled by Franklin Loehr took a balanced approach to suicide in the terminally ill. Dr. John spoke about the subject, and its complexities, at length:

> The soul chooses its time of birth. And the soul can choose when to withdraw, but on the whole it is left to the body itself to some extent.... There needs to be greater spiritual understanding before the right of an individual to choose his/her own time of death could be considered a universal right.... It's good to check with one's guides, with others, and that it be not an emotional or impulsive thing.
>
> Question: You are saying if I am terminally ill and in great pain, a burden, I could with impunity and in good conscience, take my own life?

> Dr. John: If the pain is prolonged, if the good that was to be gotten from the pain has already been gotten, there is no point in prolonging the experience. Now to know whether or not the good has been gotten will require quite a depth of spiritual insight, and is a decision that should be made gradually. But then, yes, it would not carry the usual penalties of suicide....
>
> If the life pattern is completed, and then you choose to die, choose carefully, gradually, thoughtfully, prayerfully, and preferably after talking it over with several others (probably not your doctor), then there would not be the usual penalty, the usual result for suicide. Often it would give you fewer years of misery, and a little earlier start on the progression of glory ahead.[46]

This same entity felt that there was no problem at all with ending the artificial prolongation of life through life support, and that bodies should never be maintained through such means in the first place. The following dialogue occurred between a questioner and Dr. John:

> Does the soul experience trauma when life is extended by life-support systems?
>
> In general, yes. Part of the trauma being that when the pattern for that life is over, why should the physical instrument be maintained? When the time of purposefulness has ended, then there is a certain vacuum, a certain lack, in that which lies ahead, and prolongation of the physical instrument is a painful process, part of the pain being its purposelessness. A person without a purpose is an anomaly in this purposeful creation and this purposeful world. That is part of it.
>
> Another part is that it is just a stupid thing to do.[47]

Dr. John later added:

> There are times when the taking of a life by the individual is really a spiritual advance over a continuation of a life that is meaningless, and is a detriment to others as well as to itself. But to discern which is which and the proper timing is a level of discrimination and discernment not yet reached on earth. On Our Side too, the guides and teachers on the whole do not as yet know enough, do not have enough spiritual principles, for reaching the right answer to counsel self-release, except very rarely.
>
> However, the needless prolongation of a life that really has ended is the pendulum swinging the other way, and "pulling the plug" in such a situation is not suicide and is not murder. It is a going along with the natural order of things, which natural order and right order of things had been violated by the needless prolongation of purposeless existence. But discrimination is the key, and discrimination is a large problem in this area.

> Question: How does terminal illness fit into someone taking his own life before going through the proposed agony of a slow death? Is there any karmic imbalance caused by this?
>
> Dr. John: There can be a long terminal illness which may be an opportunity to experience the love of others in the care given, and the progressive love of society providing care. Having said that, this is but one general consideration, and each individual case is an individual case. It is not possible to make a set rule in this area, and it is difficult to reach an individual decision in many of the cases.[48]

Finally, when asked about a specific case involving a woman with severe multiple sclerosis, Dr. John responded:

> If Mada and her husband and possibly the other members of her family come to a time of agreement that the condition of her body and the completion of the positive aspects of her life really indicate spiritually and logically that it would be good for her to make her transition, and if it is done with sufficient time so that all concerned come to an emotional acceptance of it as a good and glorious step out of limitation into greater health, into more life, into even a greater companionship with them, her loved ones, then if such a decision is made, well, I for one certainly would not speak against it in any way. I believe it could be a step of spiritual progression to reach such a stage.[49]

Jeanne Walker's deceased daughter, Karen, expressed an even more extreme attitude through automatic writing, making the following controversial statement:

> If you accept my premise that death is but a step into a new level of consciousness where the individual continues to grow, then the problem of the mercy killing is of considerably less significance than you have made it.... I am talking about such situations as a definite terminal illness where the individual is a vegetable or where the suffering is so intense that prolongation of life, even with drugs, is nonsensical. In such cases there can be no question but that someone there must take responsibility for the *release* of life into a new realm. I do not mean just removing life-support systems and letting the person go on but sending him on by literally destroying the physical body.
>
> Another instance where such destruction is necessary is with those individuals whose mental capacity is so limited that no learning from life-experience takes place. This is a more difficult decision than the one of terminal illness and pain, for it is hard to know how extreme the mental impairment must be....
>
> The test is this: *If quantity can no longer be gained on earth plane due to extreme physical handicaps, then coming across is necessary for growth.* Such

a termination is truly a release for the individual as well as for the purpose of evolution....

Until you learn better methods, such so-called mercy killing must be accomplished by physical (medically induced) means.[50]

Karen, who died at a young age from cancer, is one of the few channeled spirits who also directly addressed the question of what would happen if a person who assists another in suicide then takes his or her own life.[51] When asked what happens to the person who performs a mercy killing, Walker writes, Karen replied as follows:

"Suppose I had literally taken your life," he said. "Our present laws would demand my imprisonment or death. My own guilt might also have worried me. In such a case is suicide wrong?"

"It is never 'wrong,'" came the answer. "The result would depend on the person involved. First, if the true motive of the mercy killing is love, then probably the person performing it has a fairly high degree of quality. In such a case the transition is usually smooth and easy. There may be a brief period of adjustment, but such an individual quickly recognizes that he has performed a worthwhile service and makes excellent progress there. There is certainly no need of physical punishment on your place for such an act."[52]

When Karen was asked why no one had spoken of this before, she stated:

It has been said, but not often in the Western world.... The main reason it is so seldom mentioned is because most mediums color the ideas with their own opinions.... As for people taking advantage of a permissive attitude toward either euthanasia or suicide, we have little concern. Those who would kill others maliciously will not be concerned with this message. Those who would kill themselves neurotically would do so no matter what anyone said. We have *not given these people permission* but have warned them of possible serious consequences. Those who are truly ready for release may be freed by this message, and if this happens, we have performed a great service.[53]

A more ambivalent comment comes from Gildas:

The practice of euthanasia ... is not truly in keeping with living according to spiritual and karmic laws. To us things can rarely be seen as wholly right or wholly wrong, wholly black or wholly white. If this practice came into use, then it would also be used karmically on the group level and also on the individual, higher-self level.[54]

However, Gildas then pointed out that there is a difference between no longer artificially prolonging life—hence allowing a natural death to occur—and an act of euthanasia performed because a person is old and tired and finding life hard.

Abraham, channeled by Erica Reppel, spoke about the differences between euthanasia and assisted suicide as follows:

> Many people now consider euthanasia an acceptable alternative to natural death. Like suicide, it seems to solve or remove many of the problems associated with the discomforts of illness or the deterioration of old age. But in seeking to solve a problem by avoidance you can often create another that is more difficult to deal with....
>
> It is often easier to face an experience than to live with guilt....
>
> Avoiding any issue will only delay the experience of that learning. Any act that robs you of your opportunities cannot be to your benefit. ... you simply delay an opportunity for growth....
>
> When you take your own life, even when it has the approval of others or of society in general, we still consider this suicide.
>
> However, when others are involved the issue is more complex. An act of compassion by another could well involve the balancing of karma. This cannot be considered in the same category.
>
> We cannot generalize, for there are too many issues involved. But if one soul helps to take the life of another with the consent of the person being killed, then it ... is not suicide, for that person's death is taking place at the correct time.[55]

The group being, Michael, felt assisted suicide could have consequences for future lives, saying, "If a person with terminal cancer suicides and there remained five or six months of life with its attendant lessons, then that soul will experience infant death at a later time."[56]

Stephen, who spoke at length through his mother after hanging himself, felt that suicide could sometimes be the correct choice in adults (never for children), given certain sets of circumstances:

> For instance: if the thinking is truly clear and things have been planned out and thought through; if the person has accomplished their soul purpose; if it's not a cop-out to keep from doing what they came in to do; if their own inner guidance is that suicide is the correct spiritual way for them to release; if there is no doubt that it is for the very highest good for themselves or another; if it's done with much thought and prayer and not done in anger and vengeance. Lots of *ifs*.
>
> You may wonder what such circumstances could be. An elderly couple in failing health that simply cannot accomplish any more in their frail bodies, can take direct control of their lives and leave through their own choice if they are sure, beyond doubt, that they have done all they can, learned all they need to learn. Every case is different, and no one can judge the

correctness or incorrectness of it, for that falls upon the shoulders of the person making such a decision....

A terminally ill person, in great pain, having exhausted all means of being healed might choose to take control of his life rather than continue to endure suffering, or for reasons of wanting to end astronomical medical bills, for his family, simply to prolong his life for a short period.... These are just a few examples. Also taking their lives under these spiritually correct conditions can free the soul from a body where they are not making any growth. This enables them to get to the spirit plane where they can learn and grow, which often prepares them for a future reincarnation more rapidly.[57]

What Puryear channeled is clearly controversial. The reader will have noted many earlier passages by suicides stating that it is never a correct option. It is impossible to judge how much of this discrepancy is due to cultural bias (either in the sender or receiver of the channeled message), variations in the level of knowledge of the soul transmitting the information, or some other factor. Some support for this viewpoint appears in a message from a spirit known as James:

> Your question presupposes a blameless form of suicide.... Such is not the case! It may be that *individuals* choose to commit suicide, and how serious the offense is depends, not too surprisingly, on the individual's motive. If they select self-annihilation at the end of a long and varied life, merely to forestall severe inconvenience and physical pain for themselves—or better yet, for others—then *that* particular suicide *may* be entirely blameless and may, in fact, have been chosen in advance, before the life began.[58]

A spirit, suffering from Alzheimer's disease before his death, spoke in a similar vein on this topic through Suzane Northrop:

> As for me, my soul had been preparing to leave, but my body was in good working order, so I stayed longer than I probably should have. In this circumstance I have to say that if the body is not serving the soul's purpose, it might be better to move on. But let me repeat this, only the soul can make this decision and that decision must be considered very, very carefully.
>
> If others are involved, either because the individual is in no condition to decide, or because the ill person has asked for their help, all must agree. It is important that the entire family agree without feelings of guilt and trust that they, in aid of the soul, with God's guidance, and to the best of their own knowledge have made the right decision. With this, God does step in and put[s] all the soul's learning into balance.[59]

Along these lines, Michael Newton makes the interesting observation of the people he had regressed through hypnosis to the period between lives that:

> I want to add that those who escape from chronic physical pain or almost total incapacity on Earth by killing themselves feel no remorse as souls. Their guides and friends also have a more accepting view toward this motivation for suicide.[60]

Newton also states:

> Suicide by a person, young or old, whose physical state has reduced the quality of their life to almost nothing is treated differently in the spirit world than those who had healthy bodies....
>
> In my experience, souls feel no sense of failure or regret when they have been involved with a mercy death.... In the spirit world, I find that no stigma is attached to a soul leaving a terribly broken body who is released by its own hand or from that of a compassionate caregiver.[61]

Completing the spectrum of channeled attitudes toward euthanasia and assisted suicide from the afterlife is the material proposed by a team of spirits led by the deceased Jesse Holmes.[62] They proposed:

> If the medical staff is in agreement that there is no help for the physical body, that a great long period of suffering is in the future, or that the being truly has no desire to live and that there is nothing to be accomplished by his further life in his present physical body, then the individual should have the privilege of being quietly and gently put to sleep.
>
> This would allow the spirit to escape the body and come on into the worlds of spirit without the trauma, without the physical suffering, and without the great struggle that many undergo ... to be free of the physical body.[63]

It should be noted that not all suicides who take their own lives because of ill health—with or without help—later feel their decision was the right one for them. As mentioned in an earlier chapter, Bill and Judy Guggenheim tell of a message from the soul of an elderly women with cancer who had taken her own life: "She told me that suicide was not the answer. She had made that mistake herself."[64]

Other mediums have also observed that having a painful terminal illness may have spiritual benefits in itself—which cutting the life short could potentially diminish. George Anderson and Andrew Barone explain:

> Terminal illness is an ugly, cruel way to pass—there is no doubt about that. So much of our loved ones are lost even before they pass, and the

anguish of watching a love[d] one in so much pain has a lasting effect on those who are left to grieve. But once passed, these souls insist that it was necessary, both for us and for them, that the spiritual lesson of pain and suffering prior to passing be learned. They tell us that not only did they benefit from the suffering in the hereafter but that we also stand to benefit from this difficult time as it is a spiritual milestone we have passed. I can see the faces of astonishment in a discernment when a loved one in the hereafter says that they would gladly endure their pain again to gain the same reward in the hereafter. They also acknowledge that no matter how bad things got, *all* of it was necessary for the completion of their lessons on the earth.[65]

In one case of one spirit who came back, George Anderson recalls:

> The parents of a nineteen-year-old girl who passed on from scleroderma wrote to me about the agony their daughter went through as a result of her illness. The illness causes a very painful breakdown of the skin, and she suffered so much that the mother actually considered killing her so that she could escape the pain—that is how hard it was to watch her suffer. Yet when I discerned her from the hereafter she was remarkably candid about needing to have the experience on the earth, as part of her spiritual education. She stated to me (and her parents) that although she wouldn't "wish that kind of pain on a dog," she benefited from the hard lesson so much in the hereafter that, "If I had to do it again to get the same reward here, I would in a heartbeat."[66]

Finally, the spirit guide, Trio, noted that in assisted suicide, the individual's attitude or awareness at the time he or she crosses over may affect his or her transition. Trio explained the problem as follows:

> If the consciousness is aware they are intending to end with the understanding they are not separate, the crossing will be peaceful. If the intention to exit is locked into the illusion of desperation because they have not explored other ways of looking at how they participate with their purpose in the world, they will still evolve but they will find the crossing more stagnant, is the only way I can describe it.[67]

We have seen in this section that the spirit attitudes toward assisted suicide appear to run the gamut, from absolute rejection to complete acceptance. Yet if we consider them more closely, it is possible to see that the true answer may be a complex one, which leads to an "it depends" kind of answer. What is best for one may not be for another. Karma and the completion of one's blueprint may only be two of many factors that need to be weighed and considered.

WHAT SOULS WHO WERE INVOLVED IN ASSISTED SUICIDE SAY

Let us turn our attention to what those souls who successfully took their own lives through assisted suicide say about their actions in hindsight. In a few cases, the manner of death appeared to have been planned prior to their incarnation. Michael Newton describes one case where under hypnosis he was told:

> S: As we prepared to come forward into this life, I was to be the oldest child in our family so I came first. We had a long discussion just before my time. Keith said he was prepared to suffer but when he reached the point where he was totally incapacitated—when he couldn't take any more—I was to shut off his life support system and free him.
>
> Dr. N: You were going to do this in a hospital?
>
> S: We planned for that in the spirit world but then, thank God, he was sent home during his last seven weeks and that made our plan easier....
>
> After Sandy regained full consciousness we discussed her role in the death of her brother. She said when there was a particular smell, or "death odor," from Keith's throat area, she knew it was time to get ready.... Almost without thinking Sandy spoke in her brother's ear, "Keith, are you ready to go?" Then came the prearranged signal. At this moment Keith squeezed his eyes open and shut three times for the "yes" response. Calmly, she detached Keith's life support system. The doctor came to the house later, found the life support system reattached, and pronounced Keith dead.
>
> For the rest of the day, she felt no guilt. That night, lying in bed, a doubt crept into Sandy's mind about her automatic reactions, and she questioned herself. After tossing and turning she finally fell into a fitful sleep. Soon Keith came to her in a dream. Smiling with gratitude, he conveyed to Sandy that she had done everything perfectly and that he loved her. A few weeks later Sandy was meditating and had a vision of her brother sitting on a bench talking with "two monks dressed in robes." Keith turned, laughed at her, and said, "Hang in there, Sis!"[68]

Thus we see that the choice to experience assisted suicide appeared to have been made prior to incarnating, where it was discussed and an agreement made. Even so, carrying out that agreement still led to angst over whether this had been the right thing to do. It is interesting that this soul, like many traditional suicides, made a point of returning during the dream state to provide reassurance, so Sandy could let go of her guilt. However, it should be noted that Michael Newton felt that assisted suicide was a very different situation from traditional suicide, because terminating a fit body was *never* planned in advance of a lifetime. He states categorically, "Suicide is not one of these options. Suicide by a physically healthy young person is not a prearranged karmic option for anyone."[69]

It does not seem surprising that the living may often need reassurance after participating in assisted suicide. We can find other instances where this has occurred. Suzane Northrop channeled the return of a woman to her husband who had made the difficult decision of whether to terminate life support. She describes the session:

> Within seconds, standing next to him in spirit was a young woman. At first it felt like she might have been a sister, but I sensed there was a baby with her. I then heard the initial C and another name that sounded like Alice or Alison.
> Howard began nervously wiping the tears from his eyes. Alison was his older daughter. He then told me that spirit was his wife, Carolyn. I asked if he knew who the baby was. "My baby, a baby girl."
> His wife kept saying, "The baby died immediately but I went into a coma." She continued by adamantly stating that he had done the right thing, for she was no longer there. This seemed to be very important information, because she repeated it over and over again, "You did the right thing. Please don't blame yourself or feel guilt; I thank you for doing what you did. It was what I would have asked of you."[70]

This husband later explained what had happened:

> Howard knew without question Carolyn was gone. He didn't know how he knew, he just knew. The internal conflict was horrific.
> Carolyn remained on support for six months. Howard needed to know what his options were, what the prognosis might be of any recovery. He contacted a known specialist on comas at a major hospital medical center. The doctor requested a photograph of Carolyn before he went to see her. Howard thought this odd, but didn't say anything.
> The doctor then went to see Carolyn. Coming out of her room, he told Howard, "I've seen this before. It's difficult for me to explain, it's not a religious thing, but she's not there. That's all I can say."
> Howard had felt sure Carolyn had "left" the day she was put on life support. Now, finally, he knew without a doubt what to do and his decision was made; two days later he terminated support for his beloved wife....
> He hoped Carolyn would forgive him and that he was doing the right thing. Carolyn as a DP [dead person] answered his prayers, "Yes, you did, I was not there."
> I remembered Bill's grandfather as Carolyn echoed his idea. To the DPs, euthanasia is not considered murder or suicide if the soul can no longer learn, because the body is incapable of continuing as intended. In essence, the soul's learning in this particular lifetime is finished.

This is still a decision requiring deep thought and contemplation. That contemplation should involve the person whose life may be ending and then those loved ones left here.

It is clear, though, that this situation is unlike conscious suicide, where discontinuing the physical journey intentionally leaves those behind devastated and interrupts the soul's blueprint.[71]

Dealing with those in a coma is one area where consulting a reputable and conscientious medium would seem to be of value—as a chance to discuss the situation with the person in coma. It should be mentioned that other mediums have mentioned similar experiences on an informal basis, and that this is not an isolated incident. Many souls do not wish to have their physical bodies uselessly prolonged by artificial life support. Furthermore, the few messages we have from assisted suicides do not speak of regret, but instead try to reassure those left behind that all is now well and they did the right thing.

Euthanasia and assisted suicide are controversial. Although some accept such an act as a compassionate way of allowing a person to end his or her life, others fear its potential for abuse. Channeled messages also reflect this range of beliefs, with some inflexibly stating that suicide is bad even if there's a terminal illness, others suggesting it can depend on whether a person has finished accomplishing his or her tasks for that lifetime, and still other spirits advocating for the idea of choosing your own time of death. What the true answer may be could well lie somewhere in the middle ground, with "it depends."

PART II

Murder-Suicide and Suicide Bombers

12

Overview of Murder-Suicide

So far in this book, we have addressed the question: If you commit suicide, what happens after you die, according to spirit sources in the afterlife? For the remainder of this book, we will ask the further, related question: What happens after you die if you kill someone else, and, primarily, what happens if you kill someone else (or others) in the process of killing yourself? This second question will be considered in light of selected spirit sources in the afterlife. Before we turn to these spirit sources, however, we need to look at what the best of our sources *right here on Earth* have to say about the combination of self-murder and the murder of others in order to provide a foundation for weighing the contributions from the spirit realm that will follow. Therefore, the purpose for this chapter is to provide you with a better understanding of the contemporary phenomenon that has come to be known as "suicide bombers," primarily operating today in the Arab Middle East.

SUICIDE BOMBERS

Most of those carrying out these acts are Muslims who take an Islamic fundamentalist perspective on what they are doing and why they are doing it. Most of them could be fairly characterized as being willing to give their lives for political, nationalist, or territorial reasons, using extreme military-type terrorist tactics in the process. At the same time, most of these same suicide bombers may be equally characterized, and are characterized by themselves, as spiritually motivated "warriors" fighting as martyrs in a jihad, or holy war, on behalf of what they hold dear. As part of this martyred, spiritual perspective, they see their acts of murder-suicide earning them a place in the afterlife, portrayed as paradise by traditional Islamic teachings, as well as by many contemporary political leaders and virtually all Islamic-oriented terrorist organizations.

Because the near-universal extremist Islamic scenario of the noble, martyred suicide bomber fighting for a supposed just cause in order to receive Allah's love in paradise lies at the heart of so much of what is being played out on the world stage today, we have chosen to provide here a fairly detailed and, we hope, balanced picture of this suicide-bomber phenomenon together with some of its socio-historical, political, and experiential roots and contexts. We will also look at the phenomenon through the lenses of psychology and psychiatry to try and understand what may be going on inside such individuals that could lead them to carry out such extreme, life-ending acts—acts that purposefully end not only their own lives, but the lives of others as well.

Our objective is to provide you with enough information to make your own conjectures and judgments about the afterlife spirits' perspective on what may or may not be awaiting these suicide bombers once they have carried out their ultimate acts of killing both themselves and others. We also hope this chapter will help prepare you to better appreciate the purported afterlife spirit messages in the remainder of the book, which are said to come from "successful" suicide bombers and other suicide-murderers.

Neil Altman, Associate Clinical Professor in the post-doctoral program in Psychotherapy and Psychoanalysis at New York University, provides an excellent introduction to this topic:

> Sometime back I remember someone proposing that these attacks should be called "homicide bombings" rather than "suicide bombings"; the emphasis on "suicide" directs our attention away from the fact that these are attacks on other people. Yet, the proposal never caught on; the fact that the attacker arranges that he *must* die, more inevitably than any other victim, compels our attention. We have no term in English for this phenomenon: "murder-suicide" refers to cases in which someone kills another and *then* kills himself. The suicide is *secondary* to the murder.[1]

Most of these acts of homicide bombing, or suicide bombing, are taking place in the Middle East today on the part of terrorist splinter groups waging what they see to be an Islamic jihad—a righteous war of self-defense against an enemy of their religion and culture. Even though these acts of murder-suicide can be interpreted in very worldly, socio-political, and strategic power-struggle ways, they also possess a distinctive transcendental character. Altman reminds us of this now-familiar theme: "It has come to the attention of most people in the West in the wake of the September 11th attacks that Muslim suicide attackers believe that with their action they become martyrs in a holy war, thus eligible for rewards in heaven."[2]

Continuing, Altman provides us with some perspectives on the suicide-bomber phenomenon that we will examine in more depth for the remainder of this overview. He writes:

> The suicide bomber is not satisfied with either killing himself alone to make a point (as Buddhist monks have been known to do) or with killing others while preserving himself (in typical military fashion). The bomber is seeking to actualize or dramatize a *psychological* situation occurring in an interpersonal and inter-group context. He does so for an audience, an audience consisting of those who he feels are responsible for his death, a psychological death that in a sense has already occurred.
>
> What is the nature of the psychological death, the murder, that has already occurred at the time of the suicide bombing? Extreme shame, extreme humiliation, can be experienced as psychological death. People will kill and die for their honor or their self-respect, because to lose their dignity can be experienced as a fate worse than death.... Humiliation also leads to rage.
>
> One [Christian] martyr, Saint Perpetua, [2,000 years ago] was reported "to take the trembling hand of the young gladiator and guide it to her throat." By taking control of the knife, she refuses the humiliation of being helpless and demonstrates her commitment to a higher cause for which she will embrace her own death. Likewise, by killing himself, the suicide bomber undoes the indignity of having been helpless to prevent his death at the hands of another and turns the tables by killing that other.[3]

PSYCHOLOGICAL AND PSYCHIATRIC PERSPECTIVES

Let us first look briefly at what mainstream psychology and psychiatry have to say about suicide when it is coupled with murder. Marc Hillbrand, professor at the Yale University School of Medicine, writes about cases of homicide-suicide, which he calls "co-occurring aggression against self and against others" and believes to be a little-understood phenomenon, accounting for one in forty deaths in the United States and with a similar prevalence elsewhere in the world. Usually the murder occurs first, followed by the suicide of the murderer. In the U.S., 95 percent of those initiating this disturbing two-step process are males and 85 percent of those murdered are women. Usually the situation involves one person being murdered and one person doing the murdering and then committing suicide, but there are certainly cases where one perpetrator may first kill a number of people. About half of all mass-murder killing sprees end with the suicide of the killer. There appear to be a variety of causes and motives that lie behind such acts. For example, in one British study, 75 percent of the perpetrators had a history of depression.[4]

According to Leonard Berkowitz, author of a leading study on the subject, *Aggression: Its Causes, Consequences, and Control*[5]: "The most popular theory of aggression in the social sciences holds that people are driven to attack others when they are frustrated: when they are unable to reach their goals, or they do not obtain the rewards they expect.[6] The most extreme form of aggression imaginable against another is murder and the most extreme form of aggression against oneself is self-murder, or suicide. Therefore the kind of murder-suicide involved with present-day suicide bombers, for example, is a compounded, extreme act of aggression. Later, we will look at the Islamic perspective on why the suicide bombings are justified; what they say lies behind their murderous acts, including feeling thwarted, frustrated, wronged, and threatened.

Berkowitz continues: "For some the term [frustration] refers to an *external barrier* to keep someone from reaching a goal, while others think of 'frustration' as an internal emotional reaction that arises from the thwarting (as when we say we 'feel frustrated')."[7] Then he makes an interesting comment: "Strictly speaking, we can't frustrate those who have no hope."[8] This seems a paradox; the suicide bombers, as we shall soon hear, often seem to voice both frustration and hopelessness—at least hopelessness with regard to their earthly situation. Perhaps when there is hopefulness, it lies in their sense that there is a possibility that their act of murder-suicide might at least make a difference in the relatively hopeless conditions of their similarly minded fellow countrymen they leave behind. Their hopefulness, from a non-earthly perspective, lies with their assumption that their martyred death will deliver them into the welcoming and approving arms of Allah, their God.

Returning to the generally espoused traditional psychological view reported by Berkowitz that every aggressive action can be traced to a previous frustration, he nonetheless feels it is just too sweeping:

> It fails to draw the important distinction between emotional aggression and instrumental aggression. Instrumental aggression can be learned ... by seeing that this behavior pays off—and need not be derived from some prior thwarting.... [But we can say] that a barrier to expected goal attainment generates an instigation to emotional aggression—an inclination to hurt [or kill] someone primarily for the sake of inflicting injury.[9]

What ultimately lies behind the terminal behavior of a suicide bomber does not lend itself to simple analysis. Working with the Beyond Intractability Knowledge-Based Project associated with the Conflict Resolution Consortium at the University of Colorado, Boulder, Michelle Maiese says about suicide bombers:

Research shows no indication that terrorists are crazy or psychopathic or that they lack moral feelings. ... terrorists tend to have considerable insight into their own actions and are aware of how others view them. They believe that their violent actions, while somewhat regrettable, are justified and noble.... Those who commit or advocate such acts do not regard them as acts of suicide, but rather as acts of martyrdom. While suicide is associated with hopelessness and depression, the actions of the bombers are seen as a matter of heroism and honor.[10]

Whether we are looking at suicide, or at murder, or at both together as one complex act, a number of researchers and clinicians have looked at the part played by anger, as just one frame of reference for trying to understand what is going on. When Chris Cantor, a psychiatrist on the faculty of the Department of Social and Preventive Medicine at the University of Queensland, Australia, was asked by his teenage son why all people with tragic lives don't just kill themselves, his response was that "Suicide requires more than just misfortune (and depression). It usually requires acute or habitual anger directed against oneself and or others."[11] It may turn out to be more of a challenge to demonstrate that suicide bombers harbor anger against themselves as part of what lies behind taking their own lives than it is to understand the more commonsense notion that anger toward others would lie behind their killing. Then, to complicate things still further, those actually being killed might not be the most deserving of the perpetrator's anger, as in the case of those killed being fellow Iraqis or fellow Arab Muslims.

Let us turn for a moment from suicide as self-murder and look at the act of killing someone other than oneself, that is, simple murder. In 2005, psychiatrist Carl P. Malmquist published his definitive study *Homicide: A Psychiatric Perspective*, in which he says that "the overall number of homicides per year in the United States is almost as great as that of suicides."[12] He points to some 30,000 successful suicides each year in the United States, with the number of homicides rapidly catching up, at 24,000 per year and growing. He discusses the "instrumental" nature of many murders—the purposeful carrying out of the act serving as an instrument to achieve a particular goal or to have a particular effect. In this sense, Malmquist believes that homicide, and perhaps suicide as well, can play a legitimate role as seen from certain perspectives, such as in the state carrying out capital punishment, or when being part of military or civil law-and-order occupations.[13] He states that "an examination of the social meaning of a homicide is an underlying necessity in any kind of sociological research if it is to give cognizance to the psychiatric significance of the behavior."[14]

Malmquist draws a "distinction between what is described as legitimate force used to control others in contrast to the force connected with criminal violence."[15] Thus: "One implication is that it cannot be assumed that violent behavior should always be viewed as irrational."[16] Malmquist could well be referring to our present-day suicide bombers when he writes:

> For some people, these acts of mass violence may be seen as instrumental to achieving a particular goal (e.g., fostering changes in society, punishing opponents, expressing deep feelings), and the perpetrators may be perfectly willing to pay the price that accompanies the commission of the crime."[17]

But he does leave open the possibility that "some of these individuals may also have varying degrees of psychopathology."[18]

Shortly after the world-changing September 11th, 2001 World Trade Center hijacked-plane attack, John T. Maltsberger, a psychiatrist and Associate Clinical Professor at the Harvard Medical School, wrote that "there has been little in the public press attending to the suicidal aspect of the September 11 attack."[19] He points to the kinds of grandiose themes that are often evident in some suicides among mentally ill patients with whom he and his colleagues have worked. Particularly prevalent, he reports, are grandiose themes that they hold about what their suicide will do for them: "Some patients believe that they can overcome death by killing themselves and be reunited with relatives who have preceded them into the shadows."[20] This is in the case of those who are mentally ill, but he points out that psychiatrists "have little experience with grandiose suicides who are not mentally ill in the usual sense of the term."[21]

Maltsberger writes: "Today we are concerned with Islamic extremists who are convinced that what they do is for the glory of Allah, and that in dying to destroy infidels, they will be subsumed into a voluptuous heaven where 72 virgins wait to greet them."[22] Even though most suicide bombers commit their acts on an individual basis, due to their sheer number they could be seen to constitute a kind of sequential, unfolding, cumulative act of mass murder-suicide. He believes that group suicides of all kinds arise from "the power of shared belief in motivating people to stay together in going down to death, usually in pursuit of some mad dream suggested to them by an idealized leader."[23] As other examples of this, he reminds us of the case of the deaths of more than 900 following Rev. Jim Jones's orders to kill themselves in Guyana, and the case of the Heaven's Gate group members taking their own lives in 1997 at the request of their leader, Marshall Applewhite, in California.

Faced with the possibility of suicide committed by someone who is not mentally ill, Maltsberger must still wrestle with the nature of what constitutes delusional thinking: "Delusions are generally defined as fixed beliefs incapable of contravention by evidence to the contrary, with the careful exception that beliefs ordinarily accepted by other members of the patient's culture or subculture are not to be classified as delusional."[24] Given this formal psychiatric definition, he believes: "We cannot say, therefore, that the terrorists who destroyed themselves and many others on September 11 were, strictly speaking, deluded."[25] This view makes sense, given how many in the culture of the terrorists share the beliefs that underlie and justify for them the murderous suicide-bomber activity.

Echoing so many others who have studied this situation, he also points to how Islamic fundamentalists have "hijacked not only airplanes, but a generous portion of the Islamic educational system,"[26] which can then be used to create a breeding ground for the mind-set of future suicide-murderers. To most Americans they will simply be terrorists, but to their own people they will be honored martyrs. But what can lead to the supreme and awful act of purposefully killing oneself in the process of killing others? In a moment of empathy for the suicide-murderer terrorists, rarely found in the West, psychiatrist Maltsberger concludes: "When humans feel helpless enough and deprived enough and exploited enough, they will do nearly anything to change their circumstances."[27]

As *Haaretz* (magazine) journalist Amira Hass put it: "Thoughts of paradise embody the evaporation of the dream of a Palestinian state."[28] Or, as stated by Muslim psychologist Shafiq Masalra: "To be tempted to go to paradise means that life on Earth is hell."[29]

In a 2004 article, Maltsberger sheds further light on the importance of martyrdom for suicide bombers, writing about what he calls "altruistic suicide":

> One must go so far as to assert that abnormalities of the superego are usually typical of suicide. ... the consciences of heroes and martyrs, locking in the courses of action that lead to death, are abnormal also. Altruistic suicide results from an extreme conscience, however noble it may be. And in the latter case I use the term "abnormal" not to pathologize, but to suggest a conscience of such force and power that it is extremely unusual, not found among ordinary men and women.... We often reflect that close emotional attachments to others serve as a protective factor against suicide. In ordinary clinical suicide, it appears necessary that patients about to kill themselves abandon their attachments to those they love.... [They] love their ideals, their principles, (their superegos, their God, if you like) more than they love others, and more than they love themselves.[30]

City University of New York professor Elaine Hoffman Baruch takes a decidedly psychoanalytic perspective on suicide-bomber terrorists and the context in which they operate. She asks, "What does sexual repression have to do with terrorism?"[31]—given the "effectiveness of using one's own body as a weapon," with "hatred of one's sexual impulses" probably involved with suicide bombings. And: "For what else is the body as bomb if not the ultimate phallic symbol?"[32] She contends that separation from the mother, especially when violent, can lead to sexual repression and a fostering of extreme polarities that can give rise to the kind of fundamentalist state of mind possessed by World Trade Center plane hijacker and suicide-murderer Mohamed Atta and terrorist leader Osama bin Laden. According to Baruch, one can then end up searching for union with a political body to replace the mother's body.

She writes of suicide bombers:

> Although they demonstrate the theory that suicide is murder turned against the self, real murder is involved here as well—of anonymous strangers. And because the "martyrs" all look forward to a reward of 72 virgins in Paradise ... their death wish also involves the hope of delayed gratification in a sexually purified heaven.[33]

She points to two kinds of what she calls unhealthy narcissism—both overinflated and negative—which she believes bin Laden and others have displayed at different times, "exhibiting both grandiosity and abasement." She ends, saying:

> If it were willing to, the United States could help the international situation simply by recognizing its own psychological injuries to others. Boasting that we're the greatest country in the world is bound to wound the narcissism of others at the same time that it reveals an inflated narcissism of our own.[34]

Michael Gurian is a social philosopher, family therapist, and corporate consultant who has authored twenty books, many *New York Times* bestsellers. His philosophy draws upon the diverse cultures in which he has lived and studied, including the Middle East. He is perhaps best known for his ground-breaking books on child development, including *The Mind of Boys*. In the following, Gurian provides a somewhat different analysis of the suicide bomber's personality and motive:

> The male willingness to risk injury and death in a quest for self-meaning is often easiest to see in population groups whose social structures tend to crush the individual human spirit. In societies where poverty, lack of a homeland, lack of economic opportunity, or racial or social oppression

dominate, the inherent male sense of meaninglessness is amplified, as is the male's drive to earn his meaning through the highest personal risk. In these populations—especially if the males are emboldened to do so by misinterpretations of religion, as in the case of Islamic fundamentalism—young males will so attach their adolescent and adult psychology to gaining meaning through "big goals" that they may even become suicide bombers. Their calling—the route by which they gain worth in the social world—becomes physical self-annihilation for the sake of God, nation, homeland, or family.[35]

OTHER SECULAR VIEWS

We turn now to some perspectives on murder-suicide and suicide bombers other than the psychological, including the sociological and political. In his milestone work *Suicide: A Study in Sociology*, the great sociologist Emile Durkheim wrote a century ago:

> There is, therefore, for each people a collective force of a definite amount of energy, impelling men to self-destruction. The victim's acts which at first seem to express only his personal temperament are really the supplement and prolongation of a social condition which they express externally.... Each social group really has a collective inclination for the act [of suicide], quite its own, and the source of all individual inclination, rather than their result.[36]

So, how does a social group acquire such an inclination for an act such as instrumental suicide and, particularly, murder-suicide terrorism? At the heart of the field of "social learning" (or "social cognition") is the view that some people function as models who exemplify a behavior followed or imitated by others. The electronic and print media are undoubtedly the most powerful and effective means today of symbolically providing such models that lead in turn to such imitative behaviors. According to Australian university psychologists R. Warwick Blood and Jane Pirkis, "In a social learning theory of suicide there is a causal link between media coverage of suicide and actual suicidal behavior." And, particularly relevant to the culture and subculture from which the suicide bombers emerge that sees itself uniformly threatened, wronged, and humiliated: "The effect of such media influence is strongest where both the model and the observer come from the same demographic, or sociocultural/ethnic group."[37]

Suicide and murder-suicide can arise from decidedly worldly, secular motives, and need have little or nothing to do with any distinctive psychological motive, let alone to do with a spiritual or transcendental one. One should never underestimate how important a firmly held political or nationalistic cause can be when some are weighing their own, or others', life and death. In an August 2005 *Newsweek* magazine article, journalist Fareed Zakaria writes:

> If you want to understand what motivates suicide bombers, watch the recent movie "Downfall." Based on eyewitness accounts, it chronicles the final days inside Hitler's bunker. In a particularly harrowing scene, Joseph Goebbels and his wife are given the opportunity to have their six young children flee to safety. But Magda Goebbels refuses and instead drugs the kids to sleep. Then she inserts a cyanide capsule into each child's mouth and presses the jaws until the capsule breaks. When explaining why she won't allow her kids to escape, Mrs. Goebbels explains, "I can't bear to think of them growing up in a world without national Socialism."[38]

Those having a completely nonreligious, nonspiritual belief and values system can still be motivated to take their own lives as well as to take others' lives. Apparently the prospect of nothingness following one's own demise, rather than a continuing afterlife existence of some kind, is acceptable, so long as the all-too-worldly cause or principle for which one commits suicide or kills others seems enough for them.

For many of us, the terms *sin* and *evil* may come to mind when we think of people who take the lives of others as well as their own. However, at the same time, we must consider the frame of reference from which one is using such terms. What may be evil to one person may be justified and righteous to another. Someone seen as an evil enemy through one person's eyes may be seen as doing good through another's eyes. Such interpretations may be relative and subjective at their core, depending on the frame of reference from which one is doing the labeling and judging. Bear this in mind as we listen shortly to the various Islamic extremist justifications for jihad, and as we hear the case made by Western governments and media that Islamic jihad is completely unjustified, groundless murderous terrorism. The vilification of one's enemy and the lionizing of oneself can take place on both sides of a conflict. This is an important point since we are interested in what we may find after death upon entering the afterlife—what place we may have made for ourselves there as the repercussions of our earthly decisions and acts. Who on Earth truly possesses the privileged frame of reference for deciding or knowing with regard to others who make for themselves their own heaven or hell?

Ernest Becker spent a large part of his career studying the nature of evil, a term that, as suggested, can easily be wielded by each side against the other in virtually any deep-seated conflict or war-type situation. Becker writes:

All you have to do is to say that your group is pure and good, eligible for a full life and for some kind of eternal meaning. But others like Jews or Gypsies are the real animals, are spoiling everything for you, contaminating your purity.... Then you have a mandate to launch a political plague, a campaign to make the world pure.[39]

Psychiatrist M. Scott Peck reminds us that sin is not just missing the mark one sets for oneself, but it is also failing to be continually perfect; thus, we are all sinners, Palestinian terrorists and Israeli soldiers alike.[40] Peck feels that many absolutely refuse to face or admit to their own sinfulness, and they sacrifice others to preserve their own sense of perfection, projecting their own evil onto the world in a process of scapegoating.[41] For Peck, evil is the exercise of political power, which is "an imposition of one's will upon others by overt or covert coercion—in order to avoid ... spiritual growth."[42] Or, perhaps, it is to push one's own spiritual agenda on others as superior to theirs. It is interesting how, in 2005, the Muslim insurgent terrorists and most of the American leadership see each other as the perpetrators of such evil, as pushers of an agenda to replace the other's. Those on both sides are, according to Peck, likely to exert themselves "to obtain and maintain an image of high respectability. They may willingly, even eagerly, undergo great hardships in their search for status."[43] Such "hardships" can, of course, include the loss of one's own life, even when self-inflicted.

"Demonic" (or "daimonic") is another term often associated with evil. But it need not mean only evil. According to the great psychologist Rollo May, "The daimonic is any natural function which has the power to take over the whole person."[44] It is capable of functioning either creatively or destructively. May continues:

> Violence is the daimonic gone awry. It is "demon possession" in its starkest form. Our age is one of transition, in which the normal channels for utilizing the daimonic are denied; and such ages tend to be times when the daimonic is expressed in its most destructive form.[45]

Once more, it would seem that both those on the side of the suicide bombers and those whom the bombers construe as the enemy against whom their jihad is being waged, are equally "possessed," each believing their own respective brand of violence and destruction to be the only truly justified one.

Psychologist Sam Keen writes: "The problem in military psychology is how to convert the act of murder into patriotism."[46] In most conflicts, each side conducts this translation of murder into acts of patriotism, heroism, and altruism. In our present, ongoing Middle-Eastern conflict, we have the fundamentalist, extremist Islamic terrorist organizations and their suicide-murderers, and then we have the opposing military and political forces conducting murders of their own. We also have, according to the Islamic extremists, quite a history of past killings and other "evils" conducted by non-Islamic "infidels," including an array of inequities, humiliations, infringements of freedoms, encroachments, imperialist takeovers, and so on—more than justifying, in Muslim eyes, the right to kill oneself and others in the name of jihad, or holy war.

Keen notes:

> We human beings are *Homo hostilis*, the hostile species.... We are driven to fabricate an enemy as a scapegoat to bear the burden of our denied enmity. From the unconscious residue of our hostility, we create a target; from our private demons, we conjure a public enemy. ... the wars we engage in are compulsive rituals, shadow dramas in which we continually try to kill those parts of ourselves we deny and despise.... We need to become conscious of what Carl Jung calls "the shadow."[47]

If we are going to consider what may await "successful" suicide bombers and other suicide-murderers in the afterlife, we may also need to consider what awaits those in the afterlife who have killed such perpetrators as their enemy. Each side sees the other as the enemy, each passionately flying the flag of its own respective righteous justification. Each has its own respective Jungian "shadow" with which it still needs to come to terms.

Mia Bloom is Assistant Professor of Political Science at the University of Cincinnati, consultant to the New Jersey Office of Counterterrorism, and a term member of the Council on Foreign Relations. In her book *Dying to Kill: The Allure of Suicide Terror*, she studies what she calls the "self-perpetuating subculture of martyrdom,"[48] where there are always new recruits ready "to jump on the suicide bandwagon." As with many others who have recently written about this phenomenon of murder-suicide, Bloom recounts many of the same motivations lying behind what most of us can only think of as the unthinkable. From her research, she has found that people kill themselves and others for revenge, out of humiliation, or to attempt to rectify what is for them a woefully uneven and unfair situation that leaves them little recourse for action other than to choose such a deathly powerful act of suicide married to murder. They may see no other way to vent their anger, express their grievances, or make a difference. Taking lives, including their own, may present itself as the best way to bring about change where they are impassioned by an internal and external call for such change, for a way to serve their own people who are disadvantaged, deprived, and nearing hopelessness. They may be choosing to make themselves a rallying point, an extreme, eloquent symbolic act to court the hearts and convictions of their fellow countrymen. Or they may long for religious purity, for outlets for their righteous indignation about how the perceived enemies of their religion are desecrating what they have been spiritually taught and hold most dear. They feel the future of their religion, the possibility of their God in their own and in others' hearts, may be in jeopardy unless they act, and act strongly and extremely. Thus, there appear to be various grounds from which these recent suicidal murderers spring. As Bloom puts it: "The individuals who perpetuate suicide attacks have social, cultural, religious, and material incentives. These include spiritual rewards in the afterlife, the guarantee of a place with God for the attackers' families, celebrity, and even cash bonuses."[49]

After studying the major extremist organizations—simply called terrorist organizations in the West—that are recruiting and training today's suicide bombers, Bloom is not the only one to portray their sometimes coldhearted-seeming, highly worldly attitudes and ways. They compete with each other for media attention, for laying claim to the latest atrocities, and they are continually pragmatically strategizing the best action to achieve their ends. This can include conducting ongoing cost-benefit analyses: How many need to kill themselves and how many do they need to kill, and just who needs to be killed, in order to achieve the organization's goals? Jihad, with its long spiritual tradition, becomes harnessed to what can appear strictly secular socio-political tactics and ends. One face of the calculating nature of this activity is the weighing of the potential negative effects that come from killing members of one's own group, whether accidentally or on purpose. Even if completely innocent fellow Muslim civilians are targeted to be blown up in order to discourage locals from consorting with or supporting the perceived occupying enemy's presence and goals, the leaders of these organizations do not want the suicide-murdering done by the martyrs—how many get killed and who they happen to be—to work against them in the forum of public opinion, especially in the eyes of their own people, the very ones, ironically, for whom they are supposedly carrying out the murder-suicides in the first place. Shiite Muslim suicide bombers, for example, need to be careful that their purposeful killing of their fellow Sunni Muslim Iraqi citizens is perceived as religious-spiritual jihad, rather than simply being murderous sibling rivalry among regional tribal factions with long-standing grudges against each other.

Henry Bayman is an American who studied Sufism and the Islamic tradition for years with masters in Turkey. In "Prologue: Rescuing Islam from the Hijackers," which begins his 2003 book *The Secret of Islam: Love and Law in the Religion of Ethics,* he presents the views of a Westerner deeply influenced by traditional Sufi and Islamic mentoring. He is concerned about how far contemporary acts, such as suicide bombing done in the name of Islam, have strayed from the original peaceful and loving roots of Islam based on the words and ways of its prophet Muhammad. Bayman writes: "Behind every attempt to divest the Prophet from his rightful place as role model in Islam, we may discern the Base Self of the party involved trying to elevate itself to that role."[50] In light of today's supposedly spiritually based murderous suicidal activity, he asks: "Eliminate spirituality, substitute politics for that, cut out the Prophet's example, erase genuine Islamic culture and civilization—enlivened by the presence of the Prophet—eradicate love and substitute hate, and where do you end up?"[51] In answer to his own question, he points to the *Al Qaeda Training Manual,* "which blends episodes from Islamic history with CIA covert operation methods ... [and] looks like something straight out of a South American guerrilla handbook of the 1970s."[52]

Bayman was told that "Moslems are not free to interpret the Koran according to their own whim."[53] As examples of such whim, he cites the present-day leaders responsible for most of the current epidemic of suicide bombing, and draws from the political-treatise-sounding will of Ayam al-Zawahir, second-in-command to Osama bin Laden, which stipulates: "Liberating the Muslim nation, confronting the enemies of Islam, and launching *jihad* against them require a Muslim authority, established in a Muslim land, that raises the banner of *jihad* and rallies the Muslims around it."[54] But, as Bayman points out, "global *jihad* is nothing but a pipedream, since no single power, not even America or China, could win a war against the rest of the world. So what we have is a senseless war without end, with terrible loss on all sides."[55]

Al-Zawahir, bin Laden, and their followers dream of a "caliphate," which is a kind of political institution headed by a caliph, who is political leader of the world's Muslims and head of their state. However, the Prophet Muhammad only saw such a caliphate lasting for thirty years. Bayman writes: "Nowhere among the injunctions of Islam is there a requirement to create an Islamic superstate." It is just "another attempt to reduce Islam to political ideology."[56]

We are also reminded that, "according to the Koran (4:75, 22:39–40), *jihad* is primarily war *against religious persecution.*" But if this is the ultimate criterion for jihad, Bayman asks, "is someone forcing you to abandon your religion or not? Are you being subjected to forced religious conversion?"[57] He implies that this is not the case with today's suicidal terrorists and their leaders. For Bayman, "*jihad* in the Koranic sense is neither ordinary war, nor a war of conquest, nor mass murder, nor terrorism,"[58] as we are experiencing it today. And he reminds us: "Not a single Islamic authority of note condones the events of 9/11." They "violate so many ethical principles in and out of Islam that one scarcely knows where to begin."[59]

Addressing the central theme of our book, Bayman writes:

> Suicide is prohibited by Islam as a form of murder—it is self-murder ... no matter for what purpose, and is sharply distinguished from martyrdom. To be slain by the will of God and to slay oneself along with others by one's own will are two different things. God's commandment in the Koran is: "believers, do not kill (or destroy) yourselves" (4:29).[60]

He quotes Muslim authorities Hassan Mneimneh and Kana Makiya: "The idea that martyrdom is a pure act of worship, pleasing to God, irrespective of God's specific command, is a terrifying new kind of nihilism."[61] Then he returns us squarely to the suicide bombers, citing Islamic scholar Seyla Benhabib: "The erotization of death ... by destruction of one's own body in an act of supreme violence which dismembers and pulverizes it, is remarkable.... As many Koranic scholars have pointed out, there is no theological justification for this."[62]

Two more views on the terrorist suicide-bomber phenomenon that also do not involve any particular religious-spiritual dimension are presented by Robert Pape and Debra Zedalis.

Robert Pape, head of the Chicago Project on Suicide Terrorism at the University of Chicago, points out that, whatever the motivational grounds underlying their acts, suicide-murderer terrorists, and especially the usually Islamic organizations that recruit them, operate to varying degrees within a mundane context of cost analysis, damage control, and public relations. He has noted that nonsuicidal terrorism is a very different beast indeed than its suicidal counterpart.[63] Although both are attempts at coercion, ordinary terrorists may deliberately avoid causing major harm, so as not to alienate support for their cause. As Pape noted, by taking an aggressive stance, suicide terrorists can anger not only their target community, but neutral audiences, as well. Furthermore, their recent focus on the indiscriminate killing of as many innocent victims as possible, regardless of gender or age, carries with it a cost. Pape writes:

Maximizing the number of enemy killed alienates virtually everyone in the target audience, including those who might otherwise have been sympathetic to the terrorist's cause. In addition, the act of suicide creates a debate and often loss of support among moderate segments of the terrorist's community, although it may also attract support among radical elements.[64]

Debra Zedalis, a graduate of the U.S. Army War College, has held numerous positions as a civilian with the Army, including serving as Chief of Staff for the Installation Management Agency, Europe Region. Her study *Female Suicide Bombers* was originally a paper selected as part of the Carlyle Papers in Security Strategy series and made available to Department of Defense leaders, and was subsequently published by the University Press of the Pacific in 2004.

Zedalis reports that, as of 2004, murder-suicide tactics were being used by seventeen terror organizations in fourteen countries, and, although this suicidal approach only accounts for 3 percent of all terrorist incidents, it accounts for at least half of all casualties resulting from terrorism.[65] The chief point of her book is that in recent years there has been an increasing number of women joining the ranks of suicide-murderers.

According to the Institute for Counter-Terrorism, suicide bombing is defined as an "operational method in which the very act of the attack is dependent upon the death of the perpetrator. The terrorist is fully aware that if she/he does not kill her/himself, the planned attack will not be implemented."[66] In addition, this tactic "inflicts profound fear and anxiety and produces a negative psychological effect on an entire population and not just on the victims of the actual attack." It also "attracts wide media coverage and is seen as a newsworthy event."[67] Zedalis echoes the prevalent view we have already heard from other sources, that murder-suicide "offers the moral justification for committing seemingly immoral acts" since the perpetrators "see their actions as being driven by a higher order; they believe their sacrifice will provide rewards for them in the afterlife."[68]

NON-ISLAMIC SUICIDE BOMBERS

Not all suicide bombers are Islamic fundamentalists with skewed interpretations of their religion's teachings in order to justify their own self-murders and the murders of others. Once more, Robert A. Pape and his colleagues have done one of the most comprehensive studies to date on suicide terror and they found that Islamic groups account for only about one-third of all suicide terrorist attacks in the last twenty years. Rather than Islamic fundamentalism, they found foreign occupation of one's homeland to be the strongest common denominator underlying what drives individuals to commit murder-suicide within what is usually considered a terrorist framework.[69]

Like Pape and his associates, Mia Bloom is one of the few researchers to focus on terrorist suicide-murderers outside Palestine, the Arab world in general, and Iraq (which is center stage as we write this book). The centuries-old multi-ethnic and multi-religious character of Sri Lanka, a large island possession off the southeast tip of India, led in the 1940s to discrimination against the Hindu Tamil population, originally from southern India, as Buddhism was given primacy as the state religion of Sri Lanka. Many Tamils emigrated to southern India, and, of those remaining, numerous groups were formed to work toward bringing about separate Tamil independence while those with national control of Sri Lanka mounted anti-Tamil efforts to keep the country together. Out of this unrest and instability and a growing Tamil breakaway spirit for independence, the Liberation Tigers of Tamil Eelam (LTTE) organization was formed. Called the Tamil Tigers for short by the media, the group effectively used murder-suicide terror tactics from 1987 until 2001. As with other terrorist groups embracing murder-suicide, they felt they were left with little choice but to use such tactics, given the resources of their adversary. Both revenge and reaction against the domestic policies of the Sri Lanka government helped fuel their passion.

One boy being recruited for the deadly work was quoted: "This is the most supreme sacrifice I can make. The only way we can get our Eelam [homeland] is through arms. This is the only way anybody will listen to us. Even if we die."[70] In a "Black Tiger Day" speech, one LTTE leader spoke of those being trained to kill themselves as they killed their enemy:

> They have deep human characteristics of perceiving the advancement of the interest of the people through their own annihilation.... Death has surrendered to them. They keep eagerly waiting for the day they would die. They just don't bother about death.[71]

There is also a female perspective on the Tamil Tiger activity. Women were attracted to the suicidal activity because they had lost a loved one, or because of community peer pressure, or because they felt helplessness in the face of rape by members of the dominant Sri Lankan community, especially the Army, or because it was a way to assert themselves in their male-dominant culture. Acting as a human bomb was one recourse for a raped woman who could never be a mother, and family members often urged victims of rape to join the LTTE.[72] Portraits of Tamil suicide bombers range from high school and college students, to seamstresses, ambulance workers, and law school graduates. "One woman joined after her boyfriend was arrested, killed and the corpse left in the village market for the public to see."[73] One woman in a village who joins can lead to others doing the same, even when they all then face paying the ultimate price for their membership.

The most famous Tamil suicide bomber of either gender was Dhanu (also known as Gayatri). Previously gang-raped by enemy soldiers, Dhanu in May 1991 went to meet Indian Prime Minister Rajiv Gandhi, camouflaging the explosives strapped to her body under a pregnancy dress. As Bloom describes: "When he clasped her hand as she respectfully kneeled before him, she detonated the device, killing both of them and several bystanders instantly."[74] Dhanu's story soon reached mythic proportions and helped bring in new murder-suicide recruits to the Tamil separatist cause. Since a cease-fire in 2002, however, the Tigers stopped using suicide-bombing tactics.

It's important to note that, in contrast to Islamic Muslim suicide bombers, there is virtually no religious dimension, or afterlife beckoning, for the Tamil liberation movement and its suicide-murderers. It has been primarily a secular affair, done for quite worldly socio-political, nationalistic reasons. This also argues against the view that a cult of martyrdom must be exclusively associated with Islamic fundamentalism, since the Tamil suicide bombers, like the rest of the Tamils, are Hindus originally from southern India, not Muslims who follow Islam. Still, as a Hindu, a Tamil suicide-murderer may have believed as much in his or her religion's doctrine of reincarnation, or the continuation of life across lives, as the Muslim counterpart believed in an Islamic afterlife. However, if this is so, one wonders how the Hindu view of karma depicts the afterlife or next-life consequence of someone who kills him- or herself, along with others. The remainder of Part II, following this overview chapter, will provide dozens of afterlife spirit perspectives.

Here is another example, from earlier in history, that also does not fit the picture of intentionally ending one's own life to strategically end the lives of others in order to enter a welcoming transcendental reality that approves of what has been done to get there. In an eight-year study culminating in his book *My Life Is a Weapon: A Modern History of Suicide Bombing*, German journalist Christoph Reuter takes us to Japan[75] as well as the Middle East. In Japan the traditional *bushido* code of honor is epitomized in the legend of Kusunoki Masahige, an early fourteenth-century Samurai general, who, completely surrounded by overwhelming enemy forces, committed suicide along with 600 of his soldiers. Reuter traces how this bushido code of honor was continued 600 years later by the *kamikaze* phenomenon, used as a last-resort strategy toward the end of World War II. As a Japanese Vice Admiral put it in 1944, the only hope for his country at that point was to put things in the hands of "God's soldiers,"[76] who would dive-bomb their single-engine planes into American ships. Bound by their loyalty to the Emperor, by their obedience to the military, and by little more, hundreds of successful suicide pilots had a definite demoralizing effect on the American forces, who had trouble understanding how their enemy could aim their planes into such certain death.

In one pilot's suicide letter left behind, he wrote, "We become molecules in a magnet drawn inexorably toward the enemy aircraft-carrier—devoid of personality, of emotions, and, of course, of reason. We become a machine whose function is to manipulate the control column."[77] For those of us trying to understand the nature of suicide and the motives behind it, these dedicated, dispassionate kamikaze pilots seem to have had a more hauntingly meaningless relationship with death than their later afterlife-motivated suicide-bomber counterparts. As Maurice Pinguit, a French authority on the Japanese, pointed out, for those pilots going to their deaths for emperor and country it was more a matter of duty than any vision of being welcomed and rewarded in any kind of spiritual hereafter. As he put it, "They hoped neither for reward nor for Paradise."[78]

Although they were later to be referred to as god-heroes, nationalism, not religious conviction, lay behind their suicidal deeds and they appeared to possess a straightforward, grounded attitude about what they were about to do. In a letter sent to his parents shortly before his kamikaze suicide mission, one young second lieutenant wrote:

> People say that our feeling is one of resignation, but they do not understand at all how we feel, and think of us as fish about to be cooked. Young blood does flow in us. There are persons we love, we think of, and many unforgettable memories. However, with those we cannot win the war.... The great day that we can directly be in contact with the battle is our day of happiness and at the same time the memorial of our death.[79]

Bringing us full circle, Reuter makes a very interesting connection between Masahige's heroic suicide in fourteenth-century Japan, the kamikaze phenomenon 600 years later, and the beginnings of modern-day suicide-terror half a century after that. He points out that the very first recorded suicide attacks carried out in the Middle East were done by three Japanese gunmen in May 1972. They opened fire in Israel's Ben Gurion

Airport, killing twenty-four. Making no attempt to escape, two of them were killed on the spot.[80]

THE ISLAMIC PERSPECTIVE

Let us look now from an Islamic—or at least a supposedly Islamic—perspective at suicide and murder-suicide from the perspectives of the present-day phenomenon of the suicide bombers, most of whom are Middle-Eastern Arab Islamic fundamentalists.

Suicide bombers are most often associated in our minds with Islam, a religion founded by the Prophet Muhammad in the seventh century. Muslims may not have been the first to use targeted assassination in situations involving a high risk of death. Nearly two thousand years ago, two Jewish groups—the Zealots and the Sicarii—used murder to try to wrest Judea from Rome's grasp. They attacked their victims in broad daylight, using daggers hidden under their cloaks. Many were caught, tortured, and killed. However, from what we can tell, although willing to die, they did not revel in it to nearly the degree as those who followed them.

It was not until the eleventh century that suicide began to be used by Islamic fundamentalists as a weapon.[81] Then, it was used by disciples of the Persian master Alamut (known as the Assassins). They conducted raids on neighboring fortresses, knifing officials of ruling dynasties, knowing they would be killed in retribution by bodyguards.[82] Of course, their efforts were directed against Muslim rulers they viewed as usurpers.[83] Members of the Ismaili Assassins continued to be active until the thirteenth century. Over that time, many military expeditions were sent against their strongholds in Iran and Syria, but it may have been an enemy that was even more ruthless that eventually defeated them. A Mongol invasion of Iran in 1258 essentially wiped out the entire population of Ismaili in the Elburz mountains.[84] After that time the term passed out of use.

These early assassins, like the Jewish ones before them, were more targeted executioners than terrorists.[85] Each victim was a highly placed military, political, or religious figure, considered to be evil. He was the only one killed. Furthermore, the only weapon they used was a dagger. They were said to have disdained other methods that could kill from a distance. Instead, they expected (and perhaps even desired) to die at the hands of their target's bodyguards, and in so doing, earn eternal bliss. However, never did the assassin take his own life. He always died at the hands of others.

Joyce M. Davis is associate director of Radio Free Europe and was deputy foreign editor at Knight-Ridder newspapers. In her book *Martyrs:*

Innocence, Vengeance, and Despair in the Middle East, she adds to the historical and socio-political perspective on the Middle East's suicide bombers that we have developed thus far. She revisits traditional Islamic teachings and turns to leading contemporary Islamic scholars for views on suicide and murder-suicide, including the meaning of jihad and being a martyr. As with most others who have studied this field, she traces the roots of Islamic martyrdom back to the first martyr, Hussein, the Prophet Muhammad's grandson, who died in battle at the hands of overwhelming forces late in the seventh century.[86] Given the overwhelming odds against him and his followers, Hussein gave his life in that early holy war. This does not exactly satisfy our definition of suicide. It is merely righteously and heroically giving one's life in battle for a sacred cause in which one deeply believes. As Davis put it, "Muslims are not permitted by their faith to accept injustice,"[87] even if it requires taking up arms and taking lives, their own and others', in the process.

Suicide bombing appears to be growing in popularity in the Middle East at an alarming rate. Far worse than the apparent utter lack of concern at the slaughter of innocent bystanders is the apparent reveling in that fact. Before the 1980s, nationalist terrorists generally tried not to die along with their victims. The religious organizations of Hamas and Hezbollah pioneered suicide missions as they occurred in Lebanon and Israel from 1982 onward. The problem then spread around the world. Islamic fundamentalist groups have sponsored human bombings in Afghanistan, Algeria, Argentina, Chechnya, Croatia, Egypt, Kashmir, Kenya, Kuwait, Lebanon, Pakistan, Panama, the Philippines, Tajikistan, Tanzania, Turkey, the United States, and Yemen.[88]

Therefore, we particularly want to hear the Muslim perspective on suicide-bombing terrorism, especially regarding its suicidal aspect. For an Islamic perspective on suicide, we are directed to the holy book of the religion of Islam, the Qur'an (or Koran), which prohibits killing oneself: "O ye who believe! … [Do not] kill yourselves, for truly Allah has been to you Most Merciful. If any do that in rancor and injustice, soon shall we cast him into the fire."[89] On the other hand, although the predominant theme in the Qur'an is forgiveness and peace, virtually all of the suicide bombers and the organizations behind them have justified their suicides and their instrumental murdering of others in light of the following passage from the Qur'an, and others like it: "Nor take life—which Allah has made sacred—except for just cause."[90] That is, both suicide and murder become reframed as acts of acceptable, even honored and heroic, martyrdom when done for "just cause." What constitutes just cause, however, remains open to debate, and in the remainder of this overview chapter we shall look at this more closely in order to try to better understand what is in the mind and heart of a Muslim suicide bomber as he takes his or her own life and takes others at the same time. By doing so, we may be able to speculate, in light of what we have heard from the spirit realm so far in this book, about what suicide bombers bring with them into the supposed afterlife and how that might affect their experience there.

One thing is clear: For "good" Muslims, it would take a very strong adherence to their just cause for suicidal martyrdom to fly in the face of the powerful, haunting words of the prophet Muhammad, as translated by Muslim historians Sahih al Bukhari and Sahih Muslim:

> He who throws himself from a mountain and kills himself will be thrown down in the fire of hell and remain in it forever; he who sips poison and kills himself will have his poison in his hand and sip it forever in the fire of hell; and he who kills himself with a piece of iron will have his piece of iron in his hand and will be stabbed with it in his belly in the fire of hell forever.[91]

As Islamic authority Bernard Lewis states:

> Islamic law books are very clear on the subject of suicide. It is a major sin and is punished by eternal damnation in the form of the repetition of the act by which the suicide killed himself....
> The early authorities make a clear distinction between facing certain death at the hands of the enemy and dying by one's own hand.[92]

According to Kay Jamison, "In Islamic law, suicide is a crime as grave as, or even graver than, homicide."[93] Other sources support the notion that, like many other religions, Islam strongly frowns upon suicide. Lewis comments:

> The Prophet was present when a man mortally wounded in the holy war killed himself to shorten his pain. Whereupon God said: "My servant pre-empted me by taking his soul with his own hand; he will therefore not be admitted to paradise." According to another early tradition, the Prophet refused to say prayers over the body of a man who had died by his own hand.[94]

Present-day Muslim terrorist extremists appear to choose to ignore such traditional teachings of their religion. Rather, they justify their murder-suicides by making the following distinction among kinds of suicide, as described by researcher Pipes:

> Islamists consider suicide as not just legitimate, but highly commendable when undertaken for reasons of jihad (holy war). Going into war knowing with the certainty that one will die, they argue, is not suicide (intihar) but martyrdom (istishhad), a much-praised form of self-sacrifice in the path of God, a way to win the eternal affection of the houris in paradise.... Islamists find suicide for personal reasons abominable, suicide for jihad admirable.[95]

Sometimes semantics are used among the suicide bombers to exaggerate this distinction. Nasra Hassan has noted, "One condition of the interviews [with suicide bomber trainees] was that, in our discussions, I was not to refer to their deeds as 'suicide,' which is forbidden in Islam. (Their preferred term is 'sacred explosions.')"[96]

Condoning suicide for the purpose of attacking others has not generally been accepted by Muslim scholars and clerics. Philps reported in 2001:

> For the past 11 months of the intifada, Islamic scholars have debated whether blowing yourself up constitutes suicide or martyrdom. Some Saudi scholars continue to denounce suicide as a sin, but the argument has been won by the radicals who see it as a legitimate means of jihad, or holy struggle.[97]

Trying to get at some of the same distinctions from a Muslim perspective, Christoph Reuter, reporter and international correspondent for the German magazine *Stern*, conducted eight years of research on modern-day suicide bombing, which included dozens of on-site Middle East interviews. He was drawn into how the present-day phenomenon of suicide bombing has become a weapon of mass psychology in the Islamic subculture. Referring back to the protagonist in fellow-German Goethe's novel *The Sorrows of Young Werther*, he describes what German psychologists call the "Werther effect," in which those committing suicide are idolized and emulated, often on a large scale.[98] He then looks for this effect in his study of terrorism's strategic uses of suicide, murder-suicide, and martyrdom in recent years, especially in the Middle East.

As other researchers have done, Reuter emphasizes that, among the Muslims he studied, there can be many motives behind suicide bombings: The perpetrators can just be naïvely doing what they are told or conditioned to do, just following orders, or emulating attractive models. They can intentionally be carrying out strategic, functional acts to help further a quite secular cause, such as: trying to right a wrong in the world; to help their own invaded and suffering people; to help their country, or potential for a country; to carry out active retribution; to retaliate in revenge; to help defeat the perceived enemy; or to earn money that will be left to their poor families. They may be striking at an enemy they perceive to be threatening their religious faith, the great tradition of Islam. And as we see so often in cases involving Islamic fundamentalists who have embraced certain idiosyncratic interpretations of the Prophet Muhammad's teachings, the Koran, and related Islamic teachings, they give their lives as martyrs in what they have been told, and what they have told themselves, is a jihad—a righteous, honorable, and spiritually sanctioned ultimate effort on behalf of what they see themselves defending or attempting to reclaim. They see that their suicidal deaths, whether they involve killing others as well as themselves, or just killing themselves alone, will achieve a desired martyrdom that will earn the welcoming embrace of Allah and a place for themselves in paradise, which they have been told is their dwelling place following death. From such multi-faceted grounds each new suicide bomber arises.[99] As U.S. military suicide bomber researcher Debra Zedalis cites the Koran: "Think not of those who were slain in the cause of God as dead. Nay, they are alive in the presence of the Lord and are granted gifts from him"[100]

The martyrdom of becoming a suicide-murderer now permeates the Arab world, right down to the children. Jessica Stern, in her book *Terror in the Name of God*, writes:

> Suicide bombing entails a willingness not only to die, but also to kill others. The situation in Gaza suggests that murder-suicide can also be spread through social contagion. "Martyrdom operations" are part of the popular culture. For example, on the streets of Gaza, children play a game called shuhada, which includes a mock funeral for a suicide bomber. Teenage rock groups praise martyrs in their songs. Asked to name their heroes, young Palestinians are likely to include suicide bombers.[101]

Islamic-inspired suicide bombers have not only been Middle-Eastern Arabs. Mia Bloom describes the Muslim suicide-murderers in Chechnya, a republic of the Russian Federation that declared itself independent during the collapse of the old Soviet Union in 1991, but with few countries choosing to recognize its independence. To date, both Russian and Chechen sides estimate that at least a quarter-million Chechens have died in their separatist struggle against the much superior Russian forces. Once more, we have a people desiring independence and the freedom to follow their own history, beliefs, traditions, and values. Starting in 1999, in the second war between the breakaway province of Chechnya and the overwhelming Russian forces seeking to maintain control and possession, hundreds of suicide bombers were spawned. And, once more, we have the picture of a wronged people claiming the moral right to seek retribution and independence in the face of humiliating domination and subjugation. Many analysts have seen Islamic Arab influences behind the tactics taken up by Chechen Muslims against the dominant Russians, including teaching Chechens to fight in a manner much like the Palestinians.

While there have been plenty of male Chechen perpetrators, as in the case of the Tamil fighters in Sri Lanka, there has also been a marked presence of female suicides, who came to be known as the "Black Widows," since most had lost loved ones during the struggles with the Russian forces. Of seven suicide attacks carried out against Russian forces in 2004, six were by women. In October 2002, of the Chechen separatists who took 711 Russian hostages in the Dubrovka Theater in Russia, most of those strapped and wired with explosives and detonators were women. And in August 2004, a Chechen woman on each of two Russian airliners leaving Moscow blew herself up with the plane and passengers.[102]

Chechen separatist murder-suicide tactics even crossed the Russian border into neighboring Uzbekistan, which, like Chechnya, is also heavily Islamic. And in Turkey, the Marxist-influenced separatist group PKK has used suicide bombing in battling for independence against the Turkish government and its forces.

Although Chechnya is characterized by its predominant Islamic religion, the terms jihad and martyrdom, and an orientation toward an afterlife and the blessings of Allah for one's sacrificial deeds, have not played a part anywhere near as prominent for the Chechen Muslim suicides as for their Palestinian, Iraqi, and other Arab Middle-Eastern Muslim suicide counterparts. Instead, as with the Sri Lankan Tamil Tigers, the context and motivation for the Chechen suicides has been more secular than religious. Most Chechens have not seemed to embrace the cult of martyrdom as in Palestine or Iraq, and the majority of Chechens are reported to have reacted with shock and revulsion to the actions of their fellow Chechen suicide bombers, especially those who were female.

Particularly graphic and disturbing in Reuter's and others' research are the descriptions of the mass suicides, or "human wave attacks," that occurred during the Iraq-Iran war that began in 1980, as Iran realized that its most effective weapon was to throw sheer numbers of its forces at the Iraqi troops and their guns in an attempt to simply overwhelm them. The Iranians, who were often nothing more than children, and who had little or no opportunity to be trained to fight, or actually have an opportunity to fight, were led into torrents of withering Iraqi machinegun fire. Surveying a scene after one of the major battles near the Iraqi village of Karbala, observers counted more than 23,000 dead, mostly young Iranians. As Reuter described it:

> Many of them, their heads shaven, wore red headbands or scarves, and every one of them had a key around his neck—this, so they had been told, would open the gate to Paradise once they had died a martyr's death.[103]

These human wave attacks represented what may well be the worst mass self-sacrifice in recent history.[104]

So, we have the picture of tens of thousands of Iranian youth, rushing without hope toward death clutching only the promise of Islamic martyrdom and a rightful place in Allah's afterlife. Earlier, we also have equal numbers of young British soldiers in World War I willing to follow orders into certain death without a fight, and there we can only wonder what Christian or Jewish promise of an afterlife bolstered them as they passively gave their lives.[105] We have the fourteenth-century Japanese mass suicide led by Masahige giving rise to the legend of the bushido code of honor that helped inspire the later kamikaze pilots of World War II. We also have a similar story at the heart of Jewish history, when in 72 CE, as defeat appeared inevitable at the hands of the dominant, advancing Romans attacking Masada, Eleazer the zealot leader of the 960 insurgents and refugees in the fortress, led them to commit mass suicide.[106] So there have been many well-known, large-scale intentional relinquishings of life in the face of hopeless conditions of battle, and often some kind of faith in a promised afterlife following death was what helped them. But is this simply suicide under orders, or is it intentional and praiseworthy martyrdom? It would appear that this is open to debate.

Jacqueline Rose is another researcher seeking the distinction between the traditional self-murder that is suicide and suicide carried out as part of murdering others done in the name of martyrdom. A professor at the University of London reviewing a number of recent books written about suicide bombers for the *London Review of Books,* Rose writes: "According to Islam, it is a sin to commit suicide. Your life belongs to God and is only his to dispose of. Martyrdom, however, is something else."[107] She quotes the late Islamic authority Abdul Aziz al-Rantissi: "If a martyr wants to kill himself because he's sick of being alive, that's suicide. But if he wants to sacrifice his soul in order to defeat the enemy and for God's sake—well, then he's a martyr."[108] Or, as another observer puts it: "Islamic law explicitly prohibits suicide and the killing of innocents. Muslims are consequently extremely reluctant to refer to the human bombers as suicide bombers. They refer to them instead as shuhada (in singular: shahid), or martyrs."[109]

CASE VIGNETTES

This section contains a number of glimpses—case studies or vignettes—of recent suicide bombers to help us continue to build a picture of the suicide-bomber phenomenon to use as a framework for entertaining the afterlife repercussions they may face, according to the spirit sources quoted throughout this book, especially in the remainder of Part II.

First, some background for the vignettes: Who tend to become today's Middle East suicide bombers? The individuals chosen early on for these missions have tended to be young, poor men, who were recruited from refugee camps.[110] They were lured with promises of a double reward—on Earth by money given to their families and in the afterlife with the delights of paradise and being the chosen of God.

In 2002, reporters Molly Moore and John Anderson observed of the Muslim individuals who commit these acts:

> The bombers of recent months no longer fit the fairly predictable profile of even a year ago, in which the vast majority were between 17 and 22 years old, single, male and driven by radical Islamic views. At that time, most were recruited by militant leaders, then kept in isolation for several weeks of mental and technical preparation.
>
> Now, suicide bombers come from a wider cross section of Palestinian society, motivated more by nationalist than religious causes, and they tend to blend in with Israel's large Arab population. Some are older men. A few have been married. Three have been women.[111]

Even more disturbing:

> Today, militant groups are receiving more volunteers than they have equipment and missions to outfit, Palestinians say. Even Israeli officials acknowledge that Israeli and Palestinian policies have combined to make suicide bombing a growth industry.[112]

Even beyond the question of the effectiveness of these acts as terrorism, suicide bombing brings financial rewards and media attention to both the bombers and the organization that sponsors them. Many are recruited from mosques. Reporter Jack Kelly noted multiple reasons can draw individuals to become suicide bombers.[113] For some, it is about the money, and financial stability for their family. Others are drawn by the prestige they feel it will bring to them and their surviving relatives. Another group (particularly young males) are lured by the idea of the reward of unlimited sex they expect to get in the afterlife. However, there also may be an undercurrent not so much of fanaticism as despair and hate.

One member of Hamas told Nasra Hassan the following story of what they expect to happen after they have blown themselves up:

> He explained that the first drop of blood shed by a martyr during jihad washes away his sins instantaneously. On the Day of Judgment, he will face no reckoning. On the Day of Resurrection, he can intercede for seventy of his nearest and dearest to enter heaven; and he will have at his disposal seventy-two houris, the beautiful virgins of Paradise. The Imam took pains to explain that the promised bliss is not sensual.[114]

Documentary filmmaker Tom Roberts interviewed failed suicide bombers and bombmakers.[115] He found that it is an exalted position to be a martyr. But not all are caught up in the ideology of being welcomed by God, living in a paradise with many rivers, be married to seventy-two virgins, and have seventy of their relatives receive absolution and go straight to paradise. His interviews pointed out that some of the motivation falls in the category of having a life so miserable that death is preferable. Roberts noted that not all suicide bombers have the courage and rigidity of thought to go through with their operations. Nor are there as many Muslims eager to pursue this course as the terrorist organizations would have us think. Roberts noted: "The ideology that is preached, that there are thousands of men who just are desperate to go do this and blow themselves up, is actually propaganda. There are actually very few individuals who truly want to do this."[116]

In a collection of 430 Arab newspaper pieces and Internet postings of biographies of insurgents, entitled "The Martyrs of the Land of the Two Rivers," we read the following almost cartoon-like graphic depiction:

> He went out barefoot, pulling up his belt. He saw some infantrymen, shot at them, and hit around two. He had seen a dream earlier that he was killing Americans and then was martyred. God was true to him and he true to God. A plane approached spewing death. He challenged it with a Bazooka. He fired and missed. It fired and opened with its missiles the gateway to the garden. ... about 15 unbelievers were killed.[117]

In another cameo, we see Abu Osama Al Maghribi, a 26-year-old Moroccan who named his son Osama, after Osama bin Laden. The young father took the money he had saved from his restaurant work and from selling a small property he owned, and traveled from his native Tangiers to Baghdad, where he purchased a car. A friend who accompanied him describes his last minutes:

> Abu Osama came back and got his bride—his car—and flew ahead of me. I was behind him, in my car. There was a lot of traffic, and he started to maneuver between the cars as though he were on a race track going for first place. I couldn't keep up. My strength flagged, I stopped the car, and I cried. I saw him pulling away from me and drawing nearer to his target. His heart grew still to tear out the criminal hearts. He will be blessed, and the criminals will face hardship; he will rise, and they will fall. I saw a column of smoke rise 20 meters into the sky amid a deafening roar. He felled 50 infidels.[118]

Mia Bloom tells of a Lebanese teacher who secretly entered Iraq by way of Syria, hoping to become a martyr, saying, "I decided on Jihad because I wanted to stop the occupation, not out of the love of blood."[119] His anger is portrayed as being fueled by daily images on television of dying Iraqi and Palestinian women and children.[120]

Here are excerpts from the suicide letter left by Ismail Masawibi, a young Muslim martyr suicide bomber who blew up himself and others in an Israeli settlement in June 2001:

> The wish to become a martyr dominates my life, my heart, my soul.... When I hear the Qur'an's verses I become sad because I'm doing nothing to change the situation. We are a nation living in disgrace. I prefer to meet God and leave humankind behind. Therefore I have told myself that I will be with the Prophet Muhammad and his followers tomorrow.... My brothers and my family: I shall be in Paradise, where everything will be mine. So don't be sad that you've lost me. In Paradise I shall be immortal.... Greetings from a martyr who wishes to see you all again one day in the Paradise of God.[121]

Joyce Davis provides numerous cameos of martyred Muslim suicide-murderers. Pictured later as an ideal martyr, in January 2002 Loula Abboud was, at 19, the first Palestinian woman suicide bomber, becoming a legend among her people. She waited until Israeli forces drew near enough to her and then exploded herself in a single murderous moment.[122]

Another case was Wafa Idris, a volunteer medic with the Palestine Red Crescent Society, who blew herself up in downtown Jerusalem, also in January 2002, killing an 81-year-old man and wounding more than 100 others. From one perspective, there may have been traditional psychological roots for her choosing to take her own life. Depression may have accompanied the loss of her first child, which made her unable to bear further children, leading to her husband divorcing her because of her infertility, thus possibly making life without a family of her own unbearable for her. Her sister-in-law was later quoted as having been told by her, "I'm going to carry a bomb," and "I hope I will be a martyr."[123] In the months and years to follow, posters and fliers greeted the Palestinian community, championing the martyrdom of Idris, Aboud, and other women, as well as male suicide bombers, depicting the heroic virtues of their own intentional deaths and murder of others in response to the humiliations, deprivations, and injustices they felt they and their people were experiencing.

The suicide of Idris reverberated through the Arab world, in spite of the overwhelmingly male-dominant culture. In response to Idris's story, one strongly feminist-sounding editorial in a leading Egyptian periodical, *Al-Sha'ab*, on February 1, 2002 asserted:

> It is a woman who teaches you today a lesson in heroism, who teaches you the meaning of Jihad, and the way to die a martyr's death. It is a woman who has shocked the enemy, with her thin, meager, and weak body.... It is a woman who blew herself up, and with her exploded all the myths about women's weakness, submissiveness, and enslavement.... It is a woman who has now proven that the meaning of [women's] liberation is the liberation of the body from the trials and tribulations of this world ... and the acceptance of death with a powerful, courageous embrace.[124]

Reem Raiyshi of Gaza was the first recorded suicide-bomber mother. She was recruited by the Hamas terrorist organization and killed herself in her early twenties, leaving her two small children behind. Dressed in the traditional Islamic *hijab* that Muslim women wear, toting an assault rifle, and backed with images of Hamas flags, she is pictured in a December 2003 video in which she called her suicide a gift from God, announcing: "I always wanted to be the first woman to carry out a martyr attack, where parts of my body can fly all over. ... this is the only wish I can ask God for."[125]

Al Masri was described by those who knew him as the typical "good boy"—quiet, gentle, and very religiously observant. Since age 16, he had become ever more obsessed with the afterlife and how he longed to be with God, yet no one who knew him could imagine it possible that he could kill himself, let alone anyone else. Nonetheless, he felt moved to give his life as a martyr on behalf of Palestine and his people, whom he saw as— or was told were—unjustly persecuted and deprived by the Israelis and the Americans supporting them. As with so many other murder-suicide martyrs in the Middle East, al Masri was moved to join the jihad by the inspiration of both political nationalism and an unwavering allegiance to fundamentalist Islamic teachings as he interpreted them and as those who recruited him interpreted them. Interviewed after his death, his mother, Um Iyad, said:

> He would bring me cassettes to listen to, Qur'anic verses. I would listen to them and he would tell me it's the afterlife we should seek, not this life. He believed that we have another life waiting for us.... This came from God.[126]

Muhammad Atta was seen by many as the leader of the 9/11 multiplane hijacking suicide-terrorist attacks that destroyed the New York City World Trade Center buildings and other targets outside New York and took thousands of lives. Like so many other Muslim terrorists who have given their lives as martyrs participating in what they see as a righteous jihad, Atta was a well-educated, middle-class individual, not a poor, ignorant, easily manipulated individual with little to look forward to or to lose. He felt he had a duty to counter the wrongs and evils he and others saw so prevalent in the Arab world being directed at Muslims by non-Muslims. In a suicide note he left behind, he quoted from the Koran verses that had helped motivate him:

> Also do not appear to be nervous, be happy with a happy heart, be confident because you are doing a job that religion accepts and loves. And then there will be a day that you will spend with beautiful angels *[hur'aen]* in Paradise. Oh young Man keep a smiling face. You are on your way to everlasting Paradise.[127]

Joyce Davis also describes an interview with al Makdah, a Palestinian terrorist organization leader who is recruiting a young man of about 20 standing facing the camera, his forehead covered with a green headband with Koran script dedicating himself to God. With triumphant music in the background, he declares his intention to die as a *shaheed* (martyr, sometimes spelled *shahid*) and asks for God's blessings that his mission be successful. The youth appears calm and resolute, and his final words are interspersed with pictures of Palestinians in battle scenes, firing rockets from barren hilltops, apparently at Israeli soldiers below. There is not the slightest hint of hesitancy to go to his death.[128]

Finally, Pakistani Muslim writer Nasra Hassan shares what a member of Hamas, who trains young martyrs for murder-suicide missions, told him about how a typical martyr is prepared:

> We focus his attention on Paradise, on being in the presence of Allah, on meeting the Prophet Muhammad, on interceding for his loved ones so that they, too, can be saved from the agonies of Hell, on the "houris"—i.e., the heavenly virgins.[129]

Then the martyr, hesitating in the face of his mission, spoke of how close paradise now was for him: "It is very, very near—right in front of our eyes. It lies beneath the thumb. On the other side of the detonator."[130]

The Hamas trainer shows her a videotape he made of martyr-to-be al Makdah shortly before the mission that would end his life and that of many others. As she describes the scene:

> On the day of the mission the video is sent to television stations to be broadcast ... posters and even calendars are distributed, with pictures of the "martyr of the month." The Shahid [martyr] is often surrounded by green birds, which are an allusion to a saying by Muhammad, that the martyr is carried to Allah by green birds.[131]

ADDITIONAL PERSPECTIVES FROM MUSLIM SCHOLARS AND JOURNALISTS

Based on her extensive research and in-person interviews, Joyce Davis provides us with some of the reasons why so many extremist Muslims choose to wage a jihad against Israel, the U.S., and others they see as arrayed against Islam and its people—a jihad in which they are sworn to end their own lives in the process of ending the lives of others. According to Davis and her sources, they hate the U.S. for a multitude of reasons: our power and wealth and how we abuse it; our support of an anti-Muslim Israel; how our troops have defiled the holiest places of Islam; how they have been negatively affected by decades of Western colonialism; how we support corrupt and despotic Middle East leaders; how great numbers of innocent Iraqi citizens have suffered and died under U.S. sanctions and embargoes; and how we usurp their own God-given oil resources.[132]

Nonetheless, Davis points out that the world's preeminent Muslim scholars have concluded that suicide-murderers, who take the lives of noncombatants, innocents, women and children, and even fellow Muslims following the same Islamic teachings, have unforgivably distorted the religion's true teachings, carrying out actions that the Prophet Muhammad clearly prohibited in his lifetime and would abhor if he were to return today.[133]

Perhaps the only full-length book available in the West that has been written on the subject of suicide bombers by a highly respected Muslim scholar is *Suicide Bombers: Allah's New Martyrs*, by Farhad Khosrokhavar, a professor at the École des Hautes Études en Sciences Sociales in Paris, with extensive field experience as a sociologist and anthropologist in Islamic regions of the Middle East. He writes of a radicalized Islam in the face of people driven to despair in a world humiliating to them—a world that has dealt them economic marginalization and social inferiority, and where true self-realization is made impossible. Through their suicides, they have a way of asserting themselves and at the same time lethally striking back at those they see as being the cause of the inequities and obstacle to their self-realization.[134]

Based on his interviews with al-Qaeda inmates in French prisons, fellow Muslim Khosrokhavar concludes that martyrdom promises them that following death their severely handicapped lives will be replaced with a paradisaical existence: "Dying allows them to accede to dignity through sacrifice, whereas everyday life is dominated by insignificance and lack of dignity."[135]

For the young Muslim preparing for his suicidal martyrdom, preoccupation with coming death leads to a condition in which "death is seen as a voluptuous incarnation of the ideal. It is an ideal that is of value in itself." Some disciples of radical Islamism see life "as something inferior to the happiness that can be found through the annihilation of the self and other, or martyrdom"[136] Then, as organizations such as al-Qaeda isolate the future martyr in preparation for his or her death, "the martyr's desire crystallizes around Allah, [and] his ties with this world, and even with his closest relatives, are loosened."[137]

Khosrokhavar continues:

> It is common to evoke Paradise in order to overcome the fear of dying that might assail the future martyr. The emphasis is now placed on the next life, which is eternal, in a world which is infinitely better than the world in which the future martyr is living. His act has such great merit in the eyes of Allah that it washes away all his sins and promotes him to the ranks of the chosen.[138]

He concludes: "Martyrs who risk their lives for the sake of a sacred cause have a complex relationship with the Absolute. They are, in the first place, servants of the Absolute, and submit themselves to it."[139] Thus "a jihadist vision is a way of giving life a meaning by assigning a tangible end to it,"[140] and "The desire for immortality is combined with the wish to die. Shi'ites will meet Allah in their fight with the ungodly enemy."[141]

Finally, we hear from a group of senior Muslim scholars about the Islamic perspective as it relates to the suicide bombers. Ergun Capan is a Turkish Muslim scholar and editor-in-chief of *Yeni Umit,* a respected Turkish quarterly journal of Islamic sciences. In 2004, he edited a collection of essays by Islamic scholars titled *Terror and Suicide Attacks: An Islamic Perspective.* In looking at the contemporary phenomenon of murder-suicide terrorism, the ten contributors, including Capan, are unanimous in their opinion that neither suicide nor homicide is acceptable in light of traditional Islamic religious tradition and teaching. They agree that the framework of legitimacy for all Muslim individuals is the Qur'an (or Koran) and the Sunna, the latter being the sayings of the Prophet Muhammad, his actions, and the actions of which he approved. Islamic authorities are then able to cite the Qur'an as prohibiting suicide (Nisa 4:29, and elsewhere).[142]

Nevertheless, many commentators feel that Muslims today are finding themselves needing to interpret Islam according to their own experiences and feelings because of the extreme helplessness and hopelessness into which they have fallen, largely, as they see it, at the hands of a threatening non-Islamic world. For most of these Muslim scholars, jihad becomes an exception to the usual Islamic prohibitions against taking one's own or another's life. In the case of jihad, Muslims are permitted, even obligated, to defend themselves and their religion in response to invasion, oppression, and exploitation, in response to injustice, and in response to colonialism, imperialism, and the West in general. Jihad is taking personal action against such perceived threats and wrongs. Jihad is taken up to remove obstacles between humanity and God and to put spiritual nature above worldly nature. As Professor of Islamic Law Hamza Aktan defines it, "Jihad is the name of all effort, exertion, and endurance that each Muslim demonstrates in order to be bestowed with the pleasure of God."[143] It can thus even be seen as a form of worship.

Hikmet Yuceoglu, Professor Emeritus of the History of Sufism, addresses the concept of being a martyr, which goes hand-in-hand with the concept of jihad, writing:

> Martyrs are those who have followed the way that God has set out for believers, a way that leads to the blessings of God, and who have died or been killed while striving to fulfill the requirements of this way.[144]

Such individuals are then to be honored as the perfect martyrs[145] or martyrs of the afterlife.[146]

However, for Professor Aktan, each Muslim must answer for him- or herself the question, "Can one call jihad the killing of civilians, women, children, and the elderly, shooting into school buses with machine guns?"[147] And he also questions suicide bombers purposefully killing innocent civilians who are fellow Muslims, as is occurring so often today in Iraq (between Shiites and Sunnis). He then answers his own question: "These acts, for which no legal authority is responsible—cannot be seen as being jihad.... There is no foundation for these acts in either the Qur'an (Koran) or the

Sunna."[148] Yuceoglu adds, "It is obvious from the framework of the above-mentioned principles that there is no place for suicide attacks in Islam."[149]

According to Ergun Capan, he or she who "savagely kills another human being deserves God's wrath and anger and should be punished in the hereafter as if they had killed the whole humanity."[150] Adil Oksuz, a university professor of Islamic law, adds, "God is the one who gives life, thus without His permission, or without considering the regulations He has set, no one can take it away."[151] This last statement would also seem to apply to suicides, who take away their *own* God-given lives.

13

General Messages

We turn our attention now to the spirit-world afterlife perspective on combining suicide with murder, and to the present-day suicide bombers in particular. Although there are clearly nonterrorist cases that qualify, such as the Columbine High School killers in Colorado, the vast majority of suicide-mass-murder cases with unwilling victims appears to occur with terrorism. Perhaps one of the most interesting findings we shall see, however, is that, if the spirit realm is to be believed, murder-suicide may have more in common with suicide than it does with terrorism per se.

We will look at two forms of murder-suicide. One form, which appears to have similar afterlife experiences to those of traditional suicides, involves willing victims. Such murder-suicide pacts often seem to involve a single pair of individuals. A second form of murder-suicide, and one that for better or worse receives far more press, involves the murder or mass murder of unwilling victims followed by, or in close association with, the suicide of the murderer.

Before we consider the information in Part II, we need to add a word of caution. In order to avoid cultural bias, one would ideally like to report information that came through mediums who come from all religious backgrounds. This is difficult with Islam. As Jamal Hussein, a parapsychologist who lives in Jordan, has said:

> Official Islam, as a vivid example of all organized religions, bans anything that has to do with the paranormal. Even miracles, which are the paranormal that was performed by the prophets, had been rewritten in such a way that would secure its being presented with nothing that would violate the laws of nature as known to the human mind. According to official Islam, there must be no such thing as the paranormal. Anything that defies rational explanation does simply not exist.[1]

Furthermore, Islam does not simply frown upon mediumship, as do some other religions, but takes a more aggressive stance. Hussein comments:

> The phenomenon of channeling, like all other phenomena relating to the occult, is being treated with great hostility in our part of the world. According to *conventional Islam,* the occult is something you have to believe in and not to research into....
>
> Channeling in our part of the world is practiced behind closed doors....
>
> I do know of no incident where the channel has conveyed a message coming from people who claim to have taken their own lives.[2]

These observations make it clear that there may be very little, if any, available written material on deceased suicides or suicide bombers from Islamic channels. Indeed, they might not even have considered the notion that it could even be possible to communicate with these souls. Because of this, Islam will not be properly represented here, and there is therefore a greater possibility for bias regarding that religion. Nonetheless, let us see what others have had to say on the topic.

Channeled messages from suicide bombers themselves are hard to find in the general literature, perhaps in part because of the Muslim attitude toward what would be considered witchcraft, and the fact that these souls are unlikely to seek out non-Muslim mediums and channels for help. Nonetheless, we do get some hints of what suicide bombers face in the afterlife from other channeled sources. These messages speak about issues such as Islam, religious wars, self-sacrifice and martyrdom, unrealistic expectations, what happens in the astral to a body blown to bits, the importance of emotion, issues of murder and confronting your victims, and the karmic damage of harming others. Those in the spirit realm have also had words to say about terrorism, and an entire chapter is devoted to this important topic later in the book.

REFERENCES TO ISLAM

Islam is far more than simply a religion. It is an entire way of life with deep historical roots. Bernard Lewis sums up Islam best:

> In the one sense it denotes a religion, a system of belief and worship; in the other, the civilization that grew up and flourished under the aegis of that religion. The word *Islam* thus denotes more than fourteen centuries of history, a billion and a third people, and a religious and cultural tradition of enormous diversity.[3]

It is a shame that this complex and rich culture now appears to be overshadowed by its connection in many people's minds with terrorism. However, if we look at what the channeled literature says about Islam, we shall see some variation, from considering it misguided or limited in vision, to referring to it as a good religion for its time that has now been hijacked and misused. Again, it has to be kept in mind that this will be inappropriately skewed because we do not have information from Islamic channels.

Given the apparent biases noted in other channeled material, it should come as no surprise that the Spiritualist literature, which is firmly entrenched in Christianity, often sounds more like a reflection of the medium's religious orientation than it does an impartial message. With this in mind, let us look at what is purportedly said by the spirit realm regarding Islam.

In the 1700s, Emanuel Swedenborg wrote that in the third state of the afterlife, surviving spirits are taught by angels as a way of preparing them for entering heaven. This included Muslims. However, he described the situation as follows:

> The people who are at these instructional sites live in different places [in the afterlife]....
> The general arrangement is like this. Toward the front are people who have died in childhood....
> Behind them are the places where people are taught who died as adults and who in the world were drawn to truth because of the goodness of their lives.
> Behind these again are people who were devoted to Islam and had led a moral life in the world, acknowledged one God, and recognized the Lord as the essential prophet. When they let go of Muhammad because he cannot do anything for them, they turn to the Lord and worship him, recognizing his divine nature; and then they receive instruction in the Christian religion....
> Not everyone is taught in the same way or by the same communities of heaven....
> Muslims, though, are taught by angels who once adhered to that religion but have turned to Christianity. Other non-Christians too are taught by their own angels.[4]

Furthermore, Swedenborg noted that "Muslims and non-Christians are taught on the basis of doctrines suited to their grasp."[5]

A quite different view comes to us from John Edmonds and George Dexter in the mid-1800s, when a spirit suggested that if bias were eliminated the Koran could be considered to be accurate:

> I remarked that it had just occurred to me that this was the manner in which Mahomet had written his Koran. Was that so?
> It was answered:

No. He was impressed, and there are many truths in his writings. If they were divested of their admixture with materiality, or earth's materiality, they would shadow forth many scenes of the spheres here.

I asked mentally, Where is he now?

Where he is I know not; but perhaps he is in the beautiful gardens he has so graphically described. At any rate, there is some truth in what he has taught.[6]

James Padgett, who also came from a Christian background, channeled a number of letters purportedly from various spirits in the afterlife, including those said to be believers of religions other than Christianity.[7] It should be noted before we read these that the similarity in style and content of these letters—many of them devoted to speaking of their conversion from other faiths to Christianity during the afterlife—makes the true source or accuracy of the material somewhat suspect. In one case a Muslim is said to have written:

God is God, and Allah is His Name, and Mohammed is His prophet. And my name on earth was Abdullah ben Caliph. I lived more than five hundred years ago in the city of Mecca and was priest of the Mosque. I had charge of the sacred carpet of the great prophet.... In my sphere, the Mohammedans live and worship Allah and adore His prophet. Yet, I see His prophet and he is still preaching the great truths and is happy....

Well, we have found that there is no marrying here, but that each of us has one of the opposite sex to live with. And strange as it may seem to you, and stranger yet it seems to us, we do not desire more than one. Our dream of having our harems filled with beautiful houris was merely a dream. We have no harems and desire none. Our happiness is complete with only one.

(Are there Mohammedans who also reside in the hells?)

Yes, there is suffering among our faithful in the lower spheres, and darkness also. But many who have lived in that darkness are now with me in the heaven of happiness that I tell you of. God is just and He will not let a guilty one escape. We must all pay the penalties of our deeds on earth. So, you see, our prophet told us the truth about there being a paradise for us in the spirit world.[8]

Whether it is true that Muslims do not get their houris is unclear, as Padgett was also told that Buddha had recanted his belief in reincarnation—which would seem unlikely in view of the mounting evidence from Ian Stevenson at the University of Virginia and others supporting the idea.

Another letter channeled by Padgett in the early 1900s also spoke of those of different faiths living in separate spheres and the importance of love. The spirit Salaalida is said to have told him:

> I am a Moslem and lived in the time of the Crusaders, and helped defend Jerusalem from the Christians....
>
> I am an inhabitant of the highest Mohammedan heavens and am very happy and satisfied with my spiritual condition, and am still a follower of the prophet who lives in our heavens and still teaches the truths of the Father, Allah.
>
> I have no criticism to make of the Christians, believing that they are also followers of God in the way that Jesus taught, but I cannot yet believe that his teachings are the only truths of the Father. He and his followers live in different spheres from our sphere, and those whom I have met seem to be happy and are very beautiful.
>
> So, while I once was an antagonist of the Christians and hated them with all the hatred that my religion taught me to hate, yet now I see that hatred is not a thing which God recognizes as being a part of the faith and practices of His true followers.
>
> I merely came to tell you of this and to inform you that love is the ruling principle of the spiritual world where I live.[9]

Sometimes the messages that James Padgett received from Muslim spirits appeared, if more forgiving of those of other faiths, to still suggest (if only temporarily) that Islam is superior to other religions. For example, this letter from Selim:

> I am here, Selim, the Sultan:
>
> I came to tell you that I am also happy in my paradise, which my God has prepared for me. I am no longer a hater of the Christians, but love all men as I believe.
>
> I don't mean that I think all men are following the truths of God in their lives, or that they believe in God in a way that will enable them to reach the happiness which He has provided for them; but nevertheless, they are his children, and I love them as one brother should love another.[10]

Still another letter, said to come from a Muslim named Seligman, appeared to imply that he felt misled by the teachings he had received from Islam while alive:

> I come to tell you that I have made investigations since I last wrote you and find that what you told me about Divine Love is true. I have received some of It in my soul and am progressing toward the soul spheres where they tell me more of It can be found....
>
> In all the years of my pilgrimage in the spirit world I have never before learned of the existence of this Love. Our prophet never taught us of the existence of this Love or anything more than the love which we all have, nor the Way to progress with this Love. But now I know that there is such

a thing as the Divine Love, and that It is the only love that will enable us to gain the Kingdom of Heaven.

Very few of my people have any conception of the existence of such a Love....

I am so glad that I came to you when I did and had the opportunity of meeting and listening to the Christian spirits, for their teachings as well as their condition of beauty and happiness have caused my soul perceptions to open up to the Truth, and have placed my soul in such a condition that the Divine Love can flow into my soul and fill it with Its influence and the Essence of the Father.[11]

The previously mentioned Selim was purported to have echoed this sentiment, as well, stating, "Our Prophet, may Allah bless him, never taught us of any other love ... and I don't believe he knows of any other love."[12]

When we turn to more modern material, we see that the entity Michael did not believe Muhammad intended much of what is done in his name to happen.[13] Michael stated that the Prophet had developed a valuable code of ethics for his time. Unfortunately, a social code was transformed into religious dogma. Michael added, "The distortion of the teaching to accommodate the religious demands of the populace has resulted not in misunderstanding as much as misuse of the teaching."[14]

Nor does Michael appear to be alone in their belief (Michael identifying itself as a group entity—as "we") that Muhammad would not be pleased with what has become of his teachings. When asked what the spirit of Muhammad thought of the religion of Islam as it currently exists, Sheila Jones channeled this response:

Again my brother there is a great disappointment. Mohamed taught the oneness of God.... Mohamed began the saying, which is still in use today, "There is no God but God." Unfortunately upon earth today ... Islam has fallen into the trap of believing that their way and their way alone is right. They have not outgrown the "eye for eye, tooth for tooth, life for life." Mohamed set them upon a pathway of spiritual enlightenment, but as with Jesus of Nazareth, his words have been twisted to suit those who followed, to suit their ideas rather than his.

War, the war between Arab and Israelite, has been fanned into flame by the die-hards of both religions. Why? Because both believe theirs is the only way; looking upon all others as enemies rather than brothers. This religion of exclusion is very wrong and certainly not what the founder Mohamed intended.... Men believe their way and their way alone is right, that all others are condemned. If indeed one believes that another is mistaken, the way lies in trying to redeem them. Not to exclude, not to condemn, not to destroy. Modern-day Islam is reverting to a religion of fear;

it is something which, if it continues in this way, will eventually destroy itself.

For man, no matter how uneducated, how oppressed a nation may be, the spirit of freedom lies within. Within every human being, there is this desire, the desire to be free, to believe, to explore, to expand one's knowledge and one's personality. And even though one may not recognize it, the need to belong, to be of one family, to be recognized as a child of God, as a brother or sister to all mankind. Islam has come away from this, has become a repression, a fanaticism, which Mohamed did not teach. There is a possibility, that in this new age of enlightenment which is now dawning, that there will arise a messenger within Islam, who will lead men back to what Mohamed truly taught: the oneness of God, the oneness of man, and love each for the other.[15]

It is, perhaps, a shame that no such messenger from within the religion of Islam appears to have arisen.

It is always difficult to determine the significance of material when bias is likely, if not obvious. Even where there may not be religious coloration of the material, there may be some degree of cultural influence. For example, those who originally channeled Michael are from the United States. In general, the messages about Islam would seem to suggest it continues to be worshipped by adherents in the afterlife, and that those in spirit may not be pleased with the way that religion is sometimes currently practiced on the earthly plane.

FIGHTING OVER RELIGION

One of the more common and consistent messages received from the other side is that the spirit realm greatly frowns upon fighting for religious purposes. Well over a century ago, Allan Kardec asked the spirit realm about religious wars and was told:

> Such wars are stirred up by evil spirits; and the men who wage them place themselves in direct opposition to the will of God, which is, that each man should love his brother as himself. Since all religions, or rather all peoples, worship the same God, whatever the name by which they call Him, why should one of them wage a war of extermination against another, simply because its religion is different, or has not yet reached the degree of enlightenment arrived at by the aggressor?[16]

Other spirits have also expressed dismay and disapproval over the religious battles and in-fighting waged on Earth regarding the right path to God. The spirit Indira (who was apparently a Hindu from India during her lifetime) stated:

> It is with some anguish that we observe from here that there are people who would allow only a single path to God.
>
> If you were to observe all the ways there are to reach God, all the branches, all the intricacies, all the individualities, all of the different manners and aspects of greeting God, you would be overwhelmed.... *There is no single way to God.*[17]

One thing that the spirits point out to those who are certain their path is "righteous" is that just because you believe that you have lived your life correctly does not mean that you will feel the same after dying. Anne Puryear channeled this comment from the spirit of Stephen:

> There are those who piously felt they had done such good, they expected their rewards at God's throne the moment they arrived. Boy, are they disappointed when they review their life. All the judgment and deceit they've hidden is fully revealed.[18]

The fact that a religious or cultural tenet may define hurting others as right in certain situations (for example, martyrdom) does not mean that it will be judged in the same manner in the afterlife. Medium George Anderson and co-author Andrew Barone write:

> Conversely, there are some who have acted in a way that their conscience dictated and did things that hurt others, without understanding that those things were fundamentally wrong. A person who has been taught prejudices and narrow religious or political beliefs from childhood and could not recognize that they were not acting in the better interest of others will also experience the impact of their deeds from the perspective of the person they tormented or oppressed. There are also others, fully aware of their actions in committing murder or violent crime, who begin to understand the horror and damage their actions created among their victims' family. Even though they felt they had no control over their actions on the earth, they come away from the life review with the knowledge that theirs will be a long road to spiritual growth and understanding.[19]

This would seem to be pertinent to the suicide/homicide bombers. The fact that they felt during their life that this was an acceptable action does not mean they will see their actions in the same light when they have crossed over.

Eileen Sullivan received comments from the spirit of a Mr. Moon that also indicate the spirit realm's dislike of religious warfare:

> Religious wars are looked upon with much grief and concern here and we are at present attempting to reach the hearts of all those who carry on in such a disastrous manner. Their souls must pay for what they do on

Earth and they are accumulating much to be forgiven later on.... Evil created in an effort to destroy another's religion doubles the injury.[20]

Yet another such message comes to us from medium Sheila Jones, who was told by the spirit Mentor that:

> For too long man has fought over territory upon the earth, has fought to convert others to his or her own belief, but I tell you there are many roads to the kingdom of God. It matters not by what name you call God and the highest praise you can offer to the one who gave you life, is to reverence and to respect all the other forms of life in which God also dwells. This means trying to understand those whose beliefs are different from your own.[21]

Allan Kardec was told by his spirit communicators that when it comes to religion:

> The truest doctrine will be the one which makes the fewest hypocrites and the greatest number of really virtuous people—that is to say, of people practicing the law of charity in its greatest purity and in its widest application. It is by this sign that you may recognize a doctrine as true; for no doctrine, of which the tendency to make divisions and demarcations among the children of God, can be anything but false and pernicious.[22]

After the September 11th attack on the World Trade Center towers and the Pentagon, Mary Beth Anderson's father told her from the afterlife that:

> God is aware of the degree of hatred existing in the hearts and minds of men. It is that hatred, which has made this nightmare a reality in the first place. And He certainly does not condone in any way, what a minority of the global population is trying to do to all of mankind. God radiates love and peace and He wants man to mimic His example. He did not bestow upon man the blessings of a free will so that man could use it to lash out in violence against one another. God wants *all* of His children to live in peace and reap the blessings of His love.[23]

This is one case where the messages channeled from the spirit realm appear to be consistent and clear. They disapprove of fighting between religions. Strongly. They tell us there are many ways to worship, and that we should be respectful of each other's religions on Earth.

SELF-SACRIFICE AND MARTYRDOM

The spirit realm's view on self-sacrifice and martyrdom is not what many would expect. Instead, it is surprisingly disapproving. Many even refer to it as selfish! For example, Stewart Edward White reported the spirits told him: "Self sacrifice ... in the popular conception of giving up our own [life] ... is often bad. It may indicate merely laziness or a vain self-righteousness."[24]

For those suicide bombers who act out of a pure desire to be a martyr, and not merely out of blind hatred or a desire for the financial reward that goes to their families, what is reported of the fate of a fanatic? The spirit realm has a lot to say about that, as well. Ruth Montgomery notes:

> Those who are zealots in any line, whether politics or religion or whatever, and who lack tolerance for the beliefs of others will still be trying to run everything on this side, telling others how to think and act, unless they iron out those flaws of personality in the body form. In other words, we are no better and no worse than those who still inhabit physical forms. We take with us the same flaws of character, the same cravings and shackles as we had while in the stage where you are now. And until those flaws are mended, we do not advance spiritually to any marked degree.[25]

As the spirit of Arthur Ford put it: "A repentant sinner is more beloved than a righteous bigot on this side."[26]

The belief of souls that their lives had entitled them to special privileges after they crossed over is also discussed by Wilfred Brandon:

> The most lonely souls here are those whose training on Earth led to a life based on the idea that God was somehow to place them in a privileged position, at His right hand, after their death. These beings find themselves still "among those present" with no greater position, spiritually, than they occupied in Earth life. They have no compensation for their trials, such as they had imagined would be bestowed on them by a beneficent deity, and their only revenge is to spend several years in sulking.[27]

Another passage that would seem to reflect on whether martyrdom may lead to a higher place in the afterlife was channeled from Latimer by James Padgett:

> I do not think the fact that I died a martyr to my beliefs had any effect in enabling me to reach a higher sphere than I would otherwise have entered.... The manner of a man's death does not determine anything, but the manner of his living and the development of his soul qualities are what determines where he shall live in the spirit world.[28]

Thus, martyrdom alone does not appear to be sufficient to guarantee the suicide bomber a place in heaven.

Another way to consider the actions of the suicide bomber is that of human sacrifice (both of the bomber and his or her victims) performed in order to please God. Allan Kardec was told that the taking of life in the form of human sacrifice was never pleasing to God. However, he added:

> God always weighs the intention which dictates any act. Men, being ignorant, may have believed that they were performing a laudable deed in immolating their fellow-beings; and, in such a case, God would accept their intention, but not their deed. ... many among them already understood, by intuition, the wickedness they were committing, but which they none the less accomplished for the gratification of their passions."[29]

Furthermore, Kardec was told:

> Voluntary sufferings count for nothing when they are not useful to others. Do you suppose that those who shorten their lives by superhuman hardships, like the bonzes, fakirs, and fanatics of various sects, advance their progress thereby? Why do they not rather labour for the good of their fellow-creatures? Let them clothe the naked; let them comfort those who mourn.... When your voluntary sufferings are undergone only for yourselves, they are mere selfishness; when you suffer for others, you obey the law of charity.[30]

The line between martyrdom and the inappropriate taking of one's own life and that of others may be a fine one. One possible hint of how the spirit realm may lean on this issue comes from Zaher Kury, a young man whose family was forced to flee the West Bank when it became occupied by Israel.[31] He used automatic writing to receive a poem entitled "Suicide." A portion of it reads:

> To take your life, in darkness you shall dwell.
> Whether it was yours or another's blood you did spill,
> Believe me, where you go is worse than hell....
> So, before you take your life and send your spirit upon that track
> I suggest you wait until you have a heart attack.
> Same in physical life, when you commit a crime,
> There, the law states that you must do the time.
> A heavy punishment is your reward
> And not the heavenly award
> You think that taking a life is so easy to do,
> Not if you see what is in store for you
> Misery and pain, confusion and insanity are yours to gain.
> So taking a life, mostly your own,
> In God's name, you're still doing wrong.
> You, knowing that it is not yours from the start

And you, knowing that it was loaned to you straight from
   God's heart
How could you let your spirit be blown apart?
When you think of suicide this way,
You will have to say:
Suicide, is not for me to play....
Again I repeat,
Before you with suicide meet,
Think about what your spirit will greet.[32]

Although many would think that self-sacrifice and martyrdom would be lauded by those in spirit, instead we are told that it is often thought of as selfish. Furthermore, the channeled literature would seem to make it clear that this form of behavior in no way guarantees you a better place in heaven—it is the way we lived our lives, how spiritual we were, that determines what will be our situation in the afterlife. A lifetime of fanaticism and hatred will not be erased by one final deed—particularly if others are harmed by that act.

PRECONCEIVED EXPECTATIONS

Many Muslims would say the suicide bombers are in a holy war, so killing and maiming others is not a sin against them. However, channeled messages imply that those who cross over—regardless of their particular faith or religion—often find that the afterlife is not as they expected. This suggests there is a limit to how much a soul can have a self-fulfilling prophecy if it does not match reality. Emanuel Swedenborg wrote in 1758:

> Many of the scholars of the Christian world are dumbfounded when they find themselves after death in bodies, wearing clothes, and in houses the way they were in this world. When they call to mind what they had thought about life after death, the soul, spirits, and heaven and hell, they are embarrassed and say that they had been thinking nonsense.[33]

Contemporary channels note that fundamentalists are still experiencing the same chagrin at finding their expectations not met. This appears to be the case in the following transition to the afterlife, as reported by the spirit of Arthur Ford:

> At first she joyously greeted old friends and relatives, rushing from one to another. But then I noted a change. On your side she was narrow-minded, devout, and good, but she had no original thoughts. ... this plane goes against what she had been led to expect in heaven, and thus she sometimes feels that she is in the wrong place....

> Since Mabel expected harps and angels floating amid palaces and sylvan glens, she is for a time, disappointed. But that will pass.[34]

Later, Arthur Ford added through his channel:

> Now let's take the case of someone who is expecting to find angels and harps floating around in a blue sky, with marble buildings and mansions, and a high throne where God sits all day and night looking benevolently at the happy souls. This is the view of the narrow-minded church people in small towns throughout America and elsewhere, but it just isn't true. If a soul who comes over here wants to will himself into marble palaces, he will be able to do so, because they do exist in the earth and we are able to go where we choose; but it's pretty hard to conjure up angels with wings and harps, because if they exist anywhere, we've never seen them where I am now.[35]

If we believe these passages, it seems clear that there can be some degree of self-fulfilling prophecy in how a soul views the afterlife, but that there are limits to how far this can vary from the reality of the situation. Although Ford was speaking about the ideas of fundamentalist Christians, the same applies to Muslims. Medium Geraldine Cummins stated that in the afterlife this can cause them to be stuck, which she explained as follows:

> So there are numerous fanatical Christians who, though they led lives of rectitude on earth, committed certain intellectual sins. These might be summed up in the phrase "rigidity of thought," "an outlook limited by fanaticism." Briefly, they are wedded to a limited concept. In the Fourth stage of existence they must learn how to escape from such a prison if they are to make further progress. These remarks apply equally to Buddhists, Mahommedans [sic], and all those other fanatical adherents of various religions.[36]

Even the spirit of Stephen had some words to say on this topic.[37] He noted, "Many, who were so dogmatically positive their religion was correct, founder when 'heaven' isn't what they expected."[38]

Thus, it would seem clear that although a soul may experience some degree of self-fulfilling prophecy when entering the afterlife, there is a limit to how far this can go. Furthermore, fanaticism itself is a rigid style of thinking which would not seem to be conducive to adaptation and spiritual growth in the afterlife. This would be true regardless of the form of religion espoused.

DEATH BY EXPLOSION

What do we know about the impact the manner of death has on the "body" of the suicide bomber and his or her victims? Channeled comments made by deceased soldiers during both World Wars sometimes addressed the topic. Where normally there appears to be little if any problem for a soul to feel and be in good health on the other side, messages from the dead speak of the increased difficulty the soul of a body that has been blown to bits may be having when first crossing over. The spirit of Arthur Ford is reported to have said that souls damaged in such a way awaken in a state of shock and require a lot of comfort.[39] Furthermore, it may take a long time for these souls to recover and reconstruct their astral body, and they may be rather angry about having had to go through it.

Sir Oliver Lodge was similarly told by his dead son during a séance with Mrs. Leonard that:

> When anybody's blown to pieces, it takes some time for the spirit-body to complete itself, to gather itself all in, and to be complete. It dissipated a certain amount of substance which is undoubtedly theric, theric—etheric, and it has to be concentrated again. The *spirit* isn't blown apart, of course—he doesn't mean that—but it has an effect upon it. He hasn't seen all this, but he has been inquiring because he is interested.[40]

After reviewing a number of channeled sources, Robert Crookall reported similar descriptions of damage to the astral body after death by explosion, from which it takes time for the spirit to recover.[41] He notes that the experiences reported by those that pass abruptly because of blows, falls, or drowning do not appear to have this problem. Indeed, other than a brief period of unconsciousness at the moment the physical body is shed, most of those who die suddenly are awake afterwards. The sole exception to this appears to be when the body is blown to pieces. Crookall cites a number of passages in the channeled literature that suggest the astral body suffers a major shock to the system when the body is shattered by an explosion, and may require some period of time to draw itself back together. Because of this, the soul may remain unconscious for much longer than usual as it recovers.

Although this would seem to be a compelling collection of depictions, not all deaths by explosion may follow this format. James Van Praagh describes a case where an accident with a grenade turned out to be fatal:

> He is describing what it felt like when he woke up. He says that after what seemed like a couple of seconds, he came back to consciousness. He looked around and noticed he felt very different, not as fatigued as

he had been. He saw a group of his buddies standing in a circle screaming, but he couldn't hear the words until he moved in closer. They were screaming out his name. Mike! Mike! He answered, but they could not hear him. He walked over to the circle and noticed they were looking down at the remaining pieces of a human carcass. Suddenly, he had a very strange and eerie sensation through his body. He looked down at the dog tags his platoon buddy was holding. He saw his name on them....

He says he was a bit confused but realized he must be dead. He is describing a very strong sensation of peace and calmness.[42]

Unfortunately, there is nothing in the above story to tell us whether this accident was part of Mike's blueprint and was pre-planned—which could potentially explain why the transition seemed to be such a smooth one. Another view on how death by explosion might be handled could involve whether the soul was prepared for the event. This seemed to be the case when Michael Newton used regression hypnotherapy to talk to a soul who had apparently been blown up during a World War I battle:

S: My energy is a mess. It is in chunks ... black blocks ... irregular ... totally skewed out of alignment.
Dr. N: Is this because you didn't escape from your body fast enough at the moment of death?
S: For sure! My unit was taken by surprise. I normally cut loose (from the body) when I see death coming....
Dr. N: So, what do you do?
S: I ... try to help myself. I'm not doing too well, it's so scrambled. Then a powerful stream of energy hits me like water from a fire hose and it helps me begin to reshape myself and push out some of the negative crap from that battle. ... it's from my guide.[43]

Finally, here is one other aspect to the suicide bomber's death by explosion that needs to be addressed—that of an unnatural, sudden death. Robert Crookall observes:

Whereas the "Judgment"-experience of average people is described, in communications from "beyond," as being undergone fairly soon after natural death, where death is enforced in the prime of life ... it is delayed (and this, in turn, delays the next experience, i.e., the assignment).... I have not seen one case in which a communicator claims that he was killed in the prime of life who also said that his Judgment-experience followed soon after.[44]

Thus, regardless of the right or wrong of a suicide bomber's actions, there may be some delay, even if temporary, in his or her recovery after crossing over. In addition to the question of having damaged his or her astral body (which would appear to be probable for most cases, hampering the initial adjustment), it may also take longer to complete the necessary life-review and self-judgment phase—which must be finished before the spirit can move on. The end result is that the suicide bomber's unnatural death by explosion may well delay his or her spiritual advancement.

THE ROLE OF EMOTION

Another factor that may affect how well suicide bombers adjust to the afterlife is whether their personality was mired in hatred for others or was imbued with love for their God and their fellow man. One spirit explained to Jasper Swain that since the afterlife is a world based on love, those who do not have enough of that emotion are severely handicapped, and will not adapt well.[45] This makes a certain amount of sense.

The idea that love is critically important in life is not a new one. What some may not have realized, however, is that its importance carries on, perhaps taking on even greater significance, in the afterlife. James Padgett was told by his deceased wife, "The conditions of all spirits are determined by their goodness and love."[46] Moreover, as far back as the mid-1700s, Emanuel Swedenborg discussed how this could affect a soul's place in the afterlife, noting:

> *We are our love or intention after death.* All heaven is differentiated into communities on the basis of differences in the quality of love, and every spirit who is raised up into heaven and becomes an angel is taken to the community where her or his love is. When we arrive there we feel as though we are in our own element, at home, back to our birthplace, so to speak. Angels sense this and associate there with kindred spirits. When they leave and go somewhere else, they feel a constant pull, a longing to go back to their kindred and therefore to their dominant love. This is how people gather together in heaven. The same applies in hell.[47]

Swedenborg also made the observation that "outward behavior and outward worship accomplish nothing whatever; only the inner realities that give rise to these outward ones are effective."[48] In another place, he warned, "People who have been bent on revenge and have therefore taken on a savage and sadistic nature love places like morgues, and are in hells of that sort."[49]

Allan Kardec was told that the enmity between enemies or combatants during battle may not end with death.[50] He wrote that after crossing over:

> A spirit, under such circumstances, is never calm. At the first moment, he may still be excited against his enemy, and even pursue him; but, when he has recovered his self-possession, he sees that his animosity has no

longer any motive. But he may, nevertheless, retain some traces of it for a longer or shorter period, according to his character.[51]

Channel Jean Marshall speaks at length on the topic of the destructiveness of hatred. Gwyneth the Lifegiver stated through her:

> It is terrible and agonizing for us to see anyone in a state of unlovingness.... The Spirits who are in this state of uncomprehension cannot be approached, cannot receive, and cannot give anything out, except their feelings of loneliness and hatred.
>
> Hatred breeds hatred, reflects it and feeds upon it, and we have to be guarded.... Our neverending compassion can be the only way for such a Spirit to receive some little glimpse of the healing warmth and comfort of love. And from this glimmer, by slow and painful steps, such a poor soul may be brought to a new awareness, and be made whole.[52]

Former Swarthmore College Department of Religion and Philosophy chairman Jessie Herman Holmes and the Holmes Research Team observe that when a person has strong negative emotions during a lifetime, it can also harm his or her astral body.[53] Further:

> Those who have engaged in a projection of hate, disillusionment, jealousy or anger are very weak and find that they are greatly in need of assistance.... The strength, force and will of such a person who projects only *negative* forces results in tremendous illness!
>
> Such a being must now be brought to a realization of that which we here know to be the truth: what is sent out from the mind of a being still in the physical body is exactly what he will reap if he continues this way of life.[54]

Strong emotions may cause other problems, as well. Hiroshi Motoyama notes, "The stronger the suffering and hatred, the more these beings are frozen to the physical locale where they died."[55] He felt such souls can be helped from a distance, but only with difficulty. A deceased psychiatrist channeled by Suzane Northrop tended to agree that the emotions at the moment of death can affect what happens to a soul.[56] As mentioned in the chapter on the initial experience of being dead, Dr. Grossman stated:

> If we're in a state of extreme emotionalism, that is, fear from an accident, emotions felt after taking another's life, or the trauma endured from dying in war, those emotions or states of mind will travel with us through our death transition. No physical pain will be felt, but there will be variables in the immediate outcome.... However, the expectation of nothingness or fear of that nothingness, fear of the unknown, or fear of

punishment—whatever terrifies you—may keep you in a state of semi-awareness until you are ready to see the light.[57]

Thus, emotion would seem to have more of a role in how well a soul can adjust to the afterlife than one might think. It is even possible that strong negative emotions can even harm the soul itself. Michael Newton writes, "The average soul's energy will become shadowed when it has lived within a host body obsessed by constant fear and rage."[58]

HOW MURDER IS VIEWED IN THE AFTERLIFE

If we consider (as many, if not most, would) that the suicide bomber's actions are harmful to others, representing not only the willful murder of the self but that of other human beings, as well, then the issue is raised as to how this may complicate what happens to these souls in the afterlife. Murderers rarely channel messages back from the afterlife, but entities sometimes speak on this matter. Often, it can involve the question of intent, survival (as in a kill-or-be-killed situation), or karma. As with other souls, there appears to be self-judgment. Wise Owl described the serious consequences murderers face in the afterlife:

> They are shown what they have done and left to meditate on their actions. We do not accuse or condemn them. This is done by themselves, and they do so more severely than we could ever possibly do it. Even when wrongdoers are told that they are pardoned for their crimes and are assured by the spirit of the person whom they killed that they are forgiven, they often do not accept this. When they do accept it, then they are informed that they have regressed a lot ... and must return to earth at an early date to expiate their karma.[59]

An even grimmer picture of what happens to those who have committed wrongs was painted by a soul who communicated with Anthony Borgia:

> The denizens of the realms of darkness have, by their lives on earth, *condemned themselves, each and every one,* to the state in which they now find themselves. It is the inevitable law of cause and effect; as sure as night follows day upon the earth-plane. Of what avail to cry for mercy? The spirit world is a world of strict justice, a justice that cannot be tampered with, a justice which we all mete out to ourselves. Strict justice and mercy cannot go together. However wholeheartedly we may forgive the wrong that has been done to us, mercy is not given to us to dispense in the spirit world. Every bad action must be accounted for by the one who commits it. It is a personal matter which must be done alone.... Every soul who dwells in these dreadful dark realms has the power within himself to rise up

out of the foulness into the light. He must make the individual effort himself, he must work out his own redemption. None can do it for him. Every inch of the way he must toil himself. There is no mercy awaiting him, but stern justice.[60]

Allan Kardec asked the spirit realm a number of questions about murder and received the following answers:

> 746. *Is murder a crime in the sight of God?*
> "Yes, a great crime; for he who takes the life of his fellow-man cuts short an expiation or a mission; hence the heinousness of his offence."
> 747. *Are all murders equally heinous?*
> "We have said that God is just; He judges the intention rather than the deed."
> 748. *Does God excuse murder in cases of self-defense?*
> "Only absolute necessity can excuse it; but if a man can only preserve his life by taking that of his aggressor, he ought to do so."
> 749. *Is a man answerable for the murders he commits in war?*
> "Not when he is compelled to fight; but he is answerable for the cruelties he commits, and he will be rewarded for his humanity."[61]

Not all channeled souls consider murder so negatively. Some have suggested that selfishness is a far worse trait. Nora Loder was told:

> *Dark souls indicate selfishness, greed, and crime.* Crime means self-destruction by disregarding others entirely. That makes one blacker than murder. Murder may be done through an instant's insanity, *but selfishness eats deeply and steadily at the root of life itself.*[62]

The issue of selfishness (as opposed to being self-focused) was already raised by the guide that works with souls who had crossed over through autoeroticism. Along with the issue of intent, it often seems to be an important factor in a spirit's life review and self-judgment. It would seem likely that murder for greed would be considered a far less evolved action, and have potentially greater consequences, than that which resulted from mental illness or with the intent of protecting others.

When murder is a crime (and not a situation of previously agreed upon karmic payback), the perpetrator may face serious consequences in the afterlife. Sometimes, this may include prolonged periods of coma/sleep before the soul will be able to function again, let alone be able to progress. The spirit of Arthur Ford stated from the afterlife:

> Now if the soul should be tainted with horrendous sins against others (the only true sin) then that soul will lie fallow for a long time, unless it is so beset by evil that it returns to trouble those left behind.[63]

Furthermore, the karmic implications may be severe. Ford's channeled explanation was:

> The murderers are, of course, in equal torment [to suicides], having to face the horror of not being able to restore physical life to the one (the victim) who now is on this side, and suffering tortures for having robbed another of the opportunity to work out his karma in due process while in the physical body. There is no quick way to atone for such a sin against the very person of God. Thus, it is a miserable period until the person at last feels strong enough to reincarnate, with the avowed purpose of atoning in the physical world for what he did.[64]

George Meek was told that suicides tend to spend less time stuck in the lower astral than the murderers, because the harm was limited to themselves and, perhaps, their loved ones, and they quickly feel a remorse that may allow them to accept aid. However, Meek notes:

> The murderer is in much, much deeper trouble. His act in cutting short an earth life indicates that he has not only failed to learn much in his past lives, if any, but that he has not evolved spiritually in the present life. Usually he has little readiness to accept teaching when offered, so his stay on the lower astral may be from many years to many centuries of our time.[65]

Meek later adds:

> If, during your life, you caused pain, hardship, and unhappiness to others … if you were a murderer or a suicide, you will reap precisely as you have sown. You will find yourself on the lower astral levels. This most undesirable "place" has been described in religious lore by the words "purgatory," "hades" and "hell." A person who finds himself in this condition solely because of his own unwillingness to grow mentally and spiritually is totally on his own. No priest can post bail for such a person.[66]

Medium George Anderson seemed to agree with Meek about the fate of murderers.[67] When asked about hell, he replied:

> I do feel it exists. It's a very low level of existence. You have to want to put yourself there by severely breaking God's law. Murder is an example of that kind of transgression. You condemn yourself to hell by hating God and what He represents, which is all that's good and positive.[68]

Based on these assessments, it would seem clear that the suicide bomber may wind up in the lower astral for a considerable period. However, it should be noted that other channels suggest that forgiveness is a key precept in the spirit realm, and there are those on the other side who will work to rescue these souls from this situation and rehabilitate them. Furthermore, if we look at others who have committed murder-suicide on a smaller scale, we can find messages that suggest that, like other souls, they may choose spiritual work as a form of repentance. Anderson noted of one murderer who took his own life:

> But he's saying he's gotten his act together over there. This is also his own penance, of his own choice, because he committed murder and then killed himself. He really committed the ultimate wrong. He broke God's law by killing someone and then himself.[69]

One of the few cases where a murderer appears to have been directly channeled was reported by John Edmonds and George Dexter in the mid-1800s. They wrote the following account of the conversation between the soul of a murderer (through a woman medium) and Judge Edmonds:

> Are you, then, the spirit of one who was tried before me for murder, was condemned to death by me, and executed?
>
> Yes, I am he, Judge. Oh, forgive me, forgive me!
>
> Nay, *I* have nothing to forgive; but in the name of Heaven, with what purpose have you come to me?
>
> Do you know why I embraced your knees just now? Well, Judge, I was so thankful that I was removed by your mandate from my former state of ignorance and blindness into the next sphere, where I have become a man, and I am now sent here by wise ones to speak to you....
>
> He said that I must not suppose he was convicted of a bloody crime, and then sent direct to a state of happiness. Oh, no; far from that. But when his spirit was released from his vile body, made so by his evil passions, he was led to a spot, and told to choose his companions. On one side they were black and dark, blacker than himself, and distorted with evil passions. On the other, they had been vile, like himself, but they were not all dark, a little light shone upon them, and their faces were turned upward with hope....
>
> And, Judge [said he], I made my choice. I braced my heart against evil, I stood firm in the strength of my manhood to do right, and began my labor for eternity.... I have so far been able to advance upward, that I have been permitted, have been commanded, to come and speak to you on my condition....
>
> The light that is around me is yet dim and obscure, but it is becoming stronger and brighter, and will continue to grow so....
>
> My friends above are patiently waiting when I shall be divested of my grossness and darkness.... God is merciful.[70]

Here we see two important themes. First, the issue that spirits may choose what companions they belong with—and hence, their level of existence in the afterlife—and second, that, with work, they can progress spiritually.

Raymond Moody said that near-death experiencers who had "died" from causes other than suicide told him that they had received the impression, while on the other side, that murder and suicide are strongly frowned upon and may lead to severe penalties.[71] In one case he was told:

> I got the feeling that two things it was completely forbidden for me to do would be to kill myself or to kill another person.... If I were to commit suicide, I would be throwing God's gift back in his face.... Killing somebody else would be interfering with God's purpose for that individual.[72]

It should be noted that there appear to be negative karmic implications for murder even if the victim wants to die, as in a murder-suicide pact. Lifetimes are considered precious by the spirit realm. Although euthanasia and assisted suicide for individuals with a terminal illness are often considered to be tolerable by the spirit realm, taking a life away from someone who is healthy is thought to be extremely wrong. One soul, who had committed murder and then his own suicide, stated from the afterlife:

> No entity has a right to take a lifetime experience away from another spirit. I am expressing my own judgment of my act. The judgment is not from others here; it is only from me....
>
> Now that I realize the enormity of my acts, now that I know how valuable a lifetime experience is to each and every entity, the whole thing opens itself to me with the terrible clarity of one exposed to light.[73]

Another question that arises with murder is whether the suicide bomber must confront his or her victims in the afterlife. Most channeled material suggests that this probably occurs—if only as part of the life-review and self-judgment phase that all souls go through, regardless of the quality of their lives or how they died. The spirit of Frances Banks told Helen Greaves about the ultimate fate of a prominent German after World War II:

> The man had been a Nazi leader; wellknown [sic] and extremely powerful during the last war. After the downfall of Germany he had committed suicide. (I cannot give his name but it is not Hitler.) Since that time he had been "lodged in the shadows" ... "wandering in the lower places." You would no doubt refer to this dark place as the "lower astral." In any case, for twenty earth years, he had been imprisoned by his own evil.
>
> Now he had been rescued. He was conscious of his terrible cruelty and filled with remorse.[74]

As with other stressed souls, this man spent most of his time asleep. However, Frances was told:

> "In the next ward," Mother Florence was saying, "is a woman who was one of his victims, a young Jewish mother who has arrived with him. She has been bound to him by her deep hatred. But she is progressing because she had real love in her heart for her husband and child who were snatched from her. She has the power of Love in her soul. He, poor creature has not ... yet....
>
> "And," Mother Florence went on, "when he is healed sufficiently they must confront one another and learn forgiveness, understanding and charity."
>
> Our patient still sleeps.[75]

This would suggest two important issues. First, the previously mentioned importance of whether a person is capable of love, which affects progress in the afterlife, and, second, the fact that one must come to terms with those he or she harmed during the last incarnation. Souls may be locked together by hatred—a somewhat disturbing thought.

It is, perhaps, fortunate that many mediums speak of how strongly forgiveness is encouraged in the spirit realm. Of course, this may not always be without a certain amount of karmic cost to the soul who has deliberately harmed others. Allan Kardec records:

> *293. Do those who have been enemies on earth always retain their resentments against one another in the spirit-world?*
>
> "No; for they often see that their hatred was stupid, and perceive the puerility of the object by which it was excited. It is only imperfect spirits who retain the animosities of the earthly life, of which they rid themselves in proportion as they become purified...."
>
> *295. What is the sentiment, after death, of those whom we have wronged?*
>
> "If they are good, they forgive you as soon as you repent; if they are bad, they may retain resentment against you, and may even pursue you with their anger in another existence. This may be permitted by God as a chastisement."[76]

Mary Beth Anderson also reports a murder victim discussing both the issues of forgiveness and how such a crime may affect the perpetrators, in this case his brother and uncle.[77] The medium emphasizes a more traditional, punishment-oriented approach to the crime:

> He has been somewhat restless, on the other side, because he has kept all this information bottled up for so long. However, he is not bitter because he accepts the circumstances in which he finds himself. He truly believes he must find forgiveness in his heart, in order to find peace here....

Justice, in one form or another, has been served because his murderers are tormented every waking hour of every day for what they've done, and God's judgment of their actions will be served in the hereafter. They'll find no peaceful days ahead because their souls are blackened. Make no mistake, karma guarantees they will be punished for their horrific deed.[78]

George Anderson, who spent a great deal of time speaking to the deceased, observes somewhat more compassionately:

What I have learned from the hereafter is that while we choose the lessons in our soul growth here, we also can choose either unconsciously or consciously to veer off course and abandon our purpose for being here.... In instances where someone chooses a life of violence, something has gone terribly wrong in their spiritual lesson that not only can't they continue, they cannot even find the road. As these souls enter the hereafter having accomplished nothing good on the earth, theirs is a very long road to understanding in the hereafter, and they judge themselves to not be worthy right away of acceptance into the Infinite Light. It will be only after great amounts of work and redemption there that they will choose to move forward to the Light.[79]

Finally, George Anderson describes numerous cases where one of the big reasons a murder victim may return is to let loved ones know that he or she has already forgiven the killer(s), and ask that the family members let go of their pain and forgive the murderer(s). As one soul put it, "I have already forgiven and moved on.... You need to do the same."[80] Anderson later states:

What I find most extraordinary about the souls in the hereafter who pass violently is their ability to forgive and understand their attacker, and their request that we also forgive. Sometimes just by looking at how that information affects the family, I can tell that it is too tall an order for them, and it will probably never happen. But, nevertheless, the souls ask us to pray not only for them but also for their aggressors. They try to make us understand (as they do now) that no one escapes their own justice, and we are all accountable to ourselves in the hereafter. It is not necessary that we waste the time on the earth fighting for a justice that will never put things to right again.[81]

This concept may be extremely difficult for the living to accept. People often hold on to their pain and grudges with unequaled passion, as if their very lives depended upon it. Nonetheless, the literature suggests that no matter how great the harm a soul has done to others, it *can* be forgiven by those it has harmed. However, if souls are like their living counterparts, suicide bombers may find it much harder to forgive themselves for what they did than it will be for their victims to find forgiveness for them.

Taking the lives of other human beings is viewed very dimly from the afterlife. Even if those harmed are able to forgive what happened, a murderer is held accountable for his or her actions. Initial consequences can include prolonged sleep or coma, as the soul tries to adjust to the new state. Then it must face self-judgment—a detailed look at how its actions harmed another, and the wider damage caused by cutting that being's life short. Penance may involve tasks that are performed in the spirit realm, in addition to any karmic reparations that will have to be made in future lives. Clearly, this is considered a very serious matter by those in spirit.

THE KARMA OF HARMING OTHERS

A number of channeled messages would seem to hint at the idea that suicide bombers are incurring significant bad karma by their acts, and possibly simply by their desire to hurt others, as well. Michael noted that:

> Karma, as we have indicated before, is the result of removing another fragment's ability and/or right to choose for itself, and is a profoundly compelling tie between fragments until the karmic ribbon has been burned by equal payment.[82]

When asked what kinds of actions cause karmic debts, Michael replied that deliberate murder clearly incurs karma.[83] Furthermore, it is possible that it will be the bombmakers and terrorist leaders who wind up bearing the brunt of the karmic load. Michael pointed out:

> The executioner does not often bear the karmic burden.... The person responsible for the death will bear the karmic ribbon. The same is true of those in battle. The one ordering the battle will bear the burden except when a soldier steps outside of his function and engages in private slaughter.... If you take the initiative in killing, you also take the responsibility. The executioner who undertakes to make a death more painful and lingering might also create a debt for himself.[84]

Thus, the bombmaker who sends the suicide bombers out may well bear significant karmic responsibility for any carnage. Michael's other comment, about karma not always resulting from one person killing another, may also be relevant. We will later note that in some events, such as the attacks on September 11th, 2001, there may have been agreement by many of the souls to be part of this event, either as perpetrator or victim.

Most spirits suggest that contemplating harm to others (without acting on it) is not, by itself, enough to create a karmic tie. For example, the group entity known as Alexander stated:

> Karma is incurred when intent to cause harm is married to action bringing harm. Both intent and action are necessary to create karma, meaning a bond with another soul who had been harmed by your acts. Merely pondering doing harm to another without following through won't incur karma; accidentally bringing harm without the intent to do so also carries no karmic weight. Intent to do harm plus an act committing harm equals karma. Once karma is incurred, the soul committing the harm and the soul so harmed are bound in a relationship until the karmic bond is released.[85]

Thus, it would seem likely that the suicide bomber creates karmic problems for him- or herself, not only because he or she cuts his or her own life short, but also because the lives of others are forcibly taken. When this is done without prior consent of the victim(s)—such as to pay a prior karmic debt—it would clearly seem to cause the suicide bomber to take on major karmic debt. Furthermore, the victims may well end up spending future lives entangled with their aggressors. For many, this may not be a happy thought.

Alexander felt that an evaluation of how an individual soul met whatever life challenges it had to face was only the first step of the life-review process.[86] It stated:

> The next step in a life review is to examine its moral balance sheet....
> Most lifetimes balance on the "good" side of the moral equation, for great compassion and understanding are offered souls releasing earthly life. Human life is a struggle, is meant to be, and this is taken into account. If the moral balance is in the soul's favor, the soul can move on to the next step of its life review. If, however, the soul committed such heinous and brutal acts while in human form that the moral equation is in the negative, meaning that massive karma was incurred, the process of life review effectively ends as further soul growth cannot occur until the karma is cleared up.[87]

If we assume that the suicide bomber is indeed creating tremendous negative karma through his or her acts (which seems likely), then this would suggest that his or her further growth and development may come to a screeching halt until the debt is paid. Alexander (which did not espouse a traditional view of reincarnation) explained:

> You see, the process is one of gradual release of a specific personality and appearance, and reintegration with the higher self. If a specific

personality caused great harm while in human form, then before reintegration can occur that karmic debt must be paid. In this instance, a new offshoot will be created more as a vehicle for the specific personality to "try again" than for the more general purpose of mastering a life theme. The new offshoot will be linked with the imprint left by the soul upon death, for the imprint carries awareness of all relationships, all brutality committed against others. So a new life will be created, and those harmed will frequently be born in relationship to the perpetrator, each such companion also linked to its imprint, so the residue of the past brutality ripples through the new life together.

This is the closest the process comes to the traditional model of reincarnation being a recycling of the same soul from body to body. In the case of great negative karma a new bodily vehicle is prepared and, while it hosts its own soul, that soul is inextricably bound to the imprint left by the perpetrator's life and must work out the karma incurred.[88]

In some cases, channeled material suggests that the karmic debt may require that the perpetrators experience the same kind of harm they inflicted on others, in order to better understand the consequences of their actions. Allan Kardec was simply told, "He who has caused his fellow-men to suffer will be placed in a situation in which he himself will suffer what he caused them to endure."[89]

The blind hatred that appears to lie behind many such attacks may, in itself, also cause karmic damage to a soul. Arthur Ford was channeled as stating:

> The soul which lodges hatred against his brother for the reason of difference in religious belief is in truth a very sick and unhappy soul. ... for it knows, within itself, that the deeds being done in the name of "religion" are done in complete ignorance of the laws of God and payment must be made....
>
> How can one religion be better, necessarily, than another? There is only one God. It is of no matter to God how you worship Him.[90]

A. D. Mattson, commenting from the spirit realm, continued with this theme:

> Those who believe they will be rewarded in heaven by killing others on earth will have an enormous karmic debt to pay.... Religious zealots who believe that they will be rewarded in heaven for killing others on earth are rewarded only by being condemned to the Realm of Darkness.[91]

Mattson further reported that such souls were doomed to continue their destructive behavior in the afterlife for eons. Eventually, the spirits realize that what they are doing accomplishes nothing. At this point, it is possible for such souls to be rehabilitated and gradually advance toward the light to the point they could feel love and concern for others. Unfortunately, this occurs far more slowly in the spirit realm than it would have on the physical plane.

The group being Michael seemed to agree on the fact that karmic debt could be incurred.[92] It stated that the key issue was the underlying intent, whether clothed in sanctity or not. The karma is the same whether the individual is a sadistic murderer or a devout priest torturing a heretic. Malicious intent carries a heavy penalty.

This would seem to apply equally to those who equip and train the terrorist or the suicide bombers themselves. Clothing one's desire to kill and maim other souls—whether men, women, or children and regardless of their faith (many of the dead from the destruction of the Twin Towers were Muslims)—with the zealous pseudo-sanctity of martyrdom does not allow spirits to escape the karmic consequences. Indeed, Michael later observed:

> Remember that evil per se only exists in the minds of those perceiving an action. If you happen to be a young soul.... You will not hesitate to wipe out the lives that are in your way. After all, are they not evil?[93]

At one point, Michael referred to Islam as being what it called a young-soul religious movement. This is significant because Michael felt that young souls as a rule tend to have an "us" and "them" mentality that labels anyone who is perceived to be different as evil.

Medium Suzane Northrop warns:

> On earth you have options. Here in Level Two [the lower astral plane], lack of a physical body prevents any emotional or drug-induced escape. You are stuck in what many may assume to be a living hell. Someone who viciously harms another person without any conscious regret or remorse could be a prime candidate for Level Two, staying trapped in the compulsive essence of this state or act....
>
> This is not a punishment; it's merely the law of Karma—cause and effect—at work.
>
> Whatever the circumstance, the actions you have not resolved while living must still be worked out after death. And then you get to watch the reruns of what happened.[94]

Not all channeled material states that suicide and murder lead to karmic problems. The entity Lazaris felt that all such issues of debt and reparation are voluntary for the soul. It stated that there was no law of karma as such—only the karmic choices that a soul makes for itself.[95] Lazaris explained:

> You see, you may have done something dastardly in a past lifetime, and you decide, "Look, I've got to work on that. I can't let that stand.... I am choosing, I am deciding.... I want to pay for that by going through it myself."
>
> Now we ask you, if you cut off someone's finger ... does cutting off your own finger fix it? No it doesn't....
>
> Forgive yourself. As you forgive yourself and apologize to them, on whatever level you need to do that, that's what fixes it. So you may have done betraying and dastardly things in your past, absolutely. And you may have failed miserably at love, and you may have failed miserably at power, and you may have been an oppressive person, and you decided, "In this lifetime I want to deal with love, and I want to learn about oppression, and I want to deal with this and I want to deal with that, and I want to deal with power." But that's your choice—not the imposition of karma....
>
> Therefore, karma does exist as long as you believe in it, and as soon as you're willing to drop it, it's gone.[96]

The point Lazaris makes about karma involving choice may be a good one, but it tends to ignore the fact that forgiveness, particularly of the self, may be very hard for a soul to do once it has gone through the life-review and self-judgment phase of the afterlife, and has seen in detail how its actions helped or harmed others. For a murderer, the general channeling literature suggests this would include not only the life cut short, but *all of those affected* by that person no longer being alive. Where there are multiple killings, as in a successful terrorism attack or bombing, this could represent considerable weight on the conscience of the one responsible.

One spirit, channeled by Mary Beth Anderson, directly addressed the issue of the possible karmic damage terrorists involved in the September 11th, 2001 attack may have engendered:

> As a result of their actions, those who support terrorists and the terrorists themselves are unwittingly banking tremendous amounts of detrimental karma against their souls. According to God's law, they will reap what they sow. Typically, I ... prefer not to dwell on negative issues, but since I am still entitled to voice my opinion, I hope the terrorists get what they deserve.[97]

Finally, it should be mentioned that both the bomber and his or her victims could be affected by this experience in another way. They may refuse to reincarnate again for a long time, potentially hampering their continued spiritual growth and advancement. Japanese medium Hiroshi

Motoyama states, "People who die accidental, tragic deaths have a difficult time reincarnating if they hang onto the pain and terror they experienced."[98] Although he applied this statement particularly to soldiers in wartime, it would also seem to be pertinent to the sudden (and in the case of the victims, unexpected) death by explosion.

The karmic implications for blowing yourself up and forcibly taking the lives of others would seem to be significant. Such souls may be stuck for a very long time in the lower astral and suffer greatly during self-judgment. Also, in addition to the effect of the suicide itself on future lives, the bomber may create an enormous debt load to those he or she has harmed. Furthermore, there is the issue of the hatred or malicious intent that led to this act causing karmic problems.

14

Experiences in the Afterlife

It is time to turn our attention to what the experience is like for suicide-murderers and, in particular, suicide-bomber souls who cross into the afterlife. As with traditional suicides, this can be broken up into initial experiences, going to funerals, the life review, adjustment problems, interactions with victims, moving on, karma, and reincarnation. In many cases, we will see that murder-suicide does not seem to differ much from traditional suicide in terms of the basic process one has to go through in the afterlife. However depending on personalities, intent, and the number of others harmed, some stages may be much more difficult and prolonged.

Not many mediums have channeled the souls of suicide bombers or the guides that claim to specialize in dealing with them, and there is, at present, relatively little available in the written literature. Because of this, much of the information the reader will see here regarding afterlife experiences relies heavily upon new material that was obtained through seven taped question-and-answer sessions, which took place in June and July 2004 and September 2005 with mediums Nevada Shaw, Joanie, Lauren Thibodeau, and Johanna Carroll. The authors owe a debt of gratitude to these individuals for the generous donation of their time and their willingness to channel these spirits. However, it must also be noted that with such a limited source of material, there is not only a greater risk of not recognizing where the process of channeling has caused distortion, but also that the entities themselves—often said to be not far along in their spiritual development—may be more apt to communicate untruths, whether deliberately or because they simply don't know any better. Where possible, we have tried to cross-corroborate what was said to determine whether other material could back up their statements. However, in the case of some of the more extreme claims made by various spirits quoted here, you, the reader, must make up your own mind about the likelihood of their accuracy. It is with this in mind that we encourage you to proceed.

INITIAL EXPERIENCES

Johanna Carroll, of Sedona, feels that the initial crossing over for those in the September 11th, 2001 attacks was fast and equal for all involved—both terrorists and their victims:

> My feeling about that is that spiritually these souls really did sign up for that sort of mission, to be part of that. And that they didn't really suffer. This is what I got. This is my own experience. They were yanked. The spirit got yanked out of the bodies like *boom!* Almost immediately. Particularly the people on the plane. So, there wasn't a lot of suffering. It was like one, two, three, *gone!* Those were my 9/11 experiences....
>
> The very first thing I saw ... it was huge—the presence, I mean—and it was very, very loving. It was beautiful! The presence of light and spirit was very, very strong. The universe was very busy that day. And I feel that everyone was crossed over equally, including the terrorists. I feel that there were spirits there on an individual basis. But I felt very much that there was a presence from the divine realm. So, the prophets [were] working. These were not just spirits coming from the astral or the causal realm, they [were] coming from the higher elevation of the divine realm, as well. To me, they were huge. Big. Very large presences. I see the people were crossed over on a wave of light. It's like the light hand would reach out, the physical hand would touch it, and they would cross. It was very quick. One, two, three.... They were all crossed over in love. Every single one.[1]

When asked if the guides would like to say more about what happened that day, Carroll channeled:

> "The crossing was very organized and very peaceful." I hear a lot of bells chiming, which can sometimes be the energy or the vibrational shift, so it sounds like bells ringing as it goes to a higher frequency. "There were four major waves of crossing."[2]

Just as with ordinary suicides, many suicide-murderers do not seem to realize that they have died. This appears to be true for both willing murder-suicide pacts and unwilling mass murder-suicide. An example of a spirit belonging in the former group is the confused spirit who showed up in a séance in 1919.[3] It had been seventeen years since the soul had been involved in a willing murder-suicide with his sweetheart. During that time, the soul appeared to have wandered, lost, confused as to his state. The transcript reads:

> Doctor: Where did you come from?
> Spirit: I was straggling along and saw a light, so I came in.
> Dr: Can you tell us who you are?

Sp: No; I don't know.... I can't seem to remember anything. What is the matter with my head? It hurts me so badly.... It is difficult to think.... It is strange, but I can't remember my name.

Dr: How long have you been dead?

Sp: Dead, you say? Why, I'm not dead; I wish I were.

Dr: Is life so unpleasant for you?

Sp: Yes, it is. If I am dead, then it is very hard to be dead. I have tried and tried to die, but it seems every single time I come to life again. Why is it that I cannot die?

Dr: There is no actual death.

Sp: Of course there is.

Dr: How do you know there is such a thing as death?

Sp: I don't know anything. (In great distress) I want to die! I want to die! Life is so dark and gloomy. I wish I could die and forget, forget,—just forget! Why can't I die?

Sometimes I get in places (auras) but I am always pushed out in the dark again, and I go from place to place. I cannot find my home and I cannot die. What is the matter? Oh, let me forget just for a little while! Let me be free from my thoughts and this horrible darkness.[4]

Part of the problem with the transition these souls have to make may indeed lie in the manner of their deaths—by explosion. Trio is a group entity of three spirit guides (speaking as one) that appear to be specialists at dealing with the souls of suicide bombers in the afterlife. As channeled by medium Nevada Shaw, Trio made the following observation of how this experience had affected the spirit of a female suicide bomber:

> This phenomenon, the literal blowing apart of the physical being, is a trauma. It distorts in a different way, the speed and the ripping apart. The molecular structure is changed in such a way [that] the former aspect of the mind has a different way of grasping it than in other forms of death. She doesn't understand how she feels solid now. She felt the explosion in her body. For a moment she wondered if someone else would have felt the explosion in their body. It did not occur to her before. In what you would call time, she will be able to ingest the sensations of moving out of the dimension of physicality, dealing with the emotional awareness of the other individuals on the plane, dealing with the questions you propose on a more ethical basis to communicate with others. It feels like another form of an explosion to her right now—the amount of information. It's as if there is panic in her eyes still, though she does not have physical eyes. She's still feeling the sensation of panic before the explosion took place. She is caught in that place. The anxiety of being caught was more frightening to her than anything. It was a relief in a sense for the explosion to have occurred. She felt as if the duty had been achieved and she could find peace. And

there is no peace where she is now. That, of course, is not the truth. But that is what she feels.[5]

As with traditional suicides, guides attempt to greet these souls using forms they feel will be accepted by the ones they are trying to contact. In the case of fundamentalist Muslims, this may mean appearing as a virgin, angel, or holy man. Trio stated, "They just got to see the beings that they wanted to see.... One was a virgin. One was an angel."[6]

In yet another case, the greeter took a different form. The guide described how he had made contact:

> Heath: I am wondering how you showed yourself or appeared to him in order to help comfort him, make him feel comfortable enough with you to see you and communicate?
> Shaw: I was in a robe. He knew I was not military. It was in a place that he often rested.
> Heath: So you created it. And again, so then you left the place of destruction ...
> Shaw: Yes.
> Heath: ... and you created an image of a place that he was comfortable.
> Shaw: He knew I was a holy man. That is not what I look like. [I did it] for him.
> Heath: How did he know that?
> Shaw: Pictures he had seen.
> Heath: So you appeared as a holy man that he already knew?
> Shaw: Not personally. But from pictures of [him]. So, for him it felt as if he had been honored with the presence of a holy man.
> Heath: And was this a holy man who has already crossed into spirit?
> Shaw: No.
> Heath: Okay. Thank you for that information. Is this a common method you [use to] greet these souls?
> Shaw: Not in that form of this particular holy man. But to have them see what is necessary for them to be present enough to move away from what they have just experienced.[7]

Despite the initial appearances of their greeters, the bombers, like their fundamentalist counterparts in other religions, soon discover that things in the afterlife are not what they had been led to expect. For example:

> Heath: Did he know he was dead?
> Shaw: Not at first. But he does now.
> Heath: How did he figure it out?
> Shaw: Because we [guides] kept showing him different places simultaneously, and it frightened him. And he realized he wasn't able to do that, earlier, so ...

Heath: Did he see what he expected to after he died?
Shaw: No.
Heath: What did he expect?
Shaw: He expected peace.
Heath: And what did he have?
Shaw: Tremendous grief. And fear.
Heath: And was he aware of his victims?
Shaw: Just the children. And one woman. I don't know if the woman was the mother of these children or not. I don't think so.
Heath: Was he aware of anyone greeting him right away?
Shaw: One of us.
Heath: Okay. So, he did sense one of the spirits who is with us today?
Shaw: Uh huh. Not immediately. He was in fear. It was a fear of this speed. He was going very fast. There was movement for him. He was panicking. And then we stepped in to allow him to feel us. But he only saw one of us.
Heath: Okay. What did you communicate to him at that time, when you first met him?
Shaw: That he was on another plane and we were there to assist him.
Heath: And how did he react to that?
Shaw: He didn't trust us (sounding sad). But he felt calmer.
Heath: And what did you do after that?
Shaw: We showed him the children.
Heath: What did you show him about the children?
Shaw: That they were all right. He didn't understand that at first. But it calmed him down.[8]

Another experience was described by a guide as follows:

Heath: And what happened the moment after he had crossed over? Was he aware he had died?
Shaw: No.
Heath: What was he aware of?
Shaw: He was aware of the destruction. It didn't occur to him as he was looking at the destruction as to what he was looking *with*. He just felt vindicated.
Heath: And then what happened? Did anyone greet him?
Shaw: I greeted him.
Heath: And what did you tell him?
Shaw: I asked him if he understood what he was seeing.
Heath: And what did he say?
Shaw: He said it "was done. I did it." I asked him if he understood what he had really done. He said, "I blew the building up. These people will *not* live."[9]

In fact, in one channeling session, the guides that came through insisted that all terrorist souls are met by an entity, if only to make sure that their emotion does not contaminate the astral realm. This was revealed in another session with Nevada Shaw:

> Heath: With accident victims, it sometimes seems to be the case that there are no guides to greet them when they cross over. Could this also be a problem with terrorist souls?
>
> Shaw: It is not the case. We are aware when it occurs. We monitor, but we don't interfere. We are there to greet only to prevent infusion of their misperception of violence into the next realm. It's a corralling.
>
> Heath: Is that part of why you are chosen for your neutrality? Because you can contain—or what do you actually do with the energy of the emotion?
>
> Shaw: It's a force field.
>
> Heath: But then what?
>
> Shaw: To describe what this feels like is easier than to describe what it looks like. We're dealing in terms that don't exist entirely on your plane. It's like a sheet of cool glass that vibrates, circulates, and breathes around the individual's energy. *They* still have the perception that their body parts have blown apart. With their confusion, they believe every part has energetic information. It does on one level, but since they do not have the body anymore, we have to blend, letting them know their spiritual energy and soul are still intact. It's simply an image to put before them, a sensation to help them feel they are intact.
>
> Heath: And it prevents emotions from spreading into your realm?
>
> Shaw: Yes.
>
> Heath: Do you end up transforming the emotions? Or do they dissipate? Or do the terrorist souls themselves transform the emotions?
>
> Shaw: Ultimately they transform the emotions. Transformation is a catalytic event. We are responsible for holding frequency with which they can use their perception to shift and transform themselves.
>
> Heath: At what point can you let go of the force field?
>
> Shaw: When their soul recognizes they have never been shattered.
>
> Heath: Shattered, did you say?
>
> Shaw: Yes. Ultimately, this is what all that cross over deal with. You mentioned earlier other suicides and [people who die in] accidents. The guides are there as well. Those that feel confused and don't know if they are here or there, they actually do have someone to greet them—just so rapid that they don't notice. But there is always someone there to greet them. Always.[10]

One of the things many terrorists are apparently told, by those who recruit and train them, is that they will be rewarded for their act. These souls therefore cross over with certain expectations that, if the guides channeled are to be believed, are not met. In one case, the guides, in response to a question about how the terrorist souls were responding to what they found in the afterlife, explained:

> Shaw: They are confused and annoyed right now. It doesn't seem that it had the impact they thought it would have. It isn't what they expected. They are annoyed.
> Heath: Did they expect to be blessed?
> Shaw: They expected to be with God. They *are* with God. But it's not what they expected.
> Heath: Did any of them have a self-fulfilling prophecy, expecting to see the virgins and the reward and create it for themselves?
> Shaw: Yes. Two that we speak with right now expected that. We allow them to see what they would like to see, but the message that comes through is the thing that we are showing them. It's not what they expected. And what they need to hear is not what they wanted to hear (slight laugh). So it will be valuable for them.
> Heath: They got to see some of what they expected to see, but not all of what they expected to see? Is that correct?
> Shaw: Yes.
> Heath: And in what way was it not what they expected to see?
> Shaw: They expected to be rewarded for what they had done. They are still loved. They are still honored with being seen as divine beings. But they have to live through the torment. And they did not expect to see that on this side. They have to see. The next step of growth has to do with surrendering the passions to any story, whether it be about violence or power—even love. They just have to be willing to pay attention.[11]

When asked whether they had seen what they had expected when they crossed over, the terrorist souls replied:

> Carroll: No. [They say,] "Not as we were taught."
> Heath: Do the terrorists feel they were lied to?
> Carroll: No. It's like they're still holding on to what they believe to be true....
> Heath: How do they feel about the fact that things aren't as they were told it would be?
> Carroll: There's one man who is saying, "It's an interesting observation." It's like he's turning his head around in a full circle, so he gets to see all of it. It's almost like he's arguing here. "We still love. We still have people we care about. We are not without feelings. We did our job. We had a mission." I see a symbol of a moon and then I see a symbol of a star. A moon and a star. I don't know why that's there.[12]

It should be noted that the moon (particularly a crescent moon) and star have been common symbols of Islam since the 15th century.

This bewilderment over what happened to them after crossing over is a common element in terrorist afterlife experiences. As Trio put it: "It is the same confusion almost all souls that experience this encounter.... They believe it will be one outcome and it is not. It doesn't feel as if the reward is present." Nor are male terrorists the only ones who report their pre-death expectations had not been met. In discussing the spirit of a Chechen woman who was involved in downing a Russian plane, Trio noted:

> She is confused because she believes she has done a service and now it feels as if that's eluded her. She feels abandoned by men. The deeper truth for her is she has abandoned herself, but she doesn't understand what that means.[13]

FUNERALS

Not all terrorist souls attend their memorial services. In the case of one who was asked whether he went to his funeral, the guides stated:

> Shaw: We asked him. He did not choose to do that. We can do that for them.
> Heath: And why did he choose not to go?
> Shaw: He felt it was too painful. He was embarrassed. There was shame.
> Heath: Why was he ashamed?
> Shaw: He felt inappropriate. It was a dishonor for him. It was something that he felt dishonored about.[14]

The guides were later asked for more explanation of why this soul did not attend his service:

> Shaw: This is more detailed than what we discussed before. The disillusionment has to do with the structure of perception in the mind. He perceived shame and took on the sorrows of his perception of the nature of childhood and what it means to be a responsible parent. The lineage of this concept became distorted for him.
> Heath: When alive? Or afterwards, when dead?
> Shaw: Both. One preceded the other. He took it into the next realm. There is a moment that you can let go of the perception when you cross over. Many of these individuals bring misperception into the next level. That is why it takes so long to take off. These issues of shame had to do with his misinterpretation of what his responsibilities as a child, as a father, as a participant of the world, are. He took it on as his personal mistake.
> Heath: But why would a funeral particularly bring that up for him?

Shaw: He would have to witness all the misperception. He would have to witness all the lineage with each misinterpretation, with each person there to grieve.

Heath: So, at that point he had more clarity?

Shaw: He began to have more clarity. He still was holding on to the misinterpretation that shame was his responsibility. That is incorrect. It is an incorrect perception. But it is what he felt.[15]

It would seem that, much like traditional suicides, terrorist souls may choose whether to attend their memorial services. However, if they should decide to go, it could expose those souls to the distorted beliefs and emotions held by the living. For those spirits still struggling to deal with their own issues, this could be a difficult thing to face.

LIFE REVIEW

All suicide-murderers go through the life-review and self-judgment phase whether they harmed one willing victim or took the unwilling lives of many. As Trio put it:

When we harm another, it harms our self, whether it be our species, another species, or the environment. Eventually, when you move past the physical, you will experience all you have had influence in as the other's perception. It's a way of allowing us the eternal view.[16]

A pair who had committed murder-suicide explained further:

The point seems to be that whenever one takes his or her own life, the eternal truth must be wrung from the life experience until there is nothing more to wring out. Then, and only then, we may move from this entryway between the earth plane and this plane....

There is no condemnation here. We meet helpers, and they lead us step by step.

Everything I do now is directed toward understanding the eternal lessons that I must learn from reviewing my entire life. Even though I was a young man, I still must examine it all minutely. That way, the guides tell me, there will be no chance of repeating the petty thoughts that opened me to the murder/suicide.[17]

Terrorist spirits eventually appear to undergo the same life-review process as do all others in the afterlife. For some, this may involve meeting with the souls of their victims. However, as with other spirits, this period is not about judgment, but learning. Trio spoke through Nevada Shaw of what one terrorist said after his initial fear was past:

Shaw: We asked him what he would like to learn from this.

Heath: What did he say?

Shaw: How to be free from the personal torture. His own fear. He can't sleep. It doesn't matter now, but when he was alive he couldn't sleep. He realizes it doesn't matter now, but he still feels the internal torment which kept him from sleep.

Heath: Has he gone through a life-review process yet?

Shaw: Not entirely. Just bits and pieces. He doesn't want to look at the aspects of his father. He's seen his mother now.

Heath: Was this act part of his blueprint before he incarnated?

Shaw: Yes. He had two paths that were available to him, though, which he chose from.

Heath: What was the other path?

Shaw: To choose not to get involved with it. And to live with his cousin.[18]

Terrorism appears to carry special implications in the afterlife that make it different from "ordinary" murder-suicide. According to the guides, this is due to one factor—the intent. This appears to make the transition even slower, as Trio noted: "They're more confused. They don't grasp the information the guides are giving them. They don't grasp it as quickly as others do. So they can't transcend it as fast, or haven't been able to *yet*."[19] Trio described the problem through Nevada Shaw:

Shaw: The intent is a misguided notion that if they take out *many* lives, it will change decisions of other people regarding positions of power. When individuals take themselves out, with intention of removing themselves from the personal pain, sometimes they want to say good-bye, and they want someone to notice. But it is not an intent always to hurt someone else. Here there is intent to hurt others on a wide scale. Also to be noticed. But it's about a power struggle. Different.

Heath: Right. And that's clear about the intent. But how does that difference in intent impact the transition?

Shaw: Transitions for those that [kill] on a wider scale are going to have to deal with the situation. There are more lives they're going to have to connect with and feel through before they can move on. So, if, suppose, an individual commits suicide and takes many with them, opposed to an individual who murders themselves and impacts others who remain alive, there's pain on both sides. But those who take lives are going to have to live through the process of each of those individuals, even if they don't understand that. It will take, in linear terms, it would appear to take a great deal of time for they will have to understand [the impact of their actions] for each soul that they have taken before they can move on.

Heath: So, do they tend to see the life unfold of the life they took?

Shaw: Not the entire life. Only the impact of what …

Heath: Of what was cut short?

Shaw: Yes.
Heath: And how it impacted others?
Shaw: Yes.
Heath: And do they feel the emotion? The grief of those left behind?
Shaw: They do. Sometimes they hold back from it. These individuals, it's harder for [them] than others that murder, or commit murder on themselves, for there is a jaded [quality], there is a wall that prevents them from absorbing the emotion. And if they don't see the emotion they can't take the next step. It's only a fraction of a second, but they have to be able. It's like living what the other individual lives, to have to notice it, on some level, for every individual.
Heath: Also for themselves?
Shaw: Yes.[20]

One of the terrorist souls also commented on the issue of intent and seemed to touch on what Trio called neutrality. This spirit felt that his actions trying to bring down a plane were performed for the right reason, in service to humanity.[21] He claimed to have finished his life review and did not appear to be dealing with the same transition issues as some of his colleagues. He pointed out through the medium Joanie:

Because it is your perception, really, that drives your intent, he says. And if you are enlightened enough to understand that there is only one energy. It's not dark and it's not light. It's intention driven. Even in the darkest, darkest, darkest act, if the intention is pure, then the energy is healing. And he's claiming many would consider him to have been misguided, but he sees himself as always having been guided by God. And there's no mistaking that.[22]

This life-review process would appear to be slow and arduous, and may even need to be performed more than once, in various levels of depth and degree. Also, the life review may be done simultaneously with other forms of spiritual work. Spirit guides who work with terrorist souls state:

Shaw: Those that I said I do not trust are very capable of learning. They're highly intelligent. They have very complicated patterns built up of lies. That is what I do not trust. Their patterns are rooted deeper.
Heath: What kind of things do you do to work with these souls?
Shaw: With the energy we put into their essence.
Heath: Okay. What kind of energy?
Shaw: It's like a sound and they feel it in their bodies. It goes from the top of the body down what you would call the spinal column. It vibrates the body. They may or may not be aware of it....
Heath: Have they finished reviewing their life and that of their victims?

Shaw: No, they have not finished reviewing.
Heath: It's too early on?
Shaw: Yes. Some have seen them [their life and those of their victims]. I do not feel that they've absorbed it till they go through it again.[23]

This mention of instilling energy may be similar to what Michael Newton describes as the technique used by the spirit realm for dealing with those souls who repeatedly have difficulty with their lives:

> S[pirit]: Those souls who have developed severe obstacles to improvement are mended by the restoration of positive energy.
> Dr. N: Is this procedure just for Earth souls?
> S: No, young souls from everywhere may require restoration as a last resort.
> Dr. N: Are these restored spirits then allowed to return to their respective groups and eventually go back to incarnating on physical worlds?
> S: (sighs deeply) Yes.[24]

Sometimes a terrorist soul, during life review, may be confused about his karma and that of his victims. Asked how the transition of terrorists differed from that of souls who die in accidents, Trio explained:

> Perspective of intention leads to how personal stories fall away from the essence I spoke of that sticks to the being when they cross over. Those that manipulate to intentionally do harm attach themselves without perhaps realizing it to the individuals their actions ultimately harm. They end up carrying what would feel to them as double karma. There is contamination. It is not truly the case, but it would feel that way. It becomes difficult for them to distinguish what is their own, and what is someone else's karma. Ultimately it becomes a learning process that is valuable to them.[25]

The guide Joshua also discussed how the life-review process proceeds with some terrorists:

> Carroll: Interesting.... They're saying on an individual level there is a review and even in the review there is an energy of an argumentative discourse, which I think is really interesting. Well, I guess they take that with them. I'm asking him to take me to the next level, so I can see after this argumentative discourse occurs, what happens to the soul next.
> Heath: Have they finished going through this review?
> Carroll: I feel like some of them are still stuck in it, to be honest with you. I'm not able to see beyond it, which is interesting.
> Heath: In a way, you've already answered this, but I'll go ahead and ask it anyway. Do they have particular problems dealing with terrorist souls compared to other souls they help move through?

Carroll: No.

Heath: Okay. So, other souls are just as argumentative?

Carroll: They're saying it depends upon this collective belief system that you go through. Belief system, to me, is not just about religion. It's about your value system. It's vibrationally how you cross over and how much work you've done on yourself in your everyday life.[26]

We have seen in this section that suicide bombers appear to go through the same kind of life-review process as do other souls. This may be a long and difficult period, as the spirits have to review not only their own life, but that of those they had harmed, along with the impact their actions have had on others. Their progress appears to be slowed down by the strength with which terrorists hold on to their old belief patterns (and may not be helped by their argumentative nature). Only one terrorist spirit claimed to have finished his life review (which could not be confirmed through other mediums); some appeared to be in the midst of it, while many did not appear to have started the process.

ADJUSTMENT PROBLEMS

Suicide bombers may face many of the same problems adjusting to the afterlife as others who take their own life. Often, they appear to have trouble accepting that they are dead. For example:

Heath: Are they aware they are dead?

Shaw: Three of them are aware they are dead.

Heath: How many of them are not?

Shaw: Five.

Heath: Are the three who are aware they are dead aware of the five who are not?

Shaw: Yes. They see one another, but they don't communicate. For the three who know, it's part of their learning process to recognize that the others don't see yet.[27]

Other times, the issue may be one of remaining near the Earth plane for a period of time. The following response was in answer to whether these souls become stuck near the physical plane:

Shaw: Some of them do.

Heath: What determines if they are stuck?

Shaw: It's a level of mental attachment. They aren't aware of choice. It's an old lie....

Heath: And what is the old lie?

Shaw: That you are trapped.

Heath: Can they hear you when you tell them otherwise?

Shaw: They can hear it. Many of them don't understand it. It's something that needs to be repeated the way that they repeat the lie.[28]

Although many of the channeled messages from traditional suicides speak of being lost in a gray mist, at least some of the guides for terrorists appear to deny that this occurred for their charges. When asked what happens for those souls who do not complete their transitions to the afterlife, Trio described the situation as follows:

Shaw: They float as if they are resting, but their thought projections come from them. It would seem to them as if they were thinking. They would feel their body as if it were still intact. Some of them would notice visually what was familiar to them. They're not what they seem.
Heath: How so?
Shaw: It would sound more quiet, except issues that would help them make the shift would stand out. Colors would stand out. Sound would stand out.
Heath: Is that the doing of the guides?
Shaw: Not specifically. It's the phenomenon itself. This is something that can happen for all those that cross over. It's a learning technique.
Heath: Some people speak of feeling like they're in a gray mist or a place without light. Is this also seen with the terrorists?
Shaw: Sometimes. Not all. Many of those we work with have not been incurring that.
Heath: What makes the difference between those that might feel they're in a place of darkness or in a gray mist? What would make that happen?
Shaw: Part of that has to do with a decision *we* make. How quickly we would need to pull a situation up to recognition—catalytic information I discussed. Ultimately their belief of what their story is will still have to do with what they see visually. They don't have eyes anymore—just perception. The ones that maintain a stuckness in the gray you have discussed, are holding on to an old system that turns in on itself. Difficult to describe. Many of them are not so sure this exists anymore, even when they are in the midst of crossing over.
Heath: What do you mean "this exists"? What are you referring to as "this"?
Shaw: Their description of what God is. Their description of what justice is. Their description of what peace is. It's as if they are in what you would describe as a drugged state. Too numb. Many of them are not as numb as they would appear. Only those that would be in this numb place would experience this as gray.
Heath: Does that tend to be depression?
Shaw: Not always.
Heath: What else causes grayness?

Shaw: Depression is one. There is something [else], an apathy, resentment. There is a control those in this place hold on to. It's a very fine parallel of feeling they have no control but holding on to a structure that control was all they had. And now, none of it makes sense. If you are trying to monitor control from an old story, there's no truth. There is no such thing as control. This is separate from the black and gray area we were talking about. It's a complex situation to discuss.[29]

Transitions for suicide bombers appear to be very slow. When questioned about the adjustment problems these souls may face, the guides stated through the medium:

Shaw: Yes, they're very matter-of-fact.... One of them just says, "groundwork of extension." It's not very poetic, but it has something to do with patience, with understanding, with a very, very long-term shifting.
Heath: Are they saying this is a slow transition?
Shaw: For those individuals, yes. Not for the victims. It's very quick for them.[30]

For many of these spirits, confusion appears to be a common theme. In some cases, the terrorists may be separated and placed in something of a holding pattern until the guides feel they are capable of learning. This can be seen in the following question-and-answer section:

Heath: Is this usual that they separate the terrorists?
Shaw: Sometimes.
Heath: What makes the difference?
Shaw: The level of learning.
Heath: Can you explain further?
Shaw: The speed with which they absorb love.
Heath: So if they can't absorb love, you sort of group by level of …?
Shaw: It's a detainment, sort of.
Heath: Okay. And are the others simply not capable of absorbing love?
Shaw: They're capable, but not now.
Heath: I understand.
Shaw: It's a choice they make right now.
Heath: So where are they right now?
Shaw: It's a holding pattern.
Heath: How do they see the holding pattern?
Shaw: It looks similar to what they saw on Earth. But calmer....
Heath: What happens to those who cannot let go of their hatred?
Shaw: They will stay in the holding pattern.[31]

The early separation of souls in the afterlife may not be unique to terrorists but simply a normal way of dealing with those who are very unevolved or have hurt others during their lifetime. Michael Newton observes:

> I have also learned that certain souls do undergo separation in the spirit world, and this happens at the time of their orientation with guides.... Those of my subjects who have been impeded by evil report that souls whose influence was too weak to turn aside a human impulse to harm others will go into seclusion upon reentering the spirit world. These souls don't appear to mix with other entities in the conventional manner for quite awhile.
>
> I have also observed that those beginner souls who are habitually associated with intensely negative human conduct in their first series of lives must endure individual spiritual isolation. Ultimately, they are placed together in their own group to intensify learning under close supervision. This is not punishment, but rather a kind of purgatory for the restructuring of self-awareness with these souls.[32]

In another book, Newton writes:

> There are certain displaced souls who have become so contaminated by their host bodies that they require special handling. In life they became destructive to others and themselves. This spectrum of behavior would primarily include souls who have been associated with evil acts that caused harm to other people through deliberate malice. In either case these souls are taken to places of isolation where their energy undergoes a more radical treatment plan than with the typical returning soul.[33]

Interestingly enough, contrary to what earlier channeled material would suggest, death by explosion does not seem to cause any particular adjustment problems. In one interview, the guides noted that for the terrorist, "He found it exhilarating."[34] It should also be noted that the bombmakers may have even slower transitions than those they send out to kill. Surprisingly, in such cases death by explosion may actually have a certain advantage. The guides known as Trio explained, regarding bombmakers:

> The nature of their story and their control I spoke of is more complex for them. To rephrase, convoluted. It's a tighter structure that's woven like a ball of rubber bands. They are more convinced that control is necessary. They come across intact, with this story, with this lie. Those that blow apart the lie actually have an opportunity to move through it faster, for part of the story has already been blown apart, to use a metaphor.[35]

Furthermore, with bombmakers:

> Shaw: It is simply more complex to unravel them. It is more complex for them to unravel themselves. For the issue of control is very important to them and they cannot see this.
>
> Heath: Is there any difference between how they are handled as opposed to how bombers are handled?
>
> Shaw: We separate them. Their control issues are linked energetically to those that would submit themselves to control. There is a submissive factor in some that can cross over despite the lack of bodies.[36]

Thus, every soul appears to bring a certain amount of baggage to the afterlife. In the case of the terrorists, their stories may be particularly tightly wrapped and hard for the guides to unravel. This includes issues of unrealized expectations—such as having the power to name seventy relatives who may go straight to heaven or receiving seventy-two virgins. Trio spoke of this:

> Shaw: Those that come in with a direct awareness that they have crossed over must address their perception, for it falls away when the body leaves. Those that are not as evolved find it difficult to let go of their personal story. It attaches to the body. When the body is gone, there's a vacuum. Very difficult to describe this, but the essence of the story clings to the nature of the being. How quickly they can move on from this and evolve depends on how quickly they can shift the perception of the moving story.
>
> Heath: That would suggest the seventy relatives receiving absolution is a story ...
>
> Shaw: Yes.
>
> Heath: ... rather than a truth.
>
> Shaw: In one respect, yes. This is true of all people crossing over.... Each individual carries their own story. There is within that story a connection between each of them. Regardless of the connection between their lineage, and regardless of the decision that the bomber carries when he crosses over, there still is independent evolution of each soul.[37]

A soul's evolution and adjustment is described in greater detail in the following section of the same interview:

> Heath: Now that they have crossed over, do they still believe that they acted according to God's wishes?
>
> Shaw: Some do. Most are still very confused. It is not the same confusion as when they had their bodies.
>
> Heath: How so?
>
> Shaw: There's more awareness that accompanies this. They're willing to look. But as long as the stories are attached, they will not get clarity to the answer to the confusion they have. It is not as rigid, though.

Heath: Do they, now that they have crossed over, still think that God wanted them to be a martyr?

Shaw: They are not sure.

Heath: Do they feel it was God who was responsible for killing the victims?

Shaw: Some do. Some are now confused as to what they consider God. Some have been confused in thinking we are God. The explanations we give to them is [that] God is part of all of it, and in a sense we are God, which confuses them more.

Heath: Did dying let them escape their problems?

Shaw: No. Though there is more neutrality for them. They can observe the opportunity to learn, without having the pain as attached. Initially the pain was very much there. That's part of the learning process if they are still attached to the story. It helps them to recognize what their part in behavior toward others can reflect in, and around, themselves. Ultimately, it is their own reflection they have always come to see. That is what I am meaning about no good or bad. Regardless, they are going to have to deal with whatever this is and their stories. And if they are responsible for the death of someone else, they will have to reflect upon that story, as well.

Heath: Many are confused, but do some feel misled or lied to about what would happen after they died?

Shaw: Yes. Though now, they are not as emotional about it. Most of that has burnt away. They are simply looking at it now. It's another story they could attach to by being annoyed.

Heath: Is annoyance a defense they are using?

Shaw: Yes. It doesn't matter who sent them.

Heath: Have you been using sleep to help them recover?

Shaw: They do not sleep....

Heath: I should also ask if, in some ways, they felt lied to, were there ways in which they felt like they were told the truth and still feel that way?

Shaw: Seventy percent. But that's fading. That's part of the confusion. There's some uncertainty now. It takes, if we are speaking in linear terms (and it varies), four to six days in your linear time terms to accommodate past initial emotions and any sensation, physicality, confusion. Some may be confused whether they have a body or not. It takes two to four weeks to deal with the emotion of the story. Beyond that, they may move into a more neutral place. It varies.

Heath: Is that the holding zone you spoke of before?

Shaw: That is part of it. The holding pattern is a much more complex and long-term position. In linear terms it could be anywhere from a month to thousands of years. It could also be a resting place for some. But essentially it's a place that those that are still confused, but neutral, stay. There is no point for them going to the next level until they adjust.

Heath: What about those who are confused but not neutral? Where do they stay?

Shaw: It *is* the same place from our perspective—the guides. It appears to them as a different place for they would not witness the other souls. They would think they are by themselves.

Heath: What do they see?

Shaw: They see themselves as they knew themselves before. They may reflect upon the individuals they came in contact with. The flashes of this go back and forth as if it were a channel. Sometimes this confuses them. Sometimes they find it a way to move through their thoughts quickly. It is a technique we use with them to help them move past the attachment.[38]

Once again, we have seen that terrorist souls may have many of the same adjustment problems as traditional suicides. They may have trouble understanding that they are dead. Even once they do realize this, they may remain somewhat stuck and are often confused. The afterlife is not what they had expected, and it may be difficult for them to come to grips with how things truly are there. As with the life-review process, transitions appear to be slow for most of these souls. Some of this may relate to the fact they have varying capacities for love. However, guides work with these souls to help them let go of their "story" and advance spiritually.

INTERACTIONS WITH VICTIMS

Earlier channeled material suggested that those who deliberately harm others may have to confront their victims in the afterlife. When the guides of terrorist souls were asked about this, some suggested that this is a matter of choice. Trio commented through Nevada Shaw:

Heath: Are they aware of their victims?
Shaw: Yes.
Heath: Has there been any interaction between them?
Shaw: No.
Heath: Will there be interaction in the future?
Shaw: For two of them.
Heath: What makes a difference whether there is interaction or not?
Shaw: Depends on the victim.
Heath: And how is that?
Shaw: The willingness of the victim to receive the information. If it feels safe for them.
Heath: So it's the victim who chooses whether or not they interact in the future?
Shaw: Yes.
Heath: What kind of interaction would that tend to be?

> Shaw: We're with them. It's as if they have a conversation with one another, but they don't touch. The communication is—you would call it telepathic—but it's very quick. Some of them might feel it in their bodies.[39]

However, at another point in the interview, Trio suggested that the terrorists, too, have a say in whether they will have to confront their victims:

> Heath: So has he interacted with this victim yet, or is that in the future?
> Shaw: It's in the future. But this would only take place if he decides he wants the contact.[40]

It may reassure some that several mediums spoke of the speed and ease of the transition for these victims. Victims are met by guides, often taken to healing centers, and helped to understand what has happened to them before any interaction is considered with the suicide bombers. A description of such a healing center comes from a soul who considered herself a victim of the September 11th, 2001 attacks. Joanie remembers:

> There was a woman on 9/11, the sister had been a client of mine.... She had been a repeat attempter of suicide. And upon watching the first tower go down, like a lot of us, the shock of it all touched her. But when she saw the second tower, she went and got her morphine patches out and delivered herself a fatal overdose, wanting to not live in a world, as she brings it to me, where such pain exists....
> She's living on the other side in what I'm going to call a healing center. It sounds a bit contrived, but that's what it is. A place where vibration is adjusted is what she's sending me. That they work with her. I'm seeing a body lifted. An ethereal body being adjusted with light fiber network all around. And she's telling me she takes treatments. They continue to help align the light body and rebalance spiritual energy. As I tune into this I am hearing quite a bit of sound and music, all attached. It's sort of a multisensory synesthesia response that is heard, felt, experienced, seen, all in the same moment. She claims that she's spent a lot of time with people who died in the 9/11 incident. She considers herself a victim of 9/11 also. And she points out that people around the world who were caused pain by this in some sense can be considered victims. A very broad kind of perspective to take.[41]

Trio described one child victim's experience:

> Shaw: There is a child.
> Heath: Okay. Was this child one of the victims?
> Shaw: Yes.
> Heath: I thank this child for coming forward. What can it tell us about its passing?

Shaw: She misses her little friend. The boy.
Heath: Did her friend also pass over?
Shaw: Yes. But she didn't know where he went.
Heath: Okay. Was she aware of any others around her?
Shaw: Her mother. But she didn't see her at the moment.
Heath: So she didn't see her mother right away, but then she did?
Shaw: Later. When she crossed over.
Heath: Who or what was the first to greet her?
Shaw: Another one of our companions.
Heath: Looking like what?
Shaw: Looking like one of her aunties.
Heath: And what did this spirit tell her?
Shaw: That she should take her hand. It would be all right. They would take her to her mother.
Heath: And where was she reunited with her mother?
Shaw: It was on the plane we are working [on]. For the little girl, momentarily it looked like her home before it was blown. But later, that removed, and she and her mother were in a place of light....
Heath: And what was the little girl told about what had happened in terms of her death?
Shaw: She was shown what happened.
Heath: Was shown the explosion?
Shaw: Yes. She was shown who did it. It was from a place where she would not be in pain about it.
Heath: Was this after her mother was with her?
Shaw: Yes.
Heath: And what was she told?
Shaw: She was told these individuals feel differently about life and the world than you do.
Heath: And how did she feel about that?
Shaw: She was confused. Surprisingly, she wasn't too frightened. She was frightened that something might happen to her mother. She was frightened she would be separated from her mother. She didn't understand all the aspects of why these people would want to do this.
Heath: And what did you tell her?
Shaw: To look within their hearts.
Heath: And what did she see there?
Shaw: She saw that they were lost. When she saw that they were lost, it reminded her of her friend. And it reminded her of what she felt when she couldn't find her mother. So she asked, "Do they feel the same thing? Are they looking for their mother?"
Heath: And did she forgive them?
Shaw: Yes.

Heath: Was this important?
Shaw: Yes.
Heath: How so?
Shaw: She can evolve very quickly. Her mother can evolve very quickly.[42]

Later, the child's mother, who was also killed in the explosion, was discussed. For her, this death had apparently been part of her life blueprint before incarnating. Trio said through Nevada Shaw:

Shaw: The information her grandfather sought to spread was of honor for all people. His wife felt the same and taught that to her daughter.... Somehow, the daughter knew that she would have an opportunity to change the way women act, not only thought.
Heath: And she did this with her death?
Shaw: That wasn't her intention initially. When it happened and she crossed over, she realized that this was part of it.
Heath: Did that help her to forgive?
Shaw: Yes.
Heath: And has she interacted with those who were responsible for her death and that of her children?
Shaw: She has not interacted. But she has seen this man we spoke of earlier, from a distance. She is interested in contacting him.
Heath: Is he not able to contact her yet?
Shaw: We have not allowed it.
Heath: Is this the one who was farther advanced, who was concerned about the woman?
Shaw: Yes.
Heath: Okay. What is your concern if this interaction comes too soon? What would happen?
Shaw: It has something to do with the child not being able to separate the information properly. The child is very attached to her mother. She doesn't understand. The father left. He was not there in the building.
Heath: He is still alive?
Shaw: He is. The little girl would find it confusing, the interaction between the souls of her mother and this other man. Where she came from, this would be forbidden.[43]

Sometimes the victims may be more aware of the terrorists than the other way around. Joanie channeled one of the victims who had worked for a major financial company in the World Trade Center, who stated:

Joanie: I am also feeling here the energy of a gentleman, a devout Muslim actually, who was killed. ... I think he's telling me I have worked with his family. Yes, I know them. I remember who this is. Yeah. He was about

> to be married in the week after. The following Saturday he was due to get married.
> Heath: Had he planned on his blueprint to be part of this?
> Joanie: He says yes, because he was able to bring a lot of people awareness that all Muslims, just like all Christians, are not all cut from the same cloth, or believe the same way.
> Heath: Was he aware of the terrorists after he died?
> Joanie: Very much so.
> Heath: What can he tell me about that?
> Joanie: He's showing me a praying for them, and he says with them. With them. But I'm seeing it's like a gap, okay? Like a vibrational distance, it's as if, if you were to look at the scene, that they would appear to be across from each other. But they aren't. They're in different places.
> Heath: Are the terrorists even aware that he's praying with them?
> Joanie: No. Yes. Well, yes-no. Well, you understand these things. The yes part being on a soul level—yes. On a just-come-out-of-human-life, still-stuck-on-human-mentality-to-a-point level, no.[44]

The interaction that occurs may also depend in part upon the relative spiritual evolution of the souls involved. This came up in the following question-and-answer segment with a terrorist soul:

> Heath: I'm just wondering if he has interacted at all with the victims?
> Joanie: He's telling me only from a distance. He said some can come. Some can come over. He's showing me an image of the pinnacle of a pyramid. Right? And you understand stratification. If you were to draw lines through it, you'd have different levels or layers. But the people at the top of the central pyramid over on the victim's side can reach and come and meet the people at the top of the pyramid [on the terrorist side]. In other words the spiritually developed ones can approach the other spiritually developed ones. It's vibration and resonance that drive it.[45]

Thus we see that a number of factors may determine whether victims and terrorists interact in the afterlife. It may involve choice (both for the suicide bombers and their victims), respective levels of spiritual development, and even cultural constraints. Such interaction is viewed as something that can be beneficial to both parties, as it may lead to forgiveness and understanding. However, some souls may never be able to take this step.

MOVING ON

One of the more intriguing statements made by the spirit guides with regard to the terrorist attack of September 11th, 2001, was that the manner of group death caused the souls to become enmeshed. The fact that many mediums report victims coming through en masse would seem to support this notion. The explanation of what happened, and how it has affected the ability of the souls to advance spiritually, came from Trio:

> Heath: There have been a great many terrorist souls in the last several decades. Are most of them in the early stages of processing?
> Shaw: Yes.
> Heath: What has happened to the ones who were part of the World Trade Center?
> Shaw: Some of them are actually more advanced than some of the others. The impact for them catapulted them further. That seems strange, but …
> Heath: How?
> Shaw: The loss of life from a different place on the Earth and a different perspective of those souls had an impact they didn't anticipate when they crossed over.
> Heath: So they were aware of their victims?
> Shaw: Yes.
> Heath: In what way?
> Shaw: They felt the immediate observation thrust into their, I can't say bodies …
> Heath: Well, astral bodies maybe?
> Shaw: Yes. It was as if they were all meshed together in a soup, and it didn't seem familiar at all.
> Heath: So they were aware of the thoughts and feelings of others?
> Shaw: Yes. It was *not* what they anticipated. They felt desperate, as if they were drowning.
> Heath: Losing their identity?
> Shaw: Yes.
> Heath: Did they understand they were dead?
> Shaw: No.
> Heath: Are some of them still confused about that?
> Shaw: Some, but not too many. Most of them have been willing to truly look at this. Some I do not trust.
> Heath: Interesting statement from a guide. So, you feel like they may be still trying to manipulate the situation?
> Shaw: Some. Some are quite in earnest, in earnest [about] learning.
> Heath: So, the way they died, all together massively at one time, linked them in a way that others are not linked to their victims?
> Shaw: Yes. It was a fusion. The same procedure could happen in any explosion. The difference is the soul information and perception of Americans, as opposed to their own countrymen.

Heath: How did that make it different?

Shaw: The belief systems are different. It forced them into seeing and feeling something that was different.

Heath: Oh, so their expectations were less met because they were simultaneously being bombarded with the expectations of Americans?

Shaw: Yes. It's more than that. It lent them the opportunity for rapid growth because they were thrust into a belief pattern that is almost the reverse of theirs. If they can see that both belief patterns carry lies, the metaphor which surrounds them both won't matter ultimately. But they are able to see it faster than someone else because they are looking at differences that they are experiencing through their own bodies.

Heath: Did some of the victims also have this advantage?

Shaw: Yes.[46]

When the guides were asked if any of these souls had reached an "advanced stage" in their development, Shaw initially channeled that this was not the case (although, in the last session, Trio noted that one terrorist spirit had managed to complete the life review and be at a point of neutrality). However, other mediums received a different answer to this question. One spirit who came through Joanie claimed to be a bodhisattva [enlightened being], have finished his life review, and be actively working to help other terrorist souls. It is difficult to say what the truth of this situation is.

The Value of Prayer

Unlike what we saw with other forms of suicide, sleep does not appear to be used very often for healing. However, as with traditional suicides, the importance of prayer did come up—both from the guides and the terrorist souls themselves. In one case, a terrorist soul who indicated he had died in the Pennsylvania plane crash on September 11th, 2001 claimed that prayers had been arranged in advance of their actions:

And he claims there were people part of this mission who did not die in the mission, whose job was to say prayers. Right? And he's telling me the prayers were said. He's showing me mosques around the world. That there was a—I'm going to call it a network, but I don't mean al-Qaeda here—it's like, I would best be able to approach it as a prayer chain of people around the world. Some knew in advance that they were to pray at this time and event. Because it wasn't as secret, I'm being told, as people thought. It wasn't as much of a surprise. That hundreds—not dozens—but hundreds knew this was going on. And they were in charge of the prayer piece, so that the people who died, the terrorists primarily that's what they were praying for. Some had the compassionate heart, he's telling me, to pray for everyone. But that was fewer of them....

And he is pointing out that that's one of the reasons this event had to happen. That we need to understand ourselves as a collective. A collective. And that we need to pray for everyone. When this happened, I remember the very first thing I heard was, "Pray unceasing." "Pray unceasing" when I saw the first tower hit. It's as if the room just filled with [this], it was amazing. Sort of put your prayers on autopilot. Put it out that the prayer continues, because these people need it.[47]

The spirit guides known collectively as Trio also stated: "Anyone from the Earth plane that would choose to be neutral, with their own fears and patterns, can be a value to any soul that crosses over by sending light."[48] This "light" would appear to be a nonverbal, energetic form of prayer or well-wishing.

Spiritual Work

Just as with traditional suicides, service is used as a tool for spiritual advancement. This appears to be true whether only one person was murdered, or many. George Anderson refers to how an adult guilty of murder-suicide was working from the other side to help a teenager who had shot himself.[49] His report reads:

"He says there's a murder involved."
"Yes," Jeannie answered, to which Sam added, "He killed somebody."
"Oh, and then he killed himself."
"Yes."
"Oh, no wonder. He kept claiming 'It's my fault.' He kept claiming he did the same things as your son.... "
"But he's saying he's gotten his act together over there. This is also his own penance, of his own choice, because he committed murder and then killed himself.[50]

In a telephone question-and-answer session with Johanna Carroll, both the channel and a guide, Joshua, who came through her, commented on how terrorist souls can evolve. Joshua's direct comments are indicated by quotation marks in the transcript below:

Heath: And what tends to shift as evolution occurs?
Carroll: "They become closer to the soul."
Heath: And how does that manifest?
Carroll: "Their desires change."
Heath: How?

> Carroll: "Their perspective on the universal mind becomes more apparent. It is not an isolated stream of thinking. They separate themselves from the distortion, thereby allowing themselves a higher viewpoint. They are assisting many who are still crossing." That's interesting. That says to me when they have this shift, they act as a catalyst in helping others cross over through what's continuing to happen on the Earth, from their own belief system. It's almost like a designation. Familiarity, in other words.
> Heath: So, they let terrorist souls act as guides?
> Carroll: "When they reach that point in evolution." ... It's almost like a retribution. They are able to balance some of that karma on the other side by being in service and helping others to cross over. Like the first wave. And I keep hearing them say, "It is safe. It is safe." It's a sentence they have put together. "It is safe."[51]

It should also be noted that, according to the guides, some victims and terrorists are actively working on the other side to change how things are on Earth. In talking about a woman victim, Trio addressed this notion through Nevada Shaw:

> Heath: So, is that her hope that when they cross over they can start again?
> Shaw: Yes. And if they choose to go back, they will go back with different information. There is impact they can have from this side into the dimension that they're [from].
> Heath: Are some of the terrorist souls doing that?
> Shaw: A few. Most of them don't have that capacity. The victims do. But only some of them as well.[52]

Few terrorist souls appear to have evolved very far in the afterlife. As with other forms of death, these spirits may perform spiritual work, sometimes acting as guides for others of their kind, both to advance and to diminish the karma they may have taken on in their prior lifetime. However, one striking difference between their afterlife experiences and that of traditional suicides or violent deaths is that sleep does not appear to be used as a form of therapy. Furthermore, it would appear that when large groups of people die simultaneously, there may be something of an enmeshment of their souls. Perhaps surprisingly, this seems to be a spiritual advantage, as it helps them to let go of any personal stories and evolve much more quickly.

KARMA AND REINCARNATION ISSUES

In one case, when asked what the karma is of terrorism, a guide responded through Johanna Carroll: "We do not equate this with karma."[53] However, in other cases, the issue of planetary karma arise:

Shaw: It is planetary karma. Those that would be victims involved with this as easily as those who perpetrate or activate. The planet itself absorbs some of this. It is the decision Earth souls as a union decide from another realm. This becomes very complex because souls are coming and going all the time. At different time intervals is what you would describe. Peaks, we discussed earlier, have to do with how quickly the karma dissipates. It is actually a known initiative of guides from this realm, and others, to sometimes inform karma [so it] can immediately be shifted. Some individuals grasp this and can let go of karma immediately.... Even a story of what you would consider karma can be let go of. It does not need to evolve over long periods of linear time. But it would not occur on a wide basis unless many would shift simultaneously. This is not a new concept, but it is not familiar.

Heath: When you speak of many, how many would have to shift?

Shaw: It depends on what problem and where on the Earth you were discussing. If you were in [the] situation of a town shifting, 20 percent. If it's within a family, one individual can make the shift. But two or three would pull it into alignment. If we're speaking of the Earth, 70 percent.

Heath: How about of the Middle East?

Shaw: Twenty percent.

Heath: What are they at now?

Shaw: Ten percent. Most people do not realize that this is closer than they know.[54]

Other entities have also spoken about group karma. J. P. Van Hulle writes in a newsletter that the group being Michael told her:

Our karma with the Middle East began almost a century ago as our country first found uses for oil and petroleum products and had no moral qualms about vastly underpaying these countries for their natural resources.... Is this our entire fault? Of course not. There is no excuse for terrorism.[55]

The apparent absence of karma involved in terrorism might be partially due to the fact that it can be a planned part of the life blueprint for suicide bombers and their victims. The authors realize this may be a controversial idea, but if one looks at the material for murder victims, one sees that there sometimes is an agreement to allow this to happen prior to incarnating, either as an experience that will aid spiritual growth or to repay a karmic debt. In one case, when asked whether this had been part of a terrorist's blueprint, Trio replied: "Yes. He had two paths that were available to him, though."[56] As for the victims in the World Trade Center towers:

Heath: For how many had this been planned in their blueprints?
Shaw: Thousands.
Heath: The ones who were victims, how many of them have moved on?
Shaw: Thousands.[57]

One interesting point that came up in channeling sessions was that the karmic impact of terrorism may be determined in part by the victims. This is discussed in the following segment:

Heath: Will they be bound to each other in future lives?
Shaw: Some of them. Right now we're aware that two will.
Heath: And will those who choose to interact later tend to have interactions in karma?
Shaw: Yes.
Heath: So the ones who do not choose to ever communicate with people who hurt them do not have to have interactions?
Shaw: Correct.
Heath: What are the karmic implications? Does it vary from one terrorist to the next?
Shaw: Sometimes. It's a complicated issue. The karma involves an entire area, not just people, the souls. Something is shifting for the entire area.
Heath: Are we talking about the Middle East?
Shaw: Yes. And elsewhere.
Heath: And how is it shifting? Can they share that with us?
Shaw: It's like a peak. Part of the information goes up the peak. And when someone reaches the peak, the entire peak of information shifts. And whoever is not up on the peak has to make the shift then, whether they are ready or not. It's about being exposed.
Heath: Exposed to what?
Shaw: Light. But the exposure is what is not light. It's both. The light brings the exposure, then what has been hidden becomes seen. If individuals are not ready, it doesn't matter. If one of them reaches the peak, the whole thing shifts.[58]

The issue of how karma and reincarnation could interact was also discussed by guides. They explained that in the case of one terrorist who had made "good" progress:

Shaw: He has an opportunity to make a choice, whether he would like to work here, with us, or make a choice to live on another plane and continually work on his journey, or make the decision to go back to the Earth. However, if this particular soul—I'm using the example of the gentleman I spoke of earlier, with the children—if *he* decides to go back to Earth, he *will* need to go back to the same area.
Heath: And why is that?

Shaw: It's a completion with one of the victims' soul. It will come back....
Heath: Is this the woman?
Shaw: Yes.
Heath: Has he known this woman in previous lives?
Shaw: No.
Heath: If they were to incarnate again, what would be their relationship in the future.
Shaw: Brother and sister.
Heath: And what would he try to learn in that life?
Shaw: How to help her raise her children. There would be two.[59]

There was some suggestion that those who were in the September 11th, 2001 attacks may be linked together in future incarnations. Trio explained that it had to do with them dying at the same time and developing almost a group soul kind of energy:

Heath: Is the fusion that occurred the reason many psychics mention they seem to get victims coming through in multiples?
Shaw: Yes.
Heath: Is that going to affect future incarnations? Will they tend to incarnate together again then?
Shaw: Yes.[60]

A different terrorist soul noted that some work is better done in discarnate form and that the hatred focused on suicide bombers actually has impact:

Heath: Will he be incarnating again?
Joanie: Not for a long while. He's claiming that there's too much to be done. Put it this way, human form has its limitations. The work that needs to be done now is best done from that plane.
Heath: And what kind of work is that?
Joanie: Healing. Healing. Healing self and others. Lifting the vibrations of many of these terrorists. He's showing me that a lot of them are not in the same place with him. Most of them are not.... They need a lot of healing. He's saying there's remorse. It's bigger than remorse. It's soul wound, sort of. The pain of the felt hatred from people. So much hatred targeted toward these people who did this.
Heath: And they're actually feeling that?
Joanie: Yes.[61]

In yet another case, there was some suggestion that certain souls may repeatedly reincarnate in dark roles. This idea came up in the interview with Johanna Carroll:

Carroll: They're showing me one man in particular. He has a very full beard. I am in a plane, so it must have been one of the men that was in the plane. And they're giving me a flashback to another lifetime, which is a consciousness stream that he carries forward. It feels very barbaric. I see him with a big sword over his head. There are dead people at his body. So, he reincarnated again and repeated the theme of barbaric acts. It's interesting to me that he was born back in a culture which exacerbated that at some level.

Heath: Are the guides able to tell us what he was trying to master? Why he chose the recent life?

Carroll: This is very interesting. What he's telling me is, "There are energy souls"—I don't know what we'd want to call them—"that do choose the dark force as the common thread for their existence. From a spiritual perspective"—so that would be us not having any judgment on it—"in the two fields of life, which would be light and dark, there is a force that is necessary to support the dark so that the light can expand and grow, as well. Do not misunderstand this message." So, the way I am interpreting this is that he's saying we have this dualistic polarity that we're in—the light and the dark. And there are some souls—I don't know if that's the right word—that through a reincarnation process continue on the pathway of the dark so that perhaps in some way they are in service to those in the light. Odd. Let's see if there's anything else around that that I need to know. He's showing me a doorway. He's saying, "There's always an opportunity, though, to go from the dark to the light." But he's just talking about this one specific individual.[62]

It is difficult to say how much individual karma is incurred by acts of terrorism. The few spirit guides that discussed it were more apt to speak of planetary or regional karma. With this, they tell us that there is hope, for shifts appear to be occurring in the region. Some souls speak of reincarnating again, and in some cases suicide bombers may share future lives with their victims in repayment of the debt they created. However, this does not always appear to be the case, and given the very slow nature of many terrorist transitions, it might well be a long time before they are ready to return.

We have seen in this chapter that terrorist souls experience many of the same features as traditional suicides. They often do not realize they are dead. They tend to be greeted by spirits. They have the option of going to their funerals. They undergo a life review that involves dealing not only with their personal life memories, but also all the lives they have touched significantly and the thoughts and feelings of those still on Earth regarding their acts. Their transitions generally appear to be slow ones—despite the fact that terrorism has been going on for decades, few souls appear to have advanced very far. One difference is that sleep did not appear to be used as often as a form of therapy. Instead, there was more talk of these souls being kept isolated or instilled with helpful energies. However, like traditional suicides, there was talk of terrorist souls (and the planet itself) benefiting from prayer. Furthermore, like their counterparts, these spirits may voluntarily take on acts of service as part of their spiritual therapy. Ultimately, it is possible that they may return to physical life, even reincarnating alongside their victims to make amends.

15

Messages to Those Left Behind

Like other souls, terrorists and their victims sometimes have messages that they would like to pass on to those remaining on Earth. These messages can vary, although terrorists seem to have much fewer messages of regret than do traditional suicides. It should be noted that these messages are not always coming from enlightened souls, nor those who have finished their life review and let go of their personal story. Thus, we will see communications that run the gamut from angry and unrepentant to spiritual dialogues on the importance of love.

MESSAGES FROM VICTIMS

The bulk of the question-and-answer channeling sessions conducted for this book focused on getting information from those involved in perpetrating murder-suicide or from their guides. However, in a few cases, victims of a suicide bomb attack stepped forward to communicate. One such soul was a Muslim woman purportedly killed with her daughter by a terrorist explosion in Iraq. She passed on the following message via a medium:

> Heath: Is there anything that the mother would say to the terrorists?
> Shaw: It is all a waste. They're only wasting time.
> Heath: And what would not be a waste?
> Shaw: To learn how to love their family—which they don't have. To learn how to start a different way. She said they could all be families here. That doesn't serve the Earth, but they could start here.[1]

This spirit also apparently tried to communicate with her still-living husband in the dream state. Trio explained through Nevada Shaw:

> Shaw: The mother is aware of her husband and visits him.
> Heath: How does she visit him?
> Shaw: In his dreams. He doesn't always see her.
> Heath: And when she visits, what does she try to communicate to him?

Shaw: She tries to install light into his psyche to help him shift to a place of not being caught up in the violence. He has maintained a separation from it. But that's getting harder. It is not his choice to be in the middle of it. But there are very few places he can now go to avoid it. She's trying to install a sense of protection and peace that he can carry with him, because soon he will be in the midst of it and he will have to make decisions based on that.

Heath: Was that part of his blueprint?

Shaw: Yes.... He will be killed.[2]

One cannot help but be moved by the sadness of this message, should it be true.

CHANNELED MESSAGES FROM SUICIDE-MURDERERS

One difference between terrorist souls and traditional suicides is that there appear to be a lot fewer messages of regret. Indeed, the messages may range from hostile and angry, to speaking of the importance of love. Few people (at least in the Western culture) have seemed willing or interested in channeling suicide bombers. Occasionally, it has happened by accident. One woman, who was in a rescue circle after September 11th, felt that she was in contact with one of the men who flew the plane into the World Trade Center. The soul was extremely confused and upset, feeling that things had not been as he expected. Nonetheless, the vast bulk of information from these souls is filtered through the intermediary of spirit guides, which seems to make the experience less unpleasant for the mediums.

Why They Did It

Willing murder-suicide pacts do not seem to differ greatly from unwilling mass-murder-suicide plans in intent. Both groups often see it as a last resort, with no other way out possible. In the case of a couple that had been involved in a willing murder-suicide pact, Jean Foster was told they killed themselves because they falsely believed that the future held no hope for any solutions to their problems. Moreover, they said, "We had the persistent thought that the end of our earth lives would be like the beginning, that we would never do more than we were doing at that time."[3]

Nevada Shaw was told by Trio of terrorist suicide-mass-murderers: "They were aware of the pain. They thought this would take care of it. Some didn't even think of that. They just acted."[4]

Trio also acted as an intermediary spirit for two Chechen women who were apparently involved in the downing of Russian planes. One of them said the reason for performing that act was because "she felt ... she could initiate action in the way that she saw being done by males. This would gain respect. But it didn't make any difference."[5] Trio later added:

> All she could feel at the time before her passing was one focus, one purpose, to eliminate a sense of fear. But the fear itself was based on an illusion of some sort of victory that has never been clear. And for her, it's more removed, for in her society she was already apart. She didn't even feel associated with the other women. She knew she would never marry. She didn't want to. She didn't want to stay. There is a cousin. Somehow the cousin infiltrated her into this.[6]

At one point, the guides also brought through a soul who had not performed his life review yet and appeared to be early in his spiritual development. It was interesting that Trio wished this point to be clear before allowing the spirit to come forward and speak. However, here again, we see that this soul felt there had been no choice in his action. The session went as follows:

> Shaw: You will have to take this information from a place that's unevolved.
> Heath: Understood. So this is someone who has not gone through the full unfoldment.
> Shaw: Yes. Are you willing to honor what they wish to say?
> Heath: Yes. ... exactly where are they in their progress at this time and I will make note of that?
> Shaw: Very angry. Delusional.
> Heath: So, very early in the transition?
> Shaw: Very. But wanting to express.... He says, "No one understands. No one understands the commitment."
> Heath: The commitment he had?
> Shaw: Yes.
> Heath: And what was his commitment?
> Shaw: He is convinced the only way change will come about is to "flatten those that are not with Allah." Those are his words. He does not understand what Allah is.
> Heath: Uh huh. And I would take it that "Allah" is not necessarily just whether you are Islamic or not ...
> Shaw: Yes.
> Heath: ... but whether you are of his sect?
> Shaw: Yes.[7]

In one case, a terrorist soul noted that he had seen his actions as being something that served a greater purpose, one that would eventually help mankind. Joanie channeled:

> He would have gone into religious service. He keeps telling me that he would have wanted to be a cleric. He was very devoted. He lived and breathed God every day. And that wouldn't it be nice if everybody else could do that? If we did, he says, there wouldn't be a need for these catalytic, cathartic events. But we need reminders. And he considers himself to have been in the holy service as a reminder.[8]

However, the same spirit admitted that others had acted because they enjoyed the violence. Joanie said:

> But he's claiming that they see this before and since as a gift of service. Now he is pointing out to me that not all of the people who [were] the actors, shall we say, the ones who actually did this—not planned it, but died in it—were as spiritually aware as he considers himself to be.... They didn't see the glory of God kind of thing. They were more caught up in the moment.... He's telling me his focus was always, *always*, on transformation. But ... some of the others ... he was very disappointed in ... got sort of aroused ... by the violence. The thrill of the kill is how he's bringing it to me. And I don't like hearing this. So, even within this group who claimed to be devoutly in service, he separates himself out a little bit.... So, the others did not quite understand themselves as transformational elements. Participants is a better word for them. But he knew. He knew from early years that this was sort of his point in being on Earth.[9]

Death Is Not a Solution

The perpetrators of willing murder-suicide pacts sometimes (although not always) speak of death as not being a solution to life's problems. Jean Foster channeled one pair who agreed that there are better alternatives to those involving the taking of life.[10] They noted that problems are never left behind:

> The thing that we understand now that we want to tell others is that suicide need not happen to others. Our earth thoughts appeared to be bleak problems that have no solutions, but we know already that this was not true. There were ways through.[11]

In some cases, the fate of the victims may be tied to that of their aggressors in the afterlife. This may especially be true for the willing victim of a murder-suicide pact, who can sometimes be bound to the fate of his or her partner. This can include suffering from the grieving of those left behind. Jean Foster was told by a murder-suicide couple from the other side:

> Now we want to get to a far place, away from the earth families who now grieve so hard. But we must stay here (close to earth) because we teamed up with what was of earth, and we must examine the whole truth of our lives there. But it isn't pleasant entering to a new plane of life, yet being subjected to the thoughts of those who were friends and loved ones. This (contact) hurts us here, but we must stay and get the whole truth that can be learned from the review of our lives and from the thoughts of others that waft to our minds here. But it isn't pleasant.[12]

Thus, we see that, as with traditional suicides, murder-suicide is not a solution, even when the victim is a willing one. Add in an unwilling victim and, as we saw earlier, the situation becomes far worse.

Regrets

Verbalized regrets seem to be less common in murder-suicide than traditional suicide, but more common than from assisted suicides. Thus, we can see how it fits into the middle of the spectrum. This is true whether speaking of individual murder-suicide or mass terrorist attacks. In the case of the murder-suicide pair previously mentioned, Jean Foster notes they did not regret their act because they admitted to having been completely overwhelmed by their thoughts at the time.[13]

Few suicide bombers report regrets. As Joshua put it, "Regret is not part of their document."[14] When the issue did come up, it was more often for the kind of life they had had on Earth. In one case, the guide Trio explained through Nevada Shaw:

> Shaw: Some have regret, but it's not due to compassion.
> Heath. Right. Do they regret not killing more?
> Shaw: Most of them are not that at that point.
> Heath: And what are some of the regrets.... ?
> Shaw: They regret they didn't have a life they felt—what's the word? I was going to say joy but that's not right. They don't know what that means. They regret having a life that feels lost. They expected it would feel complete, and it wasn't. They regret the hole. It feels like a vacuum to them.[15]

In the case of another individual, said to be more advanced than the other terrorist souls they had worked with, Trio explained: "He regrets the loss of the children. That started opening an awareness, the regret. A quieter decision."[16] In another section of the interview, Trio went into more detail:

He says, "I am not fit to be alive. I am not fit to be a father. How could I take the lives of children—to prevent others, who could be good fathers?" He has not let go of the guilt. Should he choose to let go of the guilt, we will arrange for him to have the option to meet with the victims. If he wants that, we will make it happen.[17]

Regretting the impact their actions visited on the children was something that came up with other terrorists, making one wonder whether this might partly be a cultural issue. Joanie channeled a spirit who claimed to have been one of the hijackers killed in the Pennsylvania crash on September 11th, 2001. When asked about regrets, she reported:

He says "Yes." There's a real sadness about him. The people who had families, particularly with small children, he/they didn't anticipate or think about really. You know, people in their twenties, thirties, and forties primarily were the victims. And how much that would [cause harm], to visit this upon the children, that was not something they had thought about. But then he sort of claims there was no way around that. So, they continue to do prayer and healing. I feel him kind of alone.[18]

Carroll described similar feelings of concern with a terrorist who was in the cabin of the second plane in the September 11th, 2001 attacks, stating:

One man ... in the second plane, not in the cockpit, in the cabin with the passengers, was very frightened. He actually did have compassion, I think.... He would have been concerned about the children. I don't even know if there were children on the second plane.... And I feel that there was a spark of compassion there—not necessarily regret, but a spark of compassion. Particularly for the children. It touched him in some way.[19]

In another case, a woman terrorist seemed, if anything, to only regret that she got caught:

Shaw: There is a woman. Many do not know that she was working with them.
Heath: As a terrorist?
Shaw: Yes.
Heath: What would she like to say? Oh—I should ask what stage was she at?
Shaw: In a medium stage.
Heath: And what would she tell us?
Shaw: She is still very angry. She is angry she was caught. She is willing to look at this....
Heath: Does she have any regrets?

Shaw: She does, but she is not acknowledging it now. I'm convinced she will feel [them]. She was in an airport. She was in the United States.
Heath: And what happened?
Shaw: She was American. Someone else took her life.
Heath: So she felt she failed?
Shaw: She doesn't feel that way. She's just angry she got caught. She did manage to achieve what she was after, she just thought she was safe.
Heath: What was it she achieved?
Shaw: She killed two people who worked in a baggage room.[20]

There Are Other Options

Jean Foster channeled a murder-suicide pair who stated that spirit help is available for any and all people who want it—they only need to ask. She was told:

> But we had no idea there is this teamwork [with spirits] available, or we would have made use of it when we were in life forms. The helpers said we could have called on them even then, and they would have helped us through the problems, whatever they were.[21]

This was one of the few statements echoed by a suicide bomber. One of the more "advanced" terrorist souls stated through Trio that he wished those still on Earth, whom he had left behind, could know the following: "He would like them to see there *is* another option. But he's terrified that won't take place. We are trying to encourage him to realize if he shifts, then it's possible for others to shift."[22]

The Importance of Love

As with traditional suicides, one of the messages that came up from suicide bombers and their guides was the importance of love. Joanie channeled from a spirit who died in the September 11th, 2001 plane crash in the Pennsylvania field:

> He's saying the most important thing to keep in mind—and it's not a new message, but humanity doesn't seem to hear it so it keeps coming up in form after form—is that you really have to be [loving], the thing is love. The only thing is love. You have to do everything you do with a loving intention. If you do that, even violence serves [a spiritual purpose]. But it should be, he claims, selective and only after other means have been tried and failed. It's a last resort option.[23]

This theme was continued in another passage; when asked what the terrorist soul would like to tell other terrorists, Joanie channeled the following response:

> I have this sort of sad, head-shaking feeling, with a kind of wistful look on his face. That they don't understand. And that's why we're here.... There is only love, is what I'm getting. There is only love. And if you don't come from a place of love for humanity, then what you are doing is unenlightened. Are you serving light or are you serving darkness? He claims he chose to serve the light. And as cruel and painful as the result of this has been on many levels, from a place of intent, and he's telling me, it's almost like a place of intent—he really wants to emphasize that—from a place of intent, his intent was always and only of service and upliftment *[sic]*, hard as that is to hear. But that many of those following hereafter have been caught up in divisiveness, hatred of Americans, Western ways, all those things. They're mistaking their motive. And he would hope that they learn to see it as one color. He says that what you do to your brother you do to yourself.... He's [saying] like in a workplace, the boss should be willing to do the job of the day laborer. And he was willing to do the job. He was willing to be there and die in service with the less enlightened ones. But he has a real issue with those who will make the bombs and the weapons and send the kids off to do this—the dirty work. That they are also prayed for because they are mistaken in their motivation. That their motivation is not upliftment.[24]

Other Messages

Some terrorist souls had things they wished they could say to others who wanted to follow in their footsteps. In the case of a Chechen female terrorist, Shaw channeled the following advice through the intermediary of a spirit guide:

> To listen to the moment when their own quiet clarity speaks to them. Moments with their children. Moments with their thoughts when they are in the midst of daily activities, not distracted by talking. If it is different than what is being said, they must take a look at that rather than cover it over.... She is remembering a moment when she knew something that was different than what was being said to her when she was terrified that if she followed the information she held to be true inside, she would lose her home; she would lose the security and the support of the community; her child might be taken from her. She does not know if this actually would have occurred, but it was her fear. The hesitancy she had before. Acts of violence have always confused her. Her uncle was killed. She was angry about that. She did not feel that revenge was appropriate, but felt herself being sucked into this momentum as if it were a personal agenda.[25]

As mentioned before, the spirit guides that accompanied terrorist souls frequently noted that they were not very spiritually evolved. This came up during the following question-and-answer segment:

> Heath: Are there messages that he would say to his brothers who are still committing terrorism and suicide bombing?
> Shaw: The fear they wake up with at night is a vacancy. The fear is a lie they hold through their emotion. They must make a choice who they are going to listen to.
> Heath: And who should they listen to?
> Shaw: It's very complicated because they don't have the structure to listen to quiet thoughts. Most of these people are confused and jaded. And they are looking for somebody to guide them. They're guided by angry individuals. The voice inside has two layers. The one they can trust comes behind the emotions when it calms down. It will only show up for a second. But if they do not have the practice of being able to have that second, they won't see it.[26]

Later on, this same terrorist soul had more to say:

> Shaw: He believes that this is achievable—that love can enter more hearts. That it will be recognized. He believes this is possible. He doesn't have a sense of time with it.
> Heath: And you said he worries about what goes on on the Earth plane?
> Shaw: Yes.
> Heath: So he's aware of things?
> Shaw: Yes, he is now. He helps us monitor.[27]

Another soul said to be early in his evolution expressed continued religious fervor through the medium:

> Heath: Is there anything that the terrorists would like to tell those left behind?
> Carroll: "We pray they will rise up in the flames of service." And then there's some kind of prayer. I don't understand it. It's a speaking in some kind of other language. It feels like a prayer. Allah-ca-than-dee. Something like that is what I'm hearing.[28]

In another session, there was the hinted warning of a possible future attack:

> Shaw: He is hesitant, but there is information. It is about water. I don't know whether he is truly informed or if it is something he heard of. It was not something he was to be a participant in. But there is something about water contamination. Contamination of water.
> Heath: And this is something that is planned?

Shaw: Something that *was* planned. I don't know how reliable that is.[29]

One of the most remarkable communications came from a terrorist who claimed to have been a bodhisattva.[30] Although the medium had some doubts about the likelihood of this, Joanie dutifully passed on his words:

> I have a terrorist here! This one was in one of the planes. This fellow was in the Pennsylvania plane crash. He's saying they did this in service.... You can understand what I mean when I say certain events are catalytic. And cathartic. And people do agree in their blueprint, as you put it, to be part of them. And he's reminding me that years ago I did a channeling session ... for the public on this whole trance field. And the issue of Hitler was addressed. The basic point came that anyone who takes a job like this is a more evolved soul than we might imagine, because to take the targeted hatred that will be directed at you later requires an incredibly strong spirit and the love and support of many.... As hard as it is on the human level to understand the need for these kind of teachable moments, on an evolutionary or consciousness level that's what this is, as he sees it.[31]

At one point, this soul commented on the fact that he was playing a part, and sometimes the darker roles are what are needed for the world to advance:

> Among those, he's one of the most spiritually evolved, in his opinion. But no, he's claiming it's not opinion. It's an energy. That tough work requires tough, evolved, spiritual beings....
>
> And he's giving me the Bible for "Lest ye entertain an angel unaware." "Judge not, lest ye be judged." All that stuff. That often it's the darker side of humanity, human nature, that launches us to our true spirit. And he sees himself as being a catalyst.... But he's saying (sighs) that in the same way that people can be both religiously oriented and abusive, he realizes what he did was wrong in human terms and yet right from a spiritual perspective. Because he keeps showing me ... the world of illusion. On the stage we're only players. This time he played a terrorist.[32]

The spirit also noted that strength is required to deal with the afterlife consequences of having taken on a role that would lead to so much anger and hatred being focused his way:

> And that's why he's claiming he's strong enough to take it. That he was a much more developed spiritual being in the first place. He's showing me flowers in a garden, that some are stronger and grow taller. It's not a judgment of them being lesser beings, but an awareness that, almost in the way that genetics [works], there are certain strengths that arise under certain conditions, he had the right strengths, and under those conditions he was

able to manage it much better. But the others were, some of the younger ones in particular, and he's talking both symbolically and literally, some of the younger ones really need a lot of healing attention. So that's what he's focused on. He's seems pretty [much to be] sticking with the perpetrators.[33]

This soul indicated that he was surprised by some of the response to the September 11th, 2001 attacks. Joanie channeled:

He says, "I'm more surprised by the people who pray for me than anything else. And the power of [it]." ... He's surprised at how many people around the world pray for the perpetrators. And those are the ones that are really the transformers....

Because without them having instigated this event, coming together collectively in prayer like this for the surviving family members, for all of the people who were touched by it, for the victims, and for the perpetrators, that would not have happened. So, he sees it as a coalescing, bringing-people-together event, rather than divisive.[34]

This soul insisted that, hard as it would be for people to understand, there was a higher purpose to the September 11th, 2001 attacks.[35] This was perhaps most clear in the following statement, channeled by Joanie:

I'm seeing now an image ... he tosses a stone into a small pond. And the ripples, you know, gently, gently, gently change the surface of things at the edges. It's going to be [a long time]. Far away. But he's claiming within forty years. He's telling me two generations. In the lifetimes of many of us a surprising amount of healing can happen. He's very surprised. He's showing me a map of the world, and where this prayer wave I keep feeling, this energy emanating off the planet, a lot of this, most of it, is from the U.S. It's quite lovely to see. But what he's getting to is it's not just for the victims or the families, but for the perpetrators. That's the thing that struck him. And that's the thing he's almost proud of—for drawing out this response. Yes, a painful event on a human level, but he considers this a—oh, I'm going to have a hard time delivering this one—blessed event. But I get it. I understand it. Yeah.... And he sees himself highly evolved and given a difficult job that he feels he carried out as well as could be done.... They expected more deaths. And it didn't happen. And he considers that a grace.... Because it means that the coming together in prayer, and beginning to see yourself as part of a collective, is happening. And yes, there is pain in this. But it might, it would have been, almost paralyzing had it been ten thousand, twenty thousand people like they thought ... that had perished.[36]

One thing that made this particular entity interesting is that he seemed to distinguish himself from most of his colleagues. Furthermore, he had some strong words to say to those who think they are following in his footsteps:

>Heath: Is there anything he would say to other terrorist bombers who continue to do these attacks?
>
>Joanie: He's telling me they don't know their motivation. They're caught up in the excitement and the glory. The ego. And he sees himself as having done a service to help human consciousness evolve. But that most of the people doing this—no, he's actually saying all of the ones to follow this—are operating from a baser perspective. And he's showing me, again I see the pyramid thing, and he's pointing to the [bottom]. If you stratified it to seven levels and considered them the seven chakras you'd be down in the low levels. Hierarchically speaking, energetically speaking, we're not talking evolved energies.
>
>Heath: And he would also include the bombmakers in that?
>
>Joanie: The bombmakers? Yes.
>
>Heath: Who send the kids out.... Because it's often older people who are making the bombs and sending out very young idealists.
>
>Joanie: Right, right, right. That they are easily manipulated is the phrase. Because they, he's saying these are hopeless, sad people mostly. They really are. He's pointing out a parallel to inner-city youths. In some ways they're like that. They're folks who have no sense that there's a better future. And so they turn to lies that are angry ones. Attacking ones.[37]

In this chapter we have seen some of the channeled messages of terrorist souls and their victims. Perhaps in part because most channeling sessions were focused on getting information from those involved in perpetrating murder-suicide, only one victim really came through to talk of her concern for a husband left behind, and her attempt to communicate with him in dreams. When we turn our attention to suicide bombers, we see that relatively few of them express regrets compared to traditional suicides, and when they do, those regrets tend to be around the life they had lived or the children who were harmed by their actions. One spoke of the importance of love, and his desire that the world transform in a positive direction.

16

The Spirit View on Terrorism

It has only been in the last half century or so that we have begun to receive (or at least document) comments from the spirit realm that address the issue of terrorism. These channeled messages tend to fall into one of two major groups: first, those of general guides, and second, from spirit guides that specialize in greeting, and dealing with, the souls of terrorists. Both are interesting, since they may be considered to represent perhaps a more enlightened view of the phenomenon of murder-suicide, and give us a different perspective on what kinds of experiences those souls may have after making their transitions to the afterlife. We will look first at what has been said from the general spirit realm.

GENERAL SPIRIT VIEWS

Ruth Montgomery, who came from a strong Christian background, states that her guides addressed the question of terrorism in this manner:

> Terrorists will persist until the time draws near for the shift [in the earth's poles] and they are driven by fear to find safe hiding places, but many of them will be swept into the seas or otherwise disposed of during or shortly after the event. Until then they will continue their terrorist acts, because they are in rebellion against God's will and firmly believe that might makes right. They are a despicable breed of latter-day Atlanteans who foraged and slaughtered the innocent near the time of the sinking of that advanced continent, and they have come back to reap revenge for their own ill-doing that led to death at that time.[1]

J. P. Van Hulle channeled information from Michael after the September 11th attack. This focused not so much on the role of the terrorists as on how the experience could make the country stronger. She wrote that Osama bin Laden was a "sixth level Young King/Priest who hated the United States."[2] Van Hulle goes on to say that, according to Michael:

> The CIA had known for some weeks that something was up, but could not discover exactly what in time to prevent all of it. As it was, there were 13 more planes that the terrorists had planned to use to attack other public targets that were not hijacked, with potential hijackers detained, not only in the U.S., but also in Mexico and Canada....
>
> People have asked if Osama bin Laden is insane. He absolutely is not. He is ruthless and anti-American and backed by wealthy disgruntled individuals from a variety of areas including Libya, Syria, Iraq, and Iran....
>
> This has been a truly horrendous challenge for Americans as a people, but if we remember that each challenge here on the physical plane has a commensurately impactful spiritual gift within it, we can see our transformation to a wiser more mature nation lies within our grasp.[3]

Mary Beth Anderson feels that her deceased father helped spirits cross over on September 11th, 2001. She channeled the following message from him about that event:

> When the ground shook on Tuesday, the 11th, I received an urgent call to be of assistance....
>
> I was dismayed by the sudden influx of the masses who flooded the gates of heaven following the attack.... Even with the sudden arrival of scores of souls, I could not single out anyone who seemed confused about where they were or why they were there.... The atmosphere was businesslike and such an atmosphere is conducive to order and purpose. It not only had a calming effect on the "new arrivals," but on me, as well.
>
> Since so little time has elapsed, since the attack, there are still souls who await their audience and judgment day, but there is no sign of anxiousness or anxiety among them because they fully comprehend what has happened to them and to so many others....
>
> The spirits of men, who I like to refer to as the "old soldiers," have come together to discuss this tragedy.... [They] state, "This flagrant, blind-sided assault shall not stand. The cowardly bastards targeted innocent people to achieve their evil means. They are not their country's heroes...."
>
> In the end, justice will be served and when the scales of justice are finally balanced much will be learned as a result of the 9/11 tragedy.[4]

Thus, the few channeled messages we have on terrorism seem to suggest two things: first, that the spirit realm expresses general disapproval of terrorism, and second, that like any other life experience, good may come of it. Terrorism may sometimes provide potential for learning and spiritual growth. However, we will see in the next sections that the general channeled messages may not always apply as directly as one would think.

THE VIEW OF SPIRITS WHO
SPECIALIZE IN DEALING WITH TERRORISTS

Some guides appear to specialize in greeting suicide bombers and other terrorists when they cross over to the other side. These beings have come through several mediums to discuss how terrorists are handled in the afterlife, their view on suicide bombing, and other issues. Perhaps because channels are more comfortable dealing with these entities (said to be of a "higher" vibration that is more pleasant to connect to), the bulk of the material relating to terrorism appears to come from these spirits. In one case, the question arose regarding what kind of being would be best at guiding a terrorist. Interestingly, one of the items that came up was that such a being is very neutral. It should be noted, however, that this neutrality may not mean what human beings are used to thinking of it meaning. The guides discussed this point:

> Shaw: Behind all emotion is an awareness that nothing is good or bad. It comes from a neutral line from God. It doesn't make sense—the usual perception we carry on the other plane—though it can be achieved. The neutrality of which I speak is not the same neutrality that most people discuss. It is very difficult to put into words. It's experiential.
>
> Heath: Is it, rather than a lack of caring, an awareness of everything at once?
>
> Shaw: Rephrase your question.
>
> Heath: Neutrality. The way most people on Earth tend to approach neutrality is as a lack of emotion, or a lack of caring or concern. But could it be that a true neutrality is more an awareness of everything at once?
>
> Shaw: Yes.[5]

This would seem to be a difficult concept to understand, but would suggest that in being very neutral, these guides might also be very highly evolved.

When asked how someone was chosen to work with terrorist souls, a guide explained:

> It's a duty, but part of it is familiar. I, particularly, was on the Earth plane before and worked as a teacher. It was with children, but they were lost children, and very dangerous. The other guides have not been on the Earth. Ultimately, it doesn't matter. It would be a choice of who the individual would go to, who they could connect with more, but it doesn't matter.[6]

The guides who specialize in dealing with these souls discussed terrorism in a number of ways. In one instance, when asked the difference between murder-suicide and terrorism, they responded:

> They're saying the difference in the terrorism is that there is really not a concern on the individual level. The energy is directed at this distorted belief that they have, that it is their spiritual mission to accomplish this. It's more collective than it is singular. So, it's not about you as a person, it's beyond you as a person. It has more power than you as an individual would have.[7]

The belief that had been distorted was explored further:

> Heath: What is the distortion they need to separate themselves from?
> Carroll: [Relaying the spirit guide Joshua's response,] "The belief."
> Heath: Of?
> Carroll: Remember before when he was talking about the distorted belief. The difference between terrorists and the collective group? Terrorism as collective suicide and murder-suicide on a singular level the difference being one is a distortion of a collective belief?
> Heath: Right. But I'm trying to get at what that distorted collective belief is.
> Carroll: They're saying, "That being in service to the old system, the distortion is that through …"—he doesn't want to use the word murder, but he's walking around it, that's interesting.
> Heath: Through ending the lives of others?
> Carroll: Thank you. "That through ending the lives of others they will receive salvation. That's the distortion." And I guess, from what I've read, in that culture, you will be with Allah and have the golden kingdom and all that other [reward].[8]

Guides are quick to point out that there are distortions of the truth on both sides of the terrorism conflict. This would not be a problem were it not for the fact that we then fight over who is right or wrong. As noted earlier, the spirit realm frowns on religious wars. Moreover, Trio noted that ultimately such battle is pointless, stating: "Our perception is limited to our definition of what is divine, whose view is worth more. We *all* shall experience the other's perception eventually."[9] However, one would hope that we need not wait until the life review to be able to experience some appreciation for the viewpoints of others. This will be discussed in more detail in the chapter section on the spirit view of the solution to terrorism.

Another question that came up was on the growing role of women in terrorism. The spirit guide Trio stated through Nevada Shaw:

The women have felt the lack of power they have seen in the formation of life they have lived. A misguided approach to what they believe is a freedom and attaining of power. It is the wrong path—not from the perspective of how we look at right and wrong, which is more neutral here, but for them. Where they are before they crossed. They believed a sense of control and power is able to come through these decisions, actions, violence. Dealing with what they would consider a business decision. Being part of the decision, a cause.... There still are women that know about a different approach and they are feeling pressured, and abandoned, by women that are switching and being sucked into this old paradigm that will not survive its own chaos. Unfortunately, there is a great deal more of it probably to come before the entire approach collapses. In order for that to collapse, those that see a different approach would have to immediately step up and refuse to participate in this method. It will take an internal revolution. The women are quite capable of this, as are the men. It's set ingrained deeper in the men; it's harder for them in that society to see in a different way. It has only recently begun infiltrating the women's approach. They became disillusioned, thinking there was no other way than the violence. It's what you refer to as jaded. Ennui. The women that do not wish to participate in this approach are feeling more frightened that they will have to go deeper underground. That makes it more complicated for them to bring the truth out. It's a matter of expanding the information, the way you stay protected. The timing is crucial, but they must not bury it.[10]

When asked about the difference between suicide with the intent to murder others and individual suicide, Trio made the following distinction:

Those that perpetuate violence to intentionally include suffering from another will receive information for spiritual advancement more slowly. Their receptors in the brain have been shut down.... There is more flexibility ... to perceive a wider view once you've left the body. But it is not exclusive to that. One could perceive it in the body even if [you have] a destructive mentality, but the focus of the destructive mentality is so limited, the receptors in the brain encase it similar to the bubble in the heart.... All those who participate in suicide have their perception of why they would choose to leave. Those who include murdering another, along with themselves, pull the bubble of another into their own heart without experiencing the other's perception. It is as if the bubble never recognizes there is another bubble with them. Those that simply murder themselves do not recognize they have a choice. Eventually, whether they are in the physical or not, they will recognize they have a choice and they will always return to the divine. It is simply a matter of effective energy to realize suicide, murder, or even something as simple as a depressed thought is separate from the divine.[11]

Trio later added:

> If an individual commits violence to another, at the point of crossing, the individual who committed the violence will experience through their own perception and consciousness the experience of the one they violated. It will be as if they experience their own violation upon themselves.[12]

According to Trio, this "opening of the bubble" happens at the moment of death. However, it may take quite some time before a soul is able to deal with what his or her victims go through at that time. Shaw channeled:

> It will immediately open when the crossing takes place. However, the integration of the experience will be digested at a rate with which the individual consciousness can absorb. It will be faster without a body, but it still can appear from our view, if we were on the planet, it will appear as if it is slower than what we would have called an evolved soul.[13]

One of the more interesting comments made by guides was their observation of the common ground between traditional suicide and terrorism. Johanna Carroll transmitted the following message:

> He's saying, "The correlation of terrorism and suicide is a distortion of belief.... Suicide is an individual act. Terrorism is a collective act of suicide.... It's a collective thought of a distortion of belief, whereas an individual performing suicide is a singular distortion of a belief. Therefore," he's saying, "terrorism has a higher concentration of waves of energy behind it because the mind embraces it collectively. They embrace the distortion collectively and therefore that gives it power." He says, "It is a power nonetheless. It matters not what the end result is. It is a power," he's saying, "through the manipulation of information on both sides." He's showing me a line of heritage. And he's taking me back one, two, three, four, five lifetimes. It would be very interesting to go back in the genealogy of Iraq and see five generations ago what was happening. Because, he's saying, "That's what's been carried forward as far as distorted information. A difficult power to overcome, for their system of ideals is not as [yours]." In other words, their system of ideals has absolutely no relationship to our system of ideals so if we try to thwart this collective consciousness of suicide, which I believe is a form of fanaticism, it doesn't work.[14]

Another way that the above message can be looked at is that we are dealing with competing paradigms. A paradigm is a system of beliefs. These beliefs are such an intrinsic part of our normal, everyday worldview that we typically never even realize that we've made any assumptions. But we have.

It is crucial to recognize that paradigms are both a help and a hindrance. They help us to make sense of what is going on around us, but they also limit our perception of the world and what knowledge we can arrive at. One of the problems with the current terrorist conflict is that it represents a battle between competing paradigms. What makes this so bloody is that the paradigm itself determines what is "right." The conflict between the terrorist paradigm and that of (for want of a better term) Western civilization is ongoing. Because these belief systems are far more deeply ingrained and widespread than religion, topics that touch on these fundamentally different worldviews permit no room for compromise. Nonetheless, we will see that the guides do see some hope for a solution.

A key topic that came up was the importance of learning to listen to the inner self and the importance of love:

> If any being would take a moment and ask their deepest self why they are here, they will receive an answer. And they must ask it at different times through their life. The answer that comes up in the still moments is the one they can trust. They will get different answers that will challenge this deeper truth. They will not be able to grasp the clear answers if they are approaching it with the mistrust that they are not supported. They have to ask where the true support comes from. So many have realized they do not have support from family or society or government. So many do not believe there is support from the other realms. They need to ask what their purpose here is, and they need to ask it in the silent moments. It may divulge a different answer than what their companions tell them. They must have the courage to listen to this answer and challenge it for themselves. Their own thoughts can lie to them as other individuals can lie to them. But each being has its own story. There is a reason they have woven this story. If they choose to always go back to the first thread [love], they can make the decision to move forward clearly. The world has become very complex. It is harder now at the pace with which things move to pay attention to this original thread. But it is information that has always been there. This is not new information. Take the time to question your own thoughts. Take the time to question others' thoughts. But be willing to listen to them and see if there is something that reminds you of the original thread. This takes practice. There must always be a moment of silence in your own mind in order to hear it, in order to see it, in order to feel it. It doesn't need to be more than a moment. Once you recognize it, it's very clear. But in order to sustain it, it takes practice or it will get hidden with everything else. At that point it's very easy to get pulled into other

dimensions, other approaches, that just dissolve into nothing again. It is a very powerful time, for many people have the opportunity to move to the clarity of this thread. If they make the commitment to find it, they will. It is achievable at this time.[15]

In another part of the same interview, Trio spoke more of the importance of love, which the spirit guide referred to as the "first thread." Shaw channeled:

> What you would call love. A simple, clear, balanced thread of light that joins all things. If you are aware, you are joined with *all* things, there would be recognition that fear is an illusion, and that to believe that you are not supported is an illusion. To describe love is beyond language. But when you recognize it and experience it, all complication falls away. Many have experienced it. They don't hold on to it, but they have experienced it. It is a state of realizing there is no separation. The idea that you have to actively pursue love is an illusion. The idea that you have to perpetrate violence to get results is an illusion. The connection is eternal. The thread of love is beyond linear time. It is an experience of awareness. It is attainable at any moment and it can change everything in a moment. If people hold on to this thought—correction, if people hold on to this awareness, for it is beyond thought—they will change. It changes their molecular structure. And it doesn't matter if you are in physical form or not. The thread is the same. It is the same in all dimensions.[16]

THE MEANING OF CATALYTIC EVENTS

Some spirit guides and one terrorist soul spoke of certain events, such as the attack on September 11th, 2001, as having a divine purpose. For some, this concept may be difficult, painful, and even impossible to accept. For others, it may aid in acceptance and healing. It should be noted that we (the authors) and the mediums we interviewed and quote here make no claims about the truth or fiction of these statements. Nonetheless, the points provide food for thought.

Joshua stated through Johanna Carroll:

> "In terms of the overall universal intention around 9/11, it was to wake up the souls of mankind to love and kindness; to move away from all items of the third dimension that hold back growth....
>
> "The kinder the Earth becomes to itself as an organic body of energy, the less suicide will be necessary. For when peace dwells as a stimulation so it dispels"—it's like he's showing me little bubbles all around these spirals, vortexes, which to me represent matrices of different people. And then

he's showing me—interesting that he's giving me a number—fifty years. That, "In fifty years the great shift will have occurred....

"It's divine ordination of a different set of principles and guidelines." So, to me that means operationally, I guess, the way we run our larger system, which would be economic, government, political. When those change, he says, then the softness comes. Which I believe probably goes back to that prophecy of a million years of peace and prosperity that we're walking into. Fifty years. I'm not sure what happens in that shift. Oh, he's showing me there's like a wave a people being pushed up to the top, you know if you're riding a wave, cresting on the wave. I'm seeing people reaching up.... So, there's some kind of an uprising of people who will want to do things differently that are going to be affecting this great shift. It feels like fifty years from now it will have occurred.[17]

Nevada Shaw also received a message echoing the idea that an energy peak is about to be reached when she was channeling material about karma in the Middle East and elsewhere:

Shaw: It's like a peak. Part of the information goes up the peak. And when someone reaches the peak, the entire peak of information shifts. And whoever is not up on the peak has to make the shift then, whether they are ready or not. It's about being exposed.
Heath: Exposed to what?
Shaw: Light. But the exposure is what is not light. It's both. The light brings the exposure, then what has been hidden becomes seen. If individuals are not ready, it doesn't matter. If one of them reaches the peak, the whole thing shifts.[18]

Another such communication focusing on the positive possibilities of catalytic events for growth came through Joanie:

I have one here that, I swear, he claims, "You'd know me most recently as Moses" ... and that he had a tough job too in that lifetime. And people don't yet understand that in the same way as he bore tablets and the word of God, people don't yet understand this particular event has that kind of energy behind it. It is a message from above. So, they seem to endorse what this fellow has been saying all along. That, sad as it is, attention had to be brought to the oneness. He's pointing out (the guide, that is) that you cannot separate the intention from the act when you are in human form. It's very hard. But from where they are, the intention stands separate. And it is the creative point. And it is the healing point. And it is the stepping up to higher levels kind of thing. He's using an imagery here of a caterpillar into a butterfly. As the caterpillar's transformation happens, it doesn't realize it is growing wings until it can fly. And then it seems as natural as anything ever was. And that in time, this will seem a natural course of evolution....

Actually, what I just saw ... was a woman stepping in. You'd know her most as Guanyin, the goddess of compassion.... Now *she's* claiming, and I hadn't thought of it exactly this way, that if you were to do a sociological kind of study, you would see an increase in feminine models....

The events on 9/11/2001. If you were to track it, you would see far more interest after that in goddess cultures. Right? And Mary. And Guanyin. And name any cultural feminine face of God. That it's mother healing energy, it's compassion, that is also rising in the wake of 9/11. That pink light business? Right. And that this is one reason that this had to happen in a culture that is known to be restrictive of women in this way. It's almost as if that is a teaching tool. Many people are resonating to the lack of equal power, or the unequal power between men and women in that culture....

And I'm seeing all these references to the feminine face of God. And that this, too, is an outgrowth of this catalytic event which will over the next thirty, forty, fifty, a hundred years, help heal the planet. It's a pendulum, I'm seeing now, it's swung too far, too. I'm seeing a pendulum overlaid on a Yin Yang symbol, representing male-female. It's too far in the direction of individual, not enough in the collective. So, the out-of-balance condition required a big statement. Unmistakable. Calls for healing. All the people who've never prayed in years and years and years, and there are many I'm being reminded. People just don't do it. Many people who hadn't uttered a prayer in decades were moved to pray in the wake of 9/11. And that's the thing that's transforming the world—loving kindness extended....

She's claiming one thing she will talk about is that this is a joyful world. And one thing that she is *very* pleased about in the wake of 9/11, and other events that led up to it, I mean she's also pointing out that it doesn't stand alone, as we like to make it. I mean it's big, but there's other big stuff out there. And she's claiming that in the wake of that event, loving kindness has been heightened. People are taking love to new places. People who were unhappy in marriages are finding their lives changing. People who were unhappy in their work are willing to redirect their career to something that brings them greater joy and happiness. The whole life's-too-short sort of thing. Of course, it is everlasting so it's not too short. But people have this idea that "I need more joy," and they're finding ways to seek it and create it.... Now I have the terrorist fellow standing behind her saying, "Yes! Precisely!" This is about teaching people to create in a way where events won't touch them, but only God. That *everything* is perfection. It doesn't mean it's what you wanted to see or experience. But it's perfect....

We're just back to that caterpillar—its getting wings and doesn't know it. It feels itself stretching and moving and recreating, but it doesn't know what it's becoming yet. And it's afraid. It's scared. But the end result is beautiful. I guess we're learning to fly, just don't know it yet, we're growing wings.[19]

The reader is reminded that this emphasis on the importance of the motivation or intent behind an action came up in the earlier chapter on the spirit realm's view of traditional suicide. Silver Birch, for example, said, "In my world, the true standard is the standard of the soul's motive."[20]

Johanna Carroll channeled a similar message about September 11th, 2001 being a catalytic event, although one that we may not yet fully understand:

> They're saying, "The result of this action was less than what it was originally intended to be," which I think we all know anyway....
>
> They're showing me waves of light going across the sea, which says to me that there were people praying for peace and harmony and love toward those countries that perpetrated this. They're saying that we don't have all the information though.... They're saying—and I don't know what this means, "Particles of information are still hidden and shall not be revealed ... for another ten to fifteen years." In terms of the spiritual realm, they're saying, "This was a necessary event that was part of the plan of circumstance." That's an interesting statement, I've never heard that before. Plan of circumstance. It's almost like they're ringing. I'm hearing the bells again. Ding, ding, ding. It's kind of like a wake-up call on some level. They're saying, "This event caused a wave of energy through circumstance that perpetrated other happenings occurring." Well, we know that....
>
> They're pointing to the United States and I hear the bells ringing again. "The lesson in awareness is not what mankind embraced." How interesting....
>
> "When greed and fear are removed from the consciousness as the primary thought, then healing can occur. Until the systems that direct the flow of information are changed, only then shall the mind absorb this truth. It is a state of mind." And then they're showing me—oh, wow! How do I explain this? It's like somebody came along and took a black piece of cloth and just put it over the head. I don't know whose head this is. I think it's just a symbol of consciousness, man, and the mind. Then the eyes couldn't see. The veil separates us. We hide behind the veil. Darkness, of course, very symbolic of the void where all creation and life exists. But it is also symbolic of fear and darkness.[21]

The channeled sources are not unique in speaking of the good that can come from what happened on September 11th, 2001. P. M. H. Atwater observes:

> Growth events come in all shapes and sizes. They can be negative or positive or both; they repeat if we miss one, or they can be a series.... A growth event is any kind of sudden, unexpected twist in life that twirls you around and changes your attitudes and stretches your mind....

> Souls can unite in groups for ... a common purpose, mission, or goal. Tremendous amounts of focused energy are produced and released when souls do this, enough to influence sweeping changes in society or cause major alterations in the world at large....
>
> Groups of committed souls can "move mountains" in what they can accomplish.... Death on a massive scale sometimes followed their efforts (i.e., the sinking of the *Titanic*; the Holocaust; September 11, 2001, when planes crashed into the World Trade Center and the Pentagon)....
>
> [A]n event of great impact will unite a broad span of people.... This "pulling together" activity creates field effects.[22]

Thus, we see that at least some in the spirit realm and those who have had NDEs suggest that good may come from the violence of terrorism. These events may be the stimulus (if unwelcome) to human growth and the transformation of our worldview.

THE SOLUTION TO TERRORISM

Occasionally in the interviews conducted for this book, guides would discuss what the spirit realm's view is on how terrorism could be ended. Sometimes, prayer was mentioned. For example, one terrorist soul from the September 11th, 2001 attacks came through to say that part of why that attack had to happen was because "we need to understand ourselves as a collective. A collective. And that we need to pray for everyone."[23] Joanie also transmitted, "That's the thing that's transforming the world—loving kindness extended."[24] And in another place, as mentioned earlier, she channeled:

> He's surprised at how many people around the world pray for the perpetrators. And those are the ones that are really the transformers. Wow. I get it. I know what he's getting to. That those are the ones who are doing the transformation. They are the catalysts. They are the transformers.[25]

The power of prayer as a manifest, visible force in the spirit realm, as described by P. M. H. Atwater, was referenced in the section on special assistance for traditional suicides.[26] One terrorist soul showed a medium what prayer looked like to him on the other side.

> Did you ever watch a radiator with heat waves kind of coming off of it? They're palpable, but they're not really, you know, in color or anything. It's like heat rising. Only it's like a soft pinkish kind of heat. Only it isn't heat. It's prayer energy. Spiritual energy. And different colors come in. But I see it as a very, very soft pink and golden. Loving prayer.[27]

It is important to understand that the spirit guides say that prayer, to be most effective, must not be limited to a particular group, but extended to everyone. This is not a new concept. Nora Loder channeled in the early 1900s, "We rise or fall as a *common whole*."[28]

Another aspect to the solution appears to involve women. Shaw channeled:

> Heath: Are there any in the Islamic world who are in touch with, as with mediums, these [terrorist] souls?
> Shaw: You mean those who are living on the Earth plane?
> Heath: Uh huh.
> Shaw: Yes, but very few.
> Heath: What messages do you feel they are getting?
> Shaw: They know something is disjointed. They don't know what to do about it. They want the violence to stop. And they are meeting in secret. Many are women. They don't know how this is achievable yet.[29]

The role of women came up again in a different session:

> Shaw: The families did not know, with the exception of two. And even then, very few people in the family were aware. A brother, a cousin. Different families. The women suspected but they did not know what was planned. Many would prefer to deny that this could happen in their family.
> Heath: Why is that?
> Shaw: Many of the families are divided, though they would like to not have that be shown.
> Heath: What other things would they like not to be shown?
> Shaw: That the women are not in agreement many times. That some of the men are not in agreement many times. They cannot discuss this. There will be a time very soon when they can discuss this. It will have to be done within a large shift for the support to feel safe. But it is possible. And soon.
> Heath: When they mentioned we were at a peak …
> Shaw: Yes.
> Heath: … is that the shift that will occur when this peak moves?
> Shaw: One of them.
> Heath: What are the others?
> Shaw: Issues about women in general when the shift occurs. When one shift occurs, it becomes apparent that others are capable of occurring.
> Heath: And this is very soon?
> Shaw: In your terms, yes. Within ten years. Possibly six.[30]

These guides sometimes mentioned that they felt all human beings are attached to stories, which are often untrue. In one case, when asked what lies they would most like to see corrected, they stated:

Shaw: They do not need to carry fear [deriving from] self-hatred. It distorts everything.

Heath: Is that one of the keys behind a great many of the terrorists? This self-hatred?

Shaw: Of everyone. They just [experience] more of it on a more physical level. It's a separation which isn't true.

Heath: From others?

Shaw: From God.[31]

Yet another message from Trio was:

Shaw: We can only suggest that those who are left on the Earth plane not waste their time with circular thoughts.

Heath: Such as?

Shaw: Worries. Aggravation. Judgment. They don't have the luxury of the time. It doesn't matter whether they stay here or work on the Earth plane.[32]

During a different session, Trio spoke more of how those on the planet can work to end terrorism. Trio felt that many individuals turn to terrorism out of a false sense of discouragement:

So many individuals feel there is nothing they can do. They feel something dramatic must be the only way that a question would be noticed, that confusion would be noticed and dealt with. They have not had the upbringing, caring, or training to recognize their very presence in the opportunity of a physical body gives them the very nature to correct this issue.[33]

In fact, the living have more influence on what happens than they realize. According to Trio, there is an almost contagious quality to thought and the energy that living people transmit, whether consciously or unconsciously. This may be part of why we have seen the recent increase in mass suicide-murder—not just by terrorists, but also by school children and others. However, that same influence can also be used for good. Trio stated:

The physical body and the psyche are influenced by those around you, depending on your level of evolved experience with the divine....

For those in the physical that carry an evolved awareness, which is still their perception, can influence another for the vibration will be of a higher frequency that carries more impact. However, if it does not resonate with another's vibration, the influence will have an experience of shifting the other's body too quickly. Some individuals will be able to manifest the ability to include the new information, which becomes almost a DNA transformation. That is the closest description we can use as an explanation. The consciousness at this point does shift. The circle at that point does become a spiral. The perception changes. It is not our place to consider the perception correct or incorrect—it is simply changed. As a small example, a youngster in a family needs to have their own explorations of their perception, their viewpoint, and their physical experience and how they affect the world, whether it is small or large. Their behavior may be destructive. If the family surrounding the youngster does not have the wisdom to direct this energy to a balanced place, the entire family can fall apart and get pulled into the youngster's perception. It is valuable for a wise family to redirect the youngster's perception to move from a circle to a spiral.[34]

This influence that the living are able to exert on each other may be strongest with those who interact on an everyday basis, but does not appear to be limited to that. If Trio is to be believed, we can have some effect on others who are far away. This came up in the question-and-answer section:

Heath: It seems like mass murder-suicide is becoming much more common. And not just simply as a tool for terrorism, but among families, at schools, and other situations.
Shaw: Yes. And it is similar to what I mentioned earlier, that the physical energy of those that surround you tends to influence. It is as if the transformation physically occurs simply by who is in the room with you.
Heath: Even on the planet?
Shaw: Yes.
Heath: So, it would be up to more developed souls to focus on counterbalancing that energy?
Shaw: Within themselves first. And whomever they are in proximity to will be influenced by what they project. Eventually, that projects out into whatever your boundaries are.
Heath: Yes, but of course with psychics there can be no boundaries.
Shaw: This is correct. But the physical body on the physical plane still influences on a level I can't describe to you.[35]

To some extent, Trio said, this positive influence was already being felt. Some of the process appeared to be a letting go or release of false perceptions, which can have even greater impact when done by the living. Trio encouraged people not to wait for their life review in the afterlife to begin this work:

When the individuals cross to the other side, they have the opportunity to witness things faster, for they are taken out of the phenomenon of the chaos that surrounded them physically. If they can get past the illusions of their mind, they will see very clearly the purpose they have.

If people can concentrate on this *before* they leave the body, the opportunity of spreading this through physical bodies is actually attainable. It is something that occurs energetically, that influences the DNA. But you must be aware in order for it to shift with the speed with which we are discussing.[36]

However, Trio also stated a belief that more individuals need to be involved in this process for there to be success at eliminating terrorism:

There are large pockets of individuals that are participating with this awareness. There are too many pockets, though, that are relying on old dreams of this awareness and they have become lazy. It's a false comfort. They must actively choose to participate. It is an act individuals must consciously make every moment to be present or they will slip into complacency. Now that is as deadly as any act of violence that anyone could perpetrate. ... it won't make any difference how pure the idea is if it is not put into action. People must commit.[37]

Should that commitment occur, then, Trio noted, not only could terrorism be solved in our lifetime, but: "Something magnificent within less than twenty years can occur."[38]

Finally, Trio gave this advice on how the living can end terrorism:

Others on the planet can assist this shift by recognizing that we all hold on to the same information and we can assist the expansion of speed of the shift by holding that thought in clarity in our quiet moments, and especially when we confront our own disillusionments of any kind; to immediately go back and stop and question what is absolute truth as opposed to surface truth. Perceptive truth. None of this is very different from any other time of war, or any other time of conflict. The shift comes about in similar ways. But the speed with which it can happen now is different than it has been before. The number of individuals it could touch is different. Despite the trauma this is going to bring forth, what can help move it through is to recognize all damaging thoughts, perceptions, and actions are exposed when more light is shone upon them. There is an *enormous* amount of light flooding the planet now. If we focus on that, the expansion occurs faster, but it will appear that there is more trauma, for it is lit up. When trauma is lit up, individuals who hold on to that trauma feel compelled to explain why they are involved with trauma. It's an end and a lie. It is so much simpler to either drop into the truth or, in the case of these individuals, to participate in their death. Either way they are all being pulled into the same place of transition. It will happen no matter what the choice is.[39]

In some cases, there was mention of how terrorist souls now in the spirit realm were being encouraged to work to change those still on the physical plane, in order to create a cascade effect. Shaw channeled this comment from Trio regarding a Chechen female suicide bomber:

> The whole activity she participated in seems pointless. In remembering where she was, she doesn't yet know how it would infiltrate the minds and hearts of those who lived where she lived. To get the smallest kernel of momentum to change this. We know that this is possible. It does start slowly and expand very quickly. The commitment to stay with the truth is simple but appears complicated. It's disguised by so many layers. All humans do this. The simplicity is attainable. It's moment-to-moment commitment. She can see this.... We have suggested to her to choose one individual and to see if she could assist that individual from this side. If she starts there, it would seem attainable to her. And then she will realize that that person can assist someone, and she can assist another soul, and so on.[40]

When a guide known as Joshua was asked what the solution was, Johanna Carroll was told:

> "Prayer." And he's showing me the women. The women. I'm feeling the tears, and I can taste the salt of the women and their energy. I don't know if it's symbolic, like the divine feminine, or literally, physically, but I think it's both. That the healing will come through the women. Which I also believe is true for the United States. "A force to be reckoned with." That's true![41]

The general spirit attitude toward terrorism appears to sometimes differ from that of spirits who specialize in dealing with terrorist souls. The general attitude tends to be fairly uniformly negative, while the spirits who deal with terrorist souls tend to take a neutral approach, seeing terrorism as an experience that may not have had the wisest intent. However, they note that those involved in such events as the September 11th, 2001 attacks on United States targets may (whether knowingly or not) have acted as catalysts for good. These events have the potential to bring people together and help them grow spiritually.

What is the solution to terrorism? The guides tell us two things. First, by actively working on our own spiritual enlightenment we can help those around us to advance. And second, it is heartfelt prayer—not just for a few, but for everyone. And there may be prayers coming not only from the planet but from the spirit realm, as well. Furthermore, at least a few guides suggest that women in the Middle East, and elsewhere, may ultimately be the driving force behind whatever changes are needed for terrorism to disappear. Even as some women take on new roles as suicide bombers, others grow more weary of the violence. The spirit realm even suggests there can be optimism, that some progress is already being made, and could even be complete in the next forty or fifty years. It can only be hoped that they are right.

17

Conclusion

As we reach the end of our study, we want to briefly recap what the dead and near-dead have told us about their experiences in the afterlife and how they view suicide. Then we will review five differing perspectives on suicide and the afterlife. Finally, we will conclude this chapter by returning to some of the key themes we used to introduce this book and why they matter.

WHAT THE DEAD SAY ABOUT SUICIDE

Throughout, we have looked at what the dead tell us about three different forms of suicide—the traditional taking of one's own life, assisted suicide or euthanasia, and homicide-suicides, such as the present-day Middle-Eastern suicide bombers. As we have heard from many spirits, they, to varying degrees, generally frown upon all forms of suicide done for any reason. They point out that suicide is not a solution and can just make problems worse for the soul.

Assisted suicide, however, appears to be viewed somewhat differently than either traditional suicide or suicide bombing. In cases where a person is suffering and near the end of his or her life, the spirit realm may take a more moderate approach. In these cases, if all the soul's major life tasks have been accomplished and there is nothing further to be gained by that person or others around him or her, then the spirits say ending the life may be acceptable. In other words, they are more apt to tell us it depends upon the situation, the individual, and a host of other factors as to whether assisted suicide is acceptable in their eyes.

Based on his extensive communications with the spirit realm, Allan Kardec summarizes the general afterlife experience following successful suicide:

> Observation has confirmed the statement that the consequences of suicide are not the same in all cases; but it has also shown us that some of those consequences, resulting from the sudden interruption of life, are the

same in all cases of violent death. Foremost among these is the greater tenacity and consequent persistence of the link that unites the spirit and the body.... The consequences of violent death are, first, the prolongation of the mental confusion which usually follows death, and, next, the illusion which causes a spirit, during a longer or shorter period, to believe himself to be still living....

The affinity which continues to exist between the spirit and the body produces, in the case of some of those who have committed suicide, a sort of repercussion of the state of the body in the consciousness of the spirit, who is thus compelled to perceive the effects of its decomposition, and experiences ... intense anguish and horror; a state which may continue as long as the life which he has interrupted ought to have lasted. This state is not a necessary result of suicide; but he who has voluntarily shortened his life can never escape the consequences of his want of courageous endurance; sooner or later, and in some way or other, he is made to expiate his fault....

Religion, morality, all systems of philosophy, condemn suicide as being contrary to the law of nature; all lay it down as a principle that we have no right to voluntarily shorten our life.... It was reserved for Spiritism to show, by the example of those who have succumbed to that temptation, that suicide is not only a fault, as being an infraction of a moral law ... but is also a piece of stupidity, since no benefit is to be gained by it, but quite the contrary.[1]

As we saw in Part I, most souls are reported to go through the same initial adjustment period and life-review process, regardless of the cause of their passing. This can involve a period of sleep, which seems to vary in length from one soul to the next. Also, with life review and self-judgment, spirits talk about the need to take responsibility for our own actions. What tends to differ with the experiences of traditional suicides is that they are more apt to express a sense of regret, which is rarely reported with suicide bombers or assisted suicides. Sometimes that regret is for the tasks left undone, for the lessons unlearned, or for the family left grieving. Although those who have committed suicide acknowledge the pain and desperation that lead to taking their own life, the nearly universal message is the same: *"Don't do it!"*

Once more we return to that same refrain we have now heard so often: Suicide is seldom a solution, except perhaps in the case of terminal illness, where the suffering body has already served all of the purpose for which it was meant and of which it was capable. However, many souls feel that simply being alive may not be enough either. Medium George Anderson provides a hopeful outlook:

There is a reason why the lessons are hard. It is a reason that is closely guarded by even the most helpful of souls in the hereafter. But they promise there *is* a reason.... Knowing that there *is* a reason is sometimes the only consolation that we may have for now.... I do know this, however—if you are at least *trying* to cope and maintain even the smallest shred of faith and hope, then you have survived the lesson. If you are at least *trying* to make sense of the senseless, then you are moving toward the Light. What we live through and continue in spite of is our spiritual lesson.[2]

Furthermore, as channel Lysa Mateu points out:

Spirits teach us that no matter how devastating the circumstances, or how deep the pain, people's lives can turn around for the better, and it doesn't have to take years. By connecting with the people around them, the spirits, and themselves, and by changing the meaning they attached to what happened to them, people can change how they feel in an instant.[3]

One of the hardest things for many suicides and potential suicides to accept may be the truths channeled from many spirits, that we choose our own lives and hardships, and that we have everything we need in life to succeed. Graham Bernard reports he was told from the spirit realm that:

Immortality is a reality.
Reincarnation is a fact.
We are here because we want to be here.
The circumstances of our lives have been chosen by us as the best for our development.
Each incarnation has a goal, a purpose.
We have the equipment necessary to cope with an incarnation.
We are all responsible for ourselves alone, and our development is up to us.[4]

So, these tenets are repeated by the surviving spirits of hundreds of successful suicides: Life continues after death. Souls return again by choice to learn, to work out their karma, to refine themselves, and to evolve. Every life, no matter how difficult, was picked by that soul for a purpose. And, again, we have what it takes to master our challenges. In every difficulty lies the potential for growth. We must accept responsibility for our lives and what we make of them, whether positive or negative.

The dead tell us that the choice is ours. But suicide is rarely ever a shortcut or solution, and often it can make things much worse for the traditional suicide or the suicide bomber. Channel Kate Anders observes:

I think the key is forgiveness. It seems in all cases, no matter what the issue, it always comes down to that. I would think that suicide bombers would have that same issue. On the other hand, I think assisted-suicide for the terminally ill is somewhat different. I think that is more about fear. It seems that we can go when we are allowed to go. Often I find that people hang on (I have one particular case in mind at the moment) due to guilt or not being released by those close to them. I have worked with enough people to know that if they are completely released in love and are not afraid of dying that they go quickly.[5]

We have seen that grief by the living regarding those who have ended their own lives does not help these souls after they have left their bodies, and can even be harmful, holding them back from progressing. It may be hard for some of those left behind to let go of their grief, anger, and guilt, but this is what the spirits ask us to do. They also remind us that we are still loved and that death does not end the connection we share with them.

From the perspective of the spirit realm, intent is everything. It is fundamental to how every aspect of our life and death may be regarded. Good intentions mean a great deal. Have you considered how your words, actions, and deeds will affect others? Or have you been selfish in thinking only of yourself, such as only of your own pain? While selfishness has its place in a survivalist context where the drive to maintain and continue individual life is only natural, selfishness can also be interpreted as an act, and a state, of alienation that goes against the grain of what is said to be the greatest truth of all: that each of us spirits, physically incarnate or otherwise, is actually an aspect of the one underlying, all-encompassing Universal Spirit. We are sibling offspring of the one Creator. From the afterlife, our fellow spirits tell us that we are all part of an interconnected whole—that everything we do affects others. Because of this, they advise us to be thoughtful of the ripples that will spread from each of our decisions, for at heart we are not separate individuals, but unique, experiencing individualizations of One Being.

An important point that the spirits make about both terrorist suicide bombers and traditional suicides is that they represent cases where, either collectively or on an individual basis, people feel they are not a part of the greater whole. As one entity put it, they feel "othered." There is an "us and them," or a "me and everyone else" mentality. From the viewpoint of the afterlife, this seems to be regarded as a form of spiritual disconnection and estrangement. The spirits' solution is, in part, to suggest that we should not allow others to think they are not a part of the whole. Through prayer and loving extension of ourselves we can bring them back to a degree of unity consciousness and a sense of belonging to the common good that can help dissolve the old grounds for feeling lonely and alienated, not cared for or understood.

If there is one thing that is certain in life, it is that all of us will eventually physically die. But the channeled messages we have been considering suggest that the death of the physical body will not mean the end of consciousness, nor will it mean the end of responsibility for whatever thoughts, actions, and feelings we have had while alive. For those who believe there is no afterlife, suffice it to say that we will, of course, all eventually learn the truth of this matter for ourselves, one way or the other. However, in the meanwhile, it seems prudent to listen to these messages said to be from the spirit realm. They warn us not to become caught up in petty problems. To remember the importance of love. To not fall into patterns of disconnection and estrangement, of judgmental lack of compassion, of rigidity or hatred. To accept responsibility for our own feelings and actions, being aware of the possible consequences of them for others. To focus on learning, growing spiritually, and connecting with each other. Such messages would seem to be wise ones.

You have had the opportunity now to read the viewpoints of hundreds of spirits said to be communicating from the afterlife through many different mediums and channels, and to sense the themes and patterns that have emerged. In closing, we would like to come full circle back to some of the themes we shared with you in the Introduction chapter of this book. Our purpose, here at the end, is to leave you with some ways to think about and use the material we have presented so that it might help you personally with your *own* lives, and with your own eventual, inevitable death.

First, let's return to the subtitle of this book: "What Really Happens in the Afterlife?" Without sounding too facetious, we tend to want to respond to this question with a simple "Who knows?" That is, at present, who knows for certain what *really* happens after death? And if someone claims to know, *how* do they know, and can we feel certain for ourselves about the matter just based on *their* certainty?

FIVE PERSPECTIVES ON WHAT HAPPENS IN THE AFTERLIFE

We have offered two basic paths that can be taken, or two perspectives from which to attempt to answer the question: what really happens in the afterlife? One is the perspective of those still alive, who comprise the usual authorities we look to for our definitive understandings about the nature of reality: our traditionally trained and credentialed scientists, researchers, scholars, and academics, as well as the representatives of our different religious organizations, all of whom have their own respective beliefs, theories, arguments, and convictions with regard to the hypothesis that we actually survive physical death.

Then there is the second perspective we offered: the one of psychics, intuitives, mediums, and channels who hold what we refer to here as a "privileged" position because they say (or others say of them) that they are able to get information from, or communicate with, the afterlife that follows death, and with the spirits supposedly residing there. We also added that, just because claims are made that someone can have this privileged anomalous-information-processing capacity with respect to another kind or level of reality than current earthly existence doesn't mean that this is actually what is going on. We must come to terms in any way we choose with the authenticity, or lack of it, of what is being claimed.

When presenting psychologist Gary Schwartz's recent mediumship-based afterlife research (in the section entitled "Survival Research: A Brief Overview" in the Introduction chapter), we listed some of the different competing explanations besides the survival hypothesis that could also possibly account for what seems like privileged, even evidentiary, information from the spirit realm. And even though Schwartz and other survival researchers before him have tried to rule out these competing points of view, in truth they can never completely do so. Therefore, as we have said before, and as the saying goes, "the jury is still out" about our being able to know for certain, based on irrefutable evidence, whether we truly survive physical death.

We could also add a *third* perspective, not mentioned in our Introduction, and that is the perspective of those who have gone through the experience of their own physical death and can now tell us about what really happens after we die and what it is really like in the afterlife. Of course, we have chosen to make this kind of source the basis for most of the material in this book. Unfortunately, the only way we can be in touch with and hear from that ultimate, privileged frame of reference—from "the dead"—is by way of those holding the second perspective, that is, by way of psychics, mediums, and channels. So, in light of this, and depending on our own orientation, many of us may still find ourselves returning to the alternative explanations, besides mediumship, channeling, and the survival hypothesis, which could perhaps equally, or even better, account for what seems to be evidence of an afterlife following death and the spirit messages associated with it.

There is yet a *fourth* perspective for us to consider from which to answer the question of what really happens in the afterlife. It is related to the other three and yet is still somewhat different. It is the perspective held by any of us here on Earth who have had our own personal firsthand experience with the afterlife and its inhabitants, or with the larger transcendental or spiritual reality in general. For those of us who have had such personal experience, it is unquestionably real and true for us. Still, we would probably not consider ourselves to be psychics, mediums, or channels. We just experienced whatever we did, and it may have been a rare or even one-time thing, but it has left us deeply affected—often changed forever, usually for the better. Just one example from this fourth kind of perspective—of direct, personal, undeniable, and profound experience of a larger or different reality—is based on having had a near-death experience, or NDE. Usually, those who have had a personal experience of such an otherworldly kind cannot be disabused of it, cannot be argued out of having had it, cannot or will not have others reduce the extraordinary influence and meaning it had. These people have often told researchers that their unusual experience was, for them, not just as real as normal earthly experience—it was actually *more* real.

Virtually all of these individuals, who choose to hold on to and be deeply influenced by their own anomalous experience, cannot provide for others irrefutable evidence for its actuality as lying outside their own subjective consciousness. As a result, those who have never had such an experience tend to dismiss or explain away unearthly seeming experience as being nothing more than a matter of unsubstantiatable personal belief or faith with no grounding in a reality that goes beyond their own inner experience. Worse, we also have those in the mental health professions disposed to label and psychopathologize such anomalous experience as being just a lapse in one's normal functional connection to the only reality that we can ever be sure of, which is publicly sharable, physical, sensate, objectively real existence. Experiences associated with such entirely subjective "lapses," or disconnections from objective reality, can then be variously explained as being the product of misperception, fantasy-proneness, unbridled imagination or wishful thinking, or worse, as being hallucination, delusion, thought disorder, or even psychosis. For, after all, as the thinking goes, if it is not experienced in ordinary waking consciousness by way of the senses, and thus potentially amenable to being publicly shared and corroborated as objectively real in that way, it must be entirely self-generated by the neuronal firing patterns of one's own central nervous system.

If we believed that all anomalous or otherworldly experiences and communications could be explained entirely in such materialist, reductionist ways, we would have never written this book. If we believed that the mediums and channels we have been using were all frauds, hoaxers, or simply creating their communications in a state of dissociation, drawing only from their own unconscious material or picking it up through psychic means from sources other than surviving spirits in the afterlife, we would, once more, have never written this book. Still, since one of us is a research psychologist with thirty-two years of unbroken employment in academic doctoral programs (Klimo), and the other is a practicing physician (anesthesiologist) with a second doctorate degree in psychology (Heath), we are both traditionally trained scientists who understand, and are at least partially based in and informed by, the first of our four perspectives.

Most of the world's population today adheres to some form of religion or spiritual faith, belief system, and practice. This provides us with a *fifth* and final perspective on what may really happen in the afterlife, and how we should look at suicide. Here no demands need be made for science to provide irrefutable evidence and proof for the survival hypothesis. In most religions, what, if anything, happens after death is taught and accepted as an article of faith. Unfortunately, within this religious-spiritual domain, there has never been much agreement across systems about exactly what is supposed to happen to us and our consciousness, memory, and personality upon death and following it. Each religion or system of spiritual teaching appears to have its own story to tell. Yet all too often, each one chooses to think that its story is the only correct and acceptable one. So, is any one religion's story about death any more true than another? And, if so, how would we know? It seems we are left to choose, discern, and accept on the basis of personal faith. There is also the additional problem that each of the traditional religions or spiritual paths has its own way of admonishing, forbidding, or at least strictly limiting its followers with regard to practicing their own connection or communicative link with the larger reality, including with a populated afterlife. As a result, religious perspectives can be just as dismissive, rigid, and negatively judgmental about most of what is represented in this book as the traditional scientist or hardened skeptic.

KEY THEMES

In one respect, what we have done in this book is attempt to present an alternative religious-spiritual perspective on the topic of suicide in light of the survival hypothesis that we continue to exist following the death of our body. At the same time, what we have done could also be seen as providing some of the much-needed grounds for a possible expansion of current psychology, biology, physics, and information processing as part of an overall emerging truer, more inclusive paradigm of understanding that integrates the three basic domains—the religious, spiritual, and metaphysical; the scientific; and the personal, experiential, and phenomenological. We simply ask that you remain open to the possibility that today we may be experiencing the growing pains of just such an emerging paradigm. None of us is completely free of rigidity; each of us probably has a problem with too much pluralism, relativism, and acceptance of coequal but different paths to the same ultimate truth of the oneness of all things in the unity of Spirit. And yet the truest, most inclusive, and accurate picture may turn out to integrate and embrace all the once-separate perspectives.

The reason that we have dwelt this long in these final remarks on the whole issue of survival of death is that everything in this book about traditional suicide, assisted suicide, and murder-suicide and the present-day suicide bombers, presupposes that we are accepting or at least remaining open to the possibility that we survive death and that at least occasional communication may occur between that next world and this one. As we have said repeatedly, the jury must still remain out as far as no one yet being able to completely convince or prove irrefutably to anyone else his or her point of view, belief, faith, or personal experience. Nonetheless we can all try to remain open to each others' perspectives and what we may learn from them. In so doing, there is the possibility of mutual sensitivity and influence and the development of an eventual common ground for deeper, better understanding, shared spirit, empathy, compassion—even love.

In our Introduction, we asked you to imagine what the world would be like if we all knew we survived physical death and that karma was real. How then would we live? Would this lead us to live differently? As the authors of this book, it is our view, and our hope, that it would lead to our acting *more* responsibly, compassionately, forgivingly, lovingly. This is just another way of imagining what the world would be like if the billions of us, guided by our own respective physical-reality-transcending, traditional religious-spiritual faiths, were to thoroughly live our lives as if what our religion told us about life, death, and the nature of transcendence was, in fact, now known to be absolutely, undeniably true and real.

However, it would seem that the troubled and divisive state of our world today, and of our own inner, so often wanting, lives, are the result of all too many of us doing pretty much the *opposite:* We are *not* living our lives as if what we have been choosing to believe spiritually and have faith in had actually come true and was now *real*. Also, there are probably additional billions of us who really have *no* abiding belief or faith in a larger reality transcending the physical world and the finality of death that gives deeper meaning to all things. Any hope, then, of bringing anything like heaven to earth or earth to heaven, of having the two realms inform and imbue each other, seems rather far-fetched for today's world and its people. But it has been the purpose of this book to try and contribute what little we can to that emerging paradigm and that interpenetration of the two levels of reality, physical and spiritual.

Finally, we want to return to how this book came to be, as described in our Introduction. It began with the attempt of one of us (Klimo) more than ten years ago to try to help a fellow psychologist, who was contemplating taking her own life. Perhaps ten or twenty pages of the kind of content that comprises hundreds of pages of the present book were prepared for the purpose of doing "bibliotherapy" with her. Recall that in the helping professions this simply means giving someone things to read to serve as topics for discussion and counseling. In the case lying behind the origin of this book, the bibliotherapy was done in the service of helping that suicidal psychologist look more carefully and fully at some perspectives on what might be involved with ending her own life. These readings were from supposed channeled spirits giving their view on how suicide is not the easy or final out that the potential suicide may think it will be.

Although it is meant to operate on a much larger scale, this book can also to be used by any who read it for doing a kind of bibliotherapy for yourself or for others. For any of you who may be contemplating suicide, who know or are working with someone who may be suicidal, or someone who has had a friend or loved one who has committed suicide, we offer you this book with the hope that it might be helpful to you. Further, we would like to leave all of our fellow human spirits currently here on Earth with ways to focus on thinking about and sharing with each other our central themes of life and death, of deeper meaning, of possible continuation, of the nature of repercussion and karma, of personal meaning-making and spiritual connection. In any way you care to use it, this book is meant for your own reflection, integration, healing, and spiritual growth, both here on Earth and in any kind of experiential hereafter that may follow.

For a world with insufficient opportunities to seriously focus on and share the taboo nature of certain aspects of existence, death, and the larger reality within which they may both be embedded, we offer this book. Its theme has been that neither self-murder nor the murder of another is going to provide final resolution. Comprising the stories of many spirits, our story has been that following death we will experience the repercussions of our intentions, choices, and acts. Therefore, it would behoove us all to think seriously on these things. We have provided this transcendental story so that at least some future traditional suicides might be prevented from carrying out their acts against self and Spirit, and that yet further terrorist suicide bombers might be kept from carrying out, in the name of religion and God, their murderous acts against themselves and others. Such is our hope.

Glossary

afterlife: The non- or transphysical realm of further existence to which we human spirits are said to go following the death of our physical body. Also see **astral realm.**

astral realm: A multilevel nonphysical reality said to exist beyond the physical realm. Human beings are said to go there following the death of their physical body. Sometimes called the **bardo** or **devachan,** this is where spirits dwell between their incarnations or after they have finished incarnating. Lower levels of the astral, close to the Earth plane, are said to be dark and unpleasant locations with a heavy or dense level of vibration.

automatic writing: Handwriting or typewriting done without conscious control, the source of which is apparently not the self.

bibliotherapy: Selecting material to read to provide a focus for study, discussion, and counseling.

chakra: From the Sanskrit word *cakram* (meaning wheel or circle), the chakras are considered to be centers of spiritual energy in the human body. Classically, there are considered to be seven of these vortexes, although some channeled material suggests there may be more. Each chakra represents a different level or kind of energy (often associated with different colors).

channel (verb): To receive and convey information or energy that is said to come from neither one's own self nor from other embodied minds, nor from physical reality (as defined by current physics and physiology). Therefore, to channel is to be capable of receiving self-transcending information or messages from some nonphysically residing source or being.

channel (noun): A physically embodied, living person capable of anomalously receiving and conveying information, messages, or energy from a source, entity, or being not residing on our physical level of reality. Sometimes referred to as a "channeler." "Channel" is a more-recent (1950s onward) term for the older word "medium," with the difference being that a medium is said to work only with discarnate human spirits, while a channel may also work with other kinds of beings and sources.

channeling: The process of receiving information from some level of reality other than the ordinary physical one and from beyond the self as we currently understand it. This includes messages from any mental source that falls outside of one's own ordinary conscious or unconscious, and is not from anyone else incarnate on the physical level of reality. Classically, channeling involved an identified, or self-identified, source said to be responsible for the information coming to or through the channel.

earthbound spirit: The soul of a deceased person who is tied to the material world, whether because of ignorance or the inability to let go of the people, places, and things of his or her old life.

eternalizing: A word frequently used by Jean Foster in channeled communications. When she asked a spirit how this word was defined, she was told: "That which enters my mind as the way things are in reality. The eternalizing may be the truth or it may not, depending on which mind one pays attention to—earth-mind or God-mind."[1]

fragment: A term used by the channeled entity Michael to refer to individual souls, which are part of a group entity.

imam: Islamic term for a spiritual guide or leader.

incarnate: Possessing a physical body; being physically embodied. All human beings presently physically alive on Earth are incarnate (or incarnated). To be incarnated, then, is to come into physical-level existence within, and to operate with, a physical body. This assumes the existence of a non- or trans-physical spirit or soul that becomes incarnated, as in, "a human spirit incarnating into a physical body in order to experience a physical earthly existence." In contradistinction to *discarnate*, which means individually existing, but operating without, or outside of, a physical body. Thus, all the purported spirits heard from in this book, said to have survived physical death and be communicating back through mediums or channels, are, by definition, discarnate spirits, while all the physically embodied mediums and channels are incarnate spirits.

instrumental transcommunication: The purported communication by human spirits, said to have survived the death of their physical body and exist in an afterlife or astral realm, by means of an assortment of electronic and related equipment, including tape recorders, telephones, radios, televisions, and computers. Often these sounds and images are not heard or seen at the time of original recording, but only appear later. It is also known by its earlier term **electronic voice phenomena** (EVP) or **Raudive phenomena.** The process may involve the mediumistic abilities of the incarnate human operators.

interlife: The period between lives, after the death of one life and before reincarnation into a new body.

karma: Word derived from Sanskrit meaning a deed or action that has consequences. Used in Buddhism and Hinduism, referring to the fact that a person's thoughts and actions (both good and bad) from prior and current lifetimes will be reflected back to that soul whether in the current life or a subsequent one. Can be summed up as "what goes around comes around."

medium: A physically living individual capable of communicating with human spirits said to have survived physical death.

mediumship: The process whereby a physically living individual is able to act as a vehicle to receive communication from, or about, the spirits of human beings no longer physically alive. Mediumship is usually meant to refer to contact only with human spirits in contrast to the more recent, related term, **channeling,** which refers to communication with not only discarnate human spirits ("the dead"), but also with a variety of other kinds of sources and beings.

near-death experience (NDE): An experience reported by some people who have been clinically dead, and then returned to life. Descriptions vary slightly in detail from one person and culture to the next, but usually share some basic elements, such as feeling outside one's body, moving down a long tunnel, seeing a bright light at the end of that tunnel, and being greeted by anonymous spirits or those one knows who have already died. Regardless of its nature, the near-death experience can be a powerful and transformative experience.

psychache: a strong, psychic pain, tension, and suffering that makes life intolerable. It tends to result from one of four situations: (1) thwarted love and acceptance; (2) loss of control (with helplessness and frustration); (3) something that damages self-image (with the need to avoid shame, defeat, humiliation, and disgrace); or (4) broken key relationships and grief.

psychokinesis: The influence of a mind (whether existing only in spirit or with a body) on external objects or processes without the mediation of known physical energies or forces. It can include such things as metal bending, object movement, the production of raps, and anomalous healing.

psychomanteum: A form of mirror-gazing, scrying, or divination. As described by Raymond Moody, it involves the viewer sitting in a comfortable chair about 3 feet from a mirror that is inclined slightly backward. Usually, a curtained booth is created through the use of a black velvet drape hanging from the ceiling and encompassing the mirror and chair. The only illumination in the room is comparable to a 15-watt bulb.

regression: A hypnosis technique used to allow individuals to review their past, not only for their current life, but for previous lives, as well.

suicide bomber: Individuals who in the last twenty years have used explosives strapped to their bodies, or driven vehicles laden with explosives, to kill targeted others while at the same time purposefully taking their own lives. Most of them have been Middle Eastern Muslims (Palestinians and Iraqis, especially) following their Islamic faith, who consider themselves to be righteous martyrs fighting a holy war on behalf of their religion, their country, sect, and/or their people.

suicidology: The scientific study of suicide and suicide prevention.

survival hypothesis: The proposition that we human beings survive the deaths of our physical body, with our essence, or spirit, continuing to exist in some meaningful and conscious way in a larger reality that transcends the physical. The hypothesis usually also speculates that at least some surviving spirits are able to communicate back to us on Earth through anomalous experiences or by means of psychics, mediums, or channels.

transcommunication: See **instrumental transcommunication.**

unfoldment: This term (a combination of unfolding and evolvement) refers to the unfolding or unraveling and release of illusion. This illusion is something all souls acquire during a lifetime, as they accumulate perceptions, which are often limiting in nature. Such perceptions act to bind or encase the soul. As souls let go of these perceptions, they become able to return to their true state as part of the Divine whole. Although it is possible for some souls to do this while still incarnate, for most it occurs during the afterlife when the lack of a physical body makes the process easier. Unfoldment is a necessary step of evolution for souls to take, but it is not precisely the same as spiritual enlightenment. This is because, upon completion of unfoldment, the soul may not be fully enlightened, simply returned to its true, natural state—at whatever level of development that may be. The image Trio gave of this was of watching a tightly curled fern bud unfurl to reveal its full, expanded leaf.

References

Abd ar-Rahim ibn Ahmad al-Qadi. *Islamic Book of the Dead: A Collection of Hadiths on the Fire & the Garden.* San Francisco: Diwan Press, 1977.

Aktan, Hamza. "Acts of Terror and Suicide Attacks in Light of the Qur'an and the Sunna," in *Terror and Suicide Attacks: An Islamic Perspective,* edited by Ergun Capan, 35–43. Somerset, N.J.: The Light, Inc., 2004.

Alkhuli, Muhammad Ali. *Traditions of Prophet Muhammad.* Riyadh, Saudi Arabia: Al-Farazdak Press, 1984.

Altman, Neil. "On the Psychology of Suicide Bombing." *Tikkun,* Vol. 20(2): 15–17.

Al-Sha'ab (Egyptian periodical), February 1, 2002.

Anderson, George, and Andrew Barone. *Lessons from the Light: Extraordinary Messages of Comfort and Hope from the Other Side.* New York: Berkley Books, 2000.

Anderson, George, and Andrew Barone. *Walking in the Garden of Souls: George Anderson's Advice from the Hereafter for Living in the Here and Now.* New York: G. P. Putnam's Sons, 2001.

Anderson, Mary Beth. *Good Teachers Carry On: Lessons from the Afterlife.* St. Joseph, Mich.: Cosmic Concepts Press, 2003.

"Attackers Neither Mad Nor Desperate." *New York Times Service.* Available at http://www.iht.com, September 13, 2001.

Atwater, P. M. H. *Beyond the Light: What Isn't Being Said About Near-Death Experience.* New York: Birch Lane Press, 1994.

Atwater, P. M. H. *The New Children and Near-Death Experiences.* Foreword by Joseph Chilton Pearce. Rochester, Vermont: Bear and Company, 2003.

Atwater, P. M. H. *We Live Forever: The Real Truth About Death.* Virginia Beach, Va.: A.R.E. Press, 2004.

Atwater, P. M. H. *The Complete Idiot's Guide to Near-Death Experiences.* Indianapolis: Alpha Books, 2000.

Austen, A. W., ed. *The Teachings of Silver Birch: Wisdom from the World Beyond,* 4th ed. with a foreword by Hannen Swaffer. London: Spiritualist Press, 1978.

Ballou, John. *OAHSPE: A New Bible in the Words of Jehovih and his Angel Ambassadors.* Photographic reproduction. New York and London: OAHSPE Publishing Association, 1882. (Also known as the "Kosmon Bible.")

Barbanell, Sylvia. *When a Child Dies.* 1942. London: Spiritualist Press, 1964.

Bayman, Henry. *The Secret of Islam: Love and Law in the Religion of Ethics.* Berkeley: North Atlantic Books, 2003.

Baruch, Elaine Hoffman. "Psychoanalysis and Terrorism: The Need for a Global Talking Cure." *Psychoanalytic Psychology,* Vol. 20(4), Fall 2003: 698–700.

Beck, Aron T., A. J. Rush, B. F. Shaw, and G. Emery. *Cognitive Therapy of Depression.* New York: Wiley, 1979.

Becker, Ernest. "The Basic Dynamic of Human Evil," in *Meeting the Shadow: The Hidden Power of the Dark Side of Human Nature,* edited by Jeremiah Abrams and Connie Zweig, 186–189. New York: Jeremy P. Tarcher/G. P. Putnam's Sons, 1991.

Bentley, Edmund. *Far Horizon: A Biography of Hester Dowden: Medium and Psychic Investigator.* Facsimile. London: Rider and Company, 1951. Available at http://www.spiritwritings.com (accessed April 10, 2004).

Berg, Bruce. *Qualitative Research Methods for the Social Sciences,* Fifth Edition. New York: Allyn & Bacon, 2003.

Berkowitz, Leonard. *Aggression: Its Causes, Consequences, and Control.* New York: McGraw-Hill, 1993.

Bernard, Graham. *Why You Are Who You Are: A Psychic Conversation.* New York: Destiny Books, 1985.

Bertolote, Jose M. "Suicide in the World: An Epidemiological Overview 1950–1995," in *Suicide: An Unnecessary Death,* edited by Danuta Wasserman. London: Martin Dunitz, 2001.

Besant, Annie. *Death—And After?* Adyar, Madras, India: Theosophical Publishing House, 1893.

Bhugra, Dinesh. "Sati: A Type of Nonpsychiatric Suicide." *Crisis: The Journal of Crisis Intervention and Suicide Prevention,* Vol. 26(2), 2005: 73–77.

Bird, Frances. *The Transition, Explained: Earth Questions Spirit Answers.* Oakland, Calif.: LC Publishing Company, 1988.

Blavatsky, H. P. *Isis Unveiled,* Volume 1. Reprint. Pasadena: Theosophical University Press Online, 2003. Available at http://www.theosociety.org/pasadena/isis/iu-hp.htm (accessed April 27, 2004).

Blood, R. Warwick, and Jane Pirkis. "Suicide and the Media: Part III: Theoretical Issues." *Crisis: The Journal of Crisis Intervention and Suicide Prevention,* Vol. 22(4), 2001: 163–169.

Bloom, Mia. *Dying to Kill: The Allure of Suicide Terror.* New York: Columbia University Press, 2005.

Bongar, Bruce. *The Suicidal Patient: Clinical and Legal Standards of Care,* 2nd edition. Washington, D.C.: American Psychological Association, 2002.

Borgia, Anthony. *Life in the World Unseen.* Foreword by Sir John Anderson. London: Corgi Books, 1970.

Boulton, Peter, and Jane Boulton. *Psychic Beam to Beyond: Through the Psychic Sensitive Lenora Huett.* Marina del Rey, Calif.: DeVorss and Company, 1983.

Brandon, Wilfred. "Waiting to Reincarnate," in *The ESP Reader,* edited by David C. Knight, 420–424. New York: Grosset and Dunlap, 1969.

Brodsky, Barbara. *Aaron: Channeled through Barbara Brodsky,* revised and expanded edition. Ann Arbor: Deep Spring Publications, 1995. Available at http://www.deepspring.org (accessed April 26, 2004).

Bronisch, Thomas. "Depression and Suicidal Behavior." *Crisis: The Journal of Crisis Intervention and Suicide Prevention,* Vol. 24(4), 2003: 179–180.

REFERENCES

Brottman, Mikita. "Kurt Cobain," in *Straight to Hell: 20th Century Suicides,* edited by Namida King, 59–63. New York: Creation Books, 2004.

Buckley, Heather. *Conversations with the Beyond.* Campbell, Calif.: self-published, 1971.

Buckley, Heather. *When You're Dead, You're Livin'.* San Jose, Calif.: self-published, 1986.

Buda, Bela. "Comprehending Suicide: Landmarks in 20th-Century Suicidology" (a book review). *Crisis: The Journal of Crisis Intervention and Suicide Prevention.* Vol. 22(2), 2001: 70.

Cahagnet, L. Alph. *The Celestial Telegraph; Or, Secrets of the Life to Come, Revealed through Magnetism. Includes Volume II: The Secrets of the Future Revealed through Magnetism.* Facsimile of the 1st American edition. New York: J. S. Redfield Clinton Hall, 1851. Available at http://www.hti.umich.edu/m/moa (accessed April 27, 2004).

Cantor, Chris. "Victims and Survivors: Letters Across the Pacific." *Crisis: The Journal of Crisis Intervention and Suicide Prevention* Vol. 24(1), 2003: 37–38.

Capan, Ergun. "Suicide Attacks and Islam," in *Terror and Suicide Attacks: An Islamic Perspective,* edited by Ergun Capan, 101–118. Somerset, N.J.: The Light, Inc., 2004.

Capan, Ergun, ed. *Terror and Suicide Attacks: An Islamic Perspective.* Somerset, N.J.: The Light, Inc., 2004.

Cassem, Edwin H. Contributions to *The Harvard Guide to Psychiatry,* 3rd edition, edited by Armand M. Nicholi, Jr,, 622–623, 704–705, 713–715, 726–727. Cambridge: The Belknap Press of Harvard University, 1999.

Chino, Yuko and Kyoto Group, eds. *Sermes: The Poems of the Angels.* Translated by Stephen Brown. Tokyo: Jihi-to-Ai Publishing Co., 1984.

Choron, Jacques. *Suicide.* New York: Charles Scribners Sons, 1972.

Cooke, Maurice B. *More Answers.* Toronto: Marcus Books, 1985.

Cornette, Michelle. "Toward an Integrated Theory of Suicidal Behavior: Merging the Hopelessness, Self-Discrepancy, and Escape Theories," in *Suicide Science: Expanding the Boundaries,* edited by Thomas Joiner and David Rudd, 44. Hingham, Mass.: Kluver Publishers, 2000.

Corsini, Raymond J. *The Encyclopedia of Psychology,* 2nd edition, Vol. 3. New York: Wiley-Interscience/John Wiley & Sons, 1994.

Crawford, April. *Parting Notes: A Connection with the Afterlife.* Bloomington, Ind.: 1st Books, 2002.

Creswell, John. *Qualitative Inquiry and Research Design: Choosing Among Five Traditions.* Thousand Oaks, Calif.: Sage Publications, 1997.

Crookall, Robert. *The Supreme Adventure: Analysis of Psychic Communications.* 2nd edition. Cambridge, United Kingdom: James Clarke & Co. Limited, 1974.

Cummins, Geraldine. *The Road to Immortality: Being a Description of the After-Life Purporting to be Communicated by the late F. W. H. Meyers through Geraldine Cummins.* 1932, 4th ed. Foreword by Sir Oliver Lodge and introduction by E. B. Gibbes. London: Psychic Press Ltd., 1967.

Cummins, Geraldine. *Swan on a Black Sea: A Study in Automatic Writing: The Cummins-Willett Scripts,* revised edition. Edited by Signe Toksvig, with a foreword by C. D. Broad. New York: Samuel Weiser, Inc., 1970.

Curtis, James. *Rustlings in the Golden City.* A facsimile of the 3rd edition, revised, London: 1902. Available at http://www.spiritwritings.com/RustlingsGoldenCityCurtis.pdf (accessed April 29, 2004).

Darby and Joan. *Our Unseen Guest*. 1920. Alhambra, Calif.: Borden Publishing Company, 1979.

Dass, Ram. "Thoughts at the Moment of Death," in *What Survives? Contemporary Explorations of Life After Death*, edited by Gary Doore, 159–164. New York: G. P. Putnam's Sons, 1990.

Davis, Joyce M. *Martyrs: Innocence, Vengeance, and Despair in the Middle East*. New York: Palgrave Macmillan, 2003.

Deane, Ashayana (Anna Hayes). *Voyagers: Secrets of Amenti*, Volume II, expanded 2nd edition. Columbus, N.C.: Wild Flower Press, 2002.

Delacour, Jean-Baptiste. *Glimpses of the Beyond: The Extraordinary Experiences of People Who Crossed the Brink of Death and Returned*. Translated by E. B. Garside. New York: Delacorte Press, 1974. Originally published as *Aus dem Jenseits Zurück* by Econ Verlag.

Diamond, Stephen A. "Redeeming Our Devils and Demons," in *Meeting the Shadow: The Hidden Power of the Dark Side of Human Nature*, edited by Jeremiah Abrams and Connie Zweig, 180–186. New York: Jeremy P. Tarcher/G. P. Putnams Sons, 1991.

DiPasquale, Tony, and John Gluck. "*Psychologists, Psychiatrists, and Physician-Assisted Suicide: The Relationship Between Underlying Beliefs and Professional Behavior.*" *Professional Psychology: Research and Practice*, 07357028, Vol. 32(5), October 1, 2001: 501–506.

Dresser, Charlotte E. *Spirit World and Spirit Life*. Edited by Fred Rafferty. Facsimile. Los Angeles: J. F. Rowny Press, 1922. Available at http://www.spiritwritings.com/library.html (accessed April 29, 2004).

Dresser, Charlotte E. *Life Here and Hereafter*. Edited by Fred Rafferty. Facsimile. San Jose, Calif.: Chase & Rae Occult Book Publishers, 1927. Available at http://www.spiritwritings.com/LifeHereafter.pdf (accessed April 29, 2004).

Durkheim, Emile. *Suicide: A Study in Sociology*. Originally published 1897. Florence, Ky.: Routledge, 2002 (published as an electronic book on http://site.ebrary.com).

Edmonds, John W., and George T. Dexter. *Spiritualism*. 5th edition. New York: Partridge & Brittan, 1853.

Edward, John. *One Last Time: A Psychic Medium Speaks to Those We Have Loved and Lost*. New York: Berkley Books, 1999.

Edwards, Harry. *Life in Spirit*. Burrows Lea, Great Britain: The Healer Publishing Co. Ltd., 1976.

Egelko, Bob. "Oregon law hinges on O'Connor: Miers' withdrawal muddles court ruling on assisted suicide," *San Francisco Chronicle*, October 20, 2005, A7.

Ellis, Albert. *Reason and Emotion in Psychotherapy*, revised and updated. New York: Birch Lane Press/Carol Publishing Group, 1994.

Engelhardt Jr., H. Tristram, and Ana Smith Iltis. "End-of Life: The Traditional Christian View." *The Lancet*, Vol. 366, September 17, 2005: 1045–1049.

Fanning, Arthur. "The Awakening of Mankind." *Sedona: Journal of EMERGENCE!*, Vol. 3(9), September 1993: 18–28.

Ford, Arthur. *The Life Beyond Death: As Told to Jerome Ellison*. London: Abacus, 1974.

Ford, Arthur. *Unknown But Known: My Adventure into the Meditative Dimension*. New York: The New American Library, 1969.

Foster, Jean K. *Epilogue: Souls Review Their Lives After Death*. Kansas City, Mo.: Uni∗Sun, 1988.

REFERENCES

Gauld, Alan. *Mediumship and Survival: A Century of Investigations.* London: Granada Publishing, 1982.

Greaves, Helen. *Testimony of Light.* 1969. Reprint. Essex, England: Neville Spearman Publishers, 1985.

Grey, Margot. *Return from Death: An Exploration of the Near-Death Experience.* Foreword by Kenneth Ring. Boston: Arkana, 1985.

Greyson, Bruce. "Wish for Death, Wish for Life: The NDE and Suicide Attempts" (translated from the French, "Désir de mort, désir de vie: La NDE dans les tentatives de suicide"), in *Death Transformed: Research into Real-life Experiences of the Approach of Death (NDE)* (in French: *La mort transfigurée: Recherches sur les expériences vécues aux approches de la mort (NDE)*, edited by Evelyn-Sarah Mercier, 135–145. Paris: L'Age du Verseau, 1992. (Note: page numbers referred to in the endnotes refer to page numbers in the unpublished manuscript of the English translation provided to Klimo by Greyson October 17, 2005.)

Gross, Terry. "Documentary Interviews Failed Suicide Bombers" on *Fresh Air.* Aired June 30, 2004. Available at http://www.npr.org/rundowns/rundown.php?prgId=13&prgDate=30-Jun–2004.

Guggenheim, Bill, and Judy Guggenheim. *Hello from Heaven!* New York: Bantam Books, 1997.

Gurian, Michael. *What Could He Be Thinking: How a Man's Mind Really Works.* New York: St. Martins Press, 2003.

Haqqani, Husain, and Daniel Kimmage. "The Online Bios of Iraq's Martyrs. Suicidology." *The New Republic,* Oct. 3, 2005: 14.

Haraldsson, Erlendur, and Majd Abu-Izzeddin. "Three Randomly Selected Cases of Lebanese Children Who Claim Memories of a Previous Life." *Journal of the Society for Psychical Research,* 68.2, no. 875, April 2004: 65–85.

Hardinge, Emma. *Modern American Spiritualism: A Twenty Year's Record of the Communion Between Earth and the World of* Spirits. A facsimile of the 3rd edition. New York: The New-York Printing Company, 1870. Available at http://www.hti.umich.edu/cgi/t/text/text-idx?c=moa&idno=ACM3377.0001.001&view=toc (accessed April 29, 2004).

Hassan, Nasra. "Letter from Gaza: An Arsenal of Believers." *The New Yorker.* Available at http://www.newyorker.com/printable/?fact/011119fa_FACT1, November 19, 2001.

Heath, Pamela Rae. *The PK Zone: A Cross-Cultural Review of Psychokinesis (PK).* New York: iUniverse, Inc., 2003.

Heckler, Richard A. *Waking Up, Alive: The Descent, the Suicide Attempt, and the Return to Life.* New York: Ballantine Books, 1994.

Hendin, Herbert. "Assisted Suicide, Euthanasia, and the Right to End-of-Life Care." *Crisis: The Journal of Crisis Intervention and Suicide Prevention,* Vol. 23(1), 2002: 40–41.

Hesse-Biber, Sharlene Nagy, and Patricia Leavy. *Approaches to Qualitative Research: A Reader on Theory and Practice.* New York: Oxford University Press, 2003.

Hillbrand, Marc. "Homicide-Suicide and Other Forms of Co-Occurring Aggression Against Self and Against Others." *Professional Psychology: Research and Practice,* Vol. 32(6), Dec. 1, 2001.

Hillman, James. *Suicide and the Soul.* 1964. Dallas: Spring Publications, Inc., 1985.

Holmes, Jesse Herman, and the Holmes Research Team. *As We See It from Here.* Franklin, N.C.: Metascience Corporation Publications Division, 1980.

Holtzer, Hans. *Life Beyond: Compelling Evidence for Past Lives and Existence After Death.* Chicago: Contemporary Books, 1994.

Home, D. D. *Incidents in My Life.* 1864. Reprint. Secaucus, N.J.: University Books, Inc., n.d.

Hoodwin, Shepherd. *The Journey of Your Soul: A Channel Explores Channeling and the Michael Teachings.* New York: Summerjoy Press, 1995.

Hutton, J. Bernard. *On the Other Side of Reality.* Introduction by John Izbicki. New York: Award Books, 1969.

Jacobson, Nils O. *Life Without Death? On Parapsychology, Mysticism, and the Question of Survival.* Translated by Sheila La Farge. New York: Delacorte Press, 1974. First published as *Liv efter döden?* (Gothenburg, Sweden: Zindermans Förlog).

Jamison, Kay Redfield. *Night Falls Fast: Understanding Suicide.* New York: Alfred A. Knopf, 1999.

Jones, Sheila. *Four Spirit Teachers: Trance Talks.* Recorded by John Mainwood, transcribed and edited by John Byrne. London: Spiritualist Association of Great Britain, 1994. Available at http://freespace.virgin.net/byrne.john/fst (accessed April 27, 2004).

Kardec, Allan. *The Spirits' Book.* Translated by Anna Blackwell. Reprint of 1857 edition. Las Vegas, Nev.: Brotherhood of Life Publishing, 2002.

Keen, Sam. "The Enemy Maker," in *Meeting the Shadow: The Hidden Power of the Dark Side of Human Nature,* edited by Jeremiah Abrams and Connie Zweig, 197–202. New York: Jeremy P. Tarcher/G. P. Putnams Sons, 1991.

Kelly, Jack. "Devotion, Desire Drive Youths to 'Martyrdom.'" *USA Today.* Available at http://www.usatoday.com/news/world/june01/2001-06-26-suicide-usat.htm, July 5, 2001.

Kelway-Bamber, L., ed. *Claude's Book.* Introduction by Sir. Oliver Lodge. Facsimile. New York: 1919. Available at http://www.harvestfields.netfirms.com/Pdf/47/00.htm or (accessed April 26, 2004).

Kerkhof, J. F. M. "End-of-Life Decisions in the Netherlands, 1990–2001." *Crisis: The Journal of Crisis Intervention and Suicide Prevention,* Vol. 25(3), 2004.

Khosrokhavar, Farhad. *Suicide Bombers: Allah's New Martyrs.* London: Pluto Press, 2005.

Klimo, Jon. *Channeling: Investigations on Receiving Information from Paranormal Sources,* revised and updated. Berkeley: North Atlantic Books, 1998.

Knight, Ralph. *Learning to Talk to the World Beyond: An Introduction to the Joy of Immortality.* Harrisburg, Pa.: Stackpole Books, 1969.

Kubis, Pat, and Mark Macy. *Conversations Beyond the Light.* Boulder, Colo.: Griffin Publishing, in conjunction with Continuing Life Research, 1995.

Kupchisky, Roman. "Smart Bombs with Souls." *Organized Crime and Terrorism Watch,* Vol. 3(13), April 17, 2003: 1.

Kury, Zaher. *From a Gun to a Flower.* Castro Valley, Calif.: Unity Press, 1985. Available at http://www.zaher.com (accessed April 28, 2004).

Lair, George S. *Counseling the Terminally Ill: Sharing the Journey.* Washington, D.C.: Taylor & Francis, 1996.

Lazaris. *Lazaris Interviews Book II.* Introduction by Jach Pursel. Beverly Hills: Synergy Publishing, 1988.

Leadbeater, Charles Webster. *The Astral Plane: Its Scenery, Inhabitants, and Phenomena*. A facsimile of the 3rd edition, revised. London: William Byles & Sons, 1900. Available at http://www.spiritwritings.com/leadbeaterastral.pdf (accessed April 29, 2004).

LeBaron Jr., Garn. "The Ethics of Euthanasia. Rethinking the Ethic: A Possible Solution," available at http://www.quantonics.com/the_ethics_of_Euthanasia_by_Gran_Lebaron.html (accessed November 18, 2005).

Lees, Robert James. *The Life Elysian: Being More Leaves from the Autobiography of a Soul in Paradise*. Leicester, United Kingdom: Eva Lees, 1905.

Lewis, Bernard. *The Crisis of Islam: Holy War and Unholy Terror*. New York: The Modern Library, 2003.

Licauco, Jaime T. "Why Some People Commit Suicide." *Philippine Daily Inquirer*, December 2, 2003.

Loder, Nora M. *Afterlife Communications*. 1917. 2nd edition. Valencia, Calif.: Delta Lithograph Company, 1978.

Lodge, Sir Oliver J. *Raymond or Life and Death: With Examples of the Evidence for Survival of Memory and Affection After Death*. New York: George H. Doran Company, 1916.

Loehr, Franklin, ed. *Death with Understanding*. Grand Island, Fla.: Religious Research Press, 1987.

Loehr, Franklin. *Diary After Death*. 2nd edition. Grand Island, Fla.: Religious Research Press, 1986.

Lucas, Winifred Blake. *Regression Therapy: A Handbook for Professionals*, Volume 1: Past-Life Therapy. Crest Park, Calif.: Deep Forest Press, 1993.

Maiese, Michelle. *Suicide Bombers*, available at http://www.beyondintractability.org/m/suicide_bombers.jsp (accessed October 10, 2005).

Malmquist, Carl P. *Homicide: A Psychiatric Perspective*. Washington, D.C.: American Psychiatric Press, Inc., 2005.

Maltsberger, John T. "Grandiose Fury: Letter Across the Pacific." *Crisis: The Journal of Crisis Intervention and Suicide Prevention* Vol. 22(4), 2001: 144–145.

Maltsberger, John T. "Letters Across the Pacific: The Conscience of Martyrs." *Crisis: The Journal of Crisis Intervention and Suicide Prevention* Vol. 25(2), 2004: 88–90.

Margalit, Avishai. "The Suicide Bombers." *The New York Review of Books*, Vol. 50(1), January 16, 2003.

Marshall, Jean. *The River of Light: Teachings of Gwyneth the Lifegiver*. London: Regency Press, 1970.

Martin, Joel, and Patricia Romanowski. *Love Beyond Life: The Healing Power of After-Death Communications*. New York: HarperCollins Publishers, 1997.

Martin, Joel, and Patricia Romanowski. *We Are Not Forgotten: George Anderson's Messages of Love and Hope from the Other Side*. New York: Berkley Books, 1992.

Martin, Joel, and Patricia Romanowski. *We Don't Die: George Anderson's Conversations with the Other Side*. New York: Berkley Books, 1989.

Mateu, Lysa. *Conversations with the Spirit World: Souls Who Have Ended Their Lives Speak from Above*. Los Angeles: Channeling Spirits Books, 2000.

Mateu, Lysa. *Psychic Diaries: Connecting with Who You Are, Why You're Here, and What Lies Beyond*. New York: HarperEntertainment, 2003.

Meek, George W. *After We Die, What Then?* Franklin, N.C.: Metascience Corporation, 1980.

Merrill, William, ed. and comp. *Messages from Beyond: Moses/Glenn—Vol. 1.* Beaverton, Ore.: Deer Publishing Co., 1993.

Mertz, Lisa Ann, and Lorin W. Smith. "Where Children Are Crying: A Shaman's Work in the Afterlife," in *What Survives? Contemporary Explorations of Life After Death,* edited by Gary Doore, 233–240. New York: G. P. Putnam's Sons, 1990.

Miles, Matthew, and Michael Huberman. *Qualitative Data Analysis: An Annotated Sourcebook.* Thousand Oaks, Calif.: Sage Publications, 1994.

Moen, Bruce. *Voyages into the Unknown.* Charlottesville, Va.: Hampton Roads Publishing Company, Inc., 1997.

Montgomery, Ruth. *A World Beyond: A Startling Message from the Eminent Psychic Arthur Ford from Beyond the Grave.* New York: Coward, McCann and Geoghegan, Inc., 1971.

Montgomery, Ruth, and Joanne Garland. *Ruth Montgomery: Herald of the New Age.* New York: Fawcett Crest, 1986.

Moody, Raymond A. *Life After Life.* Reprint. New York: Bantam Books, 1977.

Moody, Raymond, and Paul Perry. *Reunions: Visionary Encounters with Departed Loved Ones.* New York: Ballantine Books, 1994.

Moore, Molly, and John Ward Anderson. "Suicide Bombers Change Mideast's Military Balance." *Washington Post Foreign Service,* Sunday, 18 August 2002, sec. 1, p. 1.

Moore, W. Usborne. *Glimpses of the Next State.* Facsimile. London: Watts and Co., 1911. Available at http://www.snu.org.uk/fb_14.pdf (accessed April 28, 2004).

Moore, W. Usborne. *The Voices: A Sequel to "Glimpses of the Next State."* Facsimile. London: Watts and Co., 1913. Available at http://www.spiritwritings.com/library.html (accessed May 1, 2004).

Moses, W. Stainton. *Spirit-Identity.* Facsimile. London: 1902. Available at http://www.spiritwritings.com/SpiritIdentity.pdf (accessed April 29, 2004).

Moses, W. Stainton. *Spirit Teachings.* 1949. 5th imprint. London: Spiritualist Press, 1976.

Mossman, Tam, ed. *Answers from a Grander Self.* Cave Creek, Ariz.: Tiger Maple Press, 1993.

Motoyama, Hiroshi. *Karma and Reincarnation.* Edited and translated by Rande Brown Ouchi. New York: Avon Books, 1992.

Myers, F. W. H. *Human Personality and Its Survival of Bodily Death.* Edited by Susy Smith. New Hyde Park, N.Y.: University Books, Inc., 1961.

Newton, Michael. *Destiny of Souls: New Case Studies of Life Between Lives.* St. Paul, Minn.: Llewellyn Publications, 2002.

Newton, Michael. *Journey of Souls: Case Studies of Life Between Lives,* 5th revised edition. St. Paul, Minn.: Llewellyn Publications, 1999.

Nicholi, Armand M., Jr, ed. *The Harvard Guide to Psychiatry,* 3rd edition. Cambridge: The Belknap Press of Harvard University, 1999.

Nickell, Molli, ed. "Dr. Peebles on Karma." *Spirit Speaks,* Vol. 1, 1985: 21–25.

Northrop, Suzane. *Second Chance: Healing Messages from the Afterlife.* Foreword by John Edward. San Diego: Jodere Group, 2002.

Oksuz, Adil. "Murder and Its Pursuit in the Qur'an and the Torah," in *Terror and Suicide Attacks: An Islamic Perspective,* edited by Ergun Capan, 131–149. Somerset, N.J.: The Light, Inc., 2004.

REFERENCES

Padgett, James E. *True Gospel Revealed Anew by Jesus,* Vol. 2, 3rd edition. Washington, D. C.: Church of the New Birth, 1965. Original title *Messages from Jesus and Celestials.*

Padgett, James E. *True Gospel Revealed Anew by Jesus,* Vol. 4. Washington, D. C.: Church of the New Birth, 1972.

Padgett, James E. *What Happens After You Die.* Compiled and introduced by David R. Lampron, edited by Michael A. Nedbal and Arthur Finmann. Santa Clarita, Calif.: FCDT Publishing, 2003.

Pape, Robert A. *Dying to Win: The Strategic Logic of Suicide Terrorism.* New York: Random House, 2005.

Peck, M. Scott. "Healing Human Evil," in *Meeting the Shadow: The Hidden Power of the Dark Side of Human Nature,* edited by Jeremiah Abrams and Connie Zweig, 176–180. New York: Jeremy P. Tarcher/G. P. Putnam's Sons, 1991.

Pelley, William Dudley. *Why I Believe the Dead Are Alive!* Noblesville, Ind.: Fellowship Press, Inc, 1972.

Phillips, M. R., X. Li, and Y. Zhang. "Suicide Rates in China: 1995–99." *Lancet,* Vol. 359 (9309), March 9, 2002: 835–840. Available at http://www.ncbi.nlm.nih.gov/entrez/query.fcgi?cmd=Retrieve&db=PubMed&list_uids=11897283&dopt=Abstract.

Phillips, P. I. *Here and There: More Psychic Experiences.* London: Corgi Books, 1975.

Philps, Alan. "New Assassins Queue Eagerly for Martyrdom." *Daily Telegraph.* Available at http://portal.telegraph.co.uk/news/main.jhtml?xml=/news/2001/09/13/wsuic13.xml, September 13, 2001.

Pike, James, and Diane Kennedy. *The Other Side: An Account of My Experiences with Psychic Phenomena.* Garden City, N.Y.: Doubleday and Company, Inc., 1968.

Pipes, Daniel. "The Jihad Menace." *Jerusalem Post.* Available at http://www.apologeticsindex.org/s37.html, July 30, 2001.

Puryear, Anne. *Stephen Lives! His Life, Suicide, and Afterlife.* Scottsdale, Ariz.: New Paradigm Press, 1993.

Putnam, Allen, comp. *Flashes of Light from the Spirit-Land, through the Mediumship of Mrs. J. H. Conant.* Facsimile. Boston: William White and Company, 1872. Available at http://www.hti.umich.edu/m/moa (accessed April 26, 2004).

"Questions and Answers." *Metapsychology: The Journal of Discarnate Intelligence,* Vol. 1(2), Summer 1985: 49–52.

Qur'an 4:29–30. Available at http://Islam.about.com/currentevents/a/suicide.

Raudive, Konstantin. *An Amazing Experiment in Electronic Communication with the Dead.* Translated by Nadia Fowler, edited by Joyce Morton, with a preface by Peter Bander. New York: Lancer Books, 1971.

Reppel, Erica. "The Journey Home." *Connecting Link,* Vol. 21, 1993: 16–19.

Reuter, Christoph. *My Life Is a Weapon: A Modern History of Suicide Bombing.* Princeton: Princeton University Press, 2004.

Richelieu, Peter. *A Soul's Journey.* Reprint. Wellingborough, Northamptonshire: Turnstone Press Limited, 1985.

Ring, Kenneth. *Heading Toward Omega: In Search of the Meaning of the Near-Death Experience.* New York: William Morrow & Co., 1984, 1985.

Ring, Kenneth. *Life At Death: A Scientific Investigation of the Near-Death Experience.* New York: Coward, McCann and Geoghegan, 1980.

Rinpoche, Sogyal. *The Tibetan Book of Living and Dying.* Edited by Patrick Gaffney and Andrew Harvey. San Francisco: HarperSanFrancisco, 1992.

Rinpoche, Sogyal. "What Survives? The Teachings of Tibetan Buddhism," in *What Survives? Contemporary Explorations of Life After Death,* edited by Gary Doore, 192–203. New York: G. P. Putnam's Sons, 1990.

Roberts, Jane. *The Afterdeath Journal of an American Philosopher: The World View of William James.* Englewood Cliffs: Prentice-Hall, Inc., 1978.

Roerich, Helena. *Letters of Helena Roerich: 1935–1939,* Volume 2. 1967. Reprint. New York: Agni Yogi Society, Inc., 1981. Available at http://www.agniyoga.org/ay_loHR2.html (originally published in Russian in 1940).

Roosevelt, Margot. "Choosing Their Time." *Time,* Vol. 165, Issue 14, April 4, 2005.

Rose, Jacqueline Rose. "Deadly Embrace." Available at: http:www.lrb.co.uk/v26/n21/print/rose01_.html, p.5 (accessed October 4, 2005).

Schwartz, Gary E., and William L. Simon. *The Afterlife Experiments: Breakthrough Scientific Evidence of Life After Death.* New York: Pocket Books, 2002.

Sechrist, Elsie R. *Death Does Not Part Us.* Virginia Beach, Va.: A.R.E. Press, 1992.

Sherwood, Jane. *Post-Mortem Journal: Communications from T. E. Lawrence.* Saffron Walden, Essex: The C. W. Daniel Company Limited, 1991.

Shneidman, E. S. *Comprehending Suicide: Landmarks in 20th Century Suicidology.* Washington, D.C.: American Psychological Association, 2001.

Shneidman, E. S. Contribution. *The Encyclopedia of Psychology,* 2nd edition, Vol. 3. edited by Raymond J. Corsini, 488–490. New York: Wiley-Interscience/John Wiley & Sons, 1994.

Smith, Suzy. *The Book of James: Conversations from Beyond.* New York: G. P. Putnam's Sons, 1974.

Stern, Jessica. *Terror in the Name of God.* New York: HarperCollins, 2003.

Stevens, Ramón. *Spirit Wisdom: Living Consciously in an Age of Turmoil and Transformation.* Ojai, Calif.: Pepperwood Press, 1995.

Stevenson, Ian. *Cases of the Reincarnation Type: Volume III Twelve Cases in Lebanon and Turkey.* Charlottesville: University Press of Virginia, 1980.

Stevenson, Ian. *Children Who Remember Previous Lives: A Question of Reincarnation.* Charlottesville: University Press of Virginia, 1987.

Stincelli, Rebecca. Website: http://www.suicidebycop.com (accessed Nov. 8, 2005).

Strauss, Anselm, and Janet Corbin. *Basics of Qualitative Research: Techniques and Procedures for Developing Grounded Theory,* Second Edition. Thousand Oaks, Calif.: Sage Publications, 1998.

Sullivan, Eileen. *Arthur Ford Speaks from Beyond.* Chicago: J. Philip O'Hara, Inc., 1975.

Swain, Jasper. *From My World to Yours: A Young Man's Account of the Afterlife.* New York: Walker and Company, 1977.

Swedenborg, Emanuel. *Heaven and Hell.* 1758. Translated by George F. Dole. West Chester, Pa.: Swedenborg Foundation, Inc., 2000.

Taylor, Ruth Mattson, ed. *Evidence from Beyond: An Insider's Guide to the Wonders of Heaven—and Life in the New Millennium.* Brooklyn: Brett Books, Inc., 1999.

Tremaine, Kit. *The Butterfly Rises: One Woman's Transformation through the Trance Channeling of Verna V. Yater, Ph.D., Kevin Ryerson and Others.* Nevada City, Calif.: Blue Dolphin Publishing, 1987.

Tribbe, Frank C., comp and ed. *An Arthur Ford Anthology: Writings By and About America's Sensitive of the Century.* Nevada City, Calif.: Blue Dolphin Publishing, Inc., 1999.

Twigg, Ena, and Ruth Hagy Brod. *Ena Twigg: Medium.* New York: Hawthorn Books, Inc., 1972.

Van Hulle, J. P. *Michael Educational Foundation Newsletter,* Vol. 1(9), September 2001. Available at http://www.mef.to/html/l_newletters.html#.

Van Praagh, James. *Talking to Heaven: A Medium's Message of Life After Death.* New York: Signet, 1999.

Viney, George. *Surviving Death.* New York: St. Martin's Press, 1993.

Walker, Jeanne. *Always, Karen.* New York: Hawthorn Books, Inc., 1975.

Wasserman, Danuta, ed. *Suicide: An Unnecessary Death.* London: Martin Dunitz, 2001.

Webster's Third New International Dictionary. Unabridged. Springfield, Mass.: G. & C. Merriam Co. Publishers, 1976.

White, Ruth, and Mary Swainson. *Gildas Communicates: The Story and the Scripts.* 1971. Reprint. Saffron Walden, Essex: The C. W. Daniel Company Limited, 1986.

White, Stewart Edward. *The Stars Are Still There.* A facsimile of the 1st edition. New York: E. P. Dutton & Co., 1946. Available at http://www.spiritwritings.com/StarsAreStillThere.pdf (accessed April 29, 2004).

White, Stewart Edward. *The Unobstructed Universe.* New York: E. P. Dutton & Co., 1940.

White, Stewart Edward. *With Folded Wings.* New York: E. P. Dutton & Co., 1947.

Whitton, Joel L., and Joe Fisher. *Life Between Life: Scientific Explorations into the Void Separating One Incarnation from the Next.* New York: Warner Books, 1986.

Wickland, Carl A. *The Gateway of Understanding.* A facsimile of the 6th edition. Los Angeles: National Psychological Institute, 1934. Available at http://www.spiritwritings.com (accessed April 28, 2004).

Wickland, Carl A. *Thirty Years Among the Dead.* Hollywood: Newcastle Publishing Company, Inc., 1974.

Wolcott, Harry. *Writing Up Qualitative Research.* Thousand Oaks, Calif.: Sage Publications, 1990.

Yalom, Irvin D. *Existential Psychotherapy.* New York: Basic Books, 1980.

Yarbro, Chelsea Quinn. *Messages from Michael.* New York: Playboy Paperbacks, 1981.

Yarbro, Chelsea Quinn. *More Messages from Michael.* New York: Berkley Books, 1986.

Yuceoglu, Hikmet. "Martyrdom—A Definition: Can a Terrorist be a Martyr?," in *Terror and Suicide Attacks: An Islamic Perspective,* edited by Ergun Capan, 86–100. Somerset, N.J.: The Light, Inc., 2004.

Zakaria, Fareed. "How to Stop the Contagion." *Newsweek,* Vol. 146(5), August 1, 2005.

Zedalis, Debra D. *Female Suicide Bombers.* Honolulu, Hawaii: University Press of the Pacific, 2004.

Notes

INTRODUCTION

1. *Webster's Third New International Dictionary,* 1233.
2. Schwartz and Simon, *The Afterlife Experiments,* 241.
3. Ibid.
4. Ibid., 242.
5. Ibid., 243.
6. *Webster's Third New International Dictionary,* 212.
7. Ibid.
8. LeBaron Jr., Garn. "The Ethics of Euthanasia. Rethinking the Ethic: A Possible Solution."
9. Klimo, *Channeling: Investigations on Receiving Information from Paranormal Sources.*
10. Ibid. Material throughout this section is based on Klimo's book.
11. Ibid., 345–352.
12. Ibid., 121–133. All other material throughout this section is also based on Klimo's book.
13. Schwartz and Simon, op. cit., 258.
14. Ibid., 268.
15. Ibid., 267.
16. Ibid., 332.
17. Roberts, *The Afterdeath Journal of an American Philosopher,* 132.

PART I – TRADITIONAL AND ASSISTED SUICIDE

I – OVERVIEW OF TRADITIONAL SUICIDE

1. Jamison, *Night Falls Fast: Understanding Suicide,* 24.
2. Choron, *Suicide,* 12–14.
3. Ibid., 18.
4. Ibid., 17.
5. Durkheim, *Suicide: A Study in Sociology.*
6. Ibid., 315 (in e-book, http://site.ebrary.com; in original edition, 263).
7. Corsini, *The Encyclopedia of Psychology,* 488.
8. Choron, op. cit., 25.
9. Corsini, op. cit., 489.

10. Choron, op. cit.
11. Corsini, op. cit., 488.
12. Ibid.
13. Ibid., 490.
14. Jamison, op. cit.
15. National Center for Health Statistics website at http://www.cdc.gov/nchs/fastats/suicide.htm (accessed August 4, 2005).
16. The University of Oxford Centre for Suicide Research website at http://cebmh.warne.ox.ac.uk/csr/profile.html (accessed December 12, 2005).
17. From website http://www.bullyonline.org/stress/suicide.htm (accessed December 12, 2005).
18. From website http://www.bullyonline.org/stress/suicide.htm (accessed December 12, 2005).
19. From Phillips et al., "Suicide Rates in China," 835. Available at: http://www.ncbi.nlm.nih.gov/entrez/query.fcgi?cmd=Retrieve&db=PubMed&list_uids=11897283&dopt=Abstract (accessed December 12, 2005).
20. Nicholi, ed., *The Harvard Guide to Psychiatry*, 713.
21. Bertolote, "Suicide in the World: An Epidemiological Overview 1950–1995."
22. Nicholi, op. cit., 623.
23. Ibid.
24. Jamison, op. cit., 272–273.
25. Ibid., 91–92.
26. Corsini, op. cit., 490.
27. Jamison, op. cit.
28. Ibid., 276.
29. Brottman, "Kurt Cobain," 61.
30. From website: http://www.owlnet.rice.edu/~reli291/jonestown/jonestown.html.
31. Shneidman, *Comprehending Suicide: Landmarks in 20th-Century Suicidology*.
32. Buda, "Comprehending Suicide: Landmarks in 20th-Century Suicidology" (a book review), 70.
33. Bongar, *The Suicidal Patient: Clinical and Legal Standards of Care*, 11.
34. Ibid., 14.
35. Cornette, "Toward an Integrated Theory of Suicidal Behavior: Merging the Hopelessness, Self-Discrepancy, and Escape Theories," 44.
36. Ibid., 46–47.
37. All quotes in this paragraph are from Cornette, ibid., 49–50.
38. Bronisch, "Depression and Suicidal Behavior," 179.
39. All quotes in this paragraph are from Bronisch, ibid., 179–180.
40. Bongar, *The Suicide Patient: Clinical and Legal Standards*, 13.
41. Ibid., 15.
42. Corsini, op. cit., 489.
43. Bongar, op. cit., 15.

44. Corsini, op. cit., 489.
45. Cassem in Nicholi, ed., *The Harvard Guide to Psychiatry*, 713.
46. Ibid.
47. Ibid., 714.
48. Corsini, op. cit., 489.
49. Bhugra, "Sati: A Type of Nonpsychiatric Suicide," 73–77.
50. Ibid.
51. From website: http://en.wikipedia.org/wiki/seppuka#well-known_people_who_committed_seppuka.
52. Ibid.
53. Ibid.
54. Heckler, *Waking Up, Alive: The Descent, the Suicide Attempt, and the Return to Life*, 2.
55. Ibid., 27.
56. Ibid., 39.
57. Ibid., 47.
58. Ibid., 49.
59. Ibid., 61.
60. Ibid., 65.
61. Ibid., 102.
62. Ibid., 39.
63. Ibid., 93.
64. Ibid., 97.
65. Ibid., 105.
66. Ibid., 107.
67. Ibid., 12.
68. Ibid., 5.
69. Ibid., 167–168.
70. Ibid., 170.
71. Moody, *Life After Life*; Ring, *Life at Death: A Scientific Investigation of the Near-Death Experience*.
72. Greyson, "Wish for Death, Wish for Life: The NDE and Suicide Attempts," 5. (Note: page numbers here for Greyson refer to page numbers in the unpublished manuscript of the English translation provided to Klimo by Greyson in September 2005.)
73. Ring, *Heading Toward Omega: In Search of the Meaning of the Near-Death Experience*, 99–100.
74. Greyson, op. cit., 3.
75. Ibid., 4, 6–7.
76. Ibid., 7–8.
77. Ibid., 8–9.
78. Ibid., 10.
79. Cassem quoting Weissman in Nicholi, ed., *The Harvard Guide to Psychiatry*, 705.
80. Cassem in Nicholi, ibid., 714.

NOTES

81. Ibid.
82. Ibid., 705.
83. Beck et al., *Cognitive Therapy of Depression;* Ellis, *Reason and Emotion in Psychotherapy.*
84. All quotes in this paragraph are from Cassem, in Nicholi, op. cit., 715.
85. Ibid.
86. Shneidman in Corsini, op. cit., 491.
87. Cassem in Nicholi, op. cit., 705.
88. Shneidman in Corsini, op. cit., 488.
89. Choron, op. cit., 145.
90. Yalom, *Existential Psychotherapy,* 33.
91. Ibid., 465.
92. Ibid., 33–34.
93. Moody, op. cit.; Ring, op. cit.
94. Yalom, op. cit., 333.
95. Ibid., 41.
96. Ibid., 122.
97. Ibid., 375–376.
98. Ibid., 465.
99. Ibid.
100. Lair, *Counseling the Terminally Ill: Sharing the Journey,* 78.
101. Ibid.
102. Ibid., 78–79.
103. Hillman, *Suicide and the Soul,* 73.
104. Ibid., 63–64.
105. Ibid., 63.
106. Ibid., 71.
107. Ibid., 75.
108. Rinpoche, "What Survives? The Teachings of Tibetan Buddhism," 198.
109. Dass, "Thoughts at the Moment of Death," 160–161.
110. Rinpoche, *The Tibetan Book of Living and Dying,* 301–302.
111. Mertz and Smith, "Where Children Are Crying: A Shaman's Work in the Afterlife," 235.
112. Jamison, op. cit.
113. Viney, *Surviving Death,* 27.
114. Blavatsky, *Isis Unveiled,* Volume 1, 344.
115. Erlendur Haraldsson, e-mail message to author, July 8, 2004.
116. Edward, *One Last Time: A Psychic Medium Speaks to Those We Have Loved and Lost,* 152–153.
117. Kate Anders, e-mail message to author, January 25, 2004.
118. Darby and Joan, *Our Unseen Guest,* 8–9.
119. Austen, ed., *The Teachings of Silver Birch: Wisdom from the World Beyond.*

120. Edward, op. cit., 51–52.
121. Ibid., 84.
122. Puryear, *Stephen Lives! His Life, Suicide, and Afterlife*, 316.
123. Gauld, *Mediumship and Survival: A Century of Investigations.*
124. A planchette is a small, movable platform that, on its own or under the fingertips of a human operator who acts as an unconscious medium, slides around a Ouija board type surface, spelling out messages ostensibly from the spirit world.
125. Ibid., 76.
126. Moses, *Spirit-Identity*, 104–105.
127. Noreen Renier, e-mail message to author, February 19, 2004.
128. Edmonds and Dexter, *Spiritualism*, 208.
129. Austen, op. cit., 132.
130. Buckley, *Conversations with the Beyond*, 10.
131. Hoodwin, *The Journey of Your Soul: A Channel Explores Channeling and the Michael Teachings*, 47.
132. Edmonds and Dexter, op. cit., 170.

2 – GENERAL SPIRIT ATTITUDES TOWARD SUICIDE

1. Edmonds and Dexter, *Spiritualism*, 123.
2. Ibid., 124.
3. Montgomery, *A World Beyond: A Startling Message from the Eminent Psychic Arthur Ford from Beyond the Grave*, 43–44.
4. Kardec, *The Spirits' Book*, 405.
5. Padgett, *What Happens After You Die*, 9.
6. White, *The Unobstructed Universe*, 238–239.
7. Moses, *Spirit Teachings*, 271–272.
8. Loder, *Afterlife Communications*, 65.
9. Curtis, *Rustlings in the Golden City.*
10. Ibid., 139.
11. Austin, ed., *The Teachings of Silver Birch: Wisdom from the World Beyond*, 185.
12. Ibid., 113.
13. Ibid., 111.
14. Montgomery, op. cit., 43.
15. Marshall, *The River of Light: Teachings of Gwyneth the Lifegiver*, 21.
16. Besant, *Death—And After?*, 99–100.
17. Kardec, op. cit.
18. Ibid., 380.
19. White and Swainson, *Gildas Communicates: The Story and the Scripts*, 131.
20. "Questions and Answers," 50.
21. Kardec, op. cit., 187.
22. Jones, *Four Spirit Teachers: Trance Talks*, chapter 13.

NOTES

23. Cooke, *More Answers*, 134.
24. Ibid., 28.
25. Ibid.
26. Ibid., 28–29.
27. Leadbeater, *The Astral Plane: Its Scenery, Inhabitants, and Phenomena*, 57.
28. Kardec, op. cit., 194.
29. Ibid., 378.
30. Jones, op. cit., chapter 14.
31. Besant, op. cit., 44.
32. Putnam, *Flashes of Light from the Spirit-Land, through the Mediumship of Mrs. J. H. Conant*, 64.
33. Ibid., 121.
34. Kardec, op. cit., 378–382.
35. Loehr, *Diary After Death*.
36. Ibid., 29–30.
37. Walker, *Always, Karen*.
38. Ibid., 95.
39. Ibid.
40. Ibid., 149.
41. "Questions and Answers," op. cit., 51–52.
42. Tremaine, *The Butterfly Rises: One Woman's Transformation through the Trance Channeling of Verna V. Yater, Ph.D., Kevin Ryerson and Others*, 49–50.
43. Sherwood, *Post-Mortem Journal: Communications from T. E. Lawrence*.
44. Loehr, ed., *Death with Understanding*, 250–251.
45. From interview session conducted by phone July 12, 2004 with medium Lauren Thibodeau.
46. Ibid.
47. Fanning, "The Awakening of Mankind," 27.
48. From interview session conducted by phone July 12, 2004 with medium Lauren Thibodeau.
49. Northrop, *Second Chance: Healing Messages from the Afterlife*, 130.
50. Anderson and Barone, *Walking in the Garden of Souls: George Anderson's Advice from the Hereafter for Living in the Here and Now*, 251–252.
51. Bentley, *Far Horizon: A Biography of Hester Dowden, Medium and Psychic Investigator*.
52. Ibid., 110.
53. Deane, *Voyagers: Secrets of Amenti*, 42.
54. Yarbro, *Messages from Michael*, 194.
55. Stevens, *Spirit Wisdom: Living Consciously in an Age of Turmoil and Transformation*.
56. Ibid., 225.
57. Yarbro, op. cit., 161.
58. Ibid., 157.

3 – WHY PEOPLE KILL THEMSELVES

1. Puryear, *Stephen Lives! His Life, Suicide, and Afterlife*.
2. Ibid., 303.
3. Ibid., 311.
4. Yarbro, *Messages from Michael*, 193–194.
5. Northrop, *Second Chance: Healing Messages from the Afterlife*, 110.
6. Fanning, "The Awakening of Mankind."
7. Newton, *Destiny of Souls: New Case Studies of Life between Lives*, 77.
8. From interview session conducted by phone July 12, 2004 with medium Lauren Thibodeau.
9. Ibid.
10. Ibid.
11. Barbanell, *When a Child Dies*, 28.
12. Moore, *The Voices*, 221.
13. Myers, *Human Personality and Its Survival of Bodily Death*, 234–235.
14. From interview session conducted by phone July 12, 2004 with medium Lauren Thibodeau.
15. Ibid.
16. Wickland, *Thirty Years Among the Dead*, 138.
17. Puryear, op. cit.
18. Ibid., 253.
19. Wickland, op. cit., 148.
20. Martin and Romanowski, *We Don't Die: George Anderson's Conversations with the Other Side*, 144.
21. Mateu, *Psychic Diaries: Connecting with Who You Are, Why You're Here, and What Lies Beyond*, 175.
22. Ibid., 179.
23. Anderson and Barone, *Lessons from the Light: Extraordinary Messages of Comfort and Hope from the Other Side*, 100.
24. Ibid., 139.
25. Twigg and Brod, *Ena Twigg: Medium*, 125.
26. Ford, *Unknown but Known: My Adventure into the Meditative Dimension*, 67–68.
27. Montgomery and Garland, *Ruth Montgomery: Herald of the New Age*, 10.
28. Van Praagh, *Talking to Heaven: A Medium's Message of Life After Death*, 175.
29. Smith, *The Book of James: Conversations from Beyond*.
30. Mateu, *Conversations with the Spirit World: Souls Who Have Ended Their Lives Speak from Above*, 87.
31. Ibid., 12.
32. Martin and Romanowski, *We Are Not Forgotten: George Anderson's Messages of Love and Hope from the Other Side*, 72–73.
33. Anderson and Barone, op. cit., 15.
34. Foster, *Epilogue: Souls Review Their Lives After Death*, 101.

35. Ibid.
36. Ibid., 103.
37. Crawford, *Parting Notes: A Connection with the Afterlife*, 205–206.
38. Lucas, *Regression Therapy: A Handbook for Professionals*, 96.
39. Northrop, op. cit., 121.
40. Martin and Romanowski, *We Are Not Forgotten*, 129–130.
41. Padgett, *What Happens After You Die*.
42. Ibid., 305.
43. Moore, *Glimpses of the Next State*, 150.
44. Foster, op. cit., 112.
45. Ballou, *OAHSPE: A New Bible in the Words of Jehovih and his Angel Ambassadors*, 137–138.
46. Moses, *Spirit Teachings*, 273.
47. Wickland, op. cit., 132.
48. Ibid., 135.
49. Wickland, *The Gateway of Understanding*.
50. Ibid., 29.
51. Ibid., 103–105.
52. Motoyama, *Karma and Reincarnation*, 76.
53. Chino and Kyoto Group, *Sermes: The Poems of the Angels*, 27.
54. Licauco, "Why Some People Commit Suicide."
55. Ibid.
56. Auerbach, personal communication, 2000.
57. Atwater, *The Complete Idiot's Guide to Near-Death Experiences*.
58. Ibid.
59. Atwater, *The New Children and Near-Death Experiences*.
60. Ibid., 70.
61. Ibid.
62. Ibid.
63. Ibid., 88.
64. White and Swainson, *Gildas Communicates: The Story and the Scripts*, 131–132.
65. From interview session conducted by phone July 12, 2004 with medium Lauren Thibodeau.

4 – TRANSITIONING TO THE AFTERLIFE

1. White, *With Folded Wings*.
2. Jones, *Four Spirit Teachers: Trance Talks*.
3. Northrop, *Second Chance: Healing Messages from the Afterlife*, 141–142.
4. Loehr, *Death with Understanding*.
5. From interview session conducted by phone July 12, 2004 with medium Johanna Carroll.
6. Ibid.

7. Rinpoche, *The Tibetan Book of Living and Dying,* 245.
8. Ibid., 252.
9. From interview session conducted by phone July 12, 2004 with medium Lauren Thibodeau.
10. Kardec, *The Spirits' Book,* 116.
11. Ibid., 159.
12. From interview session conducted by phone July 12, 2004 with medium Johanna Carroll.
13. Kubis and Macy, *Conversations Beyond the Light,* 98.
14. Martin and Romanowski, *We Are Not Forgotten: George Anderson's Messages of Love and Hope from the Other Side.*
15. Twigg and Brod, *Ena Twigg: Medium,* 125.
16. Martin and Romanowski, *We Don't Die: George Anderson's Conversations with the Other Side.*
17. Ibid., 241.
18. Jacobson, *Life Without Death? On Parapsychology, Mysticism, and the Question of Survival.*
19. Ibid., 279.
20. Ibid.
21. Swedenborg, *Heaven and Hell,* 440.
22. Ibid., 413–414.
23. Padgett, *True Gospel Revealed Anew by Jesus,* Vol. 2, 284–285.
24. Ibid., 285.
25. Roerich, *Letters of Helena Roerich: 1935–1939,* letter 17.
26. Ibid.
27. Leadbeater, *The Astral Plane: Its Scenery, Inhabitants, and Phenomena,* 55.
28. Northrop, op. cit., 147–148.
29. Sechrist, *Death Does Not Part Us.*
30. Ibid., 211.
31. Meek, *After We Die, What Then?,* 132.
32. Grey, *Return from Death: An Exploration of the Near-Death Experience.*
33. Ibid., 65–66.
34. Ibid., 68–69.
35. Ibid., 71.

5 – AFTERLIFE EXPERIENCES

1. Crookall, *The Supreme Adventure: Analysis of Psychic Communications.*
2. Wickland, *Thirty Years Among the Dead.*
3. Ford, *The Life Beyond Death: As Told to Jerome Ellison,* 112.
4. Van Praagh, *Talking to Heaven: A Medium's Message of Life After Death,* 170.
5. Puryear, *Stephen Lives! His Life, Suicide, and Afterlife.*
6. Ibid., 260.
7. Ibid., 263.

8. Mateu, *Conversations with the Spirit World: Souls Who Have Ended Their Lives Speak from Above*, 27.
9. Pike and Kennedy, *The Other Side: An Account of My Experiences with Psychic Phenomena*.
10. Ibid., 103–104.
11. Ibid., 115.
12. Ibid., 118.
13. Ford, op. cit., 106.
14. Grey, *Return from Death: An Exploration of the Near-Death Experience*, 47.
15. Delacour, *Glimpses of the Beyond: The Extraordinary Experiences of People Who Crossed the Brink of Death and Returned*, 125–126.
16. Whitton and Fisher, *Life Between Life: Scientific Explorations into the Void Separating One Incarnation from the Next*, 146–147.
17. Ibid., 147.
18. Pelley, *Why I Believe the Dead Are Alive!*, 212–213.
19. From interview session conducted by phone July 12, 2004 with medium Johanna Carroll.
20. Puryear, op. cit.
21. Ibid., 255.
22. Martin and Romanowski, *We Are Not Forgotten: George Anderson's Messages of Love and Hope from the Other Side*, 134.
23. Anderson and Barone, *Lessons from the Light: Extraordinary Messages of Comfort and Hope from the Other Side*, 137.
24. Ibid., 146.
25. Martin and Romanowski, *We Don't Die: George Anderson's Conversations with the Other Side*, 144.
26. Anderson and Barone, op. cit.
27. Foster, *Epilogue: Souls Review Their Lives After Death*, 112.
28. Ibid.
29. Loehr, *Diary After Death*, 17.
30. Puryear, op. cit., 240.
31. Darby and Joan, *Our Unseen Guest*, 236.
32. Foster, op. cit.
33. Ibid., 117.
34. Loehr, *Death with Understanding*, 143.
35. Puryear, op. cit., 240.
36. Wickland, op. cit., 135–136.
37. From interview session conducted by phone July 12, 2004 with medium Johanna Carroll.
38. From interview session conducted by phone July 12, 2004 with medium Lauren Thibodeau.
39. Abd ar-Rahim ibn Ahmad al-Qadi, *Islamic Book of the Dead: A Collection of Hadiths on the Fire and the Garden*, 50.

40. Atwater, *Beyond the Light: What Isn't Being Said About Near-Death Experience*, 11.
41. Mateu, op. cit., 25–26.
42. Swedenborg, *Heaven and Hell*, 351.
43. Moses, *Spirit Teachings*, 227–228.
44. Tribbe, comp. and ed., *An Arthur Ford Anthology: Writings By and About America's Sensitive of the Century*, 81.
45. Edward, *One Last Time: A Psychic Medium Speaks to Those We Have Loved and Lost*, 159.
46. Martin and Romanowski, *We Don't Die*, 242.
47. Martin and Romanowski, *We Are Not Forgotten*, 263.
48. Newton, *Destiny of Souls: New Case Studies of Life Between Lives*, 153.
49. Mateu, op. cit., 45.
50. Twigg and Brod, *Ena Twigg: Medium*, 125.
51. Foster, op. cit., 113.
52. Ibid., 115.
53. Ibid., 123.
54. Mateu, op. cit., 73.
55. Puryear, op. cit., 236.
56. From interview session conducted by phone July 12, 2004 with medium Lauren Thibodeau.
57. Ibid.
58. Ibid.
59. Newton, *Journey of Souls: Case Studies of Life Between Lives*, 57–58.

CHAPTER 6 — ADJUSTMENT PROBLEMS

1. Edward, *One Last Time: A Psychic Medium Speaks to Those We Have Loved and Lost*.
2. Puryear, *Stephen Lives! His Life, Suicide, and Afterlife*, 315.
3. Anderson and Barone, *Lessons from the Light: Extraordinary Messages of Comfort and Hope from the Other Side*, 152–153.
4. Ibid., 166–167.
5. Boulton and Boulton, *Psychic Beam to Beyond: Through the Psychic Sensitive Lenora Huett*, 98.
6. White, *The Stars Are Still There*, 44.
7. Wickland, *The Gateway of Understanding*, 100–101.
8. Foster, *Epilogue: Souls Review Their Lives After Death*, 102.
9. Ibid., 124.
10. Smith, *The Book of James: Conversations from Beyond*.
11. Ibid., 93.
12. Meek, *After We Die, What Then?*, 134.
13. Montgomery, *A World Beyond: A Startling Message from the Eminent Psychic Arthur Ford from Beyond the Grave*, 113.
14. Ford, *The Life Beyond Death: As Told to Jerome Ellison*, 112.

15. Ibid., 112–113.
16. Moen, *Voyages Into the Unknown*, 195.
17. Richelieu, *A Soul's Journey*, 143.
18. Loehr, *Diary After Death*, 28.
19. Abd ar-Rahim ibn Ahmad al-Qadi, *Islamic Book of the Dead: A Collection of Hadiths on the Fire and the Garden*, 137.
20. Loehr, op. cit., 51.
21. Puryear, op. cit., 240.
22. Ibid., 236.
23. Lees, *The Life Elysian: Being More Leaves from the Autobiography of a Soul in Paradise*, 65.
24. Ibid.
25. Kardec, *The Spirits' Book*, 119.
26. Motoyama, *Karma and Reincarnation*, 23–24.
27. Loehr, *Death with Understanding*, 145.
28. Wickland, *Thirty Years Among the Dead*, 135.
29. Mateu, *Conversations with the Spirit World: Souls Who Have Ended Their Lives Speak from Above*.
30. Licauco, "Why Some People Commit Suicide."
31. Ibid.
32. Loehr, *Diary After Death*, 28–29.
33. White, *With Folded Wings*, 228–229.
34. Wickland, *The Gateway of Understanding*, 33.
35. Dresser, *Life Here and Hereafter*, 222–223.
36. Sherwood, *Post-Mortem Journal: Communications from T. E. Lawrence*.
37. Ibid., 112.
38. Smith, op. cit.
39. Refers to a no longer physically living spirit who, rather than moving on with his or her new existence in the spiritual realm, remains attached or preoccupied with a particular earthly place, situation, or still physically alive person or people.
40. Ibid., 93.
41. Meek, op. cit., 134.
42. Loehr, *Diary After Death*.
43. Ibid., 51.
44. Richelieu, op. cit., 143.
45. Roerich, *Letters of Helena Roerich: 1935–1939*, letter 17.
46. Wickland, *The Gateway of Understanding*, 101.
47. Ibid., 30–32.
48. Ibid., 34.
49. Ibid.
50. Ibid., 40–41.

51. Leadbeater, *The Astral Plane: Its Scenery, Inhabitants, and Phenomena*, 57.
52. Ibid., 59.
53. Heath, *The PK Zone: A Cross-Cultural Review of Psychokinesis (PK)*.

7 – MOVING ON

1. Swedenborg, *Heaven and Hell*, 366.
2. Edmonds and Dexter, *Spiritualism*, 142–143.
3. Cahagnet, *The Celestial Telegraph; Or, Secrets of the Life to Come, Revealed through Magnetism*, Vol. 1, 55.
4. Bird, *The Transition, Explained: Earth Questions Spirit Answers*, 42.
5. Wickland, *Thirty Years Among the Dead*, 132.
6. Cummins, *Swan on a Black Sea: A Study in Automatic Writing: The Cummins-Willett Scripts*, 31.
7. Moses, *Spirit Teachings*, 274–275.
8. Chino and Kyoto Group, *Sermes: The Poems of the Angels*, 27.
9. Dresser, *Spirit World and Spirit Life*, 138.
10. Ibid., 226.
11. White, *The Stars Are Still There*, 42.
12. Anders, e-mail message to author, January 25, 2004.
13. From interview session conducted by phone July 12, 2004 with medium Lauren Thibodeau.
14. Taylor, ed., *Evidence from Beyond: An Insider's Guide to the Wonders of Heaven—and Life in the New Millennium*, 91.
15. Cahagnet, op. cit., Volume 2, 69–70.
16. Besant, *Death—And After?*, 96–97.
17. Ibid., 40.
18. Ibid., 42.
19. Loder, *Afterlife Communications*, 20.
20. Roerich, *Letters of Helena Roerich: 1935–1939*, letter 17.
21. Sherwood, *Post-Mortem Journal: Communications from T. E. Lawrence*, 112.
22. Van Praagh, *Talking to Heaven: A Medium's Message to Life After Death*, 180.
23. Ibid.
24. Northrop, *Second Chance: Healing Messages from the Afterlife*, 173.
25. Moody, *Life After Life*, 143.
26. From interview session conducted by phone July 12, 2004 with medium Lauren Thibodeau.
27. Moses, op. cit., 274.
28. Padgett, *What Happens After You Die*, 304.
29. Ibid.
30. Myers, *Human Personality and Its Survival of Bodily Death*, 327.
31. Crookall, *The Supreme Adventure: Analysis of Psychic Communications*, 241.
32. Licauco, "Why Some People Commit Suicide."

33. Motoyama, *Karma and Reincarnation*, 24.
34. Ibid., 69.
35. Anderson and Barone, *Walking in the Garden of Souls: George Anderson's Advice from the Hereafter for Living in the Here and Now*, 231.
36. Anderson and Barone, *Lessons from the Light: Extraordinary Messages of Comfort and Hope from the Other Side*, 113.
37. Ibid., 136.
38. Anderson and Barone, *Walking in the Garden of Souls*, 247.
39. Sechrist, *Death Does Not Part Us*, 227.
40. Ibid., 212.
41. Ibid., 213.
42. From interview session conducted by phone July 12, 2004 with medium Johanna Carroll.
43. Ibid.
44. Raudive, *An Amazing Experiment in Electronic Communication with the Dead*, 47.
45. Ibid., 51.
46. Ibid., 157.
47. Atwater, *We Live Forever: The Real Truth About Death*, 131–132.
48. Crookall, op. cit., 66.
49. Puryear, op. cit.
50. Ibid., 255–256.
51. Sherwood, op. cit., 111.
52. Tremaine, *The Butterfly Rises: One Woman's Transformation through the Trance Channeling of Verna V. Yater, Ph.D., Kevin Ryerson and Others.*
53. Ibid., 48.
54. Van Praagh, op. cit., 170–171.
55. Ibid., 177.
56. From interview session conducted by phone July 12, 2004 with medium Johanna Carroll.
57. Northrop, op. cit., 112.
58. Twigg and Brod, *Ena Twigg: Medium*, 126.
59. Tribbe, *An Arthur Ford Anthology: Writings By and About America's Sensitive of the Century*, 52–53.
60. Ibid., 55.
61. Martin and Romanowski, *We Don't Die: George Anderson's Conversations with the Other Side*, 242.
62. Foster, *Epilogue: Souls Review Their Lives After Death.*
63. Ibid., 119.
64. Ibid., 120–121.
65. Ibid., 130.
66. Edwards, *Life in Spirit*, 56.
67. Anderson and Barone, *Lessons from the Light*, 100.

68. Ibid., 101.
69. Ibid., 118.
70. Edward, *One Last Time: A Psychic Medium Speaks to Those We Have Loved and Lost*, 159.
71. Montgomery, *A World Beyond: A Startling Message from the Eminent Psychic Arthur Ford from Beyond the Grave*, 121.
72. Anderson and Barone, *Lessons from the Light*, 129.
73. Puryear, op. cit.
74. Anderson and Barone, *Lessons from the Light*, 102.
75. Foster, op. cit., 134.
76. Ibid., 127.
77. Puryear, op. cit.
78. Newton, *Destiny of Souls: New Case Studies of Life Between Lives*, 155.
79. Ibid., 157.
80. Loehr, ed., *Death with Understanding*.
81. Ibid., 43.
82. Ibid., 48.
83. Stevenson, *Children Who Remember Previous Lives: A Question of Reincarnation*.
84. Stevenson, *Cases of the Reincarnation Type*, 95–96.
85. Motoyama, op. cit., 19.
86. Ibid., 5–6.
87. Ibid., 99–100.
88. From interview session conducted by phone July 12, 2004 with medium Johanna Carroll.
89. Ibid.
90. From interview session conducted by phone July 12, 2004 with medium Lauren Thibodeau.
91. Haraldsson and Abu-Izzeddin, "Three Randomly Selected Cases of Lebanese Children Who Claim Memories of a Previous Life."
92. Ibid., 69.
93. Stevenson, Ian. *Children Who Remember Previous Lives*.
94. Ibid., 221.
95. Tucker, e-mail message to author, July 9, 2004.
96. Lucas, *Regression Therapy: A Handbook for Professionals*.
97. Ibid., 242–243.
98. Ibid., 374.
99. Newton, op. cit., 162.
100. Lucas, op. cit., 392.

8 – MESSAGES OF REGRET

1. Wickland, *Thirty Years Among the Dead*, 152.
2. Twigg and Brod, *Ena Twigg: Medium*, 126.

3. Richelieu, *A Soul's Journey,* 142–143.
4. Guggenheim and Guggenheim, *Hello from Heaven!.*
5. From interview session conducted by phone July 12, 2004 with medium Johanna Carroll.
6. Edward, *One Last Time: A Psychic Medium Speaks to Those We Have Loved and Lost,* 159.
7. Wickland, op. cit., 133.
8. Mateu, *Psychic Diaries: Connecting with Who You Are, Why You're Here, and What Lies Beyond,* 1–2.
9. Van Praagh, *Talking to Heaven: A Medium's Message of Life After Death,* 177–178.
10. Ibid., 178.
11. Ibid., 179–180.
12. Wickland, op. cit., 138.
13. Ibid., 140.
14. Wickland, *The Gateway of Understanding,* 102–103.
15. Van Praagh, op. cit., 170.
16. Mateu, *Conversations with the Spirit World: Souls Who Have Ended Their Lives Speak from Above,* 158.
17. Puryear, *Stephen Lives! His Life, Suicide, and Afterlife,* 257.
18. Ibid., 314–315.
19. Anderson and Barone, *Lessons from the Light: Extraordinary Messages of Comfort and Hope from the Other Side,* 113.
20. Ford, *Unknown but Known: My Adventure into the Meditative Dimension,* 67.
21. Taylor, ed., *Evidence from Beyond: An Insider's Guide to the Wonders of Heaven—and Life in the New Millenium,* 122.
22. Northrop, *Second Chance: Healing Messages from the Afterlife,* 111–112.
23. From interview session conducted by phone July 12, 2004 with medium Lauren Thibodeau.
24. Guggenheim and Guggenheim, op. cit., 236.
25. Ibid., 237.
26. Lucas, *Regression Therapy: A Handbook for Professionals,* 96.
27. Ibid., 395.
28. Ibid.
29. Twigg and Brod, op. cit., 182.
30. Newton, *Destiny of Souls: New Case Studies of Life Between Lives,* 153.
31. Mateu, *Conversations with the Spirit World,* 14–15.
32. Ibid., 27–28.
33. Ford, *The Life Beyond Death: As Told to Jerome Ellison.*
34. Ibid., 112.
35. Mateu, *Conversations with the Spirit World,* 27.
36. Guggenheim and Guggenheim, op. cit.
37. Ibid., 364.
38. Darby and Joan, *Our Unseen Guest,* 191.

39. Mateu, *Conversations with the Spirit World*, 37–38.
40. Foster, *Epilogue: Souls Review Their Lives After Death*, 127.
41. From interview session conducted by phone July 12, 2004 with medium Johanna Carroll.
42. Merrill, ed. and comp., *Messages from Beyond*, 148–149.
43. Van Praagh, op. cit., 157.
44. Austen, ed., *The Teachings of Silver Birch: Wisdom from the World Beyond*, 61–62.
45. Montgomery, *A World Beyond: A Startling Message from the Eminent Psychic Arthur Ford from Beyond the Grave*, 119.
46. Whitton and Fisher, *Life Between Life: Scientific Explorations into the Void Separating One Incarnation from the Next*, 46–47.
47. Newton, *Journey of Souls: Case Studies of Life Between Lives*, 68.
48. Whitton and Fisher, op. cit., 136
49. Boulton and Boulton, *Psychic Beam to Beyond: Through the Psychic Sensitive Lenora Huett*, 97–98.
50. White and Swainson, *Gildas Communicates: The Story and the Scripts*, 131.
51. Myers, *Human Personality and Its Survival of Bodily Death*.
52. Ibid., 313.
53. Van Praagh, op. cit., 163.
54. Newton, *Destiny of Souls*, 154–155.
55. From interview session conducted by phone July 12, 2004 with medium Lauren Thibodeau.
56. Ibid.
57. Ibid.
58. Padgett, *What Happens After You Die*, 305.
59. Foster, op. cit., 114.
60. Ibid., 126.
61. Ibid., 130.

9 – MESSAGES TO THE SUICIDAL

1. Guggenheim and Guggenheim, *Hello from Heaven!*, 311–312.
2. Home, *Incidents in My Life*.
3. Ibid., 53.
4. Wickland, *The Gateway of Understanding*, 107.
5. From interview session conducted by phone July 12, 2004 with medium Lauren Thibodeau.
6. Ibid.
7. Wickland, op. cit.
8. Guggenheim and Guggenheim, op. cit., 312–313.
9. Mateu, *Psychic Diaries: Connecting with Who You Are, Why You're Here, and What Lies Beyond*, 180.
10. Ibid., 293.

NOTES

11. Foster, *Epilogue: Souls Review Their Lives After Death*, 121.
12. Martin and Romanowski, *Love Beyond Life: The Healing Power of After-Death Communications*, 175–176.
13. Richelieu, *A Soul's Journey*, 143.
14. Nickell, "Dr. Peebles on Karma," 25.
15. Kelway-Bamber, ed., *Claude's Book*, 16–17.
16. Crookall, *The Supreme Adventure: Analysis of Psychic Communications*, 240–241.
17. Northrop, *Second Chance: Healing Messages from the Afterlife*, 110.
18. Twigg and Brod, *Ena Twigg: Medium*, 126–127.
19. Foster, op. cit., 130.
20. "Questions and Answers."
21. Montgomery, *A World Beyond: A Startling Message from the Eminent Psychic Arthur Ford from Beyond the Grave*, 137.
22. Mateu, op. cit., 69.
23. Swain, *From My World to Yours: A Young Man's Account of the Afterlife*, 53.
24. Wickland, *Thirty Years Among the Dead*, 136.
25. Mateu, *Conversations with the Spirit World: Souls Who Have Ended Their Lives Speak from Above*, 46.
26. Kubis and Macy, *Conversations Beyond the Light*, 96–97.
27. Smith, *The Book of James: Conversations from Beyond*, 161–162.
28. Wickland, *Thirty Years Among the Dead*, 133–134.
29. Guggenheim and Guggenheim, op. cit., 313–314.
30. Anderson and Barone, *Lessons from the Light: Extraordinary Messages of Comfort and Hope from the Other Side*, 102.
31. Ibid., 115–116.
32. Puryear, *Stephen Lives! His Life, Suicide, and Afterlife*, 305.
33. Mateu, *Conversations with the Spirit World*.
34. Guggenheim and Guggenheim, op. cit., 235–236.
35. Martin and Romanowski, *We Don't Die: George Anderson's Conversations with the Other Side*, 144–145.
36. Foster, op. cit., 103.
37. Moody, *Life After Life*, 143.
38. Ibid.
39. Grey, *Return from Death: An Exploration of the Near-Death Experience*, 67–68.
40. Atwater, *Beyond the Light: What Isn't Being Said About Near-Death Experience*, 16–17.
41. Meek, *After We Die, What Then?*, 17.
42. Ibid., 132.
43. Atwater, *The Complete Idiot's Guide to Near-Death Experiences*, 73.
44. Mateu, *Conversations with the Spirit World*, 17.
45. Ibid., 28–29.
46. Ibid., 49.

47. Ibid., 159.
48. Grey, op. cit.
49. Wickland, *The Gateway of Understanding*, 106.
50. Mateu, *Conversations with the Spirit World*, 64.
51. Ibid., 51.
52. Ibid., 37.
53. Ibid., 63.
54. Ibid., 65.
55. Foster, op. cit., 103.
56. Ibid., 104.
57. Ibid., 135.
58. Tremaine, *The Butterfly Rises: One Woman's Transformation through the Trance Channeling of Verna V. Yater, Ph.D., Kevin Ryerson and Others.*
59. Ibid., 50.
60. From interview session conducted by phone July 12, 2004 with medium Johanna Carroll.

10 – MESSAGES TO THOSE LEFT BEHIND

1. Viney, *Surviving Death*, 45.
2. Anderson and Barone, *Walking in the Garden of Souls: George Anderson's Advice from the Hereafter for Living in the Here and Now*, 231.
3. Edward, *One Last Time: A Psychic Medium Speaks to Those We Have Loved and Lost.*
4. Holtzer, *Life Beyond: Compelling Evidence for Past Lives and Existence After Death.*
5. Ibid., 64–65.
6. Guggenheim and Guggenheim, *Hello From Heaven!*, 328.
7. Moody and Perry, *Reunions: Visionary Encounters with Departed Loved Ones*, 107.
8. Developed by psychiatrist Raymond Moody, a psychomanteum is a small, very dimly lit, curtained room within a room, where a person sits facing a mirror angled so he or she does not see his or her own reflection. Many report seeing spirits of deceased people they knew when alive. This apparatus is especially used to help clents who are grieving the recent death of a loved one.
9. Ibid., 107–108.
10. Ibid., 109.
11. Cahagnet, *The Celestial Telegraph; Or, Secrets of the Life to Come, Revealed through Magnetism*, Volume 2, 70.
12. Northrop, *Second Chance: Healing Messages from the Afterlife*, 111.
13. Martin, and Romanowski, *Love Beyond Life: The Healing Power of After-Death Communications.*
14. Ibid., 50–52.
15. Guggenheim and Guggenheim, op. cit.
16. Ibid., 309.
17. Barbanell, *When a Child Dies*, 29.
18. Sechrist, *Death Does Not Part Us*, 156–157.

19. Anderson and Barone, *Lessons from the Light: Extraordinary Messages of Comfort and Hope from the Other Side*, 136.
20. Holtzer, op. cit., 86.
21. Puryear, *Stephen Lives! His Life, Suicide, and Afterlife*, 226.
22. Moody and Perry, op. cit.
23. Ibid., 73.
24. Puryear, op. cit., 241.
25. Barbanell, op. cit.
26. Guggenheim and Guggenheim, op. cit., 238.
27. Northrop, op. cit., 120
28. Anderson and Barone, *Lessons from the Light*, 113–114.
29. Schwartz and Simon, *The Afterlife Experiments: Breakthrough Scientific Evidence of Life After Death*, 83.
30. Van Praagh, *Talking to Heaven: A Medium's Message of Life After Death*, 170.
31. Ibid., 175–176.
32. Twigg and Brod, *Ena Twigg: Medium*.
33. Ibid., 125–126.
34. Northrop, op. cit., 226–227.
35. Crawford, *Parting Notes: A Connection with the Afterlife*, 206.
36. Montgomery and Garland, *Ruth Montgomery: Herald of the New Age*, 10–11.
37. Martin and Romanowski, op. cit., 156.
38. Buckley, *When You're Dead, You're Livin'*, 179–180.
39. Ibid., 180.
40. Ibid., 182.
41. Barbanell, op. cit.
42. Swain, *From My World to Yours: A Young Man's Account of the Afterlife*, 55–56.
43. Fleming, e-mail message to author, July 24, 2005.
44. Ibid.
45. Knight, *Learning to Talk to the World Beyond: An Introduction to the Joy of Immortality*, 145.
46. Mateu, *Conversations with the Spirit World: Souls Who Have Ended Their Lives Speak from Above*, 44–45.
47. Puryear, op. cit., 217.
48. Ibid.
49. Ibid.
50. Anderson and Barone, *Lessons from the Light*, 128.
51. Foster, op. cit., 113.
52. Mateu, *Conversations with the Spirit World*, 134–135.
53. Puryear, op. cit., 227.
54. Anderson and Barone, *Lessons from the Light*, 141.
55. Ibid., 142.

56. Puryear, op. cit.
57. Ibid., 265.
58. Martin and Romanowski, *We Are Not Forgotten: George Anderson's Messages of Love and Hope from the Other Side,* 73–74.
59. Ibid., 130.
60. Ibid., 155.
61. Anderson and Barone, *Lessons from the Light,* 112.
62. Ibid., 115.
63. Van Praagh, op. cit., 161–162.
64. Northrop, op. cit., 116.
65. Martin and Romanowski, *We Don't Die: George Anderson's Conversations with the Other Side,* 237.
66. Crawford, op. cit., 206.
67. Mateu, *Psychic Diaries: Connecting with Who You Are, Why You're Here, and What Lies Beyond,* 179.
68. Anderson and Barone, *Lessons from the Light,* 144–145.
69. Wickland, *The Gateway of Understanding,* 105–106.
70. Van Praagh, op. cit., 175.
71. Hutton, *On the Other Side of Reality,* 155–157.
72. Ibid., 159.
73. Mateu, *Conversations with the Spirit World,* 68–69.
74. Ibid., 76.
75. Ibid., 81.
76. Jacobs, personal communication, May 4, 2004.
77. Hardinge, *Modern American Spiritualism: A Twenty Year's Record of the Communion Between Earth and the World of Spirits,* 434.
78. Martin and Romanowski, *We Are Not Forgotten,* 131.
79. Ibid., 155.
80. From interview session conducted by phone July 12, 2004 with Lauren Thibodeau.
81. Ibid.
82. Anderson and Barone, *Lessons from the Light,* 129–130.
83. Edward, op. cit., 72.
84. Puryear, op. cit., 244.
85. Ibid., 315.

11 – ASSISTED SUICIDE

1. Roosevelt, "Choosing Their Time."
2. Ibid.
3. Durkheim, *Suicide: A Study in Sociology,* original edition, 294.
4. Egelko, "Oregon law hinges on O'Connor: Miers' withdrawal muddles court ruling on assisted suicide, A7.
5. Roosevelt, op. cit.

6. Kerkhof, "End-of-Life Decisions in the Netherlands, 1990–2001."
7. Egelko, op. cit.
8. Ibid.
9. Cassem, in Nicholi, ed., *The Harvard Guide to Psychotherapy*, 726–727.
10. DiPasquale and Gluck, "*Psychologists, Psychiatrists, and Physician-Assisted Suicide: The Relationship Between Underlying Beliefs and Professional Behavior*," 501–506.
11. Ibid.
12. Ibid.
13. Cassem, op. cit., 704–705.
14. Ibid., 726.
15. Ibid., 704.
16. Ibid., 813.
17. Ibid., 727.
18. Hendin, "Assisted Suicide, Euthanasia, and the Right to End-of-Life Care," 40.
19. Ibid.
20. Ibid.
21. Ibid., 41.
22. Stincelli, from website: http://www.suicidebycop.com (accessed November 8, 2005).
23. Ibid.
24. Ibid.
25. Engelhardt and Iltis, "End-of-Life: The Traditional Christian View," 1045.
26. Ibid.
27. Ibid.
28. Ibid., 1047.
29. Ibid., 1045.
30. Ibid., 1046.
31. Kardec, *The Spirits' Book*, 380–381.
32. Moore, *Glimpses of the Next State*, 63.
33. Ibid.
34. Austen, ed., *The Teachings of Silver Birch: Wisdom from the World Beyond*.
35. Ibid., 187.
36. Marshall, *The River of Light: Teachings of Gwyneth the Lifegiver*, 21.
37. Phillips, *Here and There: More Psychic Experiences*, 203–204.
38. Ford, *The Life Beyond Death: As Told to Jerome Ellison*.
39. Ibid., 113.
40. Ibid.
41. Brodsky, *Aaron: Channeled through Barbara Brodsky*, chapter "Leaving the Incarnation."
42. Ibid.
43. Van Praagh, *Talking to Heaven: A Medium's Message of Life After Death*, 154.
44. "Questions and Answers."
45. Ibid.

46. Loehr, ed., *Death with Understanding*, 250–251.
47. Ibid., 257.
48. Ibid., 263–264.
49. Ibid., 268.
50. Walker, *Always, Karen*, 145–146.
51. Ibid.
52. Ibid., 148.
53. Ibid., 150.
54. White and Swainson, *Gildas Communicates: The Story and the Scripts*, 132.
55. Reppel, "The Journey Home," 18.
56. Yarbro, *Messages from Michael*, 194.
57. Puryear, *Stephen Lives! His Life, Suicide, and Afterlife*, 243–244.
58. "Questions and Answers," op. cit., 51.
59. Northrop, *Second Chance: Healing Messages from the Afterlife*, 130–131.
60. Newton, *Journey of Souls: Case Studies of Life Between Lives*, 58.
61. Newton, *Destiny of Souls: New Case Studies of Life Between Lives*, 153.
62. Holmes and the Holmes Research Team, *As We See It from Here*.
63. Ibid., 56.
64. Guggenheim and Guggenheim, *Hello From Heaven!*, 314.
65. Anderson and Barone, *Lessons from the Light: Extraordinary Messages of Comfort and Hope from the Other Side*, 44–45.
66. Anderson and Barone, *Walking in the Garden of Souls: George Anderson's Advice from the Hereafter for Living in the Here and Now*, 249–250.
67. From interview session conducted by phone September 3, 2005 with channel Nevada Shaw.
68. Newton, *Destiny of Souls*, 375–376.
69. Ibid., 235.
70. Northrop, op. cit., 132.
71. Ibid., 133–135.

PART II – MURDER-SUICIDE AND SUICIDE BOMBERS

12 – OVERVIEW OF MURDER-SUICIDE

1. Altman, "On the Psychology of Suicide Bombing," 15.
2. Ibid., 15–16.
3. Ibid.
4. Hillbrand, "Homicide-Suicide and Other Forms of Co-Occurring Aggression Against Self and Against Others."
5. Berkowitz, *Aggression: Its Causes, Consequences, and Control*.
6. Ibid., 30.
7. Ibid., 31.
8. Ibid.

9. Ibid., 32.
10. Maiese, *Suicide Bombers.*
11. Cantor, "Victims and Survivors: Letters Across the Pacific," 37.
12. Malmquist, *Homicide: A Psychiatric Perspective*, ix.
13. Ibid., 354–355.
14. Ibid., 356.
15. Ibid., 357.
16. Ibid., 358.
17. Ibid., 359.
18. Ibid.
19. Maltsberger, "Grandiose Fury: Letter Across the Pacific," 144.
20. Ibid.
21. Ibid.
22. Ibid.
23. Ibid.
24. Ibid., 145.
25. Ibid.
26. Ibid.
27. Ibid.
28. From Jacqueline Rose's *London Review of Books* article "Deadly Embrace," available at http:www.lrb.co.uk/v26/n21/print/rose01_.html, p.3.
29. Ibid.
30. Maltsberger, "Letters Across the Pacific: The Conscience of Martyrs," 90.
31. Baruch, "Psychoanalysis and Terrorism: The Need for a Global Talking Cure," 698.
32. Ibid., 699.
33. Ibid.
34. Ibid., 700.
35. Gurian, *What Could He Be Thinking: How A Man's Mind Really Works*, 48.
36. Durkheim, *Suicide: A Study in Sociology*, 315–316.
37. Blood and Pirkis, "Suicide and the Media: Part III: Theoretical Issues," 164.
38. Zakaria, "How to Stop the Contagion," 40.
39. Becker. "The Basic Dynamic of Human Evil," 187.
40. Peck, "Healing Human Evil," 177.
41. Ibid., 178.
42. Ibid.
43. Ibid., 180.
44. Diamond, "Redeeming our Devils and Demons," 182.
45. Ibid., 182–183.
46. Keen, "The Enemy Maker," 199.
47. Ibid., 198.

48. Bloom, *Dying to Kill: The Allure of Suicide Terror*, 88.
49. Ibid., 85.
50. Bayman, *The Secret of Islam: Love and Law in the Religion of Ethics*, xliii.
51. Ibid., xlv.
52. Ibid., xl.
53. Ibid., xliii.
54. Ibid., xlvii.
55. Ibid., xlviii.
56. Ibid., l.
57. Ibid., liii.
58. Ibid.
59. Ibid., liv.
60. Ibid., lv-lvi.
61. Ibid., lvi.
62. Ibid.
63. Pape, *Dying to Win: The Strategic Logic of Suicide Terrorism*.
64. Ibid., 11.
65. Zedalis, *Female Suicide Bombers*, 1.
66. Ibid., 5.
67. Ibid., 14.
68. Ibid., 19.
69. Pape, op. cit.
70. Bloom, op. cit., 63.
71. Ibid., 64.
72. Ibid., 160.
73. Ibid., 159.
74. Ibid.
75. Reuter, *My Life Is a Weapon: A Modern History of Suicide Bombing*.
76. Ibid., 132.
77. Ibid., 131.
78. Quoted in Reuter, ibid., 130.
79. Kupchisky, *Smart Bombs with Souls*, 1.
80. Reuter, op. cit., 136.
81. "Attackers Neither Mad Nor Desperate."
82. Philps, "New Assassins Queue Eagerly for Martyrdom."
83. Lewis, *The Crisis of Islam: Holy War and Unholy Terror*.
84. Pape, op. cit.
85. Lewis, op. cit.
86. Davis, *Martyrs: Innocence, Vengeance, and Despair in the Middle East*, 16–17.
87. Ibid., 197.

88. Hassan, "Letter from Gaza: An Arsenal of Believers"; Lewis, op. cit.
89. *Qur'an* 4:29–30, quoted on http://Islam.about.com/currentevents/a/suicide.
90. Ibid.
91. Alkhuli, *Traditions of Prophet Muhammad,* 70–71.
92. Lewis, op. cit., 152–153.
93. Jamison, *Night Falls Fast: Understanding Suicide,* 14.
94. Lewis, op. cit., 153–154.
95. Pipes, "The Jihad Menace."
96. Hassan, op. cit., 3.
97. Philps, op. cit., 1.
98. Reuter, op. cit., 13.
99. Ibid.
100. Quoted in Zedalis, op. cit., 24.
101. Stern, *Terror in the Name of God,* 52–53.
102. Bloom, op. cit., 153–156.
103. Reuter, op. cit., 35.
104. Ibid., 36.
105. Ibid.
106. Bloom, op. cit., 10–11.
107. Rose, "Deadly Embrace," 5.
108. Ibid.
109. Margalit, "The Suicide Bombers," 2.
110. Lewis, op. cit.
111. Moore and Anderson, "Suicide Bombers Change Mideast's Military Balance," 1.
112. Ibid.
113. Kelly, "Devotion, Desire Drive Youths to 'Martyrdom.'"
114. Hassan, op. cit., 5.
115. Gross, "Documentary Interviews Failed Suicide Bombers." (Roberts was a guest on the *Fresh Air* program.)
116. Ibid.
117. Haqqani and Kimmage, "The Online Bios of Iraq's Martyrs: Suicidology," 14.
118. Ibid.
119. Bloom, op. cit., 168.
120. Ibid., 168–169.
121. Reuter, op. cit., 91.
122. Davis, op. cit., 67–72.
123. Ibid., 78.
124. *Al-Sha'ab,* February 1, 2002.
125. Davis, op. cit., 215.
126. Ibid., 107–108.

127. Text available at http://abclocal.go.com/ktrk/news/100401_news_will.html.
128. Davis, op. cit., 154.
129. Margalit, op. cit.
130. Ibid.
131. Ibid.
132. Davis, op. cit., 191–192.
133. Ibid., 202.
134. Khosrokhavar, *Suicide Bombers: Allah's New Martyrs*, 45.
135. Ibid., 49.
136. Ibid., 59.
137. Ibid., 65.
138. Ibid., 68.
139. Ibid., 140.
140. Ibid., 215.
141. Ibid., 148.
142. Capan, ed., *Terror and Suicide Attacks: An Islamic Perspective*, 102.
143. Ibid., 27.
144. Quoted in Capan, ibid., 88.
145. Ibid., 89.
146. Ibid., 94.
147. Ibid., 28.
148. Ibid., 41.
149. Quoted in Capan, ibid., 100.
150. Ibid., 104.
151. Ibid., 144.

13 – GENERAL MESSAGES

1. Hussein, e-mail message to author, July 23, 2005.
2. Ibid.
3. Lewis, *The Crisis of Islam: Holy War and Unholy Terror*, 3.
4. Swedenborg, *Heaven and Hell*, 391–392.
5. Ibid., 392–393.
6. Edmonds and Dexter, *Spiritualism*, 153.
7. Padgett, *What Happens After You Die*.
8. Ibid., 75–76.
9. Ibid., 102–103.
10. Ibid., 221.
11. Ibid., 149.
12. Ibid., 227.
13. Yarbro, *Messages from Michael*.
14. Ibid., 185.

15. Jones, *Four Spirit Teachers: Trance Talks*, Chapter 17.
16. Kardec, *The Spirits' Book*, 288.
17. Tremaine, *The Butterfly Rises*, 55.
18. Puryear, *Stephen Lives! His Life, Suicide, and Afterlife*, 236.
19. Anderson and Barone, *Lessons from the Light: Extraordinary Messages of Comfort and Hope from the Other Side*, 27.
20. Sullivan, *Arthur Ford Speaks from Beyond*, 173.
21. Jones, op. cit., Chapter 8.
22. Kardec, op. cit., 336.
23. Anderson, *Good Teachers Carry On: Lessons from the Afterlife*, 154.
24. White, *With Folded Wings*, 55–56.
25. Montgomery, *A World Beyond: A Startling Message from the Eminent Psychic Arthur Ford from Beyond the Grave*, 145.
26. Ibid., 139.
27. Brandon, "Waiting to Reincarnate," 422.
28. Padgett, *True Gospel Revealed Anew by Jesus*, Vol. 4, 303.
29. Kardec, op. cit., 287–288.
30. Ibid., 303.
31. Kury, *From a Gun to a Flower*.
32. Ibid., 47–48.
33. Swedenborg, op. cit., 256.
34. Montgomery, op. cit., 12.
35. Ibid., 67.
36. Cummins, *The Road to Immortality: Being a Description of the After-Life Purporting to be Communicated by the Late F. W. H. Meyers through Geraldine Cummins*, 65–66.
37. Puryear, op. cit.
38. Ibid., 236.
39. Sullivan, op. cit.
40. Lodge, *Raymond or Life and Death: With Examples of the Evidence for Survival of Memory and Affection After Death*, 195.
41. Crookall, *The Supreme Adventure: Analysis of Psychic Communications*.
42. Van Praagh, *Talking to Heaven: A Medium's Message of Life After Death*, 99–100.
43. Newton, *Destiny of Souls: New Case Studies of Life Between Lives*, 89.
44. Crookall, op. cit., 46–47.
45. Swain, *From My World to Yours: A Young Man's Account of the Afterlife*.
46. Padgett, *What Happens After You Die*, 9.
47. Swedenborg, op. cit., 364.
48. Ibid., 379.
49. Ibid., 374.
50. Kardec, op. cit.
51. Ibid., 249.

52. Marshall, *The River of Light: Teachings of Gwyneth the Lifegiver*, 71.
53. Holmes and the Holmes Research Team, *As We See It from Here*.
54. Ibid., 68.
55. Motoyama, *Karma and Reincarnation*, 76.
56. Northrop, *Second Chance: Healing Messages from the Afterlife*.
57. Ibid., 142.
58. Newton, op. cit., 93.
59. Phillips, *Here and There: More Psychic Experiences*, 39.
60. Borgia, *Life in the World Unseen*, 151–152.
61. Kardec, op. cit., 309.
62. Loder, *Afterlife Communications*, 21.
63. Montgomery, op. cit., 32.
64. Ibid., 44.
65. Meek, *After We Die, What Then?*, 132.
66. Ibid., 146.
67. Martin and Romanowski, *We Are Not Forgotten: George Anderson's Messages of Love and Hope from the Other Side*.
68. Ibid., 289.
69. Ibid., 145.
70. Edmonds and Dexter, op. cit., 235–237.
71. Moody, *Life After Life*.
72. Ibid., 144.
73. Foster, *Epilogue: Souls Review Their Lives After Death*, 107.
74. Greaves, *Testimony of Light*, 50.
75. Ibid., 52.
76. Kardec, op. cit., 174.
77. Anderson, op. cit.
78. Ibid., 93.
79. Anderson and Barone, *Walking in the Garden of Souls: George Anderson's Advice from the Hereafter for Living in the Here and Now*, 120.
80. Anderson and Barone, *Lessons from the Light*, op. cit., 171.
81. Ibid., 172.
82. Yarbro, *More Messages from Michael*, 275.
83. Yarbro, *Messages from Michael*, op. cit.
84. Ibid., 168. "Karmic ribbon" is the channeled entity Michael's term for the line, tie, or bond of connection or attraction that exists between two spirits (incarnate or discarnate) representing the karmic indebtedness of one to the other. Until the debt is paid or burned off, such a karmic relationship will remain, joining the two.
85. Stevens, op. cit., 224.
86. Ibid.
87. Ibid., 225.

88. Ibid., 225–226.
89. Kardec, op. cit., 313.
90. Sullivan, op. cit., 136.
91. Ibid., 142.
92. Yarbro, *Messages from Michael*, op. cit.
93. Ibid., 174.
94. Northrop, op. cit., 148–149.
95. Lazaris, *Lazaris Interviews Book II*.
96. Ibid., 188.
97. Anderson, op. cit., 157.
98. Motoyama, op. cit., 107.

14 – EXPERIENCES IN THE AFTERLIFE

1. From interview session conducted by phone July 12, 2004 with medium Johanna Carroll.
2. Ibid.
3. Wickland, *Thirty Years Among the Dead*.
4. Wickland, *Thirty Years Among the Dead*, 149.
5. From interview session conducted July 28, 2004 with medium Nevada Shaw.
6. From interview session conducted June 26, 2004 with medium Nevada Shaw.
7. Ibid.
8. Ibid.
9. Ibid.
10. From interview session conducted July 3, 2004 with medium Nevada Shaw.
11. From interview session conducted June 26, 2004 with medium Nevada Shaw.
12. From interview session conducted by phone July 12, 2004 with medium Johanna Carroll.
13. From interview session conducted July 28, 2004 with medium Nevada Shaw.
14. From interview session conducted June 26, 2004 with medium Nevada Shaw.
15. From interview session conducted July 3, 2004 with medium Nevada Shaw.
16. From interview session conducted by phone September 3, 2005 with medium Nevada Shaw.
17. Foster, *Epilogue: Souls Review Their Lives After Death*, 106–107.
18. From interview session conducted June 26, 2004 with medium Nevada Shaw.
19. Ibid.
20. Ibid.
21. From interview session conducted by phone July 5, 2004 with medium Joanie.
22. Ibid.
23. From interview session conducted June 26, 2004 with medium Nevada Shaw.
24. Newton, *Journey of Souls: Case Studies of Life Between Lives*, 159.
25. From interview session conducted July 3, 2004 with medium Nevada Shaw.

26. From interview session conducted by phone July 12, 2004 with medium Johanna Carroll.
27. From interview session conducted June 26, 2004 with medium Nevada Shaw.
28. Ibid.
29. From interview session conducted July 3, 2004 with medium Nevada Shaw.
30. From interview session conducted June 26, 2004 with medium Nevada Shaw.
31. Ibid.
32. Newton, *Journey of Souls,* op. cit., 49.
33. Newton, *Destiny of Souls: New Case Studies of Life Between Lives,* 93.
34. From interview session conducted June 26, 2004 with medium Nevada Shaw.
35. From interview session conducted July 3, 2004 with medium Nevada Shaw.
36. Ibid.
37. Ibid.
38. Ibid.
39. From interview session conducted June 26, 2004 with medium Nevada Shaw.
40. Ibid.
41. From intervew session conducted by phone July 5, 2004 with medium Joanie.
42. From interview session conducted June 26, 2004 with medium Nevada Shaw.
43. Ibid.
44. From intervew session conducted by phone July 5, 2004 with medium Joanie.
45. Ibid.
46. From intervew session conducted June 26, 2004 with medium Nevada Shaw.
47. From intervew session conducted by phone July 5, 2004 with medium Joanie.
48. Ibid.
49. Martin and Romanowski, *We Are Not Forgotten: George Anderson's Messages of Love and Hope from the Other Side.*
50. Ibid., 145.
51. From interview session conducted by phone July 12, 2004 with medium Johanna Carroll.
52. From an interview session conducted June 26, 2004 with medium Nevada Shaw.
53. Ibid.
54. From interview session conducted July 3, 2004 with medium Nevada Shaw.
55. Van Hulle, *Michael Educational Foundation Newsletter.*
56. From interview session conducted June 26, 2004 with medium Nevada Shaw.
57. Ibid.
58. Ibid.
59. Ibid.
60. Ibid.
61. From interview session conducted by phone July 5, 2004 with medium Joanie.
62. From interview session conducted by phone July 12, 2004 with medium Johanna Carroll.

15 – MESSAGES TO THOSE LEFT BEHIND

1. From interview session conducted June 26, 2004 with medium Nevada Shaw.
2. Ibid.
3. Foster, *Epilogue: Souls Review Their Lives After Death*, 105.
4. From interview session conducted June 26, 2004 with medium Nevada Shaw.
5. From interview session conducted July 28, 2004 with medium Nevada Shaw.
6. Ibid.
7. From interview session conducted June 26, 2004 with medium Nevada Shaw. "Unfoldment" refers to the unfolding (or unraveling) and release of illusion, which is a necessary step for souls to take to evolve. According to Trio, souls become bound or encased by old "stories" they collect as truths during their lifetimes. Much of the life-review process is devoted to helping souls let go of these limiting (and often false) perceptions. Unfoldment does not appear to be the same as spiritual enlightenment, although it is a necessary step in that direction and allows the soul to return to its true state as part of the whole. The image Trio gave of this was watching a tightly curled fern leaf unfurl.
8. From interview session conducted by phone July 5, 2004 with medium Joanie.
9. Ibid.
10. Foster, op. cit.
11. Ibid., 106–107.
12. Ibid., 106.
13. Ibid.
14. From interview session conducted by phone July 12, 2004 with medium Johanna Carroll.
15. From interview session conducted June 26, 2004 with medium Nevada Shaw.
16. Ibid.
17. Ibid.
18. From intervew session conducted by phone July 5, 2004 with medium Joanie.
19. From interview session conducted by phone July 12, 2004 with medium Johanna Carroll.
20. From interview session conducted June 26, 2004 with medium Nevada Shaw.
21. Foster, op. cit., 106.
22. From interview session conducted June 26, 2004 with medium Nevada Shaw.
23. From interview session conducted by phone July 5, 2004 with medium Joanie.
24. Ibid.
25. From interview session conducted July 28, 2004 with medium Nevada Shaw.
26. From interview session conducted June 26, 2004 with medium Nevada Shaw.
27. Ibid.
28. From interview session conducted by phone July 12, 2004 with medium Johanna Carroll.
29. From interview session conducted June 26, 2004 with medium Nevada Shaw.
30. From intervew session conducted by phone July 5, 2004 with medium Joanie.
31. Ibid.

32. Ibid.
33. Ibid.
34. Ibid.
35. Ibid.
36. Ibid.
37. Ibid.

16 – THE SPIRIT VIEW ON TERRORISM

1. Montgomery and Garland, *Ruth Montgomery: Herald of the New Age*, 264–265.
2. Van Hulle, *Michael Educational Foundation Newsletter*.
3. Ibid.
4. Anderson, *Good Teachers Carry On: Lessons from the Afterlife*, 151–153.
5. From interview session conducted July 3, 2004 with medium Nevada Shaw.
6. From interview session conducted June 26, 2004 with medium Nevada Shaw.
7. From interview session conducted by phone July 12, 2004 with medium Johanna Carroll.
8. Ibid.
9. From interview session conducted by phone September 3, 2005 with medium Nevada Shaw.
10. From interview session conducted July 28, 2004 with medium Nevada Shaw.
11. From interview session conducted by phone September 3, 2005 with medium Nevada Shaw.
12. Ibid.
13. Ibid.
14. From interview session conducted by phone July 12, 2004 with medium Johanna Carroll.
15. From interview session conducted July 28, 2004 with medium Nevada Shaw.
16. Ibid.
17. From interview session conducted by phone July 12, 2004 with medium Johanna Carroll.
18. From interview session conducted June 26, 2004 with medium Nevada Shaw.
19. From intervew session conducted by phone July 5, 2004 with medium Joanie.
20. Austen, ed., *The Teachings of Silver Birch: Wisdom from the World Beyond*, 111.
21. From interview session conducted by phone July 12, 2004 with medium Johanna Carroll.
22. Atwater, *We Live Forever: The Real Truth About Death*, 47–49.
23. From intervew session conducted by phone July 5, 2004 with medium Joanie.
24. Ibid.
25. Ibid.
26. Atwater, op. cit.
27. From intervew session conducted by phone July 5, 2004 with medium Joanie.
28. Loder, *Afterlife Communications*, 63.

29. From interview session conducted June 26, 2004 with medium Nevada Shaw.
30. From interview session conducted July 3, 2004 with medium Nevada Shaw.
31. From interview session conducted June 26, 2004 with medium Nevada Shaw. Although in the broader spectrum of things, fear always creates problems, in this particular instance, Trio said that souls are often driven by a refusal to accept accountability for their self-hatred. Instead, they harbor an illusion that they loathe something other than themselves, when in fact, it's self-hatred. This self-loathing stems in large part from a false perception of being separate from others. However, for people to admit this feeling (and self-imposed isolation) would require them to take responsibility for it.
32. Ibid.
33. From interview session conducted July 28, 2004 with medium Nevada Shaw.
34. From interview session conducted by phone September 3, 2005 with medium Nevada Shaw.
35. Ibid.
36. From interview session conducted July 28, 2004 with medium Nevada Shaw.
37. Ibid.
38. Ibid.
39. Ibid.
40. Ibid.
41. From interview session conducted by phone July 12, 2004 with medium Johanna Carroll.

17 – CONCLUSION

1. Kardec, *The Spirits' Book*, 382.
2. Anderson and Barone, *Lessons from the Light: Extraordinary Messages of Comfort and Hope from the Other Side*, 8.
3. Mateu, Psychic Diaries, 81–82.
4. Bernard, *Why You Are Who You Are: A Psychic Conversation*, 197–198.
5. Anders, e-mail message to author, January 25, 2004.

GLOSSARY

1. Foster, *Epilogue: Souls Review Their Lives After Death*, 116–117.

Permissions

This page is an extension of the copyright page.

Excerpts from *George Anderson's Lessons from the Light* by George Anderson and Andrew Barone, copyright © 1999 by George Anderson & Andrew Barone. Used by permission of G. P. Putnam's Sons, a division of Penguin Group (USA) Inc. Excerpts from *Walking in the Garden of Souls* by George Anderson and Andrew Barone, copyright © 2001 by George Anderson & Andrew Barone. Used by permission of G. P. Putnam's Sons, a division of Penguin Group (USA) Inc. Excerpts from *Good Teachers Carry On* by Mary Beth Anderson reprinted with the permission of Cosmic Concepts Press. Excerpts from *We Live Forever* by P. M. H. Atwater reprinted with the permission of A.R.E. Press. Excerpts from *One Last Time* by John J. Edward, copyright © 1998 by John J. Edward. Used by permission of Berkley Publishing Group, a division of Penguin Group (USA) Inc. and Dystel & Goderich Literary Management. Excerpts from *Return from Death: An Exploration of the Near-Death Experience* by Margot Grey (Arkana 1985. Copyright © Margot Grey, 1985). Reproduced by permission of Penguin Books Ltd. Excerpts from *Hello from Heaven!* by William Guggenheim III and Judith A. Guggenheim, copyright © 1995 by William Guggenheim III and Judith A. Guggenheim. Used by permission of Bantam Books, a division of Random House, Inc. Excerpts from *The Spirit's Book* by Allan Kardec reprinted with the permission of Brotherhood of Life, P. O. Box 46320, Las Vegas, NV 89114-6320, www.brotherhoodoflife.com. Excerpts from *Death with Understanding*, edited by Franklin Loehr, reprinted with the permission of the Religious Research Foundation, www.religiousresearch.org. Excerpts from *Diary After Death*, second edition, by Franklin Loehr, reprinted with the permission of the Religious Research Foundation, www.religiousresearch.org. Excerpts from *Regression Therapy* by Winifred Blake Lucas reprinted with the permission of the author. Excerpts from *Love Beyond Life* by Joel Martin and Patricia Romanowski reprinted with the permission of Sarah Lazin Books. Excerpts from *We Are Not Forgotten* by Joel Martin and Patricia Romanowski, copyright © 1991 by Joel Martin and PAR Bookworks, Ltd. Used by permission of G. P. Putnam's Sons, a division of Penguin Group (USA) Inc., and the authors. Excerpts from *We Don't Die* by Joel Martin and Patricia Romanowski, copyright © 1988 by Joel Martin & PAR Bookworks, Ltd. Used by permission of Berkley Publishing Group, a division of Penguin Group (USA) Inc. and Sarah Lazin Books. Excerpts from *Conversations with the Spirit World* by Lysa Mateu reprinted with the permission of the author. Excerpts from *Psychic Diaries* by Lysa Mateu reprinted with the permission of HarperCollins Publishers and the author. Excerpts from *After We Die, What Then?* by George W. Meek reprinted with the permission of Ariel Press. Excerpts from *A World Beyond* by Ruth Montgomery, copyright © 1971 by Ruth Montgomery. Used by permission of Coward-McCann, Inc., a division of Penguin Group (USA) Inc. Excerpts from *Answers from a Grander Self*, edited by Tam Mossman, reprinted with the permission of the author. Excerpts from *Karma & Reincarnation* by Dr. Hiroshi Motoyama, copyright © 1993 by Dr. Hiroshi Motoyama. Reprinted by permission of HarperCollins Publishers. Excerpts from *Destiny of Souls* by Michael Newton , Ph.D. © 2000. Llewellyn Worldwide, Ltd. 2143

PERMISSIONS

Wooddale Drive, Woodbury, MN 55125-2989. All rights reserved. Excerpts from *Journey of Souls* by Michael Newton, Ph.D. © 2000. Llewellyn Worldwide, Ltd. All rights reserved. Excerpts from *Second Chance* by Suzane Northrop reprinted by permission of the author. Excerpts from *What Happens After You Die* by James E. Padgett, copyright © 2003. Reprinted by permission of Foundation Church of Divine Truth (FCDT) Publishing, P. O. Box 802694, Santa Clarita, CA 91380-2694. Excerpts from *Stephen Lives! His Life, Suicide, and Afterlife* by Anne Puryear, copyright © 1992, 1996 by Anne Puryear. Reprinted with the permission of Pocket Books, a division of Simon & Schuster Adult Publishing Group. Excerpts from *A Soul's Journey* by Peter Richelieu reprinted by permission of HarperCollins Publishers Ltd. © Peter Richelieu 1953, 1958. Excerpts from *Death Does Not Part Us* by Elsie R. Sechrist, copyright © 1992 by Elsie Sechrist. Reprinted by permission of A.R.E. Press. Excerpts from *Talking to Heaven* by James Van Praagh, copyright © 1997 by James Van Praagh. Used by permission of Dutton, a division of Penguin Group (USA) Inc. Excerpts from *Gildas Communicates* by Ruth White and Mary Swainson, published by C. W. Daniel. Reprinted by permission of The Random House Group Ltd. Excerpts from *The Gateway of Understanding* and *Thirty Years Among the Dead* by Carl A. Wickland reprinted by permission of Health Research Books.

The authors have made every effort to trace the copyright holders of *Four Spirit Teachers* by Sheila Jones, *Spirit Wisdom* by Ramón Stevens, and *Always, Karen* by Jeanne Walker. If you have such information, please contact North Atlantic Books.

About the Authors

Jon Klimo, Ph.D., has been core professor in the clinical program at the American Schools of Professional Psychology (ASPP), Argosy University, at its San Francisco Bay Area campus in Point Richmond, California, since 1998. He has done extensive research, writing, and teaching in parapsychology, consciousness studies, alternative medicine and anomalous healing, new paradigm thought and new science, metaphysics, the transpersonal domain, and UFO/extraterrestrial studies. He wrote what is widely considered the definitive study on the phenomenon of channeling, *Channeling: Investigations on Receiving Information from Paranormal Sources*, first published by Jeremy P. Tarcher & St. Martin's Press in 1987, translated into six languages, and expanded into a new edition and published by North Atlantic Books in 1998. Klimo regards this book as a kind of Rosetta stone for looking at many related anomalous phenomena as well as for rethinking our current understating about the brain, mind/consciousness, and the nature of reality, physical and beyond.

With undergraduate and graduate degrees from Brown University and a doctoral degree in psychology from Rosebridge Graduate School (now the ASPP) he has been teaching full time in doctoral programs for the past thirty-two years, chairing over 200 dissertations in the process. From 1974–1982 he was a professor at Rutgers University's Graduate School of Education, where he was the founding director and principal faculty member for the Creative Arts Education Program. He was next a professor at Rosebridge Graduate School, during which time he worked with masters and doctoral candidates preparing to become licensed counselors and clinical psychologists. From 1991 to 1998 he designed, developed, and was chief instructor in one of only two doctoral-level specialization programs in parapsychology in the United States.

Klimo has published dozens of articles and given hundreds of public presentations. He recently completed a four-year research grant for the study of using technological means to receive and record voices and images from purported human spirits who have survived the deaths of their bodies (i.e., "EVP" or "ITC" research), and is vice president of the United States Psychotronics Association, and a member of the Parapsychological Association. Dr. Klimo has also appeared on more than one hundred radio programs and twenty television programs, usually as an authority on channeling, parapsychology, consciousness studies, the otherworldly (extraterrestrial) studies, and spiritual/metaphysical subjects.

Pamela Rae Heath M.D., Psy.D., received her doctoral degree in psychology specializing in parapsychology from Rosebridge Graduate School of Integrative Psychology (now the American School of Professional Psychology, Argosy University, San Francisco Bay Area Campus) in 1999. She presented her dissertation work, a phenomenological study of the experience of performing psychokinesis, at the Parapsychological Association Convention at Stanford University, and has since published *The PK Zone: A Cross-Cultural Review of Psychokinesis (PK)*, as well as articles on this subject in the *Journal of Parapsychology, Iridis,* and the *Australian Journal of Parapsychology*. She is a certified Master Hypnotherapist, a cofounder of the Paranormal Research Organization, a board member of the California Society for Psychical Research, full member of the Parapsychological Association, associate member of the Society for Psychical Research, and an investigator with the Office of Paranormal Investigations. She has made television appearances both as a parapsychologist and as a psychic.

Dr. Heath obtained a bachelor's degree in psychology from the University of Missouri in Columbia in 1976, and an M.D. from the University of Texas Medical Branch at Galveston in 1980. She became Board Certified in Anesthesiology in 1985 and practiced medicine at a variety of locations, including serving as Chief of Anesthesia in Humana Hospital-Abilene, as Director of Education for the Anesthesia Department and a member of the Surgery Faculty in Orlando Regional Medical Center, on the faculty of Anesthesia at the University of Florida in Miami, and for two years as Chief of Anesthesia at Chinle Hospital on the Navaho Reservation. After she began having spontaneous psychic experiences in the early 1990s, she returned to graduate school to study these experiences in depth.

Dr. Heath currently lives in Alameda, California and divides her time between writing, practicing medicine, and doing field investigations. She has been a guest lecturer on psychic phenomena and experiential research at a variety of locations.